147 Traditional Stories
for Primary School Children to Retell

Chris Smith PhD

storytelling schools
where every child is a storyteller

Hawthorn Press

147 Traditional Stories for Primary School Children to Retell © 2014 Chris Smith

Chris Smith is hereby identified as the author of this work in accordance with section 77 of the Copyright, Designs and Patent Act, 1988. He asserts and give notice of his moral right under this Act.

Hawthorn Press

Published by Hawthorn Press, Hawthorn House,
1 Lansdown Lane, Stroud, Gloucestershire, GL5 1BJ, UK
Tel: (01453) 757040   Fax: (01453) 751138

E-mail: info@hawthornpress.com

Website: www.hawthornpress.com

All rights reserved. No part of this book may be reproduced, stored in a retrieval system or transmitted in any form by any means (electronic or mechanical, through reprography, digital transmission, recording or otherwise) without prior written permission of the publisher.

UK Edition 147 Traditional Stories for Primary School Children to Retell © Hawthorn Press 2014

Cover illustration © Shirin Adl

Illustrations by Shirin Adl

Cover design and typesetting by Lucy Guenot

Printed by Berforts Information Press Ltd, Herts, UK

Every effort has been made to trace the ownership of all copyrighted material. If any omission has been made, please bring this to the publisher's attention so that proper acknowledgement may be given in future editions.

The views expressed in this book are not necessarily those of the publisher.

Printed on environmentally friendly chlorine-free paper manufactured from renewable forest stock.

British Library Cataloguing in Publication Data applied for.

ISBN 978-1-907359-39-2

FSC MIX Paper from responsible sources FSC® C013262

About the author

Chris Smith PhD

Chris Smith, PhD, is a storyteller, educational trainer and founding Director of Storytelling Schools. Chris loves helping to make education more joyful, effective and engaging, especially in areas of social deprivation where good education can make such a difference to future life chances. For the last ten years Chris has been researching and developing the Storytelling Schools idea in UK schools. Chris has also been a father, musician, exhibition designer, performer, monk, UN manager, human ecologist, surfer and writer. He currently divides his time between a house in Oxford and a wood in Devon. For more information on Chris see: www.storysmith.co.uk

Storytelling Schools

Storytelling Schools is a group of educationalists who are passionate about the power of storytelling to transform education and learning. We were founded in 2013 to promote the storytelling schools model throughout the UK and beyond. By systematically learning storytelling skills at school, students can receive an education that builds confidence and fluency in spoken language, raises standards of reading and writing, and provides an engaging way to learn other subjects in the curriculum, all in a method that is enjoyable and inclusive.

Storytelling Schools make information, resources and training available for teachers who wish to adopt this approach in their school.

Our founders are Chris Smith, Adam Guillain, Pie Corbett and Nanette Stormont.
For more information see our website at **www.storytellingschools.com**

Acknowledgements

The stories in this collection are all traditional stories that have evolved over the centuries by being told, retold, retold, and sometimes written down. Behind all these tales stand tens of thousands of storytellers who have adapted the tales to suit their own styles and purposes, all part of the still-evolving story.

Many of these stories are quite popular in England, told by storytellers in schools, festivals and story circles throughout the country. I have told all of these stories myself and tried to bring my own storyteller's voice to the written text. However, doubtless I have picked up phrases and ideas from others, as is the way with traditional stories, so thanks to all the tellers of these tales whom I have seen and heard over the years.

I'd like to name a few storytellers who have been particularly inspiring and influential to me over the years, and whose voices I have no doubt sought to imitate and integrate into my own telling. Thanks to Ben Haggarty, Daniel Morden, Hugh Lupton, Jan Blake, Sally Pomme Clayton, Vergene Gulbenkian and Eric Maddern. Thanks to Merry, Lucy and Claire at Hawthorn Press for making the book happen, and in particular to Martin Large for his support and advice. Thanks to the Story Museum, Oxford for generously helping with the editing of earlier drafts of this collection. Much appreciation to Alida Gersie and Hugh Lupton for their advice and feedback when preparing this book.

Finally I'd like to acknowledge the stories themselves. They come alive when told and retold out loud. They like to be shared, changed, played around with and enjoyed. With your help, may they go forth and multiply.

Contents

Introduction
How to Use this Collection   ix

Chapter 1
Year 1 Stories

Monkeys and Hats – India	2
The Little Red Hen – England	4
Three Little Pigs – England	6
The Birth of Jesus – World (Christian)	8
The Gingerbread Man – England	10
Bat Learns to Dance – origin unknown	12
Three Billy Goats Gruff – Norway	14
The Noisy House – Britain	16
The Giant Turnip – Russia	18
The Wooden Baby – Czech Republic	20
Goldilocks and the Three Bears – Britain	22
The Fox's Sack – England	25
The Princess and the Pea – Denmark	28
Skinny Old Lady – Africa	30
The Freedom Bird – Thailand	33
Snip-Snip – European (Jewish)	36
The King and the Moon – Dominican Republic	39
The Magic Porridge Pot – Germany	41
The Sweet-Talking Potato – Africa	44
Stone Soup – Switzerland	46
A Husband for Miss Mouse – Myanmar	48
Awongalema – Africa	52
The Lion's Roar – India (Buddhist)	54
Goose Girl's Wings – China	57
Mouse and Lion – Greece	60
The Nest and the Web – Islam	62
The Dancing Harmonica – USA	63
The Talkative Turtle – Native American	66
Bandits and Berries – China	68
The Thirsty Frog – Aboriginal (Australia)	71
More! – USA	73
Little Red Riding Hood – France	74
Jack and the Beanstalk – Britain	76

Chapter 2
Year 2 Stories

The Stonecutter – China	82
The Unlucky Man – England	85
The King and the Cockerel – Iraq	88
The Bird and the Forest Fire – India (Buddhist)	92
Honey and Trouble – Africa	94
How Coyote Brought Fire to Earth – Native American	97
The Snake and the Frog – USA	100
The Talking Skull – Africa	101
The Elephant's Fury – Asia (Buddhist)	103
The Island of Fairies – Scotland	106
The Bee's Treasure – Japan	108
The Pied Piper of Hamlyn – Germany	111
The Pedlar of Swaffham – England	113
Strength – Africa	115
Sleeping Beauty – Germany	118
Rumpelstiltskin – Germany	120
Cinderella – Germany	124
The Magic Paintbrush – China	130
Snow White – Germany	132
The Two Dragons – Wales	136

Chapter 3
Year 3 Stories

The Marriage of Ganesh – India	142
Cap of Rushes – England	145
Lazy Jack – England	147
Baba Yaga's Black Geese – Russia	150
Three Brothers and the Polar Bear – India/Arctic	152
Three Dolls – India	154
The Lighthouse Keeper and the Selkie – Scotland	157
Death in a Nutshell – Scotland	159
The Fox and the Healer – Native American	162
Jack and the Dancing Trees – England	164
Little Burnt Face – Native American	167
The Monk and the Thieves – Chile	169
The Story Bag – Korea	171
How a Boy Learned to be Wise – Uganda	174
Persephone – Greece	178
The Wooden Horse – Greece	180

SHORTER STORIES:

Half a Blanket – Scotland	182
Fruit of Love – Native American	184
One Wish – Ireland	186
Birth of Athena – Greece	187
The Lode Stone – England	189
The Scorpion and the Frog – India	191
Three Wishes – Sweden	192

Chapter 4
Year 4 Stories

The Blind Man and the Hunter – West Africa	196
The Birth of Osiris – Egypt	200
Prometheus – Greece	202
The Eagle Who Thought He Was a Chicken – Native American	204
How Butterflies Came to Be – Native American	206
Icarus – Greece	208
The Shepherd's Dream – Ireland	211
The Piper's Boots – Scotland	213
Midas's Wish – Greece	216
Midas and Apollo – Greece	218
Theseus and the Minotaur – Greece	220
The Woman of the Sea – Scotland	224
How Jerusalem Began – Palestine and Jewish	226
Odysseus and the Cyclops – Greece	228
The Four Dragons – China	230
The Land of the Deep Ocean – Japan	233
Rama and Sita – India	236

SHORTER STORIES:

The Building of St Paul's Cathedral – England	238
Feathers in the Wind – Jewish	239
Heaven and Hell (1) – Japan	240
Heaven and Hell (2) – European	241

Chapter 5
Year 5 Stories

The Hunter and the Leopard – West Africa	244
The Boots of Abu Kassim – Iraq	246
Who is the Thief? – Japan	248
Beowolf – England	251
The Tiger's Whisker – Indonesia	253
The Apple Tree Man – England	255
Godmother Death – Mexico	258
The Weaver's Dream – China	261
The Prince and the Birds – Spain	264
Jumping Mouse – Native American	269
Jack and Jackie – Ireland	272
The House That Has Never Known Death – Germany	274
Why the Seagull Cries – Native American	276

Shorter Stories:

Luckily Unluckily – China	279
Language Lesson – England	281

Nasseradeen Tales – Iran

Looking on the Bright Side	283
Stop Eating Sweets	284
Hitting the Target	285
Nasseradeen and the Perfect Wife	286
The Neighbour's Cockerel	288
Nasseradeen's Nail	289
Nasseradeen and the King's Hunting Party	291
Nasseradeen Speaks Truth	292
Nasseradeen and the Light	293
Nasseradeen Teaches Justice	294
Who Do You Trust?	295
Nasseradeen and the Turnips	296
Cause and Effect	297
Nasseradeen Teaches Empathy	297

Chapter 6
Year 6 Stories

Children of Wax – Africa	300
Warrior – Egypt	302
Baldur – Norway	309
Ericython – Roman	312
Quetzalcoatl Brings Chocolate to Earth – Aztec	314
Skeleton Woman – Inuit	318
The Boy who Learned to Shudder – Germany	320
The Woodcutter and the Snake – Serbia	325
Three Questions – Russia	328
Gawain and the Green Knight – Britain	331
Mother Sun and Her Daughters – Argentina	334
Five Wise Trainings – India	336
Gawain Gets Married – Britain	340
Everything You Need – Iraq	344
Gilgamesh – Iraq	348
A Drop of Honey – Iraq	352

Shorter Stories:

Who is the Husband? – India	356
What Happens When You Really Listen! – India	357
The Power of Stories – India	358
The Diamond Dream – India	359
Bird in Hand – India	361
Traveller at the Gates of a City – USA	362

Appendices
Classification of Stories

Topic	365
Value	368
Plot Type	371
Story Genre	374
Country or Region of Origin	377
Story Titles in Alphabetical Order	380

Sources and Resources   382

Introduction

How to Use this Collection

Why This Collection?

A Riddle

What is it that, when you give it away, you keep it?
It moves from place to place and changes as it moves.
Without it there is no past or future,
No reason or meaning.
What is it?

Learning to tell and improvise stories is a wonderful and natural way to learn. Such storytelling builds language, knowledge, thinking skills, feeling skills and confidence in communication. It can also form the basis for raising standards in writing: if you can't say it you won't be able to write it.

This is a collection of stories for retelling in Storytelling Schools where oral storytelling is a key way that children learn. If you want to know more about this approach then see the companion volume, *The Storytelling School: Handbook for Teachers*, Hawthorn Press, which explains the methods in detail, or visit the Storytelling Schools website: www.storytellingschools.com.

This collection has come out of more than ten years' experience working with schools that adopt this method of learning. It was clear early on that, in order to become Storytelling Schools, teachers needed great stories in a form that was easy for them to learn and retell to their classes. They needed stories that matched up with the age and abilities of their classes, and which fitted with the topics they were teaching.

The result is this book, where teachers can go looking for the stories they need. All the stories are tried and tested in the sense that they have all been told many times by me and they have all been retold by teachers and students in Storytelling Schools around the country.

To be successfully retold by busy teachers, the stories need to be short, simple and quick to learn. I have written them with this in mind:

➤ Keeping them generally short so they can be read and absorbed efficiently
➤ Emphasising the main plot elements or 'bones' of the story, for tellers to flesh out as they wish
➤ Using storyteller's language and adding in key bits of description and dialogue that help the plot flow.

All stories come with some tips on how to approach retelling. Feedback from trials of this book in more than 100 schools strongly endorsed the value of this approach.

In Storytelling Schools training we use a model called the three I's, devised by Pie Corbett, to explain how storymaking works. The three I's are:

➤ Imitation, where we copy
➤ Innovation, where we begin to adapt and change the thing we learned
➤ Invention, where we remix what we have learned into something seemingly new

This applies well to the process of learning to tell a story:

- First a student will copy the words and style of the story they have heard
- Later they start to add and change bits of the story so it works better for them
- When students invent their own stories they will remix ideas from stories they already know.

These three stages are not discreet but form a continuum from word-for-word memorisation to free-form improved storymaking.

The stories in this volume are there to be innovated upon. Just as I found a way to adapt these stories for retelling to my audiences, so teachers and their students will do the same. This kind of storytelling is more like jazz than classical: storytellers improvise details around a given basic plot just as jazz players improvise around a given set of chord changes.

Consequently these are not retellings where the words in the story are remembered word-for-word. Neither are they tellings where the exact details of description, dialogue and character are preserved. These stories have been changed to suit my own storyteller's voice and the audiences of primary children they have been told to. Teachers are welcome to start by imitating my own voice as a start before developing their own style and approach to telling.

When stories are retold and innovated upon by children they soon start playing around with new characters, settings and plot ideas. In the Storytelling School that is all encouraged, as the students develop their own way of telling and developing the story in a way that is satisfying for them. If *Little Red Riding Hood* becomes *Little Blue Motorbike Helmet*, all well and good. If the forest becomes a park or council estate, all well and good. This is the oral tradition: we drink in ideas about character and plot and then retell in new and satisfying ways.

In this way students learn to develop fluency with language and narrative, adjusting and adapting to their purposes.

Storyteller Abbi Patrix once taught that each story told is a unique interaction of story, storyteller, audience and place. These stories have evolved in this way.

For example, in this book you will find lots of little songs popping up here and there. That's an example of a way I like to innovate when telling to primary children. Music and song brings engagement, enjoyment and imagination and is a great way of getting your audience involved.

For some folklorists this might raise the question of authenticity: should we always be true to the 'origin' of the tale? With this approach the answer is an emphatic no! We are working with oral tradition where stories mutate and change in the telling. If you want to read scholarly texts of exactly how a story used to be told, then this is not the book for you!

I have included detailed notes on various sources for these stories so that the process of discovery and refinement can be transparent. These will also help direct teachers to alternate sources for the class to research where suitable, plus clips to watch and listen to on the web.

What is in this Collection?

I have organised the stories by notional year group for easier reference. This is just a guide, as most stories can be adjusted so that they are suitable for younger or older audiences once the teacher gets the hang of this. However, the chapters give you a good place to start looking.

There are sets of appendices at the end of the book, which classify the stories in various ways for easy reference when looking for a suitable story.

The categories are:
- Topic
- Value
- Plot Type
- Story Genre
- Country or Region of Origin
- Story Titles in Alphabetical Order

In addition each story comes with brief tips for telling and a set of sources and references signposting alternative sources and versions as needed.

Groupings by Age

This collection has been divided into six chapters, one for each primary school year from Year 1 to 6. This may make life simpler for your school. You can go along with the scheme and allocate stories to each year group from the relevant chapter.

However, in practice most of these stories can be adapted for any age, so the groupings are in some ways arbitrary. If you find a suitable story you can adapt it to your class.

Also, most stories need to be adapted to the aptitude of the class. If a class is new to storytelling they will need a simpler story than a class that has been telling stories regularly for a few years. Classes where the school entry has a high spoken language competence may need more challenging stories than those where the entry cohort has less developed language skills.

It is fine to select stories from other year groups and adapt them for your situation. With a bit of practice this becomes second nature. One important element in selection must be the teachers themselves. It's best to tell stories you really like: in a collection of 147 stories it should always be possible to find a few.

Plot Type

My colleague, Adam Guillain, has developed a way of teaching about plots using the 'seven basic plots' idea developed by Christopher Booker in his seminal work, *The Seven Basic Plots*. The idea is that there are seven main plot patterns that most stories fit into, and one great way of learning to create new stories is to get to know how these patterns work.

These seven basic plots are:

Voyage and Return
Quest
Defeat the Monster
Rags to Riches
Comedy
Tragedy
Rebirth

We have classified each story by basic plot type so that teachers can select stories for teaching a particular plot if and when they wish to.

In reality, these plot types are not always so clear cut, as stories often contain several plot elements, but nevertheless it can be very helpful for students to have these plot ideas in mind when they write.

Story Genre and the Ladder to the Moon

The great storyteller, Ben Haggarty, introduced me to the idea of 'The Ladder to the Moon' – a storyteller's classification of types of oral tradition story. Tradition has it that storytellers sometimes tell stories in the sequence of the Ladder to the Moon as a way of progressively raising the level of language and imaginative immersion during a storytelling session.

For those for whom this is useful I have also classified the stories in this way, loosely based on the ladder idea.

Namely:

➤ Folktale (no magic)
➤ Fable (may have talking animals but no real magical characters)
➤ Stories of How and Why (the genre that explains why things are the way they are)
➤ Wondertale (magic realms but no gods)
➤ Legends (historical reference to place or time, but no active gods)
➤ Myth (gods involved as main characters)
➤ Creation Myth (the world and its contents are created)

Values

Often teachers will want to use stories to illustrate something about values or morals as part of personal and social education. Stories can be a great way to do this, so I have classified the stories by some of the main values that may be connected to the story. This can also be useful if a particular issue comes up in the class or for school assemblies on a given theme.

Topics

Many schools have a particular topic or project focus every half-term (six or seven weeks) and like to link their story to that topic. For example, if you are doing Forces as a topic you might teach 'The Giant Turnip' to a KS1 group, or, if you are doing Amazing Journeys as a topic, you might teach 'Gilgamesh' for Year 6. I have taken some of the most common topic themes and linked them to stories which might be used for that purpose.

Teaching Story Features

In the Storytelling School students learn to retell stories as a way of learning about stories and about how to make good ones. Teachers often will use a story to teach key storytelling features like:

Setting
Character
Dilemma
Mood
Description, etc.

I have not classified stories for this purpose as most stories have sections which illustrate these features. We leave it up to the teacher to pick a story and then pick a section where a particular language feature can be taught.

Teaching Language Features

Similarly, teachers will sometimes use stories to illustrate particular language features (use of connectives, adverb clauses, sentence starters, and so on). Again, I have not classified the stories according to particular language features as it is simple enough to add these features to any story that you use.

How to Use the Stories

Tell Them for Retelling

If you want your class to tell these stories themselves, the best thing is for the teacher to tell the story to them. Advice on how to do this is set out in *The Storytelling School Handbook*, but basically you might try this:

If you have an audio or DVD version of the story being told, listen to it. Otherwise read the story aloud at least three times to get the sound of the story going.

Draw a story map of the story, showing main moments in the narrative – just a quick sketch with stick figures and simple outlines.

'Step' the story: with each step speak a word or sentence with a gesture to remember a key moment in the story. Practise this till you can do it fluently.

Practise telling it alone or to a friend until you are comfortable with your version.

Remember this is not usually word-for-word memorisation. The point is to tell the story in your own way using your own words. Try standing up and letting your body move as you tell. You may be surprised what a difference it makes.

Teach Them the Story

Once you have told the class the story, you can teach them to tell it themselves. With the exception of choral stories where the story is chanted by a group word for word (used sometimes in Foundation and Year 1), most of these stories can be learned in the same way as the teacher learned it. After hearing the story told, the class will map it, then step it, then practise speaking the story in small groups. This can be remembered with the initials HMSS – Hear, Map, Step, Speak.

Links to Literacy

Once learned, the story can be deepened with drama, role play, poetry, visual arts and other activities so that the words and ideas are developed and clear. The students will often use the story as a basis for writing and/or story innovation. See *The Storytelling School: Handbook for Teachers* for detailed methods and approaches.

Reading

The stories can be used as a reading resource in the classroom. Once students have got the hang of storytelling you can give them stories to learn by reading the text first. Some students might read the text after learning to tell it. For those who struggle with reading this might ease the process of decoding.

All stories may be photocopied and distributed within the school for this purpose and for homework.

Chapter 1

Year 1 Stories

Monkeys and Hats – India	2
The Little Red Hen – England	4
Three Little Pigs – England	6
The Birth of Jesus – World (Christian)	8
The Gingerbread Man – England	10
Bat Learns to Dance – origin unknown	12
Three Billy Goats Gruff – Norway	14
The Noisy House – Britain	16
The Giant Turnip – Russia	18
The Wooden Baby – Czech Republic	20
Goldilocks and the Three Bears – Britain	22
The Fox's Sack – England	25
The Princess and the Pea – Denmark	28
Skinny Old Lady – Africa	30
The Freedom Bird – Thailand	33
Snip-Snip – European (Jewish)	36
The King and the Moon – Dominican Republic	39
The Magic Porridge Pot – Germany	41
The Sweet-Talking Potato – Africa	44
Stone Soup – Switzerland	46
A Husband for Miss Mouse – Myanmar	48
Awongalema – Africa	52
The Lion's Roar – India (Buddhist)	54
Goose Girl's Wings – China	57
Mouse and Lion – Greece	60
The Nest and the Web – Islam	62
The Dancing Harmonica – USA	63
The Talkative Turtle – Native American	66
Bandits and Berries – China	68
The Thirsty Frog – Aboriginal (Australia)	71
More! – USA	73
Little Red Riding Hood – France	74
Jack and the Beanstalk – Britain	76

Monkeys and Hats

This is a great starter story with lots of physical copying. Every time the monkeys copy the hat-maker you can get your audience to join in and do the same thing, making monkey noises at the same time. I can remember where I heard this one first, as it is very popular and much loved. You can find one simple version in Hugh Lupton's The Story Tree. *This story is all about having fun together. Try and tell it that way.*

Once, not twice, not thrice...

There was a hat-maker. He made tall hats and short hats, fat hats and thin hats, green hats and blue hats ... all sorts of hats.

One day he was walking through the forest on the way to market carrying a basketful of hats on his head to sell in the market. As he walked he sang a song.

> *I am going to market, to market, to market,*
> *I am going to market, to sell my hats.*

It was hot day and the hat-maker felt tired so he decided to have a rest. He lay down under a tree with his basket of hats next to him and fell asleep.

When he woke up, he looked in the basket and ... all the hats were gone. He looked behind trees and under bushes but there was no sign of his hats.

Then he heard the sound of a monkey chattering above his head. He looked up and saw, sitting on a branch high up above his head, a crowd of monkeys, each one wearing one of his hats.

Furious, he shook his fist at them and shouted, 'Give me back my hats!'

Now monkeys love to copy and all of the monkeys did the same thing back to him, shaking their fists and shouting back in monkeytalk.

This made the hat-maker even more cross. He shook his finger at the monkeys, 'If you are making fun of me then you'll be sorry!'

The monkeys copied him, wagged their fingers and shouted back in their own language.

'If you don't give them back, then I'll go and get my bow and arrow and shoot you one by one!'

He made as if to shoot an imaginary weapon and the monkeys just followed suit.

'Please,' he begged, his hands clasped together in prayer, but again they just copied.

This went on for a while, until finally he gave up.

Taking off his own hat he threw it onto the ground. 'I give up!' he shouted.

All the monkeys in their trees took of their hats and threw them down onto the ground.

Delighted, the hat-maker picked them up, put them in his basket, and walked off to town singing his song.

That evening the hat-maker told his son what had happened with the monkeys, and after that the monkey story was his son's favourite.

'Tell me, Dad! Tell me the one about the monkeys and the hats!'

The son grew up and became a hat-maker just like his dad. One day he was walking through the forest with a basketful of hats, singing a song. He decided to have a rest. He lay down under a tree and fell asleep, and when he woke up … his basket was empty.

Knowingly, he looked up into the tree and smiled at the monkeys wearing his hats.

He waggled his finger at them. 'I know how to get the hats back,' he called up, and the monkey waggled their fingers back at him.

He poked his chest confidently, 'My dad told me this story!' And again they copied.

He took off his hat, and threw it down, but the monkeys didn't move a muscle.

'Come on you stupid monkeys!' he called. 'Copy that!'

But they didn't.

The largest of the monkeys, grey and long-haired, hung his hat on the branch and climbed down the tree until he stood face to face with the hat-maker's son.

'You think you are clever,' said the monkey, waggling his finger at the son, 'because your dad told you stories. Well, our dad's told us stories too, and this time we're keeping the hats!'

And the monkeys disappeared into the forest with the hats. The hat-maker's son went home with nothing to sell in the market.

That's why stories are so important…

You never know what you will learn from one, and when it will come in handy!

The Little Red Hen

This is a repeating story, which can easily be told communally with actions for each line. It's a very popular story for learning the communal method. The web is full of examples of children telling the story in this way to give you ideas for actions. I first heard this from Pie Corbett, whose way of telling has become very well known around the UK and beyond. It's a good story to teach about living things and life cycles as well as about food and about the benefits of helping others.

To make it meaningful it's often good to explain the sequence before you start telling: planting, watering, cutting, grinding, kneading, baking and eating. The class can learn an action for each step to make it more fun and memorable.

Once upon a time there was a Little Red Hen who lived on a farm with a bull, a cat and a rat. One morning the Little Red Hen woke up and decided to grow some wheat, to make some bread, to eat when she was hungry.

She went outside to the field.
'Who will help me plant the seeds?' said the Little Red Hen.

'Not me,' said the Bull.
'Not me,' said the Cat.
'Not me,' said the Rat.

'Oh well, then I suppose I'll have to do it myself,' she said.
And so she did, planting all the seeds.

Time passed.

'Who will help me water the seeds?' said the Little Red Hen.
'Not me,' said the Bull.
'Not me,' said the Cat.
'Not me,' said the Rat.

'Oh well, then I suppose I'll have to do it myself,' she said.
And so she did, watering all the seeds.

Time passed and the wheat grew.

'Who will help me cut the wheat?' said the Little Red Hen.
'Not me,' said the Bull.
'Not me,' said the Cat.
'Not me,' said the Rat.

'Oh well, then I suppose I'll have to do it myself,' she said.
And so she did, cutting all the wheat herself.

Time passed.

'Who will help me grind the wheat?' said the Little Red Hen.
'Not me,' said the Bull.
'Not me,' said the Cat.
'Not me,' said the Rat.

'Oh well, then I suppose I'll have to do it myself,' she said.
And so she did, grinding all the wheat herself.

Time passed.

'Who will help me bake the bread?' said the Little Red Hen…
'Not me,' said the Bull.
'Not me,' said the Cat.
'Not me,' said the Rat.

'Oh well, then I suppose I'll have to do it myself,' she said.
And so she did, baking the bread herself.

Time passed.

'Who will help me eat the bread?' said the Little Red Hen.

'I will,' said the Bull.
'I will,' said the Cat.
'I will,' said the Rat.

'Oh no you won't!' said the Little Red Hen. 'I'll eat it myself.'
And so she did, eating all the bread herself.
It tasted good!

Three Little Pigs

Once there were three little pigs who lived with their mum.
(three fingers for three, press nose for pig)

One day she said,

'Off you go and build your own houses.

(shoo off with hand, mime roof with arms)

Remember to build them strong.'

(clench fists for strong)

The first pig built his house out of straw.

(one finger for first, roof for house, mime thin straw)

Along came the wolf and said, *(mime claws and jaws for wolf)*

'Little pig, little pig, let me come in.'

'Not by the hair of my chinni chin chin!'

(shake head and scratch chin)

'Then I'll huff and I'll puff and I'll blow your house down!'

The wolf huffed and puffed and blew the house down *(huff and puff)*

and he ate up the little pig. *(eating)*

The second little pig built his house out of wood.

Along came the wolf and said,

'Little pig, little pig, let me come in.'

'Not by the hair of my chinni chin chin!'

'Then I'll huff and I'll puff and I'll blow your house down!'

The wolf huffed and puffed and blew the house down

and he ate up the little pig.

The third little pig built his house out of bricks.

Along came the wolf and said,

'Little pig, little pig, let me come in.'

'Not by the hair of my chinni chin chin!'

'Then I'll huff and I'll puff and I'll blow your house down!'

The wolf huffed and puffed but he couldn't blow the house down.
(mime a lot of futile huffing)

So the wolf went home and the third little pig was glad. *(big smile)*

The Birth of Jesus

I helped create this story with the Foundation Team at St John Fisher School, a pioneer Storytelling School in Oxford. It's good for communal chanting, with an action for each line. Make up your own actions. It can be used for a whole school assembly at Christmas.

A long long time ago
Mary was going to have a baby
They walked and walked and walked and walked
And slept in a stable

> *Snow is falling*
> *Stars are shining*
> *Halleluya baby Jesus*

In the cold of the dark dark night
When everyone was sleeping
Jesus was born to Mary
And lay in the straw of a manger

> *Snow is falling*
> *Stars are shining*
> *Halleluya baby Jesus*

Who's that knocking at the stable door?
LOOK it's the shepherds
What will they give to baby Jesus?
Sheepskins and wool

Snow is falling
Stars are shining
Halleluya baby Jesus

Who's that knocking at the stable door?
LOOK it's the three wise men
What will they give to baby Jesus?
Gold, frankincense and myrrh

Snow is falling
Stars are shining
Halleluya baby Jesus

Who's that knocking at the stable door?
WE ARE, WE ARE
What will we learn from baby Jesus?
Joy, love and hope

Snow is falling
Stars are shining
Halleluya baby Jesus

The Gingerbread Man

Once upon a time (*open hands*) there was a little old lady (*mime dress*) and a little old man (*mime beard*) who lived together in house. (*mime roof*)

One day the little old lady said, 'I'm going to bake a gingerbread man.'
(*mime gingerbread man: hand and feet out and mouth open*)

She mixed and pressed and put the dough in the oven. (*mime*)

Then she heard a knocking from inside the oven. (*knock*)

She opened the door (*mime*) and out jumped the gingerbread man. (*mime*)

'Stop!' said the old lady. (*hold up hand*)

> *Run run as fast as you can*
> *You can't catch me I'm the gingerbread man* (*mime running*)
> *The old man can't catch me* (*mime beard*)
> *And you can't catch me* (*point finger for you*)

He ran and he ran and he ran (*mime running*)
until he came to a:

1. Cat (*mime whiskers*)
'Stop!' said the cat. (*hold up hand*)

> *Run run as fast as you can*
> *You can't catch me I'm the gingerbread man* (*mime running*)
> *The old man can't catch me* (*mime beard*)
> *The old lady can't catch me*
> *And you can't catch me* (*point finger for you*)

2. Dog (*mime ears*)
(repeat whole sequence)

3. Cow (*mime horns*)
(repeat whole sequence)

4. River and a Fox (*mime flowing water and fox's tricky tail with hand*)

'Jump on my tail!' said the fox, 'And I'll carry you over the river.'
The gingerbread man jumped on his tail. (*mime the jump with a hand onto your tail*)

'Jump on my back,' said the fox, 'I'm sinking in the water.'
And the gingerbread man jumped on his back. (*mime hand jump onto your back*)

'Jump on my head,' said the fox, 'I'm sinking in the water.'
And the gingerbread man jumped on his head.
(*mime hand jump onto your head*)

'Jump on my nose,' said the fox, 'I'm sinking in the water.'
And the gingerbread man jumped on his nose. (*mime*)

The fox shook his nose
The gingerbread man flew up into the air
And down into the fox's mouth. (*mime all this into your mouth*)

And that was the end of the gingerbread man.

Bat Learns to Dance

This can be chanted or told as a participative story. There is lots of clear physicality. You can let your class make up the dances. I am not sure where it comes from; it's very popular with UK storytellers.

Once a baby bat was hanging on the roof of its cave next to her mum and dad in the middle of winter.
'I'm cold,' shivered the bat, and fell off onto the floor.

There she met a worm.
'I'm cold,' she said. 'How can I get warm?'
'When I am warm,' said the worm, 'I go wiggle waggle wiggle waggle.'
(*do the dance and have them copy*)
'Thanks,' said the bat and the bat wiggled and waggled too. (*copy*)
'That was good,' she thought, 'but I am still cold!'

Next she came to a fly on the wall.
'I'm cold,' she said. 'How can I get warm?'
'When I am warm,' said the fly, 'I go buzz buzz buzz with my wings.'
(*do the dance and have them copy*)
'Thanks,' said the bat and the bat buzz buzz buzzed too. (*copy*)
'That was good,' she thought, 'but I am still cold!'

Repeat for anything you like ... spider spin, bird flap, and so on.

Next she came to a ghost.
'I'm cold,' she said. 'How can I get warm?'
'When I am warm,' said the ghost, 'I go wail wail wail and sway sway sway.'
(*do the dance and have them copy*)
'Thanks,' said the bat and the bat wailed and swayed. (*copy*)
'That was good,' she thought, 'now I am nice and warm.'

She flew back to her mum and dad.
'Look Mum! Look Dad! I know how to get warm. I dance like this:

Wiggle waggle

Buzz buzz

Wail and sway

'Well done!' said Dad.
'Well done! said Mum.

And they all went to sleep!

Three Billy Goats Gruff

Here's a version with a little song to liven it up. Use any tune you like. Can be communal or participative. Get the class to practise different voices for the characters.

Once upon a time there were three Billy Goats Gruff. (*three fingers, horns, gruff-frown and stroke chin*)
A big billy goat gruff. (*big horns*)
A middle billy boat gruff. (*medium horns*)
And a tiny billy goat gruff. (*tiny horns*)

They decided to go to a lovely green grassy hillside.
On the way they sang a song:

> *We're going to a hill where the grass is long and green.*
> *We're going to the hill it's the best we've ever seen.*
> *We're going to a hill where the grass is green and long.*
> *We're going to a hill, that's why we sing this song.*

On the way they came to a bridge where a troll lived.
A big mean foolish troll. (*mime troll body and face*)

First the small Billy Goat Gruff went trip trap trip trap across the bridge.
'Wait!' said the troll, 'I'm going to eat you up.' (*troll body and voice*)
'O I'm very small and thin (*small voice and horns*)
You don't want to eat me!
My big brother comes next.
He's much bigger and better to eat.'
'OK,' said the troll, 'I'll wait.'

Next the middle Billy Goat Gruff went trip trap trip trap across the bridge.
'Wait!' said the troll, 'I'm going to eat you up.'
'O I'm very small and thin
You don't want to eat me!
My brother comes next
He's much bigger and better to eat.'
'OK,' said the troll, 'I'll wait.'

Last the big Billy Goat Gruff went trip trap trip trap across the bridge.
'Wait!' said the troll, 'I'm going to eat you up.'
'OK,' said the big Billy Goat Gruff, 'just try.'
The troll jumped onto the bridge and ran at the Big Billy Goat.
The big Billy Goat Gruff butted the troll into the air and down into the valley.

The three Billy Goats Gruff went off to the green hillside singing their song:
(*sing song as above*)

and ate lovely green grass. (*mime eating*)
It tasted sooooo good! (*lick lips*)

Four leaf clover
Our story's over.

The Noisy House

I heard this from Megan Davies, who can't remember which storyteller she heard it from. It's a great little story that can be adapted to any environment to fit with your child's home area.

Once there was a boy called Jack who lived in a house...

where the floor went creak (*make arm into floorboard and move it as you creak*)
the tap went drip drip (*thumb touches second finger – move down as you say drip*)
and the wind blew whhhhh whhhh whhhh (*wave hands back and forth as you go whhhhh*) through the holes in the windows.

This is too noisy, thought Jack. (*hands on ears*)
I need help.

So Jack went (*move hand up and down in time with this chant*) up the hill and down the hill and up the hill and down the hill and up the hill and down the hill and down the hill and up...

(*you can add details of your community here if you like. Down the road, over the park, into the shopping centre and so on*)

...until he came to the housing office. (*do a roof for the housing office with your arms*)

He said to the housing man (*maybe knot a tie for the housing man*)

'My house is too noisy. (*roof for house, then fingers in ears*)
The floor goes creak, the tap goes drip drip and the wind blows whhh whhh whhh through the holes in the windows.'

'Get a cat,' (*fingers mime whiskers*) said the man. (*mime tie*)

So Jack bought a cat and went home.
He went up the hill and down the hill and...

When he went inside
The floor went creak, the tap went drip drip, the wind blew whhh whhh whhh through the holes in the windows and the cat went meow.

This is too noisy, thought Jack.
I need help.

So Jack went (*move hand up and down in time with this chant*) up the hill and down the hill and up the hill and down the hill and up the hill and down the hill and down the hill and up...

...until he came to the housing office. (*do a roof for the housing office with your arms*)

He said to the housing man (*tie*)

'My house is too noisy. (*roof for house, then fingers in ears*)
The floor goes creak, the tap goes drip drip, the wind blows whhh whhh whhh through the holes in the windows and the cat goes meow!'

'Get a dog,' said the man. (*show dog with fingers as ears on head*)

So Jack got a dog, then he went up the hill and...

Repeat for:
Cow (*show horns with fingers on our your head, go moo*),
Horse (*show galloping hooves with your hands, go nayhhhh*)
Anything else chicken, monkey, elephant...

Until...
He said to the housing man

'My house is too noisy. (*roof for house, then fingers in ears*)
The floor goes creak, the tap goes drip drip and the wind goes whhh whhh whhh though the holes in the windows and the cat goes meow, the dog goes woof, the cow goes moo and the horse goes nhaaaay!'

'Get rid of all the animals,' said the man.
So the boy took all the animals back to the animal shop, and then he went home.

Up the hill and...

The floor went creak, the tap went drip and the wind blew through the windows.
This is nice and quiet, he thought.
I like it here.

Crick crack cring
The story's done its thing.

The Giant Turnip

This is a very popular story from Russia, with many, many written versions including one from Tolstoy himself, who used it to illustrate the power of working together. In this retelling there's a little song or chant that you can sing each time they try and pull up the turnip. It can be a very physical story with the class miming all the actions. I have added suggestions for movements in brackets.

Once upon a time there was a farmer.
He lived in a house (*mime roof*) with his
Wife (*mime skirts*)
His son Jack (*mime beard*)
His daughter Jill (*mime pigtails*)
His sheepdog (*mime dog ears*)
And a mouse (*mime mouse teeth and claws*)

One day he took a seed and planted it in the ground. (*mime planting*)
Every day he watered it. (*mime watering can*)

The roots went down (*fingers down*)
and the shoots went up. (*fingers up*)

The seed was soon the size of a nut, (*show with index finger*)
a tomato, (*show with finger and thumb*)
a potato, (*fist*)
then a man's head, (*show size with two hands*)
and still it kept growing.

One day the farmer's wife said, 'Pull that turnip up! I want to cook it.'

So the farmer went out and took hold of the turnip top and pulled and pulled (*mime pulling*). As he pulled he sang this song:

> **Heave-ho, heave-ho! Pull the turnip free.**
> **Heave-ho, heave-ho! We'll have it for our tea.**

He sang and he pulled, he pulled and he sang, but the turnip would not budge.

He called out to his wife. 'Can you help me?'

And the farmer grabbed the turnip,
the wife grabbed the farmer,
and together they pulled and sang.

> *Heave-ho, heave-ho...*

They sang and they pulled, they pulled and they sang. But the turnip would not budge.

The wife called to her son, Jack, 'Come and help.' The farmer grabbed the turnip, the wife grabbed the farmer and Jack grabbed his mother, and together they all pulled and sang.

> *Heave-ho, heave-ho...*

They sang and they pulled and they pulled and they sang... But the turnip would not budge.

Jack called out to his sister, Jill, for help.

The farmer grabbed the turnip...

Repeat for sister Jill, the sheep dog, the mouse and anything else you like till:

The farmer grabbed the turnip,
The wife grabbed the farmer,
Jack grabbed the wife,
Jill grabbed Jack,
The sheep dog grabbed Jill,
The mouse grabbed the dog,
And they all pulled and sang.

> *Heave-ho, heave-ho! Pull the turnip free.*
> *Heave-ho, heave-ho! We'll have it for our tea.*

...and this time, the enormous turnip popped out.

The wife chopped it up (*mime this*)
put it in a stew (*stir it*)
and that night they all enjoyed a delicious bowl of turnip stew. (*mime eating*)

Afterwards they sang

> *Heave-ho, heave-ho! We pulled the turnip free.*
> *Heave-ho, heave-ho! We've had it for our tea.*

Heave-ho. Heave-ho
Now it's time to go

The Wooden Baby

This one is a bit crazy, which most children really love. There is lots of scope to make up things that the baby eats. You might simplify it a bit for communal chanting or use it this way for participative telling. I've heard it a few times from several storytellers. There's a great neolithic version in Ben Haggarty's great graphic novel, Mezolith.

Once upon a time there was a little old lady who had no children at all. Not even one! One day she was feeling sad that she would never be a mother and said to herself,

'I wish I had a baby, even if it was a toy baby, even if it was only a wooden baby.'

The next morning a wooden baby was sitting on the bed. The old lady was happy and cuddled the baby for a while then put it on the table and went outside to work in the garden.

While she was working the wooden baby started to move. It climbed down off the table, opened the cupboard, and started to eat. Soon it had eaten all the bread and cake and biscuits in the cupboard.

The old lady heard a noise from the kitchen and rushed in to see what was happening.

She saw the wooden baby standing by the cupboard.
'Who are you?' she cried. 'And what have you done?'
'I am the wooden baby,' came the reply, 'and I've eaten all the food in the cupboard and now I'll eat you up too!'

The wooden baby ate up the little old lady, growing bigger as he ate. Then he went outside where he saw a boy on a bicycle.

'Who are you?' cried the boy, 'and what have you done?'
'I am the wooden baby,' came the reply, 'and I've eaten all the food in the cupboard, I've eaten the little old lady, and now I'll eat you up too!'

The wooden baby ate up the boy on the bicycle, growing bigger and bigger as he ate, then walked on down the road ... until he saw a policeman.

'Who are you?' cried the policeman, 'and what have you done?'
'I am the wooden baby,' came the reply, 'and I've eaten all the food in the cupboard, I've eaten the little old lady, I've eaten the boy on the bicycle, and now I'll eat you up too!'

The wooden baby ate up the policeman, growing bigger as he ate, and then walked on down the road until he saw a...

(*Repeat for teacher, baker, butcher, street cleaner, or add fictional characters Simpsons, Harry Potter, or footballers, or other celebrities, whatever you class would enjoy.*)

Finally the enormous baby came to a garden, and in the garden was an old lady with a pointed hat and a pointed nose. She was a wise old lady.

'Who are you?' cried the wise old lady to the enormous wooden baby, 'and what have you done?'

'I am the wooden baby,' came the reply, 'and I've eaten all the food in the cupboard, I've eaten the little old lady, I've eaten the boy on the bicycle, I've eaten the policeman ... etc. and now I'll eat you up too!'

'Oh no you won't!' said the old lady.

Quick as a flash she poked a needle into the wooden baby's tummy and the baby burst open like a balloon. POP!

Out came:
...the policeman, the boy on the bicycle, the little old lady and all the bread and cake and biscuits from the cupboard.

They said, 'Thank you, wise old lady,' and all went home for tea.

And the little old lady never wished for a wooden baby again.

Goldilocks and the Three Bears

Once upon a time, in the middle of a deep green forest, there was a cottage.

In the cottage there lived three bears.
A daddy bear (*show how tall*)
A mamma bear (*show how tall*)
And a baby bear. (*show how tall*)
They loved each other lots and lots. (*touch heart*)

Inside the cottage there were three porridge bowls. (*cup hands*)
The baby bear had a tiny bowl (*show sizes with hands*)
The mamma bear had a middle-sized bowl
And the daddy bear had a big bowl.

Inside the cottage there were three chairs. (*show with hands or mime sitting*)
The baby bear had a tiny chair (*show sizes with hands*)
The mamma bear had a middle-sized chair
And the daddy bear had a big chair.

Inside the cottage there were three beds. (*mime sleeping*)
The baby bear had a tiny bed (*show size with hands*)
The mamma bear had a middle-sized bed
And the daddy bear had a big bed.

One morning mama bear cooked porridge for breakfast and poured it into the three bowls. (*mime stirring and pouring*)
It was too hot to eat (*mime spoon and hot mouth*)
so they went for a walk. (*mime walking*)

As they walked through the forest they sang a song:

> *We're three bears, three bears, living in our cottage in the wood*
> *Three bears, three bears, living here together feels so good.*

While they were out walking a selfish little girl with golden hair was walking though the forest, and singing a song:

Goldilocks, Goldilocks, what can I steal today?
Maybe some food, maybe some money, maybe a game to play?

She smelled porridge, and thought, 'Hmm, I'm hungry.
Maybe that's my breakfast?'
She followed the smell to the cottage, (*mime sniffing*)
peeped in through the window (*mime peeping*)
lifted the latch (*mime lifting*)
and stepped into the cottage. (*mime stepping*)

Goldilocks went over to the kitchen table where the porridge was cooling.
First, she tried the porridge in the big bowl but it was too hot.
'Too hot! Too hot!' she shouted and pouted.
Next, she tried the porridge in the middle bowl but it was too cold.
'Too cold! Too cold!' she shouted and pouted.
Finally, she tried the porridge in the tiny bowl and it was just right.
'Ahh!' she said, 'Just right!' She smiled and gobbled it all up.

After that she thought she would sit down.
First, she sat down in the big chair, but it was too hard.
'Too hard!' she shouted and pouted.
Next, she sat down on the middle chair, but it was too soft.
'Too soft!' she shouted and pouted
Finally, she sat down on the tiny chair.
'Ahh!' she said, 'Just right!'

But the girl was too heavy,
and the chair fell to pieces
and Goldilocks fell on the floor.

'Oh bother!' she shouted and pouted. 'That's no good!'

Goldilocks went upstairs to the bedroom.
First, she tried the big bed, but it was too high at the head.
'Too high!' she shouted and pouted.
Next, she tried the middle bed but it was too low at the head
'Too low!' she shouted and pouted.

Finally, she tried the tiny bed.
'Ahh!' she said, 'Just right!' And fell asleep.

A while later the three bears came back from their walk still singing their song:

> *We're three bears, three bears, living in our cottage in the wood*
> *Three bears, three bears, living here together feels so good.*

They lifted the latch and went into their cottage,

First, they went over to their bowls.
'Someone's been eating my porridge!' roared the daddy bear.
'Someone's been eating my porridge too!' shouted the mamma bear.
'Someone's been eating my porridge too!' squeaked the baby bear, 'and they've eaten it all up!' and began to cry.

Next, they went over to their chairs.
'Someone's been sitting in my chair!' roared the daddy bear.
'Someone's been sitting in my chair!' shouted the mamma bear.
'Someone's been sitting in my chair!' squeaked the baby bear, 'and it's fallen to pieces!'
The baby bear started to cry again.

Finally, they went to the bedroom.
'Someone's been sleeping in my bed!' roared the daddy bear.
'Someone's been sleeping in my bed! shouted the mamma bear.
'Someone's been sleeping in my bed!' squeaked the baby bear, 'and she's still there!'

The three bears roared and Goldilocks jumped up out of bed, jumped out of the window, and the three bears never saw her again.

Chit, chat
That's the end of that!

The Fox's Sack

Here's a funny and tricky story that's good for older Foundation kids. There's lots of suspense when the sack opens. Find your foxy voice!

Once upon a time there was a hungry fox with an empty sack.
He said, 'I wish my bag was full of food.'

Just then a bee buzzed past.
BZZZZ
The fox grabbed the bee and popped it in the sack,
Put the sack over his shoulder and walked down the road singing:

> *Nobody knows it*
> *Nobody knows it*
> *Nobody knows what's in this sack but me.*

He came to a house and knocked on the door.
A short lady opened the door.
'Hello, Mr Fox,' she said, a little frightened.
'Hello,' he said. 'I need a place to leave my sack while I visit my friend. Can I leave it here?'
'OK,' she said, nervously.
'But whatever you do, don't look in the sack!'
'What's in it?'
'Just don't look!'
He put the sack down in her room and went away.
She stared at the sack singing her song:

> *I want to know*
> *I really want to know*
> *I want to know what's in the sack.*

She tiptoed over and opened the sack.
BZZZZ
Out came the bee.

Later the fox came back.

'Here's your sack,' said the short lady.
'Where's my bee?' said the fox.
'It flew out of the sack and my chicken ate it,' said the woman.
'Well then, I'll take the chicken,' said the fox, and he picked it up and put it in the sack.

He trotted off to the next house in the street and knocked on the door.

A tall lady answered.
'Yes?'
'Hello,' he said. 'I need a place to leave my sack while I visit my friend. Can I leave it here?'
'OK,' she said, nervously.
'But whatever you do, don't look in the sack!'
'What's in it?'
'Just don't look!'
He put the sack down in her room and went away.
She stared at the sack singing her song:

> *I want to know*
> *I really want to know*
> *I want to know what's in the sack.*

She tiptoed over and opened the sack.
Out jumped a chicken.
Puk puk puk puk puk
Out into the yard and away down the road went the chicken chased by the tall lady's pig.

Later the fox came back.

'Here's your sack,' said the tall woman.
'Where's my chicken?' said the fox.
'It flew out of the sack and my pig chased it away,' said the tall woman.
'Well then, I'll take the pig,' said the fox, and he picked it up and put it in the sack.

He trotted off to the next house in the street and knocked on the door.

A thin lady answered.
'Yes?'
'Hello,' he said. 'I need a place to leave my sack while I visit my friend. Can I leave it here?'
'OK,' she said, nervously.
'But whatever you do, don't look in the sack!'
'What's in it?'
'Just don't look!'
He put the sack down in her room and went away.
She stared at the sack singing her song:

> *I want to know*
> *I really want to know*
> *I really want to know what's in the sack.*

She tiptoed over and opened the sack.
Out jumped a pig.
Oink oink oink
Her little boy chased the pig away down the road.

Later the fox came back.

'Here's your sack,' said the thin woman.
'Where's my pig?' said Mr Fox.
'It jumped out of the sack and my son chased it away,' said the thin woman.
'Well then, I'll take your son,' said the fox and he picked him up and put him in the sack.

He trotted off to the next house in the street and knocked on the door.

A fat lady answered.
'Yes?'
'Hello,' he said. 'I need a place to leave my sack while I visit my friend. Can I leave it here?'
'OK,' she said, nervously.
'But whatever you do, don't look in the sack!'
'What's in it?'
'Just don't look!'
He put the sack down in her room and went away.
She stared at the sack singing her song:

> *I want to know*
> *I really want to know*
> *I want to know what's in the sack.*
> *But I won't look.*

The fat lady started making biscuits with her two daughters, mixing the batter and cutting out the shapes. Soon the biscuits were baking in the oven and a lovely smell spread around the house.

'Mum, I want a biscuit!' said a daughter.
'Me too!' said a voice from the sack.

The fat lady opened the sack and out jumped the boy.
'Mr Fox put me in there!'
'You go and hide under the bed,' she said and she called her big black dog and put him in the sack.

Mr Fox came back, picked up the sack and walked away.
He heard a growl from the sack.
'I'm hungry,' he thought. 'Time to eat the boy.'
He put the sack down, put in his paw and ... 'OWW! He bit me!' shouted Mr Fox.

The dog jumped out and chased the fox into the woods, then bit him on the tail.
'OWW!' said Mr Fox. 'That hurt!'

The fox went into his den and was safe but sore.
The dog went home and they all ate the cookies together.

Fox sat in his lair singing:

> *Everyone knew*
> *Everyone knew*
> *Everyone knew what was in my sack but me.*

The Princess and the Pea

This is a silly little story that connects with the princess in us all! Play it for comedy. Check out the excellent Three Rapping Rats *by Kaye Umansky for a rap version!*

Once upon a time there was a prince.
He lived in a palace with his dad and mum, the king and queen.

One day his dad said, 'Son, it's time you got married. Let's find you a wife!'

The prince said, 'Dad, I only want to marry a real princess.
Lots of girls pretend but I want a real one.'

'No problem!' said the king. 'I'll find you one.'

The king sent messages that he needed a real princess, so women came from all over the land to visit. Soon there was a long queue outside the palace gates. One by one the young women met the prince with their lovely hair and lovely eyes and fine clothes.

To each one the prince asked the same question: 'Are you a real princess?'

Some said, 'Yes' and some said, 'No' and some said, 'Maybe'.

'I don't think you are a real princess,' he said, and one by one the prince sent them all home.

Then one rainy night there was a knock on the palace door and in stepped a young woman. 'I'm a princess,' she said, 'and I need a place to stay for the night.'

The queen looked closely at the woman and said, 'Welcome. You go and sit by the fire and we'll get your bed ready.'

The princess sat by the fire and the prince came to say hello.

'Are you a real princess?' he asked.

'Oh yes, definitely!' she said.

'Good,' he said, but still wasn't sure.

The queen told the servants to make up a bed with ten mattresses, one on top of the other, with a hard dried pea under the bottom mattress. Then the servants showed the princess to her bed and they all went off to sleep.

The next morning at breakfast the princess came down with tired eyes.

'What's the matter, dear?' asked the queen.

'Oh, I couldn't sleep a wink! That bed was so uncomfortable! There was something hard in it, which kept poking and prodding me all night. I feel bruised all over!'

'Wonderful!' said the queen.

'Not wonderful!' said the princess.

'Wonderful!' said the queen, 'Because now we know that you are a Real Princess.'

'Well, I knew that already!' the princess said.

The prince and princess had breakfast together and then lunch and then supper.

'You are so really a real princess,' said the prince.

'And you are really a real prince,' she replied.

Soon the prince and princess were married and guess what they had at the banquet?
Pea soup.

Snick snack
That's the end of that.

Skinny Old Lady

My colleague, author and storyteller Adam Guillain, introduced me to this fine African story. Make it playful and funny but with scary animals.

Once there was a skinny old lady who was very hungry.
She decided to visit her mum on the other side of the forest. Her mum was a really good cook.

In the forest she knew there were three animals who would try and eat her – the Lion, the Bear and the Tiger – but even so, she walked off into the forest singing her song:

> *I'm hungry*
> *I'm hungry*
> *I'm going to see my mum*
> *When I get here she'll give me*
> *Some food to fill my tum*

First she came to the Lion.
'Who's coming into my forest?' he roared and jumped out in front of her.
'I'm going to eat you up!'
'Oh, you don't want to do that!' said the old lady, laughing. 'I'm much too thin. Wait till I come back from visiting my mum and I'll be big and fat and much better to eat!'
'Do you promise to come back?' asked the Lion.
'I promise,' said the skinny lady and she went on her way singing her song:

> **I'm hungry...**

Next she came to the Bear.
'Who's coming into my forest?' he roared and jumped out in front of her.
'I'm going to eat you up!'
'Oh, you don't want to do that!' said the old lady laughing. 'I'm much too thin. Wait till I come back from visiting my mum and I'll be big and fat and much better to eat!'
'Do you promise to come back?' asked the Bear.

'I promise,' said the skinny lady and went on her way singing her song:

I'm hungry...

Next she came to the Tiger.
'Who's coming into my forest?' he roared and jumped out in front of her.
'I'm going to eat you up!'
'Oh, you don't want to do that!' said the old lady, laughing. 'I'm much too thin. Wait till I come back from visiting my mum and I'll be big and fat and much better to eat!'
'Do you promise to come back?' asked the Tiger.
'I promise,' said the skinny lady and she went on her way singing her song:

I'm hungry...

She came to her mum's house and ate and ate and ate till she was as round as a ball, then she set off home with her basket.

On the edge of the forest she stopped by some spiders' webs and picked off some flies.
'Spider,' she said, 'if I give you these flies will you help me?'
'OK,' said the spider. He ate the flies and hopped into her basket.

Next she took some eggs from a bird's nest and called out, 'Snake! Snake! Come!'
The snake came over.
'Will you help me if I give you these?'
'OK,' said the snake. He ate up the eggs and slithered into her basket.

Finally she saw a piece of rotten meat on the path, covered in fleas. She picked it up and put it in her basket and went into the forest singing her song:

Going home
Going home
Now I'm round and fat
Going home
Going home
As happy as a cat

First she came to the Tiger.
'Who's that coming into my forest?' he roared.
'It's me again,' she said. 'I am big and round now.'
'Good!' he said, and was about to eat her up when the spider jumped out of the bag and bit him on the nose.

'OWW!' he roared and ran away.

The old lady went on along the path singing her song...

Going home...

Next she came to the Bear.
'Who's that coming into my forest?' he roared.
'It's me again,' she said. 'I am big and round now.'
'Good!' he said and was about to eat her up when the snake jumped out of the bag and bit him on the tummy.
'OWW!' he roared and ran away.
The old lady went on along the path singing her song...

Going home...

Finally she came to the Lion
'Who's that coming into my forest?' he roared.
'It's me again,' she said. 'I am big and round now.'
'Good!' he said and was about to eat her up when she threw the old meat at him. The fleas jumped off and started to bite him all over.
'OWW!' he roared and ran away.

The old lady went on along the path singing her song till she got home, sat down and laughed and laughed and laughed.

Ho ho ho
Now it's time to go.

The Freedom Bird

This is another participative story that is fun to join in with. It has a simple repeating form that makes it easy to learn. It's good for all ages. I learned it first from David Holt. You can find a version written in the excellent Ready-to-Tell Tales *by David Holt and Bill Mooney. Like the Monkeys and Hats story it needs to be told with humour and playfulness.*

The birdsong is important in this story. You can use any tune you like; personally I like to use the teasing chant that is popular in UK playgrounds, but any tune will do. You need to find a sound to evoke birdsong, then shivering, then bubbling, then earth. The song makes the whole thing work with the audience joining in.

Once there was a hunter. He was a fine hunter. He was a proud hunter. His eyes were sharp and his aim was true. One day he was walking through the forest when he came to a tree. Perched on the top branch of the tree was a bird with a golden beak, a red head, blue wings and a yellow tail.

'What a beautiful bird!' he thought. 'I won't kill it. I'll let it live.'

Just as he was walking away from the tree, the bird pushed back its wings (*audience, you push back yours*), stuck out its beak (*audience, you stick out yours*) and sang this song (*sing with me*).

    NAA NAA N NAA NAA

The hunter did not like the sound of the song. He wondered if the bird was making fun of him.

'Don't sing that again, or you'll be sorry,' he called up to the bird.

But the bird (*get them to join in again*) pushed back its wings, stuck out its beak and sang the song again.

    NAA NAA N NAA NAA

Chapter 1   Year 1 Stories   147 Traditional Stories

'Once more,' he shouted, 'and you are dead meat!'

When the bird sang the song again the hunter aimed his bow and arrow and shot the bird straight though the heart. (mime the shooting)

The bird fell to the ground and lay there still and unmoving.
'That'll teach you,' said the hunter. He put the bird in his sack, threw the sack over his shoulder and started off for home.

As he walked he heard a very muffled sound coming from inside the sack (sing it through your hands)

NAA NAA N NAA NAA

The hunter felt a little irritated and resolved to put a stop to the annoying song as soon as he got home. Inside his kitchen he put the bird on the table and plucked it (*mime this*). It was cold in the hut, and the hunter noticed that the plucked bird was shivering. Then a shivering sort of song came from the plucked bird.

(*sing it in a shivery voice*)
BRR BRR B BRR BRR

'I wish this bird would shut up,' he fumed. 'I'll cook it, then that'll be the end of it!'

He chopped up the bird into 100 pieces (*mime this*) (not 99, not 101, but 100) and dropped them into a pot of water that was bubbling in the stove. He was just thinking about what else to put in the stew when a bubbly sound came from the pot.

BBL BBL B BBL BBL

Exasperated now, he took the pot into the garden, dug a hole, poured all the bits of bird into the hole and filled it in. He was walking back to the hut when a very earthy sound came up through the ground. The ground seemed to be singing the song now. (*try a deep voice*)

MMM MMM M MMM MMM

Fuming and furious he dug the bird bits up, put them in a wooden box, tied it up with string and flung it into the river which flowed past the bottom of his garden. He watched it float away, smiled, and lay down in his hammock for a well-earned rest.

A few days later some fishermen, downstream, were fishing in the river, throwing in their nets and pulling them out (*mime this*), when they saw a box floating down the river. They caught it, slowly undid the string and opened the lid.

As the lid opened, to their wonder and amazement, 100 birds flew out, each with a golden beak, red head, blue wings and a yellow tail.

'Wow!' they said. 'What was that?'

A few days later the hunter was hunting in the woods when he came to that same tree where he first met the bird. Perched in the top branches of the tree he saw 100 birds, each with a golden beak, red head, blue wings and a yellow tail. They sang down to him:

NAA NAA N NAA NAA

'Hmm,' he thought, 'I know what those birds are. I've heard about them but never seen one before. They must be Freedom Birds, because they say that however hard you try and kill one or keep them quiet, they just keep on coming back and singing the same song.'

So the hunter didn't try and kill any more Freedom Birds, and from then on, at least in that forest, the hunter and the Freedom Birds lived happily ever after.

Snip-Snip

I have worked a lot with this delightful story, which is sometimes known as The Blue Coat. It's great for all ages and has lots of places for improvisation, making up things that happen to the child as he/she gets older. Get the audience to help make it up and they will add elements that retell it in their own environment. It's full of learnings about stories and life. There is a much simpler version called The Blue Coat in Hugh Lupton's The Story Tree.

Introduction

This is a story about someone who had something that he really loved to wear. When he wore it he felt good. He felt happy. How many of you have favourite clothes that you love to wear? (*hear a few with prompts like what colour and so on*)

The story is about a tailor. Who can tell me what a tailor is and what he does? (*explain*)

Now here's the story:

Once there was a boy called Jack. He loved his mum and loved his dad but most of all he loved his granddad. His granddad was a tailor, someone who makes clothes by cutting out cloth and sewing it together again. When Jack was just five years, on his birthday, his granddad gave him a present. It was a coat.

(*Loop A begins here, repeating for jacket, t-shirt, tie and button and anything else you want to add.*)

'Thanks very much, Granddad!' he said. 'That's a lovely coat!'

Jack loved it so much he wore it all the time. When his friends saw him in the street they said, 'Jack, that's a really fine coat, where did you get that?'

'My granddad made it for me!' said Jack proudly. 'He's a tailor!'

'Lucky you!'

Jack wore the coat at home and at school, in the park and in the shops, in the garden and ... where else do you think he wore it? Where else might he go? (*Take suggestions, with prompt. Where are the places that you might go?*) Do you know what ... he even wore the coat on top of his pyjamas when he went to bed! He couldn't get to sleep without the feel of the coat on his cheek.

Time passed and Jack got bigger. He got taller. His arms got longer, his feet got bigger and he needed new shoes, his legs got longer and he needed new trousers... (*continue with other things that grew! Get Jack to grow up each time.*)

But the coat didn't grow. It began to split and tear and got old and smelly and didn't fit him at all. One day his mum said, 'Jack! That coat doesn't fit you anymore. Let's chuck it away and get you a new one. '

Jack shook his head.

'No, I love this coat. Granddad made it, Granddad will fix it!'

So he went off to his granddad's shop and said, 'Mum wants me to throw away the coat, but I love the coat. What shall we do?'

His granddad took the coat and began to snip with his scissors and stitch with his needle. (*demonstrate this and have them copy your gestures. If you like, sing the song from the tape with them*).

As he worked he sang this song:

> *Snip snip snip, this is what I do*
> *Snipping here, snipping there, making something new.*
> *In and out and in, this is how I sew.*
> *Sewing things together, that's what I know.*

When he had finished, he handed back to Jack the loveliest jacket he had ever seen.

(*From here repeat the story back to loop A for jacket, t-shirt, tie, and button – or anything else you want to add*)

Then one day Jack looked down and the button was gone. He was miserable. He loved that button so much. He looked in all the places he had been with the button (remember them with your audience), but couldn't find it. Finally he went to his granddad and told him what had happened.

His granddad took a pen and paper and started writing (*get them to mime writing too*), then handed the paper to Jack, who read what was written.

'Granddad! This is our story of the coat and the jacket and the t-shirt and the tie. Why have you written this?'

'Jack, I think you are old enough now to understand. Nothing in this world lasts forever. But if you love something and you lose it, put it in a story, and then every time you tell the story you'll see the thing that you have lost. Maybe that will help.'

Jack put the story in his pocket and went out into the street. When he met a friend he told them the story. Every time he told it he saw the coat and jacket and t-shirt in his imagination and felt better.

From that day to this the story has been told to remind us that if you love something and you lose it, try putting it in a story and telling it to a friend. Sometimes it will help you feel better.

Snip snip
Snap snap
That's the end of that!

PS If suitable you can add an ending where, later, the granddad dies and Jack tells the story again, this time to remember his granddad. It can be a great way to introduce the subject of death and dying when they come up.

The King and the Moon

This is a lovely, silly story about thinking things through. Play it for comedy.

There was once a king who had everything. He had beautiful clothes, plates of silver and stables with a thousand horses. But still wanted more. He was never happy. He always got what he wanted and was very angry if he didn't.

He'd say, 'Bring me what I want now, and if you don't I'll have your head on a spike.'

Late one night he was gazing at the moon. He saw the man in the moon. He saw the rabbit in the moon. He saw the frog in the moon. He decided that what he really wanted was to be able to touch the moon (so beautiful!). Then he would be really happy. He started to sing:

> *I want to touch the moon. I want to touch the moon.*
> *I want to touch it soon. I want to touch the moon.*

He asked all the carpenters in the land to build a tower to the moon.
So they chopped down a forest and sung this song while they were chopping:
(*chop and sing*)

> *He wants to touch the moon. He wants to touch the moon.*
> *He wants to touch it soon. He wants to touch the moon.*

When the forest was cut down they sawed up the wood. As they sawed they sang...
(*saw and sing*)

And they made thousands of boxes, hammering nails into the wood. As they hammered they sang... (*hammer and sing*)

Carefully they began to pile the boxes one on top of another. As they piled they sang...
(*pile and sing*)

Day by day the tower grew higher and higher. Soon it reached the clouds. Soon it was nearly at the moon. One night the king began to climb. As he climbed he sang...
(*climb and sing*)

> *I want to touch he moon. I want to touch the moon.*
> *I want it soon. I want to touch the moon.*

He climbed higher and higher.

The chief carpenter called out a warning, 'Be careful your majesty, the tower is beginning to wobble!'

For a while there was no reply. At long last they could hear the king from above the clouds.
'Fiddlesticks!' he shouted rudely. 'I just need one more box!'
'There are none left, your majesty,' replied the carpenter.
'Then pull one out from the bottom!' shouted the king.
'Are you sure?'
'Do as you're told or I'll have your head on a spike!'

Now everyone could see what would happen if they pulled a box from the bottom of the tower, but no one dared to say anything because they were scared of the king.
So they pushed and pushed and pushed and as they pushed they sang:

> *He wants to...*

A moment later the tower came crashing down. Wham! Bam! Smack! The king landed on the ground with an almighty wallop. He lay on the ground seeing stars. He sang to himself:

> *I nearly touched the moon... I wanted it too soon...!*

So let that be a lesson to you all!
What is that lesson anyway? (*take suggestions*)

Ponder and pout
It's time to work it out!

The Magic Porridge Pot

Here's another old favourite. In this tale the description is important. The audience has to see the events quite clearly. I worked out this version with Beth Wooldridge from SS Mary and John's School in Oxford, one of the first Storytelling Schools in the country. Thanks, Beth. Some schools retell it as The Magic Chocolate Pot, to make it sweeter. Whatever your topic, you can put it in the pot!

Once upon a time there was a forest.
In the forest was a village.
And in the village lived a little girl and her mum.

Early one morning the little girl's mum woke up and looked in the cupboard for some food. The cupboard was empty.

The mother said, 'Daughter, go and find some food in the woods.'

The little girl took her basket and walked into the forest.

She walked and she walked and she walked singing her song:

> *I'm so hungry*
> *Need something in my tum*
> *I'm so hungry*
> *I want to help my mum*

Until she came to some blackberry bushes.

She picked and she picked and she picked until her basket was full of fat, juicy blackberries.

She set off for home singing:

I'm so hungry
Need something in my tum
I'm so hungry
I want to help my mum

On the path she met a thin old woman with no teeth.
She looked at the girl and smiled, 'I'm hungry. Can I have some blackberries?'

The little girl looked at the old woman and wanted to help her.

'Of course! You can have as many as you like!'

The old woman put her hand in the basket and ate some berries.

'Thank you,' she said, 'and now I will help you. Take this pot and when you get home say, 'Fill pot! Fill!' and it will fill with porridge. When it is full say, 'Stop pot! Stop!' and it will stop filling. OK?'

'Thanks!' said the girl and went home singing her song:

I'm so hungry...

At home she put the pot on the table.
'Fill pot! Fill!' she said and the pot filled with porridge.
When it was full she said, 'Stop pot! Stop!' and it stopped filling.

They ate up the porridge and were happy.

After that, every day they'd eat porridge from the magic pot. They were never hungry.

One day the little girl went off into the forest to get more berries.

While the little girl was away, her mother sat at home looking at the pot and felt hungry. 'Fill pot! Fill!' she said and the pot filled with porridge.

When it was full she said, 'That's enough! Stop it!'
But the pot didn't stop. Porridge flowed over the side.

'Please stop!' she said, but porridge flowed onto the floor.

'Stop now!' she shouted as porridge flowed out of the door.

Soon the whole village was covered in porridge.

When the little girl came back with a basket full of blackberries she saw porridge everywhere and people standing on the roofs to keep away from the porridge.

'Tell that pot to stop!' they shouted.

The little girl smiled and said, 'Stop, pot! Stop!' and the pot stopped.

All the villagers had to eat their way back indoors but nobody minded. After all, it was the sweetest, creamiest porridge in the whole wide world.

The Sweet-Talking Potato

Here's a Ghanaian folk tale, with a simple silly repeating motif. Pie Corbett made this story popular with his version 'The Papaya that Spoke.' It is more frequently told with a yam as the initiating vegetable. I like to use a sweet potato just because young UK children are perhaps more likely to know what a potato is!

The story has a simple repeating form that you can escalate as the characters get more and more incredulous. Also, it's easy to innovate the story using your own sequence of talking objects and animals. Great fun!

Once upon a time there was a farmer.
One day he felt hungry so he went out to pick a sweet potato.
As he picked it up, to his amazement, the sweet potato spoke.

'Hands off!' it said.

The farmer looked at his dog. 'Did you say that?' said the farmer.
'No,' said the dog. 'It was the potato!'
'Aaaaargh!' screamed the farmer 'A talking dog!' and ran away as fast as his legs could carry him.

He ran and he ran till he came to a market, where he met a man selling chickens.
'Why are you running so fast when the day is so hot?' asked the fisherman.

'First a potato spoke to me and then my dog spoke to me!' replied the farmer.
'That's impossible!' said the man. 'Dogs and potatoes can't talk!'
'Oh no it isn't!' said a chicken.
'Aaaaargh!' screamed the farmer. 'A talking chicken!' and ran off.

He ran and he ran till he came to a shop, where he met a baker selling loaves of bread.
'Why are you running so fast when the day is so hot?' asked the baker.

'First a potato spoke to me, next my dog spoke to me and after that a chicken spoke to me!' replied the farmer.
'That's impossible!' said the baker.
'Oh no it isn't!' said a loaf of bread.
'Aaaaargh!' screamed the farmer. 'A talking loaf of bread!' and ran off.

He ran and he ran and he ran till he came to the town, where he met the king sitting on his throne.
'Why are you running so fast when the day is so hot?' asked the king.

'First a potato spoke to me, next my dog spoke to me, after that a chicken spoke to me and finally a loaf of bread spoke to me!'
'That's impossible!' said the king. 'Get out of here, you foolish man!'

The poor farmer walked home feeling foolish.

The king said to himself, 'How silly of him to imagine that those things can talk!'

There was a long silence – and then the throne spoke!

'How true, Your Majesty. Whoever heard of a talking potato?'

Tic tac ting.
The story's done its thing.

Stone Soup

This one needs attention to character. Maybe it's a good story to tell to introduce the idea of character and how you show it with voice and body – here it's a tricky traveller and a gullible old woman.

Once there was a poor man who travelled from place to place with his son.
One day they came to a new village with no money to buy food.
'I'm hungry,' said his son.
'Don't worry, son,' the father said. 'We'll soon get something to eat and a place to stay.'
'But how?' said the son. 'We haven't got any money.'
The father looked to his son and smiled. 'I'll show you how to make something from nothing.'

He picked up a stone from the road. 'With this stone, I will get us food and a place to stay for the night. Watch and you will learn.' He put the stone into his pocket and they walked to a cottage and knocked on the door.

A little old woman answered. 'Can I help you?' she said.

'No,' said the traveller. 'But we can help you. We come from a country called Estonia and in Estonia we make a very special dish called Stone Soup. We make it with very special stones like this.' He took the stone from his pocket and showed it to her. 'Can we make some for you and give it to you as a present?'

The old woman was very interested and invited them in and soon the stone was boiling in a pot of water.

After a while the traveller tasted it. 'Mmm, the stone soup is almost ready,' he said. 'It just needs an onion.'

'I have an onion,' cried the old woman. She chopped it up and threw it into the pot.

After a while longer the traveller tasted it. 'Mmm, the stone soup is almost ready,' he said. 'It just needs a couple of carrots.'
'I have some carrots,' cried the old woman. She chopped them up and threw them into the pot. (*repeat for potatoes, turnips, meat, salt, etc.*)

'That's ready now!' said the man, and they all dined on delicious soup. Then the traveller put the stone into his pocket and made ready to leave.

'Wait,' said the old lady. 'I want to cook stone soup again and I can't without a special stone. I'll buy it off you for a gold sovereign.' The traveller didn't look keen.

'Two gold sovereigns,' said the old woman. Again the traveller looked unimpressed.

'Three!' she begged.

And so the traveller and his son checked into the finest hotel in town, slept in big, comfortable beds and in the morning had a fine, big breakfast.

The son learned his lesson. And that was that.

A Husband for Miss Mouse

This is a sweet, repeating story with a circular form. You can show both character changing and element descriptions in the telling, with comedy/irony at the end. Make sure you have a mouse voice! In the story there are seven repeats – good practice for everyone.

Once upon a time there was a little mouse who liked strong things. She liked strong smells, strong tastes, strong opinions and strong boxes.

One day her father said, 'Little Mouse, it's time for you to get married, go and live in a new nest and raise your own family. Why not marry the mouse who lives in the barn? He really likes you and is a good man. Why not marry him?'

Little Mouse thought about it.

'No. He's just a weak little mouse. I'd like to marry something really strong. I'd like to marry the strongest thing in the world.'

Just then the sun shone on her face.

'I know,' she said. 'I'll marry the sun. It's the strongest thing in the world. Nothing can stop the sun.'

She stretched her arms up to the sun. 'You look really hot! Sun, will you marry me?'

She sang him a song:

> *Sun, Sun, will you marry me?*
> *You are so fine and strong.*
> *Sun, Sun, will you marry me?*
> *You are where I belong.*

The sun smiled down at her and said, 'You're very kind, but I am not the strongest thing. Cloud is stronger than me. When Cloud comes along I can't shine on the Earth anymore. Cloud is stronger.'

'Oh!' said Little Mouse. 'Then I shall marry a cloud. Clouds are the strongest things in the world. Stronger than the sun.'

She looked up at a cloud and stretched out her hands. 'You look really big and soft. Cloud, will you marry me?'

She sang him the song:

Cloud, Cloud, will you marry me?...

The cloud smiled down at her and said, 'You're very kind, but I am not the strongest thing. The wind is stronger than me. When the wind comes along it just blows me away. Wind is stronger.'

'Oh!' said Little Mouse. 'Then I shall marry the wind. Wind is the strongest thing in the world. Cloud is stronger than Sun but Wind is stronger than the Cloud.'

She looked up at Wind and stretched out her hands. 'You look really fast. Wind, will you marry me?'

She sang him the song:

Wind, Wind, will you marry me?...

Wind smiled down at her and said, 'You're very kind, but I am not the strongest thing. The hill is stronger than me. When I blow against the hill I can't move it and have to go round. Hill is stronger.'

'Oh!' said Little Mouse. 'Then I shall marry Hill. Hill is the strongest thing in the world. Cloud is stronger than Sun, Wind is stronger than Cloud, but Hill is stronger than Wind.'

She looked up at Hill and stretched out her hands. 'You look really solid. Hill, will you marry me?'

She sang him the song:

Hill, Hill, will you marry me?...

Hill smiled down at her and said, 'You're very kind, but I am not the strongest thing. The bull is stronger than me. When he pulls the plough through my soil I just get turned over. There's nothing I can do. Bull is stronger.'

'Oh!' said Little Mouse. 'Then I shall marry Bull. Bull is the strongest thing in the world. Cloud is stronger than Sun, Wind is stronger than Cloud, Hill is stronger than Wind, but Bull is stronger than Hill.'

She looked up at Bull and stretched out her hands. 'You look really muscled. Bull, will you marry me?'

She sang him the song:

Bull, Bull, will you marry me?...

Bull smiled down at her and said, 'You're very kind, but I am not the strongest thing. Rope is stronger than me. When he pulls me I have to go where he wants. There's nothing I can do. Rope is stronger.'

'Oh!' said Little Mouse. 'Then I shall marry Rope. Rope is the strongest thing in the world. Cloud is stronger than Sun, Wind is stronger than Cloud, Hill is stronger than Wind, Bull is stronger than Hill, but Rope is stronger than Bull.'

She looked up at Bull and stretched out her hands. 'You look really long. Rope, will you marry me?'

She sang him the song:

Rope, Rope, will you marry me?...

Rope smiled down at her and said, 'You're very kind, but I am not the strongest thing. The mouse in the barn is stronger than me. When he nibbles me I fall apart. There's nothing I can do. Mouse is stronger.'

'Oh!' said Little Mouse. 'Then I shall marry Mouse. Mouse is the strongest thing in the world. Cloud is stronger than Sun, Wind is stronger than Cloud, Hill is stronger than Wind, Bull is stronger than Hill, Rope is stronger than Bull, but Mouse is stronger than Rope.'

She looked across at Mouse, who was sitting on an acorn and listening very carefully. 'You look really good. Mouse, will you marry me?'

She sang him the song:

> **Mouse, Mouse, will you marry me?...**

Mouse smiled. 'Yes,' he said. 'I will marry you. Would you like to dance?'

They took each other in their arms and danced and sang. Around them the sun shone, the clouds drifted, the wind blew, the hill stayed put, the bull ploughed and the rope tugged.

They all smiled at the dancing mice and sang along with them.

'Good luck, Mr Mouse!' they all said, and smiled.

The story is simple but the pattern is quite a lot to remember so here is a summary:

PATTERN REMINDER

Husband	Quality
Sun	Hot
Cloud	Soft
Wind	Fast
Hill	Solid
Bull	Muscled
Rope	Long
Mouse	Good

Awongalema

My friend and colleague Adam Guillain taught me this story, which he learned when he lived in Zanzibar. It can be fun to explore with all the animals you want. Children love choosing their own and adapting the story as it is told. You can experiment with ways to evoke the various animals with voice and gesture.

Once upon a time, in the forests of Africa, there was no rain, nothing much grew, and the animals were all hungry. They gathered around a huge acacia tree.

The lion said, 'This tree will give us fruit if we can remember its name.
Does anyone know its name?'
All the animals shook their heads.
'Who will go and learn the name from the mountain spirits?' asked the owl.
'I will,' said the cheetah.
'Hurray!' cheered the animals.

Cheetah ran and he ran and he ran and he ran as fast as the wind till he came to the top of the mountain.
'Mountain spirits, talk to me. Tell me the name of the old, old tree.'
'Awongalema!' they called.
'Awongalema!' He answered and ran down the mountain as fast as he could.

On the path he crashed into an ant hill and got bitten all over.
'OWWWW!' he roared, and brushed away all the ants.
When all the ants were gone he had forgotten the name.

Back at the tree they said, 'Have you learned the name?'
'No,' he said. 'I forgot,' and hung his head.
'Then who will go and learn the name from the mountain spirits?' asked the owl.
'I will,' said the lion.
'Hurray!' cheered the animals.

Lion ran and he ran and he ran and he ran as fast as the wind till he came to the top of the mountain.

'Mountain spirits, talk to me. Tell me the name of the old, old tree.'
'Awongalema!' they called.
'Awongalema!' he answered and ran down the mountain as fast as he could.

On the path he crashed into an ant hill and got bitten all over.
'OWWWW!' he roared, and brushed away all the ants.
When all the ants were gone he had forgotten the name.

Back at the tree they said, 'Have you learned the name?'
'No,' he said. 'I forgot,' and hung his head.

(*Repeat for other fast animals – gazelle, tiger, etc.*)

Finally owl said, 'Let's try a slow animal.'

They sent the tortoise.
He didn't run. He went plod plod plod as slow as a slug till he came to the mountain top.
'Mountain spirits, talk to me. Tell me the name of the old, old tree.'
'Awongalema!' they called.
'Awongalema!' he answered and plodded down the mountain as slow as a slug.

When he got home the animals all cried, 'Did you remember the name?'
'Awongalema,' he said and the tree was covered with fruits.

They all ate and ate and were happy.

The Lion's Roar

Here's a Buddhist fable from Asia that's a lot like Chicken Licken but with a different ending. Here the main character gets more and more frightened and spreads the fear to others, so you need to panic when you tell this one! The lion is the wise one you always wanted. Add animals as needed. The original story is with a monkey but for some reason I like it with a rabbit. Up to you!

Once a nervous rabbit was lying in the shade of a mango tree in the heat of the midday sun. He was worrying about the end of the world and what would happen if the Earth split open.

Suddenly he heard a crash.

'Oh no!' he thought. 'It's going to happen! The Earth is splitting open!'

Terrified at the thought of being swallowed by the Earth, he jumped up and ran away as fast as his little legs could carry him. He ran over hills and valleys and valleys and hills until he came to a gazelle.

'Are you alright?' asked the gazelle. 'You look frightened.'

'No, I'm not alright,' said the rabbit. 'I'm running away because the Earth back there is splitting open and it's going to swallow everything up!'

'Oh, no!' wailed the gazelle. 'I'd better tell my friends. We're coming with you!'

(*Repeat loop A starts here*)

Terrified at the thought of being swallowed by the Earth, the rabbit and the gazelles ran away as fast as their legs could carry them. They ran over hills and valleys and valleys and hills until they came to an ostrich.

'Are you alright?' asked the ostrich to a gazelle. 'You look frightened.'

'No, I'm not alright,' replied the gazelle. 'I'm running away because the Earth back there is splitting open and it's going to swallow everything up!'

'Oh, no!' wailed the ostrich. 'I'd better tell my friends. We're coming with you.'

(Repeat loop to here then back to A for rhinos, elephants and any other animals you fancy)

Then...

Terrified at the thought of being swallowed by the Earth, the rabbit, gazelles, ostriches, rhinos and elephants ran as fast as their legs could carry them. They ran over hills and valleys and valleys and hills until they came to a lion.

The lion gave a great ROAR and all the animals stopped.

'Are you alright?' he asked an elephant. 'You look frightened.'

'No, I'm not alright,' replied the elephant. 'I'm running away because the Earth back there is splitting open and it's going to swallow everything up!'

'How do you know?' asked the lion.

'The rhino told me,' replied the elephant.

'How did you know?' said the lion to the rhino.

'The ostrich told me.'

'And how did you know?' said the lion to the ostrich.

'The gazelle told me.'

'And how did you know?' said the lion to the gazelle.

'The rabbit told me.'

'And how did you know?' said the lion to the rabbit.

'I heard it,' replied the rabbit. 'I was lying under a tree when I heard a loud bang and I knew the Earth was splitting open.'

'Hmmm. What kind of tree was it?'

'A mango tree, I think.'

'Jump on my back. Let's go and visit the tree.'

The rabbit jumped up and the lion bounded back to the tree, over hills and valleys and valleys and hills. There the lion saw a ripe mango on the ground.

'You see that, little rabbit,' said the lion. 'That's what made the noise.'

The rabbit was glad.

'Thank you,' said the rabbit.

He hopped off the lion's back, picked up the mango, and began to eat it.

Oh how sweet it tasted!

Goose Girl's Wings

I first read this tale in a version called The Magic Wings *by renowned storyteller Diane Wolkstein, author of more than 20 books in her lifetime. This is a sweet and intriguing story from China with clear repetition and a song for all the characters to sing. As with many folktales it takes a poke at pride and privilege and can lead to good talking points.*

Once there was a poor goose girl who looked after a flock of geese. She fed them, sang to them, nursed them when they were sick and looked after the goslings. She was out in winter and summer, always caring for them.

Sometimes they would fly up into the sky and sometimes she wished she was flying too.

One springtime she watched the flowers blooming.

'How I wish I could fly like my geese,' she said. 'I'd love to see springtime from the sky.'

She stood in a field with her geese, poured water from the stream on her back and wished that she could grow wings. She flapped her arms as if they were wings and sang a song:

> *If I had wings and I could fly then I would fly so high*
> *I would fly so high till I touched the sky* (repeat)

As she was singing and flapping a shopkeeper's daughter walked by.

'What are you doing, you ignorant girl?' she called out, nastily.

'I'm trying to grow wings,' said the goose girl, 'so I can fly up and see the world from the sky.'

'Ignorant girl!' said the shopkeeper's daughter. 'Girls can't fly!'

The shopkeeper's daughter went home and thought about it. 'What if you can grow wings?' she thought. 'I want to be the first one with wings, not that silly girl! Just in case, I'll try too.'

She stood in the garden, poured milk on her back, flapped her arms and sang the song:

If I had...

As she sang the judge's daughter went by.

'What are you doing, you ignorant girl?' she called out, snootily.

'I'm trying to grow wings,' said the shopkeeper's daughter, 'so I can be the first to fly.'

'Ignorant girl!' said the judge's daughter. 'Girls can't fly!'

The judge's daughter went home and thought about it. 'What if you can grow wings?' she thought. 'I am the daughter of a judge. If anyone is to fly it should be me and not the daughter of some little shopkeeper! Just in case, I'll try.'

She stood in the garden, poured wine on her back, flapped her arms and sang the song:

If I had...

As she sang the princess went by.

'What are you doing, you ignorant girl?' she called out.

'I'm trying to grow wings,' said the judge's daughter, 'so I can be the one who flies higher than everyone else.'

'Ignorant girl!' said the princess. 'Girls can't fly!'

The princess went home and thought about it. 'What if you can grow wings?' she thought. 'If anyone flies it should be a princess, not that silly girl! Just in case, I'll try.'

She stood in the palace garden, poured perfume on her back, flapped her arms and sang the song:

If I had...

Lots of people saw the princess, but didn't dare speak to her. Soon all the girls in the country were standing outside, flapping their arms and singing the song.

Up in heaven the Goddess of Wishes heard the songs. 'I only have one pair of wings. Who shall I give them to?'

She flew down to the princess, the judge's daughter, the shopkeeper's daughter and the goose girl, and asked each one why they wanted to fly. Each told the truth. All but one wanted to be better than others. One wanted to see the beauty of spring.

Then the Goddess sniffed each girl. One smelt of heavy perfume, one of old wine, one of smelly milk and one of clear stream water.

Moments later the goose girl felt herself lifting off the ground as she flapped and sang, higher and higher above the Earth. Soon she was joined by her flock of geese as they sang together their joy for spring.

Mouse and Lion

Here's a retelling of one of Aesop's wonderful fables. I learned this first from Venerable Amaranatho, a monk friend, who was using it to teach about friendship. When telling it make sure to emphasise the drama of the mouse in the claws of the lion and then the drama of the lion caught in the hunter's net.

Once there was a mouse who lived with her family in a hole in the corner of a cave. A lion lived in the cave.

One day the little mouse decided to go out looking for food. She waited till the lion was asleep and then ran across the cave.

Just then the lion opened one eye, reached out his paw and WHACK, caught the mouse by its tail.

'Oh look,' said the lion. 'A snack before breakfast!'

'Please don't eat me,' said the mouse. 'I am so small and not worth eating. Let me live and I will be your friend and help you when I can. Will you let me live?'

The lion thought about it. He wasn't very hungry so he nodded.

'OK,' he said. 'I'll let you live.'

Little mouse went off to look for food, her heart beating fast.

That day a hunter was hunting in the forest and set an animal trap with a big net. The lion walked into the trap and was caught hanging in the air in the net.

Little mouse came along.

'Now I will help you,' she said.
'How can you help me when you are so small?' said the lion.

Little mouse chewed through the net with her sharp teeth and soon it fell open. The lion escaped and from that day the lion and the mouse were best friends.

(You can play a game like rock, paper and scissors using hunter, mouse and lion. This can be done with three gestures: muscles for a hunter, claws for a lion and little teeth for a mouse, or something like that.

One way to play is with two teams. They stand in line back to back and each team chooses one of the characters. At the count of 1, 2, 3 they jump around and show their gesture and sound. The winners then chase the losers back to the wall or some kind of safe home. If a loser is touched before they reach home they join the winner's team.)

The Nest and the Web

This is a simple story from the life of the Prophet Mohammed, about a miracle on his journey from Mecca to Medina that saved his life. It's well known and loved by many Muslims.

Once, the prophet Mohammed was teaching his message in the city of Mecca, but not everyone liked what he said. Some plotted to kill Mohammed and one night a group of killers surrounded his house and waited to kill him with knives and swords.

Mohammed had been invited by friends to go and live in another city, Medina, and that night he decided he would leave. He walked out of the house with his wife, Aisha, and by some miracle the killers did not see him.

Mohammed and Aisha set off straight away on the road to Medina, walking and walking all day in the hot desert sun. That evening they found a cave, slipped inside and fell asleep, exhausted.

While they were sleeping a spider came and worked through the night spinning a huge web across the front of the cave and a family of birds carried their nest into the cave entrance with little chicks just hatched still in the nest.

The group of killers were following their tracks in the sand, and the next morning they arrived at the cave entrance.

'They can't be in there,' said one. 'Look at that spider's web. It's been there for weeks.'
'Yes,' said another, 'and look at that nest, those birds would have flown if anyone was in the cave!'
'Let's keep going,' said the third. 'They must be further on down the road.'

So the killers went on down the road and never found Mohammed and Aisha.

A few days later Mohammed and Aisha arrived in the city of Medina where they were welcomed by all. Mohammed was safe to teach his message.

The Dancing Harmonica

I love this story. It's funny, silly and involves dancing. You can dance as a storyteller and get your class to dance too. (I tell it as a harmonica story because I can play one and dance at the same time. Change it for any instrument you can have a go at that works with the story. It could be a drum – just bang it! Virtuosos not needed!) Or you could play a tape of an instrument at that time in the story and dance to it yourself. Have fun!

Once upon a time, in a house on a hill, there lived a boy called Lazy Jack.

Every day Jack sat by the fire warming his hands (show this) as his mother worked, sweeping and cleaning and cooking (show this). Every day she asked him to help with the housework (say this) and everyday he said he was too tired *(say this)*.

Finally she swept him out of the house. (*show this*)
'Don't come back till you're ready to help!'

He rolled down to the bottom of the hill and lay on the ground, waiting to see what would happen. A few minutes later an old lady walked past him with a smile on her face.

'Are you Lazy Jack?' she asked. When he nodded she said, 'Then I've got a present for you.' And she handed him a harmonica. 'It will get you in and out of trouble if you play it.'

He put it in his mouth and started to play a jig. (*you play a bit*)

A while later a lady walked along carrying a basket of fruit and bread from the market singing a song:

> *I am going to market to market to market*
> *I am going to market to sell my fruit*
> (sing and sway with basket on head)

As soon as she heard Jack's music she started dancing. It was a wild dance, jumping and twisting and kicking out her legs. (*show this*)

'Stop the music!' she shouted. 'It's making me dance! I can't stop!'

But Jack kept playing, enjoying watching her dance till the fruit and bread fell from her basket to the floor.

Finally she stopped and ran away, shouting, 'I'll get my husband onto you!'

Jack collected up all the fruit and bread and started to eat an apple. (*mime*)

Soon after, the woman's husband arrived with a big stick.

'You're in trouble!' he shouted and ran towards Jack, who calmly put the mouth organ in his mouth and started to play. The man started dancing, jumping up and down and twirling the stick about his head (*show this*). He danced and danced till his legs hurt so much, and he begged Jack to stop.

When the music finished, he ran away shouting, 'I'll get a policeman!'

Jack was just munching on a pear (show) when a policeman came running towards him waving a truncheon shouting, 'Give back the fruit!' (*show*)

Jack started playing and the policeman danced and danced in his big boots (*show*) till he cried for Jack to stop. When Jack stopped the policeman ran away.

'Now I've got something for mum,' he thought. He walked up the hill to his house and walked in with a basket of food, which he handed to his mother.

'Where did you get that?' she asked.

'It's the magic harmonica. When I play this whoever hears can't stop dancing!'

'Let me see!'

She took the harmonica and put it in her pocket.

Jack went back to the fire and warmed his hands.

'Jack, will you help me with the sweeping?'

'No, Mum, I'm too tired!'

So she started to play the harmonica and Jack started to dance (show). He danced until his legs hurt too much. 'Please stop, Mum!' he begged. 'I'll help.'

And for the first time in his life, Jack swept the floor.

From then on every time his mum wanted him to help, she just patted her pocket and Jack did as he was asked.

And so they all lived happily ever after.

Crick crack
That's the story of Jack.

The Talkative Turtle

This is a much-told tale. I can't imagine why teachers like it. Quiet you lot! To make it work you have to get into the character of the turtle and chatter away all the time. That's what makes it funny ... and then sad. Dovie Thompson tells a lovely version of this teaching tale (very relevant for storytellers).

There was once a turtle who talked a lot. He talked all day and he talked all night. Yabber yabber yabber. (*show with hand yabbering*)

The turtle was friends with two geese. Every winter the geese flew south to a warm beach and came back in springtime. The turtle missed them when they were away and had no one to talk to.

One winter, when it was time for the geese to fly south, the turtle felt sad.

'It's not fair!' he complained. 'I have to stay here in this cold place. I want to go with you. Let me, please!'

'But you can't fly,' said a goose. 'Don't worry, we'll be back to see you again in the spring.'

'But I want to go with you now!' said the turtle and went on talking and talking about it.

The two geese made a plan. 'We'll get a stick, carry it between our two beaks and you can hang onto it with your mouth,' they suggested.

'Yes!' cried the turtle, excitedly. 'What a good idea!'

'But there's one problem,' said a goose. 'You must never open your mouth. You must keep it shut for the whole journey otherwise you'll fall. Do you think you can do that?'

'Yes, yes, yes!' shrieked the turtle.

So the geese found a large stick, clamped it between their beaks and the turtle held onto it with his mouth.

The two geese soared up high into the air. The turtle looked down and saw other friends.

'Look at meeeeeeeeeeeee!' CRASH!

As soon as he opened his mouth he fell down from the sky, crashing against the ground.

His shell cracked to pieces.

'Awww!' he moaned.

Today, if you ever look at a turtle's shell, you can still see the joins where the pieces of the turtle's shell have been joined back together, reminding us all that it's good to think before you speak.

Bandits and Berries

Here's another great Chinese tale looking at kindness and helping, with lots of places for physicality and descriptions. There's a lovely version of this by Linda Fang in More Ready-To-Tell Tales *by Holt and Mooney.*

Once there was a forest.
In the forest there was a cottage.
In the cottage a mother lived with her young son living off their land as best they could.

One year there was no rain, and crops dried out in the field. Mother and son were hungry, and the mother grew ill, spending all day in bed.

One morning the boy went off to the family field looking for something to cook for his mother's lunch, leaving the mother at home.

When he came back with a dried old cabbage, he saw that something was wrong. All the chickens and rabbits in the courtyard had gone and inside the kitchen there were broken pots on the floor.

He ran upstairs to his mother who was lying on the bed in tears.

'What happened?' he said.

'Bandits came and took all our food and money. They've left us with nothing!'

He looked around the kitchen and saw that it was true.

'Don't worry, Mum,' he said. 'I'll go out into the forest and pick some berries for us to eat today. I'll take care of everything. You just rest.'

The mother smiled and lay back in bed. The boy took two baskets and set off into the forest. After a while he came to a bush. Some of the berries were black and ripe, and some were red and sour, not quite ripe.

'I'll pick the sweet berries for my mum,' he thought. 'She needs them most. I'll be fine with the sour berries.'

So the boy picked all the berries on the bush, putting the sweet berries in one basket and the sour ones in the other. As he worked he sang:

> *Sweet berries for my mama*
> *Sour berries for me*
> *Sweet berries for my mama*
> *That's how things should be*

When both baskets were full he started walking back home when a man jumped out in the road pointing a knife at him. It was a bandit!

'You have to pay if you want to use my road!' he said.

The boy hid the baskets behind his back.
'I don't have any money,' he said.

'What's behind your back?' asked the bandit. 'Show me!'

The boy showed him the baskets. The bandit grabbed both. He tried the black berries.

'Hmm sweet!'

'Don't you dare take them!' shouted the boy. 'Those are for my mum!'

The bandit tried the other basket and frowned. 'Sour! I don't like those!'

'Those are mine,' said the boy. 'You can have those if you like. I'll be fine.'

The bandit started eating the sweet berries and the boy began to cry.

'Don't be a baby!' the bandit said. 'Be happy. Sing that song you were singing right now.'

The boy sang his song:

> *Sweet berries for my mama*
> *Sour berries for me*
> *Sweet berries for my mama*
> *That's how things should be*

As the bandit listened a tear formed in his eye and ran down his cheek.

'What's the matter?' asked the boy.

'You've reminded me of my mum. I left her alone when I ran away to become a bandit. You are a good son. I wish I had been like you. Here, take the berries to her.'

The boy went off home singing his song and they ate the berries for supper.

In the morning the boy opened the front door and saw a sack of rice on the doorstep.

On it was a note.

'This is to help you both through the hard times,' it said.

They were never troubled by bandits again.

Clip clip
Clop clop
Clip clop
It's time to stop.

The Thirsty Frog

This Aboriginal tale is very popular with teachers, linking well to topics about water, the environment and animal life. This is a quest kind of plot, problem-solving to save the world and save yourself. Good practice for life! There's a lovely version in The Barefoot Book of Animal Tales. *The nub here is the suspense – first failure and then success, so don't rush this bit. Make it really important. Also make it funny, especially at the end. This is a good chance to practise your dancing skills. Have a drink and have a go.*

In the beginning there was huge frog. He went CROAK.
He was as big as a mountain and as wide as the sky.
The frog was thirsty.
He drank up the streams, but he was still thirsty.
He drank up the rivers, but he was still thirsty.
He drank up the lakes, but he was still thirsty.
He drank up all the seas, and he was still thirsty.
He drank and drank till there was no water left, then he closed his mouth and sat still, full of water.

No sea for the fish.
No clouds for the rain.
No water for the soil.
Nothing to drink.

All the animals got together and sang a song:

> *What shall we do?*
> *What shall we do?*
> *The frog's drunk all our water*
> *How shall we get him to open his mouth?*
> *I really think we ought-a.*

Owl said, 'The frog has got all the water. We have to get him to open his mouth so we get some water back. What shall we do?'

Cat went to the frog and said, 'Please open your mouth, or we will all die.'
But the frog kept his mouth shut.

The nightingale went to frog and said, 'Would you like to sing with me?'
She sang him a song, but he kept his mouth shut.

Parrot went to frog and told him some jokes, but he kept his mouth shut.

Badger brought some delicious food. 'Would you like to eat?' But the frog kept his mouth shut.

This went on for a while (*make some up*).
Nothing seemed to work. Then little snake had an idea. He slithered over to the frog's belly button and started to dance in it. His tail tickled the frog.

He started to grin.
Then he smiled.
Then he started to shake all over.
Finally he opened his mouth and went:
'HA HA HA HA HA!'

All the water spouted out of his mouth and went down the mountains into the streams. The streams filled the rivers, the rivers filled the lakes and the lakes filled the seas.

'Hooray!' called the animals. 'WATER!'
And they all danced with the clever little snake.

> *What did we do?*
> *What did we do?*
> *To open the frog's mouth*
> *We danced on his belly.*
> *We danced on his tum*
> *And all the water came out!*

Pip pip
Pout pout
The story's just run out.

More!

Here's a salutary tale about greed, desire and addiction. Save it for a rainy day. We can all identify with her somehow. The key to telling it is to have a bigger and bigger tantrum, with the mum getting more and more flustered. This is adapted from Carol Birch's lovely version, which I found in Joining In *by Teresa Miller, from the excellent Yellow Moon Press in the USA.*

Once there was a little girl who lived with her mum and dad next to a jewellery shop. One birthday her mother bought her ten lovely glass bracelets – all the colours of the rainbow. She smiled, slipped them over her wrist, admired them for a moment, and then frowned, stamped her foot and sang out:

> *I want more!*
> *I want more!*
> *I'll stamp my foot*
> *Till I get what I want!* (repeat)

Her mum was the type that was keen to please. 'OK darling, if that makes you happy!' Mum rushed round to the shop, bought another ten bangles and handed them over. 'Good!' said the girl, smiled for a moment and then frowned:
> *I want more!...*

'OK darling, if that makes you happy!'

Her mum went back to the shop and got a box full of bangles. The little girl slid them on until they went from her wrists to her shoulders, and then all the way up her legs. When she has put them all on she said:
I Want More!...

'Oh well! It's her birthday!' thought her mum and went round and bought some bigger bracelets. They slipped over her hips and over her head – more and more until she was completely covered in lovely glass bangles.

When the last bangle was on, her mother stood and admired her daughter, waiting for a little thank you. But the bangles were too heavy and, trying to balance, the little girl leaned to one side. The weight of the bangles pulled her down and she fell onto the floor with a glassy crash. Every single glass bangle broke. The little girl sat there, shocked, in a pile of rainbow glass and sighed. 'Maybe next time I'll just have the ten bangles,' she said. 'They were really nice!'

Little Red Riding Hood

Of course there are lots of ways to tell this one. It's much loved for its dramatic end and many-layered symbolism. Here's one way to do it – with an emphasis on fearfulness and tragedy. I think it is a mistake to airbrush death from all our great stories. We can't do that with death in real life, however hard we try. Stories help us reflect on this. If you are interested, have a look at Jack Zipes's wonderful book on this story. There are loads of amazing versions. This version relies on danger and fear, so please tell it that way.

Once there was a little girl called Little Red Riding Hood, who lived with her mum in a cottage on the edge of a dark forest. She had a red cloak and hood, which she wore all the time, so people called her Little Red Riding Hood. One day her mother called her to the kitchen.

'Little Red Riding Hood, your grandmother is sick. I want you to take this basket of eggs and milk to her on the other side of the forest.'

'Do I have to?' said Little Red Riding Hood. 'I'm scared of the forest. I don't want to go.'

'Yes, you have to go,' replied her mum firmly. 'You are old enough now to go to the forest by yourself, but remember, go straight to her cottage and never stray from the straight path.'

Little Red Riding Hood nodded and set off along the path as her mother waved goodbye.

Soon after she entered the forest she came to a fork in the road, where the path split in two directions. Standing next to the path she saw a huge brown wolf, staring at her with hungry eyes and licking his lips.

'Where are you going?' he growled slowly.

'I'm taking this basket of food to my gran in the woods,' she answered, nervously.

The wolf was about to eat her up when he heard the sounds of hunters, and ran away.

The wolf ran off down the straight path and Little Red Riding Hood wandered down the winding way. After a while she saw some wild flowers growing under the trees next to the path and, stepping onto the dark brown soil, she started picking flowers and making a bouquet for her gran.

Some time later, flowers in hand, she arrived at the cottage, lifted the latch, and stepped inside.

Inside she saw someone in her gran's bed. It didn't look much like her gran but it was dark inside and Little Red Riding Hood thought maybe her gran looked odd because she was ill.

'Get into bed to keep me company,' said the voice from the bed. Obediently, Little Red Riding Hood climbed in. She looked at the strange and yet somehow familiar face beside her.
'What big eyes you have!' she said.
'All the better to see you with, my dear.'
'What a big nose you have!'
'All the better to smell you with, my dear.'
'What big ears you have!'
'All the better to hear you with, my dear.'
'What big teeth you have!'
'All the better to EAT YOU WITH!'

And the wolf gobbled her up.

And that's the end of that.

Jack and the Beanstalk

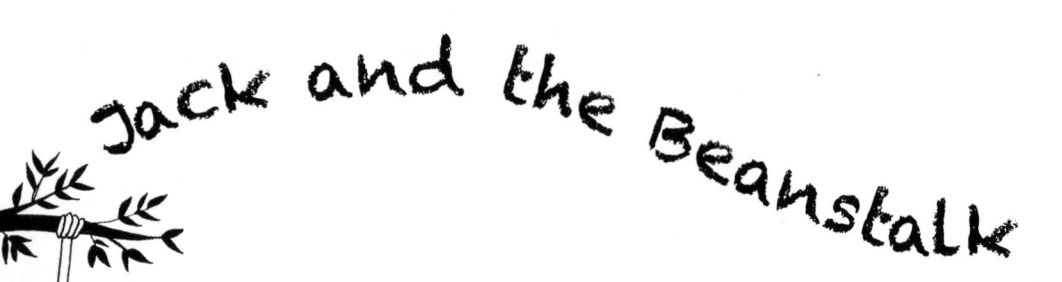

Once your class has got the hang of telling simple stories, let them try this full version of Jack and the Beanstalk. I've taught this to four-year-olds who retold it easily, so keep expectations high! I like this one because it includes the back story of Jack's father, which then makes sense of the rest of the plot. Without it, I find the story weaker. Enjoy!

Once there was a boy called Jack, who lived with his mum in a little cottage. They were very poor.

Sometimes Jack would say, 'Mum, where's Dad?'
Then his mum would shake her head and cry, saying nothing.

One day his mum said, 'Jack! Take our old cow to market and sell it for a good price so we can buy some food.'

Jack walked off to town with the old cow singing a song:

> *I am going to market, to market, to market.*
> *I am going to market to sell my cow.*

On the road he met a man carrying some coloured beans.

'What are they?' asked Jack.
'Magic beans,' said the man.
'Can I have some?' asked Jack.
'I'll swap for the cow,' said the man.
Jack nodded and took the beans home to mum.

'Look, Mum! I've got some magic beans!'
She was angry and threw them out the window.
'Go to bed!' she shouted. 'You silly boy!'

The next morning there was a huge beanstalk outside the window going up into the sky.

Jack climbed up singing his song:

> *Climbing the beanstalk, the beanstalk, the beanstalk.*
> *Climbing up the beanstalk to get to the top.*

He climbed through the clouds till he came to the top of the stalk, and stepped onto a sky land and saw a lovely old lady with golden wings.

'I am your angel,' she said. 'I'll tell you about your dad. He was a rich man but a giant killed him and took all his treasure. The giant lives in that castle. Go there and take what is yours!' She pointed to a castle at the top of the hill.

When Jack got there he saw an old lady peeling potatoes.
'Go away!' she shouted. 'Or my husband will eat you!'
'I'm hungry!' said Jack, 'Let me eat first.'
'OK. Come in.'
Jack was sipping his soup when he heard the giant coming – Boom boom boom.

Jack hid in the cupboard.

In came the giant. 'Fee fi fo fum! I smell the blood of an Englishman!'

'Oh no!' said his wife. 'That's just the smell of your supper. Here, have some.'

The giant supped on his supper and then said, 'Bring me my hen!'

The giant's wife put the hen on the table and the giant said, 'LAY!' and it laid a golden egg. He said, 'LAY!' again and it laid another, and another and another till he fell asleep.

Jack slipped out of the cupboard and took the hen down the beanstalk and gave it to his mum. They were rich.

Time passed.

Jack grew restless.

One day Jack climbed up the beanstalk singing his song:

Climbing the beanstalk, the beanstalk, the beanstalk.
Climbing up the beanstalk to get to the top.

He climbed through the clouds and walked to the castle.

When Jack got there he saw the old lady peeling carrots.
'Go away!' she shouted. 'Or my husband will eat you!'
'I'm hungry!' said Jack. 'Let me eat first.'
'OK. Come in.'

Jack was sipping his soup when he heard the giant coming – Boom boom boom.

Jack hid in the cupboard.

In came the giant. 'Fee fi fo fum! I smell the blood of an Englishman!'

'Oh no!' said his wife. 'That's just the smell of your soup. Have some.'

The giant supped on his soup and then said, 'Bring me my money!'

The giant's wife put the gold and silver coins on the table and he counted it all then fell asleep.

'That's mine!' thought Jack, and he slipped out of the cupboard and took the money home.

Time passed.

One day Jack climbed up the beanstalk singing his song:

Climbing the beanstalk, the beanstalk, the beanstalk.
Climbing up the beanstalk to get to the top.

He climbed through the clouds and walked to the castle.

When Jack got there he saw the old lady peeling parsnips.
'Go away!' she shouted. 'Or my husband will eat you!'

'I'm hungry!' said Jack. 'Let me eat first.'
'OK. Come in.'
Jack was sipping his soup when he heard the giant coming – Boom boom boom.

Jack hid in the cupboard.

In came the giant. 'Fee fi fo fum! I smell the blood of an Englishman!'

'Oh no!' said his wife. 'That's just the smell of your soup. Here, have some.'

The giant sipped on his soup and then said, 'Bring me my harp!'

The giant's wife put the harp on the table.

The giant said, 'PLAY!' and it played lovely music.

The giant fell asleep.

'That's mine!' thought Jack and slipped out of the cupboard, picked up the harp and ran out. The harp started playing and the giant woke up.

'Stop thief!' he shouted and chased Jack to the beanstalk, then down the stalk.

Jack got down first, grabbed an axe and chopped down the beanstalk.

The giant fell down DEAD.

And Jack and his mum lived happily ever after.
Four leaf clover
This story's over.

Chapter 2

Year 2 Stories

The Stonecutter – China	82
The Unlucky Man – England	85
The King and the Cockerel – Iraq	88
The Bird and the Forest Fire – India (Buddhist)	92
Honey and Trouble – Africa	94
How Coyote Brought Fire to Earth – Native American	97
The Snake and the Frog – USA	100
The Talking Skull – Africa	101
The Elephant's Fury – Asia (Buddhist)	103
The Island of Fairies – Scotland	106
The Bee's Treasure – Japan	108
The Pied Piper of Hamlyn – Germany	111
The Pedlar of Swaffham – England	113
Strength – Africa	115
Sleeping Beauty – Germany	118
Rumpelstiltskin – Germany	120
Cinderella – Germany	124
The Magic Paintbrush – China	130
Snow White – Germany	132
The Two Dragons – Wales	136

The Stonecutter

I really love this story. It has so many levels of meaning for all ages. I added a little song to lighten the whole thing up, and it's easy to fit physical movements to the song when the class joins in for chipping, sun, cloud, wind and mountain.

The key to the story is making the character a bit foolish, getting grumpy and then enthusiastic about his next wish before another disappointment. You can also play around with the things that he sees during each phase of the story and what he likes doing. You might also play versions of stone, paper and scissors using the gestures and idea in the story.

Once there was a stonecutter who worked all day cutting stone into blocks in a quarry at the foot of a mountain. One day, as he was working under the hot midday sun, feeling the back of his neck getting hotter and hotter, he looked up into the sky.

'I am just a stonecutter!' he said to himself. 'If only I was important. If only I was the sun, the most important thing in the world! I wish I was the sun.'

Up in the sky the Goddess of Wishes heard him. She smiled and sang a little song while dancing around on a cloud. (*teach them the dance and song*)

> *Stonecutter, stonecutter, chip chip chip*
> *The sun in the sky it shines so bright*
> *Sister cloud she gives us rain*
> *And brother wind blows day and night*
> *Mountain mountain big and strong*
> *And the little stonecutter chips all day long*
> *Chip, chip, chip chip chip*

Then, something amazing happened. By the goddess's magic, the stonecutter became the sun!

'Wow,' he said to himself. 'I like this. I am big and hot and the most important thing on the planet. Without me everything would die.'

Happily he shone down on fields making the crops grow, on forests, on sunbathers and on solar panels. He felt so useful and good. Then a cloud came between him and the earth.

He frowned.

'Hmm,' he said to himself. 'The sun is important but cloud is more important. The cloud can stop the sunshine. I wish I was a cloud!'

Up in the sky the Goddess of Wishes heard him. She smiled and sang her little song while dancing around on a cloud.

Then, something amazing happened. By the goddess's magic, the stonecutter became a cloud!

'Wow,' he said to himself. 'I like this. I am big and cool and fluffy and soft. I am the most important thing on the planet. Without me everything would die!'

Happily he floated over the earth, raining down on fields and forests, making rivers and lakes. He saw people drinking his water. He felt so useful and good. Then the wind blew him away over the sea.

He frowned.

'Hmm,' he said to himself. 'A cloud is important but the wind is more important. The wind can blow the cloud anywhere! I wish I was the wind.'

Up in the sky the Goddess of Wishes heard him. She smiled and sang her little song while dancing around on a cloud. (*sing it*)

Then, something amazing happened. By the goddess's magic, the stonecutter became the wind!

'Wow,' he said to himself. 'I like this. I am light and fast and everywhere. I bring air to everything. Without me everything would die.'

Happily he blew around the world, spinning windmills, speeding sailboats and bringing air to the plants and animals of the world.

Then he came to a mountain and … it wouldn't move. He had to go round it.

He frowned.

'Hmm,' he said to himself. 'The wind is important but the mountain is more important. The mountain can stop the wind. I wish I was a mountain!'

Up in the sky the Goddess of Wishes heard him. She smiled and sang her little song and danced her dance.

Then, something amazing happened. The stonecutter became the mountain!

'Wow,' he said to himself. 'I like this. I am big and heavy and invincible! I am the strongest and most important. I bring soil to everything. Without me everything would die.'

Happily he did nothing. Huge and solid, he watched the world go round as trees grew on him and birds nested in his crevices.

Then he heard a sound:
Chip chip chip chip chip

He frowned and looked down at a stonecutter in the quarry.

'Hmm,' he said to himself. 'The mountain is important but the stonecutter is more important. The stonecutter can chop down the mountain. I wish I was a stonecutter!'

Up in the sky the Goddess of Wishes heard him. She smiled and sang while cloud dancing.

Then, something amazing happened. The stonecutter became himself again!

'Wow,' he said to himself. 'I like this. I am a stonecutter! The sun is in me from the food I eat; cloud is in me from the water I drink; wind is in me from the air I breathe; mountain is in me from the crops that grow in the soil. They are all part of me and me of them! What could be more important than that!'

Happily he chipped away at the stone, singing his song:

> *Stonecutter, stonecutter, chip chip chip*
> *The sun in the sky it shines so bright*
> *Sister cloud she gives us rain*
> *And brother wind blows day and night*
> *Mountain mountain big and strong*
> *And the little stonecutter chips all day long*
> *Chip, chip, chip chip chip.*

The Unlucky Man

This is a great starter story that many storytellers use. There are five characters to evoke, and the plot has a lovely twist at the end. Practise your character voices and do try and sing the song – it adds joy to the whole thing and makes the ending stronger. You can tell it as tragicomedy. Make up the moans that work for you and your class! Probably it's good to remember the wording of the final line to add impact.

Once there was a man who was always moaning to his friends.

'My house is too small! My job is too boring! I don't have enough friends! I'll never get married! Why am I so poor? Why am I so lonely? … I just don't have any luck!'

His friends got fed up with listening to his moaning, so finally one said, 'Why don't you go and ask the wise man at the top of the sacred mountain?'

The unlucky man agreed and set off for the mountain walking as fast as he could. As he walked he sang this song:

> *I am so unlucky.*
> *Unlucky as can be.*
> *I'm so unlucky.*
> *Nothing works for me.*

He walked and he walked and he walked until he came to the mountain. He began to climb.

As he climbed he sang his song, *I'm so unlucky…*

After a day he came to a thin, sick old wolf lying on the ground next to the path.

'Where are you going?' asked the wolf.
'To ask the wise man at the top of the mountain why I don't have any luck.'
'Oh, well would you ask him why I am so thin and weak too?'

'OK,' said the unlucky man and continued up the mountain singing his song, *I'm so unlucky...*

After another day he came to a thin, leafless tree.

'Where are you going?' asked the tree.
'To ask the wise man at the top of the mountain why I don't have any luck.'
'Oh, well would you ask him why I am so thin and leafless?'
'OK,' said the unlucky man and continued up the mountain singing his song, *I'm so unlucky...*

After another day he came to cottage by the path. A lovely young woman was standing in the doorway. She smiled at him and waved.

'Where are you going?' she asked.
'To ask the wise man at the top of the mountain why I don't have any luck.'
'Oh, well would you ask him why I am so sad and lonely?'
'OK,' said the unlucky man and hurried off up the mountain singing his song, *I'm so unlucky...*

At the top of the mountain, he entered the hut of the wisest of men.

'I've come to ask you why I don't have any luck.'

'You have lots of luck!' said the wise man. 'You just have to look around you to find it.'

'Great!' said the unlucky man, smiling, 'I'll go home right now and start looking!'

Then he remembered the three questions from the others and asked them to the wise man, who gave his answers.

Soon after this the unlucky man was running down the hill keen to go home and find his luck. As he ran he sang:

>*I'm so lucky*
>*Lucky as can be*
>*I'll just look around*
>*So my luck I'll see*

On the way down the hill he came to the cottage.
'Did you ask him?' asked the lovely young woman.
'Yes, he says you are lonely and should find a husband.'
She blushed a little and looked him up and down.
'Well, are you married? We could be married. Would you like that?'
'I'm sorry,' said the unlucky man impatiently, 'but I have to rush off home to look for my luck. I don't have time now.'

So off he went down the mountain singing his song, *I'm so lucky...*

A day later he came to the tree.
'Did you ask him?' asked the tree.
'Yes, he says you are weak and thin because there is a box of treasure buried under your roots so they can't grow. Ask someone to dig it up and you will be fine.'
The tree swayed and smiled.
'Would you dig it up for me? If you do you can have all the treasure! Would you like that?'
'I'm sorry,' said the unlucky man impatiently, 'but I have to rush off home to look for my luck. I don't have time.'

So off he went down the mountain singing his song, *I'm so lucky...*

A day later he came to the wolf.
'Did you ask him?' asked the wolf.
'Yes, he says you are ill because you are hungry, so you should eat the first fool that comes along.'

So the wolf did just that!

That was the end of him
And this is the end of this story.

The King and the Cockerel

This little Iraqi story is another good one to start with. It has simple repetition and loads of potential for story invention within the story frame, by making up dreams for the king every time he falls asleep. Children love doing this. Get the class to join in with the cockadoodledoo, the repeating phrases and the sounds of the various items and animals that appear. This is all about the pain of not being listened to and determination to be taken seriously. It's good for any storytelling class.

Once there was a little cockerel. A brave little cockerel. A smart little cockerel. He lived in a little cottage with a kind old lady. They were very poor. Every day the cockerel would go down to the bottom of the cottage garden and go scritching and scratching around in the soil, looking for something to eat.

One day he was scritching and scratching around when he saw something glittering on the ground. It was a gold coin! The little cockerel was so happy. 'I'll give the coin to my kind old lady, and then we can buy a real feast,' he thought.

Just then, the king came walking down the street past the house, with a crown on his head and his nose in the air. He saw the gold coin, stepped over the fence, picked it up and put it in his pocket.

'That's not fair!' shouted the cockerel. 'That's my coin. Give it back! That's not fair!'

But the king paid no attention. He stepped back over the fence walked away back to the palace.

That evening the king was going to bed. He got into his silk pyjamas, put on his velvet sleeping hat, slipped under his soft clean sheets and put his head down on a pillow of the finest softest feathers. He was just dropping off to sleep when the little cockerel hopped up onto his bedroom windowsill.

Cockadoodledoo! Cockadoodledoo!
I'll scream and shout
With all my might
That's not fair! That's not right!
Give me back my coin!
Cockadoodledoo! Cockadoodledoo!

'Guard! Guard!' shouted the king. 'Get rid of this cockerel. I'm trying to sleep!'

A guard came in, grabbed the cockerel by the neck, and took it outside into the palace gardens.

In the garden was a big water tank with heavy lid on top. They opened the lid, threw the cockerel inside, and shut the door again, thinking that the cockerel would drown.

But the clever, brave little cockerel opened his mouth and ... GLUG GLUG GLUG GLUG ... he swallowed all the water in the tank!

When the guard came back a while later and lifted the lid of the tank, the little cockerel flapped his wings and flew up past him, up into the sky.

A while later the king was snoring loudly, his four fat chins wobbling backwards and forwards as he slept. He was just in the middle of a delightful dream about a fantastic food feast, when...

Cockadoodledoo! Cockadoodledoo!
I'll scream and shout
With all my might
That's not fair! That's not right!
Give me back my coin!
Cockadoodledoo! Cockadoodledoo!

'Guard! Guard!' shouted the king. 'Get rid of this cockerel! I'm trying to sleep!'

A guard came in, grabbed the cockerel by the neck, and took him down to the palace kitchens.

In the kitchen was a huge oven, full of burning wood. The guard opened the oven door, threw the cockerel inside and closed the door, thinking they would be eating roast cockerel for supper. But the clever little cockerel, the brave little cockerel ... he opened his mouth and … SSSSSSSSSSSS … out came all the water he had drunk in the tank, putting out the fire and cooling down the oven till the cockerel was quite cool.

A while later when the guard came back and opened the oven door, expecting to find supper. The little cockerel flapped his wings and flew up past him, out of the kitchen window and up into the sky.

A while later the king was in the middle of a dream about gold and jewels. He was counting all of his money, coin by coin when…

> *Cockadoodledoo! Cockadoodledoo!*
> *I'll scream and shout*
> *With all my might*
> *That's not fair! That's not right!*
> *Give me back my coin!*
> *Cockadoodledoo! Cockadoodledoo!*

'Guards! Guards!' called the king. 'Get rid of this cockerel! I'm trying to sleep!'

A guard came in, grabbed the cockerel by the neck, and took him down to the bottom of the palace gardens. They walked up to a large white wooden box with the sound of buzzing coming from it … it was a beehive.

The guard opened the top of the beehive and threw the cockerel inside, and then closed the top again, thinking the cockerel would get stung to death. But the clever little cockerel, the brave little cockerel … he opened his mouth and …GAH GAH GAH GAH GAH … he swallowed all the bees in the beehive.

Later, when the guard came back and opened the beehive door, the little cockerel flapped his wings and flew up past him, out of the kitchen window and up into the sky.

A while later the king was just in the middle of a dream about cockerels, when…

> *Cockadoodledoo! Cockadoodledoo!*
> *I'll scream and shout*
> *With all my might*
> *That's not fair! That's not right!*
> *Give me back my coin!*
> *Cockadoodledoo! Cockadoodledoo!*

'Guards! Guards!' called the king. 'Get rid of this cockerel! I'm trying to sleep!'

Five guards came in and tried to grab the cockerel, but this time he was too quick for them, flapped his wings and circled above them close to the ceiling. The guards started jumping up trying to catch the cockerel, knocking over the chairs, tables, mirrors and vases as they jumped.

Then the clever little cockerel, the brave little cockerel ... he opened his mouth and CA CA CA CA CA... all of those bees he had swallowed came buzzing out of his mouth and started stinging the guards who were trying to catch him.

'Owww! Owww! Your majesty, I've got stung on the elbow!' cried one.

'Ouch! My leg hurts!' cried another.

'Oh no! My nose!' cried a third.

Imagine the racket! Five guards jumping around the king's bedroom, wailing about their bee-stings.

The king had enough!

'QUIET!' he shouted. 'Guards, go and get that gold coin and give it to the cockerel, or I'll never get any sleep!'

So the guards gave the coin back and the cockerel took it home to the kind little old lady. She was so happy. She went shopping and they had a fantastic feast of the most delightful food, and lived happily ever after.

Shnick schnack shnoo!
The storytelling's through!

The Bird and the Forest Fire

Here is an Indian fable from the Buddhist tradition, in this case illustrating qualities of faith and determination and their ability to triumph against the odds. It can be fun to get the audience to join in with all the sounds of the forest and the fire, and then the sound of water hissing and fizzing on the flames. It can be quite a gentle and tender tale, speaking to fears and hopes for the future and how alone this can leave us. I like the way Rafe Martin tells this and similar stories in his book The Hungry Tigress.

Once there was a forest and in that forest there was a tree and in the tree there lived a little bird. The little bird loved her home. She loved the leaves, the branches, the tree and the whole forest. It was her home.

One day the little bird smelt something strange. She flew up, high over the canopy and saw in the distance a fire, a great snake of flames and smoke coming towards her. She called down to her friends, 'It's a fire! We must do something!' But all her friends just ran away.

'Run away with us!' they called. 'Otherwise you will die!'

'No!' said the little bird. 'I love my home. I won't leave it. I'll do everything I can to save it.'

As her friends ran, she flew down to a stream by the tree in which she lived and dipped her wings into the water. She then flew up above the fire and tipped her wings, releasing the droplets of water. The water hissed and fizzed away in the flames in an instant. Then, she flew back to the stream and again wetted her wings before returning to the fire.

She did this time and time again with the fire getting closer and closer to her tree.

Up in the heavens, the gods looked down and laughed at the little bird.

'Who does she think she is?' said one.
'She'll soon be cooked!' laughed another.

But one god, the Eagle God, admired the little bird.
He opened his wings, swooped down from heaven and joined the little bird as she flew between stream and fire.

'Listen, little bird,' said the Eagle God. 'You must fly away! You can't put the fire out. It's too big and you are too small. You will die!'

'I don't care if I die,' cried the bird. 'I love my home and I will do what I can to save it.'

Tears filled the Eagle God's eyes as he listened to the brave little bird. They dripped from his eye and down into the fire, hissing and fizzing in the fire. The tears got stronger and faster and soon there was a stream of tears flowing onto the fire. The stream became a river and soon the fire was gone, put out by the Eagle God's tears.

The Eagle God returned to heaven and the little bird to her tree and the next spring, new green shoots peeped up through the carpet of ash on the forest floor.

Honey and Trouble

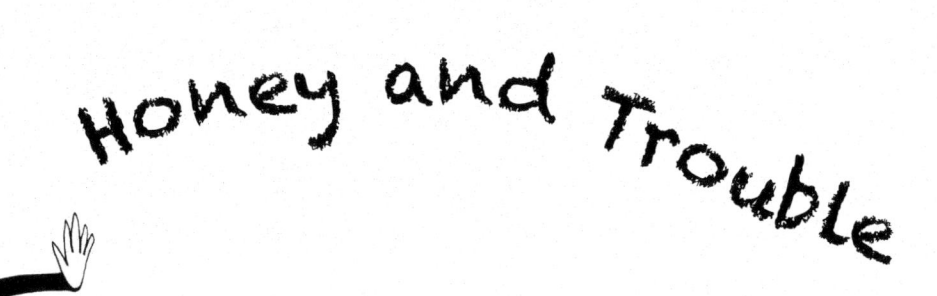

Honey and Trouble is another very popular and brilliant story that works on many levels. Children love the comedy of misunderstanding, something all children know about. There are loads of versions of this story, which is told by many tellers. I like Hugh Lupton's version in Tales of Wisdom and Wonder *from the excellent Barefoot Books. At another level the story is about how we can repeatedly bring trouble on ourselves, albeit unintentionally. It's a great comedy story and good for memorable retelling.*

Once there was a woman who kept bees and made honey. One day she was walking through the forest to market singing a song with a pot of honey on her head.

> *I am going to market, to market, to market*
> *I am going to market to sell my honey*

She started to imagine what she would buy with the money when she sold her honey: a new dress for herself, toys for her children, a new hat for her husband ... she was so busy imagining these things and singing that she didn't notice a rock in the middle of the path. Her foot caught the stone and she fell down. The pot of honey fell down to the ground and shattered into a hundred pieces.

She wailed up to the sky, 'Why do you give me so much trouble?' She turned around and walked back towards home, muttering.

Above the path where the pot broke a young monkey was sitting. He hadn't started school yet and so didn't know very many words. When he heard the woman cry out he thought, 'I wonder what that means? I wonder what trouble is?'

He climbed down from the tree, put his finger in the sticky liquid and licked his finger. 'OOO I like this!' he said to himself. 'This must be trouble. I like this. I like trouble a lot! It's really sweet!'

He ate up all the sweet liquid from the ground, and when he had finished he wanted more, so he went off to see his friend the elephant.

'Brother Elephant,' he said. 'I've found out my favourite thing in all the world. I've found out what I really love best. I really like trouble, and I wondered if you have some that you can give me.'
'Are you sure?' said the elephant, a little puzzled.
'Oh yes! Certainly!' nodded the monkey.
'Alright then, I'll give you some,' said the elephant with a shrug. The elephant swung back his trunk and whacked the little monkey on his bottom. The monkey flew through the air, crashed into a tree and lay on the ground, bruised and confused.

'Why did Brother Elephant do that?' he said to himself. 'I'll go and ask Brother Lion.'

He found his friend the lion sitting under a tree.
'Brother Lion,' he said. 'I've found out my favourite thing in all the world. I've found out what I really love. It's trouble. I really like trouble, and I wondered if you have any that you can give me.'
'Are you sure?' said the lion, curious.
'Oh yes! Certainly!' nodded the monkey.
'Alright then, I'll give you some,' he said with a shrug. Lion opened his mouth wide and bit the little monkey on the leg. Monkey ran away crying and bleeding.

'Why did Brother Lion do that?' he said to himself. 'I only wanted some trouble. I'll go and ask Brother Bull.'

Bull was eating grass in a field by the river.
'Brother Bull,' he said. 'I've found out my favourite thing in all the world. I've found out what I really love. It's trouble. I really like trouble, and I wondered if you have any that you can give me.'
'Are you sure?' said Bull.
'Oh yes! Certainly!' nodded the monkey.
'Alright then, I'll give you some, if that's what you really want.' The bull butted the monkey with his long sharp horns, sending the monkey rolling along the ground and crashing into a wall.

'Why did Brother Bull do that?' he said to himself. 'It makes no sense. I'll go and ask the wise monk of the forest.'

The monkey went to the wise monk's hut, knocked and went in. The wise monk was sitting on the floor meditating.

'Brother Monk,' he said, once the monk had opened his eyes. 'I've found out my favourite thing in all the world. I've found out what I really love. It's trouble. I really like trouble, and I wondered if you have any that you can give me.'
'Are you sure?' said the monk brightly.
'Oh yes! Certainly!' nodded the monkey.
'Alright then, I'll give you some. Take this black bag to the desert. When you can't see any trees, open it. It's full of trouble.'

The monkey dragged the big black bag out into the desert and started to open it.

'It doesn't smell like trouble,' he thought as he pulled open the bag and looked inside.

RUUUFFFF!

Out jumped three big black dogs. They chased the monkey across the desert. He ran and ran and ran and ran until he saw a tree. He climbed the tree and waited for the dogs to go away, then he went home.

Back home, he told the story to his mother. She laughed and laughed. 'You poor thing!' she said. 'It's not trouble you want. It's honey. I've got some in the kitchen right now!'
She came back with a jar of sweet liquid. The little monkey dipped his finger in and tasted it.

'So that's not trouble!' she said smiling. 'That's honey!'

How Coyote Brought Fire to Earth

This Native American story, from the Karok people, is one of those 'how things got to be the way they are' stories. This one, as a heroic quest, has plenty of drama and excitement as our hero and his friends are chased by a monster and make good. It needs to be told with pace once the action starts. I'm not sure where I first heard this one, which is very popular with UK storytellers. I like to tell the chase scene with a drum in the background for atmosphere.

In the beginning, the world and all its creatures were made. Most animals were made with fur which kept them warm at night, but humans were made with hardly any fur at all.

At night they huddled and shivered and many of their children died from the cold.

The humans called a meeting of all the animals and asked for help. All the birds and animals of the forests turned up and listened.

'We need warmth at night,' said the human chief. 'If we don't then we will die. The nights are colder and colder and we have no fur. The sun warms us by day, but we need a piece of it at night. Can anyone bring us a piece of the sun?'

All the animals looked at one another, as if it was a silly question. Then Coyote popped up and said, 'Leave it to me. I'll see what I can do.'

He trotted out of the forest, up through meadows and mountains, into the sky then through the door in the sky into the sky world. There he crept carefully and slowly towards the blazing sun.

When he got there he saw that the sun was a great blazing fire, watched carefully by the guardians of the fire, huge giants with hands as big as mountains and legs as long as rivers, eyes blazing never blinking, watching the fire on guard for thieves.

Coyote hid behind a bush and watched. For a long time nothing happened, then he heard the fire guardian call out, 'I'm hungry, brother, come and take my place.'

The flaming giant stood and walked away from the fire towards his hut and moments later a second fire guardian – even larger that the first – came out of the hut and took his brother's place. Coyote watched and waited. A while later the brother called out that he was hungry and walked towards the hut. A third brother came out and took his place.

Coyote thought and thought till he had a plan, then turned and was about to return to the forest when his claws touched a leaf which rustled softly.

The guardian had huge ears and could hear almost everything.

'Who is there?' boomed his voice. 'Who comes to steal my fire? I will not allow it! Show yourself and I will spare you. Run and I will burn you up with fire breath!'

Coyote ran away as fast as his legs could carry him, back to the forest and the gathering of humans and animals.

'I can help you,' he said, 'but I need help. White Crow, White Squirrel and Singing Frog offered to help.

Coyote whispered his plan to them and they nodded and went off into the forest. Coyote went back up through the meadows and mountains up into the sky and through the sky door, then crept with all his stealth to the sun fire.

Coyote hid behind a bush, watching and waiting. When a guardian called out to his brother and walked towards his hut, Coyote nipped out from hiding, took a piece of fire in his mouth and crept away towards the sky door.

When the next guardian came to the fire he looked for a moment and bellowed out, 'Who has been stealing my fire? Where is the thief?' He sniffed the air, smelled the trail of the fire and began to run after Coyote with huge giant strides.

Coyote rocketed through the sky door and down towards the Earth with the guardian close behind. As he ran his face started burning, then his fur, till he was completely on fire, blazing down through the sky with the guardian close behind. By the time he reached the mountain his fur was black all over.

Just then the guardian caught up and reached out to grab Coyote, but at that moment White Crow was waiting. 'Here!' shouted Coyote, and threw the fire to Crow, who caught it in his beak and flew off down the mountain. His white feathers caught fire as he ran, burning until they were as black as night.

The guardian chased Crow on down through the rocks and stones of the mountain till they came to a meadow where Squirrel was waiting.

The giant was just about to reach out and catch Crow when Crow called out, 'Here, Squirrel! Your turn!' He threw the fire to Squirrel, who caught it on his paws and ran off down through the meadows chased by the guardian. Soon his fur caught fire, burning until his fur was ash grey.

As he reached the forest Singing Frog was waiting. 'Here!' shouted Squirrel and threw the fire to Singing Frog, who swallowed it in his throat and went off hopping through the forest. As he hopped he felt his throat burning.

The guardian was about to reach him when Frog called out to Tree, 'Here! Your turn!' Frog coughed out the fire, which flew through the air towards Tree, which opened his trunk and let fire go inside, then closed up again so that the guardian couldn't find the fire.

And from that day, fire has lived inside wood. If you don't believe me, make a bonfire and see where the fire comes from!
And from that day until now, the frog lost his lovely singing voice. All he can do is croak.
And from that day crows are black and squirrels are grey.
And as for the guardians of the sun – they are still up in the sky guarding the sun. Sometimes they look down at the fires on earth and grumble about the time that Coyote stole their fire. That's where thunder comes from.

The Snake and the Frog

Here's our first tall tale in the collection. I like to tell it in the first person to add to the credibility of it. It can lead to very interesting discussions. There is a version by Jon Spelman in that lovely collection of Holt and Mooney, More Ready-To-Tell Tales. *Spin it out with all sorts of detail to add to the suspense.*

I am a traveller. Last year I was travelling in the Amazon rainforest, when I saw something I will never forget. I was quietly by the river watching the forest and its amazing wildlife. Monkeys in the trees. Huge birds gliding above the canopy. Huge lizards down on the edge of the river.

Then I saw this huge bright green frog sitting on a rock by the water's edge. It was the biggest frog I've ever seen; as big as a small dog!

As I watched it an enormous black snake, as thick as my leg, slithered onto the rock next to the frog.

The frog looked at the snake. The snake looked at the frog. The frog croaked and the snake hissed. I knew they were going to fight. At the exact same moment, they attacked each other.

The frog grabbed the snake's tail and began to swallow it just as the snake grabbed the frog's back legs and started to swallow them too.

At one end each was gripping and swallowing while at the other end each was wriggling and trying to get free.

They fought and fought, the frog swallowing more and more of the snake's long body, the snake swallowing the back legs, then the body of the frog. Finally, all that was left of the two creatures were their heads.

Amazingly, at the exact same instant, they both swallowed. A moment later both had disappeared.

I wonder where they went?

The Talking Skull

This is a very common and popular African tale, discussed in some depth in Pantheon's African Folktales *by Roger Abrahams. It is a brooding kind of story with a nice twist at the end to add to the sense of doom! It's good to explore the desert environment during the story, to give a sense of place and atmosphere. Find a good voice for the skull!*

Once a traveller was walking through the desert when he noticed a human skull, bleached white in the sun, nestling in the sand.

He said out loud, to no one in particular, 'What are you doing here?'

To his amazement, the skull spoke! 'Talking brought me here,' it said. 'Be warned! Talking will bring you back here too if you don't keep your mouth shut!'

Leaving the skull behind, the traveller walked to the next village where he told everyone about what had happened.

Word of the story reached the king and he summoned the traveller to court.

'What's all this nonsense I hear about a talking skull?' said the king.

'It's true, your majesty,' said the traveller. 'It talked to me. I swear it on my life.'

'So be it,' said the king. 'Take me to this talking skull. Your life depends on it.'

And so the hunter led the king to the place where the skull still lay in the sand.

'Here it is, your majesty,' he said, then turned to the skull.

'What are you doing here?' the traveller asked the skull. 'Tell the king like you told me.'

But the skull said nothing. 'Come on!' said the traveller, feeling worried. 'Talk!'

But the skull said nothing.

The king signalled to his guard, who drew his sword and chopped off the traveller's head with one blow.

A few months later, another traveller was walking through the desert when he noticed two skulls in the sand. He said out loud, to no one in particular, 'I wonder what you are doing here?'

The skulls replied, 'Talking brought us here and be warned, talking will bring you back here too if you don't keep your mouth shut.'

Hmmm...

I wonder what happened next?

The Elephant's Fury

Here's another popular Buddhist fable showing how the stories we hear affect who we become. It can lead to great discussions about wise and unwise friendships. The story itself needs strong action when the elephant is on the rampage, and then suspense and curiosity when the wise man starts to investigate. There's lots of opportunity for descriptions of ancient India.

Once in ancient India, there was a white royal elephant. In those days, to own a white elephant was considered extremely good luck. The people of the city were delighted that their king had such an elephant, and the king was delighted too.

Every day the elephant's trainer would slowly ride him around the streets of the city so the people could admire and enjoy the sight of him. Sometimes they would stop and the elephant would gently pick fruits from a tree and pass them, with his truck, out to children. Sometimes he would gently pick flowers and hand them out to the crowd without damaging a single petal. The king was delighted to own such an elephant. It gave people confidence that all was well with them and their king.

There were so many stories about the elephant: how he saved children from drowning in the river. How he chased away a lion that was attacking a mother and baby. How he found hidden treasure in the royal palace. In the evenings the people would come to his stables, say prayers, leave flowers and ask for the elephant's blessing on their lives.

Then one day everything changed. The elephant woke up one morning and began trumpeting, as if he was screaming with pain. He ran out into the street bellowing, his eyes rolling and his truck waving in the air. When anyone came close he would swing his huge trunk at them. Most backed off fast but one got too close – his back was broken with one blow.

A royal carriage pulled by six horses came towards the elephant and he charged it, flipping it up into the air with his huge tusks, as the horses whinnied and scattered.

When the elephant approached the marketplace he charged at the crowds, crushing the market stalls and terrifying the people.

In the evening the elephant returned to his stables and lay down on his bed of straw to sleep. Everyone hoped he would be better the next day, but – on the contrary – he seemed wilder and more dangerous. He charged at huts, flattening them and the people inside. He kicked out at anyone and anything within range, And always with that same bellowing scream that chilled the hearts of the citizens.

The king called an urgent meeting of all the elephant specialists in the city (and there were many) but none could explain the change in their beloved elephant. So the king sent a message to a wise old hermit who lived in the forest.

The wise old hermit took one look at the elephant and asked about where he lived. After looking around the stables he said, 'Give me a couple of days. I'll see what I can do.'

That evening the hermit hid himself in the stables between two bales of straw, and waited. Around midnight the door creaked open and in came a group of men armed to the teeth with swords and knives and clubs. Each carried a heavy sack. They were robbers.

They sat against the wall opposite the elephant, who watched them, without moving, one eye half open as if he was pretending to be asleep. The robbers poured out the contents of their sacks onto the floor in a big pile. There was gold, silver, money, silk, incense, jewellery – a glittering pile of treasures. Then their leader, a big man with a wide moustache, got out a bottle of rum and they started to drink.

The hermit listened as the robbers talked and drank.

One remembered how, as a child, he had lived alone as a beggar and how rich boys had kicked and spat on him. Another how he had been double-crossed time and time again and how now he trusted no one except himself. Another talked about the time someone had tried to kill him but he had stabbed him first.

All night the robbers drank and swapped stories about their world – a world where they were surrounded by enemies and danger and the best thing to do was kill before you were killed.

The next morning the hermit went to the king and said, 'Collect together the kindest, wisest and most compassionate men in the city and, every night, once the elephant is asleep, let them meet up in the stables. Let them talk together, swap stories about life and how they live it. This will solve your problem.'

So the king did as the hermit suggested and within a week the elephant had returned to its old peaceful ways, bringing confidence and delight to the city and its people.

(*optional*)

The hermit explained it like this to the king:

'We are all made from the stories that we hear. If, day after day, we hear stories of fear and hate, then we will take them as our teachers and become fearful and hateful. If we hear stories of kindness and gentleness then these will become our teachers and we will become kind and gentle. Just as we need healthy food to have a healthy body, so we need wise stories to keep our minds healthy. The elephant had been listening to stories of killing and betrayal, and they changed him into a killer. Once he started listening to wise and kind stories, his wisdom and kindness soon returned.

'You are the king. Make sure that your people have, not just good food for their bodies, but good stories for their minds. Do this and your city will prosper.'

The king did as he was asked and the city remained happy and prosperous for as long as he ruled over them.

The Island of Fairies

Here's a delightful legend from Wales. Islands are a common topic and this is a fine island story. Imaginary Worlds is another. Both work well with this story. You can paint a detailed picture of the island as each storyteller sees it and start project work from there. Emphasise the magic and wonder of discovery at the beginning. Spin out the mystery at the beginning of the story.

Once there was a fisherman who lived by the sea. His wife died soon after they were married and he missed her very much. Every Sunday he would go to the grave of his wife, leave some flowers and look out over the sea for a while. One day he was standing there, staring out into the sea, when he saw something strange. Out near the horizon there was an island, with hills and valleys and a lighthouse, as clear as anything. He was amazed! He'd never seen it before!

'Interesting!' he thought, 'I shall go there.'

He went down to the beach and set off in his rowing boat. But when he looked for the island he couldn't see it.

'How strange!' he thought.

He went back to the graveyard and looked again, and the island had gone.

He was puzzled. It made no sense. Then he stepped onto exactly the same place where he had first seen it and he could see the island again! He stepped forward and it disappeared. He stepped back and it reappeared.

'I can only see it,' he thought, 'when I'm standing on this piece of grass.'

He took out his penknife and cut up the square of grass he was standing on, then went down to the harbour and sat on the grass as he rowed out towards the island. Sitting on the grass he could see the island clearly!

He rowed into the harbour and called out to the people, who looked at him in a friendly way. They had beautiful, shining hair, sparkling eyes, and little wings poking out of their backs. They were fairies!

They were very excited. A young one said, 'How did you find us? We've never met a human before!'

'I stood on this grass,' said the man. 'Up in the graveyard.'

There was a hush. All the fairies had heard stories about the magic grass. The stories were true!

The fisherman ate fairy cakes, danced fairy dances and drank fairy wine.

A young fairy said, 'Please take this bag of gold and in return give us the grass. If other humans see us they will do us harm.'

The man saw that this was true so he gave them the grass and rowed home with his bag of gold. He still went to the graveyard every week, but now, when he looked out to sea, he knew the fairy island was there even if he couldn't see it.

Four leaf clover,
The story's over.

The Bee's Treasure

Here's a Japanese story that echoes the English story, the Pedlar of Swaffham (later), but with more comedy and drama. The character of the dreamer is important in this story. You can make him seem foolish and determined and the rich man a bit nasty and greedy.

Once, not twice, not thrice, there was a man who wanted a dream. He'd never had a dream, and when he heard about his friends' dreams he felt sad that he was missing something.

'Oh, I wish I could have a dream too!' he thought.

Then he had an idea. He went to a friend who had lots of dreams and said, 'Can I buy your last dream? I've never had one and I want one so much.'

'Don't be silly!' said his friend. 'Nobody buys dreams. You have to dream them.'

'Well I want to buy one. Why not?'

So the man paid his friend for the dream.

Now, the man who bought the dream was very poor, and he was always struggling to make ends meet, so when his wife found out that he had spent their precious little bit of money on someone else's dream, she was very upset.

'How could you be so foolish?' she asked. 'What are you thinking? Why would you want to buy someone else's dream?'

'I think this dream could be worth something. I was watching my friend sleeping, and listen ... just as he was woke up, he yawned, and a little bee flew out of his nose. Then, he told me his dream. It was about a jar of gold, and this jar of gold was buried underneath a nandin bush, and the nandin bush was next to a tall pine tree, which was at the foot of a little mountain in the gardens behind a big mansion. And he said this mansion belongs to the richest man in Osaka. And I really think I have to go there, and so that's why I bought the dream.'

His wife was still upset, but anyway the man set off on his journey. It was a long way to Osaka. It was 400 miles to get there, and it took many days. He had to sleep along the side of the road, and begged for food.

Well, when he arrived in Osaka, the man began asking the people in the streets there, who was the richest man in the city. He went to the house and knocked on the door of a vast mansion. A servant answered.

'Do you have a little mountain in your back garden?'
'Yes, we have.'
'Is there a big pine tree by the mountain?'
'Yes, there is.'
The man was getting more excited with every question.
'And, is there a nandin bush beside the pine tree?'
'Yes, there is.'

Now, the man who bought the dream was really delighted. And he asked if he could stay there for the night. So they let him stay. That evening he told the rich man all about the dream that he had bought, and all about the jar of gold. And he said he would share some of the gold with the rich man if he would only have his servants help dig up the jar the next day.

After everyone was in bed, the rich man thought, 'Could there really be this jar of gold?' He woke up his servants and he told them to begin digging under the nandin bush. Late in the night, they finally came to the top of a jar. Now, the rich man was planning to take this gold for himself, but when he opened the jar, just a little bee flew out. Otherwise the jar was empty.

The rich man laughed and laughed, and then he ordered his servants to bury the jar again. The next morning, the man who bought the dream was very excited. He went out with the servants, and began digging under the nandin bush, hoping to find the jar. For the servants, the digging was easier this time. Finally, they found the top of the jar, and the man who bought the dream screamed with delight, 'There it is! This is it!'

The man who bought the dream slowly uncovered the jar and slowly and carefully removed the top. And then he gasped. He could not believe his eyes. The jar was empty!

Now the man who bought the dream didn't know what to do. He felt so foolish because he had bought this dream that turned out not to be true. He was completely broken-hearted. And with his head down, he thanked the rich man and set out on his journey back home. He was so distressed that he even thought of not returning to his wife. How could he face her now? He had spent their last few coins on a worthless dream that wasn't even true. So he took a long, long time to get home, thinking over and over that he should not go.

The man who bought the dream had no other place to go, and he knew that he loved his wife no matter how poor they might be. So he finally arrived back in his own village.

As he came close to his house, his wife saw her husband through the window, and she came running out.

'Husband!' she said. 'I'm so happy to see you. A few days after you left I heard a bee buzzing in the attic. I went up and a little bee flew out of the door. I looked at where the bee had been and there was a pile of gold coins in the corner of the attic. We are rich!' 'Gosh!' said the man who bought the dream. 'That dream was good value after all!'

Snip snap
That's the end of that!

The Pied Piper of Hamlyn

Here's a famous legend about promises and honesty. Once children have learned the story they can work from the famous poems too, if you like. If you can play a recorder or flute a little that really adds to the story. Tell it like a legend so refer to place and time at the beginning.

Once, there was a town called Hamlyn in Germany. It is still there today.

The main street is called the silent street: why is that? There it was forbidden to play music. If you go into the church, this is written in the church book:

> *In the year 1284 after the birth of Christ*
> *From Hamlyn were led away*
> *One hundred thirty children, born at this place*
> *Led away by a piper into a mountain.*

If you look at the windows of the church, they tell the story of what happened…

Once, the town of Hamlyn was full of rats. They ate the bread from the table. They ate the grain in the store. They ate the fruit from the trees. Nobody visited Hamlyn because it was so nasty and full of dirty rats, so business was poor.

Worst of all, the rats carried the plague, a disease caused by the fleas that lived on the rats. Every year hundreds of people died after being bitten by the fleas.

One day a man came into the town wearing a coat of many bright colours and playing a flute, so they called him the Pied Piper, meaning 'many coloured piper'.

He said he could get rid of all their rats, forever, if they paid him thirteen bags of gold.

The mayor said it was too much.

'Take it or leave it!' said the Piper.

'We'll take it!' said the mayor. 'Do you need a contract?'

'No,' said the Piper. 'You pay or you will be sorry.'

The Piper began to play his tune and as he did all the mice and rats came and listened until the street was like a river of rats, jumping up and down as if dancing to the music.

He walked out of town with a long tail of rats behind him.

The Piper walked into the river and stood, playing, up to his waist in the water.

The rats followed and were soon drowned.

He returned and asked for his gold and the mayor made excuses.

'I'm sorry, we don't have any gold. Come back next year. Anyway, it only took you ten minutes...'

'Pay or you will be sorry!' the Piper snarled. He turned on his heel and left the town.

A few days later he returned with a strange red hat and hunter's clothes. This time, when he played, the children came out of the houses and started to dance to his music.

Before the parents realised what was happening, the Piper led them out of the town and into a mountain.

The parents ran out after the children and followed the footsteps, which led to a cave in the mountain. Inside there was no sign of them. The mountain had swallowed them up. The children were never seen again.

Some say that if you go to that cave today, and listen very carefully, you can still hear the children dancing to the flute deep inside the mountain.

The Pedlar of Swaffham

This story is a popular English legend from Norfolk. It echoes The Bee's Treasure *story told earlier. You might teach them both together and compare. You can tell this one as comedy, as drama, or a bit of both.*

Once, in the village of Swaffham, there lived a poor pedlar called John Chapman. He travelled from place to place selling this and that. He was very poor. Back home there were holes in the roof of his cottage, no glass in his windows and no money in his pocket.

In the summer months, John Chapman would snooze at the bottom of the garden under an old apple tree. One night he had a dream.

In the dream a voice said, 'John Chapman. You must travel to London, and find London Bridge. Wait there and you will find your fortune.'

The next day he set off for London. He travelled day and night, night and day and day and night again until at last he was standing on London Bridge.

John Chapman stood there a whole day and nothing happened except that his toes grew colder and colder.

He waited another day and again nothing happened except that his stomach became empty.

He waited almost the entire third day when a policeman passed by. 'What are you doing hanging around here all the time?' he asked.

'I had a dream that I needed to come to London Bridge to find my fortune,' John Chapman told the policeman.

'You're stupid!' sneered the policeman. 'Dreams don't mean anything. Why, last night I had a silly dream about a place called Swaffham! I mean – where's Swaffham? And who is this chap I've never heard of called John Chapman? I dreamed that at the bottom of his garden was an old apple tree where a pot of gold was buried. What nonsense!'

'I see,' said John Chapman. 'Thank you for your advice.'

John Chapman went straight home. He travelled day and night, night and day and day and night again until he got home. He found a spade and dug around his old apple tree.

Sure enough he found a pot of gold coins.

Now, John Chapman's cottage has a roof that doesn't leak, windows with glass and money in his pocket.

'How strange,' he thought, soon after. 'To think I dreamed for so many years of finding my fortune and it was here at home all the time.'

Strength

I love this story. It's a great way to introduce the themes of violence and weapons, which are sadly so important in this modern world. You can play with the various animals, finding voices and gestures to embody them, and then get in character for the serious competitive man. Leave plenty of talking time afterwards. You can find a lovely version of this in Margaret Read MacDonald's excellent book Peace Tales, which is full of excellent stories about war and peace. It is from West Africa, so you can see it there if you like.

Once, when the world was new, the animals of the world got together in the forest.

'What shall we do?' said Bird.
'Let's play a game!' said Monkey.
'How about a competition?' said Owl.
'I know,' said Elephant, 'let's have a competition to see who is the strongest.'

All the animals of the world were there, and seven of them joined the competition: Gorilla, Deer, Leopard, Bull, Elephant and Man.

All the animals sat under the shade of a tall wide tree, and waited.

First Gorilla stood up and sang a song in a deep gorilla-like voice.

He sang a song to the audience:

> *I am so strong.*
> *As strong as strong can be.*
> *Watch what I can do.*
> *There's no one stronger than me!*

Gorilla climbed a small tree and tied it in a knot, then climbed down.

'Strong! Strong! Pretty strong!' he chanted and pounded his fists on his chest. The animals chanted with him and copied the pounding.

Next, Deer jumped up and sang the song in a high little voice:

> *I am so strong.*
> *As strong as strong can be.*
> *Watch what I can do.*
> *There's no one stronger than me!*

The deer ran three miles into the forest and got back in just a few minutes. She wasn't even out of breath.

'Strong! Strong! Pretty strong!' she chanted, jumping up and down in the air. The animals chanted with her and jumped up and down too. They were having fun.

After that was Leopard. He sang the song in a smooth leopard purr:

> *I am so strong.*
> *As strong as strong can be.*
> *Watch what I can do.*
> *There's no one stronger than me!*

Leopard opened his claws and dug into the ground with earth flying everywhere. 'Strong! Strong! Pretty strong!' he chanted, waving his claws in the air. The animals chanted with him and copied his claw-waving.

Next was Bull. He sang the song, then lowered his horns and ploughed the ground.

Then Elephant sang, then leaned on a group of trees and knocked them all over.

Finally Man jumped up and sang:

> *I am so strong.*
> *As strong as strong can be.*
> *Watch what I can do.*
> *There's no one stronger than me!*

He did somersaults, cartwheels and back flips.

'Strong! Strong! Pretty strong!' he chanted, but the animals didn't join in. They were quiet.

'What?' shouted Man.

'Not very strong,' said Owl and all the animals nodded.

'OK,' he said angrily, 'watch this!'

He climbed up a tree and threw down coconuts. Strength! Strength! That was strength!

'Strong! Strong! Pretty strong!' he chanted. The animals shook their heads. Not really.

Now Man was furious. 'I'll show you strength!'

He pulled out his gun and Bang! He shot the Elephant.

He smiled, confidently. 'Strong! Strong! Pretty strong!'

He looked around but the animals had gone.

Deep in the jungle they huddled together.
'Did you see that?' asked Gorilla
'Was that strength?' asked Deer.
'No,' said Bull, 'that was death. DEATH.'

From that day animals run from men.

They have learned that some men do not know the difference between strength and death.

Sleeping Beauty

I feel there is something really important in teaching our children the original stories, before they were adapted by Disney studios and other eminent movie makers. The originals have a power and also a plot integrity which are quite different from the new versions. Here's a version of Sleeping Beauty based around the Grimm narrative.

Once there was a king and queen whose first child, a daughter, had just been born. The king and queen were so happy they threw a great party and invited all the lords and ladies of the land. Twelve wise women were invited and each gave a gift to the baby, one at a time. A thirteenth was not invited. She had been forgotten.

She stormed into the party and shouted out, 'This baby will be cursed. On her fifteenth birthday she will prick herself with a spinning wheel spindle and fall down dead. That is my gift to your child!'

One of the wise women softened the gift. 'Let it not be death, let it be a deep sleep of a hundred years,' she said.

The king ordered that all the spinning wheels be burned and this was done, so everyone had to spin wool by hand.

When the princess was fifteen years old she was wandering around the palace and came to an old storeroom. Inside there was an old woman spinning thread. 'What's that?' asked the princess.

'Have a go,' said the old woman, grinning.

The princess took the thread and pricked her finger on the spindle. Before her blood had hit the ground she had fallen into a deep sleep.

Everything in the palace fell into the same sleep: the king and queen, the servants, the dogs and cats, the flies and spiders. Every creature fell asleep and just stopped where it was, frozen in time.

A hedge of thorns grew up around the castle and soon it was hidden from view, hidden from the road. Young men heard the story of the princess and she became known as 'The Thorn Rose Princess'. They tried to cut their way through the thorns to find her but none of them succeeded. The thorns closed around them, killing them with a thousand cuts. In this way one hundred years passed.

Then a prince decided to try his luck. When he approached the hedge all he found was a wall of sweet blooming flowers – the thorns were gone! He walked into the castle where everything was still. He walked past the sleeping dogs, the sleeping soldiers and the frozen servants until he came to the sleeping princess. 'This must be Thorn Rose,' he said, and, finding her beautiful, kissed her on the lips.

At that moment she opened her eyes and the whole castle came back to life, as if the hundred years were just the blink of an eye.

Soon they were married and lived happily to the end of their days in contentment.

Rumpelstiltskin

Here's another classic, loosely based on the Grimm text. Bringing the characters alive is the key here: the king, the girl and the little old man. He needs to be pretty crazy for the story to work. Spin out the drama in the guessing sections. For other Grimm sources I really like the recent Routledge Grimm: Complete Fairy Tales.

Once there was and once there was not ... a poor miller, who made his living grinding wheat into flour. He felt sad that he was not more important and would make things up to impress people. Do you ever do that? Anyway, one day he was delivering bags of flour to the palace when he happened to meet the king, who invited him in for a cup of tea.

'Do you have a daughter?' asked the king, biting on a biscuit.
'Oh, yes indeed!' said the miller. 'And she is not only beautiful, but she is a fine spinner! She knows how to spin straw into gold!'
'Is that true?' asked the king, suspiciously.
'Most certainly!' said the miller.
'Then bring her to me immediately. If she can do this I will marry her. If not, then ... off with her head!'

The next morning the miller arrived with his daughter and the king took her to a room in the cellar with a strong oak door and no windows. Inside were a spinning wheel and a pile of straw.

'You have until tomorrow to spin this straw into gold,' said the king. 'Succeed and I will marry you. Fail and you die!'

The miller's daughter was locked in the room. She sat on the straw and began to cry.

After a while a little man appeared in the room. He was tiny like a doll with a strange grin and fiery eyes.

'Can I help?' he said.
'I need to spin the straw into gold,' she said.

'What will you give me if I do it for you?' he asked.
'Gosh! My necklace?'
'OK!'

He sat at the spinning wheel and started to spin. As he spun he sang:

> *I'm not very big and I'm not very bold*
> *But I am the only one*
> *Who can spin this straw to gold!*

When the king unlocked the door and came into the room he was amazed and astonished. He was delighted with the reels of gold, but he wanted more. So he took the miller's daughter into a larger room that was also full of straw, and again told her to spin all the straw into gold or he would have her killed.

Again, after the king locked the door, the miller's daughter started to weep until the funny little man appeared.
'What will you give me this time?' he asked.
'My ring?' she said.
'OK!'

He spun all night singing his song:

> *I'm not very big and I'm not very bold*
> *But I am the only one*
> *Who can spin this straw to gold!*

In the morning the king came in again, and was delighted by the gold. He took the miller's daughter to an even bigger room. 'You have till morning!' he said.

As soon as she was left alone and started to cry the little man appeared.

'What will you give me now?'
'I have nothing left to give you,' she sobbed.
'Then promise me,' he said, 'if you ever become queen, to give me your first child.'

She thought to herself, 'That will never happen. The king will never marry a poor miller's daughter!' So she promised and the little man spun and sang through the night:

I'm not very big and I'm not very bold
But I am the only one
Who can spin this straw to gold!

The king came into the room in the morning and, delighted with the gold, he married the miller's daughter the very next day.

Soon her belly was swelling and within a year she was a mother. She was so happy, she had forgotten all about her promise to the funny-looking little man. Then one day he appeared in her room.

'Time to keep your promise!' he said.
'Oh I cannot,' she said. 'I love my baby! I am the queen. What can I give you instead?'
'I don't need anything,' said the little man, 'but I'll give you a chance. I'll give you three days to find out my name. Get it right and you can keep the baby. Fail and he is mine.'

The little man did a little jig on the spot and then disappeared.

The queen immediately summoned her servant and sent him off to find out the name of the man. At the end of the first day the servant had no news and when the little man came she tried guessing:
Adam, Alistair, Alfred? NO!
Bill, Bob, Barney? NO!
Chris, Colin, Conroy? NO!

She only got as far as 'I' when he said, 'That's enough! But you can try again tomorrow.'

The next day the servant had no news and when the little man came the queen started again from J:
Jack, John, James? NO!
Keith, Kenneth, Kurt? NO!

She only got to 'T' when he said, 'That's enough. One more day to go!'

He did a little jig on the spot and disappeared.

The next evening the servant came back. 'Your majesty, I was in a wood today and found a tiny cottage with a little fire outside. A little old man with a big grin and fiery eyes was dancing around it singing this song:

> *I'm not very nice and I'm not much fun*
> *But soon I'll have the queen's first son.*
> *It's really very sad and it's really such a shame*
> *And Rumpelstiltskin is my name.*

That night the queen was ready for him.
'Last chance!' he said.
Is it Uriah? NO!
Is it Victor? NO!
Is it William? NO!

The little man was dancing in a circle he was so excited.
Xavier? NO!
Yuri? NO!
Zac? NO!

Now he was jumping up and down. 'Give me the baby! Give me the baby!'

'One more guess?' said the queen.

She did a little dance and sang this song:

> *You're not very nice and you're not much fun*
> *But you won't have the queen's first son.*
> *It's not very sad and it's really not a shame*
> *'Cos Rumpelstiltskin is your name!*

The little man went bright red in the face and stamped his foot deep into the ground. He tried to pull it out so hard that he split himself in two.

So that was the end of him.

Cinderella

This is so well known it can easily become a caricature when told. For it to work properly you need to somehow capture the selfishness of the sisters and the goodness of Cinderella. As a Grimm-type version it will be interestingly different from the one the students are most familiar with.

Once there was a city where a man lived with his beloved wife and daughter. When the wife fell seriously ill she called her daughter to her bed and said, 'Daughter, I will die soon. I want you to live your life with patience and kindness. In this way you will find happiness.'

Soon after that the mother died and every day her daughter went to her grave watering its flowers with her own tears.

Winter came and snow covered the grave and by the time it had melted the father had married again. His new wife brought with her two daughters. The two families moved together into the father's house.

The daughters had beautiful faces but their hearts were cold and cruel. They took away the daughter's fine clothes and forced her to stay in the kitchen dressed in rags and doing the work of cleaning and cooking all day. At night she slept on the kitchen floor by the fire in the cinders. For this reason they called her Cinderella.

The father was so full of grief for his lost wife and full of hope for his new one that he hardly noticed what had happened to Cinderella.

One day the father was going to town and asked the daughters what they wanted him to buy.
'A new dress,' said one stepdaughter.
'Fine jewels,' said the second.
Cinderella said, 'Father, just bring me the first twig that knocks against your hat on the way home.'

The father went to town and bought a dress and jewels, then on the way home a hazel twig knocked against his hat and he brought it back to Cinderella.

She took the twig and planted it on her mother's grave. She visited the twig three times a day and watered the twig with her tears. It grew into a fine beautiful bush. One day a beautiful bird appeared in the tree. Cinderella was so happy to see the bird; she told it all her troubles and felt that in the bird she had a friend at last.

One day the king announced that it was time for his son to marry and that for three evenings there would be a royal dance to which all the young women of the land were invited. The prince would choose his bride from one of them.

The two stepsisters were excited about the royal dance and ordered Cinderella to help them get ready. She combed their hair, laced their dresses, shined their shoes and brought their shawls. When they were ready she went to her stepmother and said, 'Let me go to the dance too?'

'Certainly,' said her stepmother. 'Just do this job for me.'

She took a pot of lentils and emptied them into the ashes of the fire. 'Pick out all the lentils in two hours, and you can go,' she said.

Cinderella stepped outside into the garden and called up to the sky:

> *Birds of the sky, give me a chance,*
> *Help me now so I can dance.*

She called and called and one by one a huge flock of birds came into the kitchen and picked out the lentils from the ashes and popped them in a dish.

She took the dish to her stepmother.
'So can I go to the dance now?'

'Yes of course. I just have one more job for you.' She took two pots of lentils and emptied them again into the ashes. 'Sort them in an hour and you can go,' she said.

Again Cinderella went outside and called up to the sky:

> *Birds of the sky, give me a chance,*
> *Help me now so I can dance.*

Within half an hour the lentils were sorted and Cinderella took them to her stepmother. 'Can I go now?'

'No!' she said. 'You have nothing but rags to wear!' and turned her back on her.

Cinderella went off to her mother's grave and began to weep by the hazel tree. When the bird appeared she said:

> *Hazel tree, hazel tree,*
> *Help to set my spirit free.*
> *Hazel tree, hazel tree,*
> *Help me join the dance.*

A dress of gold and silver appeared with slippers of silk and gold. She slipped them on and went off to the palace.

When Cinderella entered the room the prince was immediately enchanted and for the rest of the evening he danced only with her. The sisters and stepmother didn't recognise her at all. Everyone said she was the most beautiful.

Finally Cinderella told the prince she had to go home. The prince said he would walk her back, curious to see where she lived. Just as she got home Cinderella felt frightened. 'What will happen when he goes to my house and sees me in rags? What then?' So she ran into her garden and hid in her father's pigeon house, locked the door, and then jumped out of the back window. She went to her mother's grave, left the dress there and went home in rags.

Meanwhile the prince was waiting patiently outside the pigeon house door. After a while Cinderella's father came out and asked the prince what was happening.
'There is a girl in the pigeon house,' said the prince. 'Who is she?'

The father brought an axe and chopped open the pigeon house but there was no one inside.

When the father returned home Cinderella was there as usual by the fire in her rags, covered in ashes.

The next day Cinderella helped the stepsisters get ready for the dance, listening to them complaining the whole time about the girl who danced with the prince. 'She wasn't as pretty as us!' said one with an ugly scowl.

Once they had gone Cinderella went to the hazel tree and sang:

> *Hazel tree, hazel tree,*
> *Help to set my spirit free.*
> *Hazel tree, hazel tree,*
> *Help me join the dance.*

A more beautiful outfit appeared; Cinderella slipped into the dress, slipped on the slippers and soon was dancing with the prince in the palace. He danced with her all night, with everyone watching, but the stepsisters were blinded by jealously and did not recognise Cinderella.

Again the prince walked Cinderella home, but just as they reached the house she panicked again and jumped up into the branches of a tall pear tree. While the prince waited for her to come down she slipped away, left the clothes on her mother's grave and returned to the kitchen in rags.

Later her father came out and asked the prince what had happened.
'Who is the maiden in the tree?' he asked.

The father brought an axe and chopped down the tree but she was gone by then.

When he got home Cinderella was by the fire in rags, covered in ashes.

The next day the sisters went off to the dance and Cinderella returned to the grave:

> *Hazel tree, hazel tree,*
> *Help to set my spirit free.*
> *Hazel tree, hazel tree,*
> *Help me join the dance.*

The clothes were even lovelier and soon she was dancing with the prince again.

This time the prince had a plan. He had covered the palace staircase with sticky tar. Around midnight Cinderella slipped away to go home, but as she ran down the staircase one of her silk slippers stuck on the tar. She was in such a rush that she left it behind!

The next day the prince went to Cinderella's house with the slipper and asked to see the father. 'I will marry the girl whose foot fits this slipper,' he said.

The eldest daughter took the shoe. 'Just a minute,' she said and went into the next room with her mother.

Her foot was too big, but her mother said, 'Cut off your toe!' When you are queen you will not need it at all!' The sister cut off her toe and slipped in her foot, then went back to the prince, who agreed that the slipper fitted and so they should be married.

She jumped on the back of his horse and together they rode back towards the palace, but as they passed the mother's grave the white bird flew around the prince's head, singing to him:

> *Turn and look, turn and look,*
> *See the blood, see what's true.*
> *Turn and look, turn and look,*
> *Your true bride waits for you.*

He turned and saw blood dripping down onto the ground. 'You're a false bride,' he said and returned to the home.

Next, the second sister tried the shoe and slipped away to the back room. This time her heel was too big and her mother said, 'Cut it off! Cut it off! You won't need it when you are queen.' The sister took the knife and chopped off the back of her heel so that the shoe fitted and went back to the prince, who agreed that the slipper fitted so they should be married.

Riding back together the bird flew from the mother's grave and sang:

> *Turn and look, turn and look,*
> *See the blood, see what's true.*
> *Turn and look, turn and look,*
> *Your true bride waits for you.*

He turned and saw blood dripping into the earth. 'You're a false bride,' he said, and returned her home.

The prince asked the father if he had any other daughters.

'Ah, yes!' he said. 'The youngest. She helps in the kitchen.'

'Bring her to me!' commanded the prince.

'Oh no!' said the stepmother. 'She's much too dirty!'

'Bring her now!' he commanded and Cinderella was brought to the prince in her rags.

The shoe fitted perfectly and at that moment the prince recognised her.

'This is my true bride,' he said.

As they rode home the bird sang down to the prince:

> *Turn and look, turn and look,*
> *See there no blood, see what's true.*
> *Turn and look, turn and look,*
> *Your true bride is with you.*

And they were married. And they danced and danced. He became king. She became queen. This story became their joy.

And as for the sisters? At the wedding all they could do was scowl and mutter. Afterwards, on the way home, two birds flew down and pecked out their eyes, so they never had to look at Cinderella and the prince again.

The Magic Paintbrush

This is a much-loved wondertale from China about helping others and protecting yourself. There are many variations of the story, among them a wonderful printed version by Julia Donaldson with illustrations by Joel Stuart. I suggest reading that book later, once the children are familiar with this version.

Once upon a time, there was a young man called Ma Liang. He was poor and kind and helped a rich man to tend cattle. He liked drawing and drew pictures everywhere. One night, he dreamed that an old man gave him a magic paintbrush and asked him to use it to help poor people. When he woke up, he found the magic paintbrush in his desk.

From that day on, he used the paintbrush whenever people needed help. When he saw that people had no water to use in the fields, he drew a river and the river came to life. People could bring water from the river to the field and save a lot of time and energy.

When he saw it was difficult for people to till lands, he drew a cow and the cow came to life. People could use the cow to till lands very easily.

When he saw people were hungry, he painted them food to eat.

When they needed a home, he painted a house.

Whenever he saw the people's troubles, he would use his magic paintbrush to help.

Soon, many people knew about the magic paintbrush.

One day the rich man heard that the magic paintbrush could bring anything to life. He decided to steal the paintbrush and use it to get rich.

He sent the police to Ma Liang's home and took him to the prison. Then the rich man got the magic paintbrush and felt very happy.

He invited a lot of his friends to come to his home and showed them the magic paintbrush. He drew a lot of pictures, but nothing happened. He was angry and summoned Ma Liang.

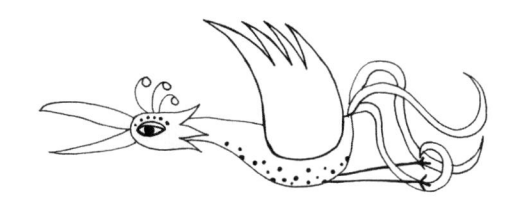

When Ma Liang came, he said to him, 'If you draw some pictures for me and turn them to life, I will set you free.'

The young man knew that he was a bad man in the village. Of course he did not want to help him. He had an idea. He said to the bad man, 'I can help you, but you should obey your words.'

The bad man felt very happy and said, 'I want a golden mountain. I will go there to gather gold.' The young man drew a sea first.

The bad man was angry and said, 'Why did you draw a sea? I do not want this. I want a golden mountain. Draw it quickly!'

Then the young man drew a golden mountain, which was far away from the sea. The bad man saw that and felt very happy. He said, 'Draw a big ship quickly! I want to go there to gather gold!'

The young man smiled quietly and drew a big ship.

The bad man jumped into the ship first and a lot of his family and friends jumped in too.

When the ship sailed to the middle of the sea, the young man drew a large wave and it destroyed the ship. So the bad man and his friends died.

After that, the young man lived with his family happily and kept on helping the poor people. In this way the magic paintbrush was known by everyone.

Snow White

This text is based again on the Grimm version of the story. It has a beautiful poetic rhythm, which is wonderful for storytelling. Again the differences from the more well-known versions will be interesting for the class. Enjoy this amazing classic tale.

Once, in deep midwinter, a sad queen sat on her balcony sewing, looking out at the white snow-filled landscape. 'Oh I wish I had a child!' she whispered to herself.
Just then she pricked her finger and three drops of red blood fell down onto the snow beneath her feet. As she looked at the blood on the snow she said to herself, 'Oh, how I wish that I had a daughter with skin as white as snow, lips as red as blood, and hair as black as a beetle's back.'

Soon after that, the queen's belly began to swell, and by the next year's snow a baby girl was born. 'Look!' said her mother. 'She is as I wished: skin as white as snow, lips as red as blood, and hair as black as a beetle's back. We will call her Snow White.'

Soon after this the queen died.

Before the winter's snow had melted the king had taken a new wife. The new queen was vain and cruel. Every morning she'd stare into her mirror and ask, 'Mirror, mirror on the wall, who's the fairest of them all?' Each time the mirror would give the same answer, 'Queen, Queen this is true, the fairest one of all is you.'

Time passed and Snow White grew more and more lovely, while the queen grew older and began to wrinkle. One day she asked, 'Mirror, mirror on the wall, who's the fairest of them all?' The mirror answered, 'You, my queen, are fair; it is true. But Snow White is now fairer than you.'

The queen summoned the huntsman. 'Take that Snow White into the woods and kill her, then bring me her heart so I know she is dead.'

The huntsman took Snow White deep into the forest, then stopped and said, 'The queen asked me to kill you, but I cannot. You are not safe in the palace so you must go and find a new home, away from her. Leave now!' He shot a boar, cut out its heart and took it back to the queen who cooked it and ate it happily with garlic and butter. She thought Snow White was dead.

Meanwhile, Snow White thanked the huntsman and ran off into the wood, wondering if she could survive in the wilds. All day she ran and she ran, full of fear, until she arrived at a little cottage. She tiptoed inside. In the cottage was a tiny table with little plates piled high with food. There were seven little chairs and seven little beds. Because she was so hungry, Snow White ate a few vegetables and a little bread from each little plate and from each cup she drank a bit of milk. Afterwards, because she was so tired, she lay down on one of the little beds and fell fast asleep.

Later, seven little men arrived home from work. They saw Snow White asleep and stared at her in silence. 'She is so beautiful!' said one. 'So lovely!' said another.

The next morning Snow White woke up, and saw the dwarves looking at her. They smiled and she felt safe. She explained how she ended up in the cottage and they asked her to stay with them.

Snow White lived happily with the dwarves. Every morning they went off to the mountains looking for gold. Every morning they said, 'Don't forget, don't let anyone in when we are away. It might be the queen!' In the evening when they came back home Snow White had their meal ready and their house tidy.

Now the queen, believing that she had eaten Snow White's heart, could only think that she was again the most beautiful woman of all, but one day she stepped before her mirror and said, 'Mirror, mirror, on the wall, who in this land is fairest of all?'
It answered, 'You, my queen, are fair; it is true. But Snow White is still fairer than you.'

The queen dressed up as a pedlar and visited the cottage. 'Dresses for sale!' she called. 'Dresses for sale!' Snow White let her in. The queen said, 'Try this corset! I'll lace it up.' But she laced it up so tight that Snow White couldn't breathe and she fell down unconscious. The queen went home thinking Snow White was dead, but she was wrong. When the dwarves came back they unlaced her dress and she could breathe again.

The next day the queen asked the mirror the same question and again it said that Snow White was the fairest.

This time she came as a pedlar and called up to Snow White, 'Combs and brushes! Something to make you beautiful!' Snow White let her in and the queen stuck a poison comb in her hair. Snow White collapsed and the queen went home thinking Snow White was dead. But that night when the dwarves came home they took out the comb and Snow White came back to life.

Again the queen asked the mirror and again she got the same answer, so she set off in disguise with a basket of fruit. Snow White let her in and the queen gave her an apple. When Snow White bit into it she collapsed on the floor and the queen went home.

Back at home she asked her mirror, 'Mirror, mirror, on the wall, who in this land is fairest of all? It finally answered, 'You, my queen, are fairest of all.' She laughed and laughed.

When the dwarves came home that evening they found Snow White lying on the ground. She was not breathing at all. She was dead. They lifted her up and looked at her longingly. They talked to her, shook her and wept over her. But nothing helped. The dear child was dead, and she remained dead.

They laid her on a bed of straw, and all seven sat next to her and mourned for her and cried for three days. They were going to bury her, but she still looked as fresh as a living person, and still had her beautiful red cheeks.

They said, 'We cannot bury her in the black earth,' and they had a transparent glass coffin made, so she could be seen from all sides. They laid her inside, and with golden letters wrote on it her name, and that she was a princess. Then they put the coffin outside on a mountain, and one of them always stayed with it and watched over her.

One day a prince entered the woods and happened upon the dwarves' house, where he sought shelter for the night. He saw the coffin on the mountain with beautiful Snow White in it, and he read what was written on it with golden letters.

Then he said to the dwarves, 'Let me have the coffin. I will give you anything you want for it.' But the dwarves answered, 'We will not sell it for all the gold in the world.' Then he said, 'Then give it to me, for I cannot live without being able to see Snow White. I will honour her and respect her as my most cherished one.'

As he thus spoke, the good dwarves felt pity for him and gave him the coffin. The prince had his servants carry it away on their shoulders. But then one of them stumbled, and this dislodged from Snow White's throat the piece of poisoned apple that she had bitten off. Not long afterward she opened her eyes, lifted the lid from her coffin, sat up, and was alive again. 'Good heavens! Where am I?' she cried out.

The prince said joyfully, 'You are with me!'

He told her what had happened, and then said, 'I love you more than anything else in the world. Come with me to my father's castle. You shall become my wife.'

Snow White loved him, and she went with him. Their wedding was planned with great splendour and majesty.

Snow White's wicked stepmother was invited to the feast, and when she had arrayed herself in her most beautiful garments, she stood before her mirror, and said, 'Mirror, mirror, on the wall, who in this land is fairest of all?' The mirror answered, 'You, my queen, are fair; it is true. But the young queen is a thousand times fairer than you!'

Not knowing that this new queen was indeed her stepdaughter, she arrived at the wedding. They heated up iron shoes in the fire till they were red hot then forced them onto the queen's feet. She danced and danced, screaming, until she died.

That's the end of that.

The Two Dragons

This story comes from the mediaeval Welsh Mabinogean collection, first written down in 14th century. This story is part of a chapter called Llud and Llevellis. It is a popular story in Oxford. I live quite near the place where they say the dragons were found!

You can use a map when telling the story to show where the king travelled. I use a singing bowl to model the sound of the land.

Once there was a king of Britain named Llud. He was a strong king with a good heart. He built a high wall around the city of London so his people would be safe inside.

One day he said to his wife, 'Could I have something to eat?'
She scowled and said, 'No, get it yourself!'

'Strange,' he thought, 'she never did that before.'

Then he said to his son, 'Can you help me for a minute?'
The son shouted, 'No, I'm busy and I don't want to! Go away!'

The king walked around the city and noticed that everywhere people were angry and arguing.

The king went to the wise man with a long beard, who said:
'It's not just you. Children no longer listen to their parents. Wives no longer listen to their husbands. Husbands don't listen to their wives! Everyone is angry and cross.'

'Why?' asked the king.

'Listen to the heart of the land and you will find the answer!' said the wise man.

He sang this song to the king:

> *Listen to the heart,*
> *Listen to the heart,*
> *Listen to the heart of the land.*
> *Something's wrong*
> *Something's gone*
> *We need to understand.*

The king put his ear to the ground and heard a faint sound of screaming.
'The land is unhappy,' he thought, 'but where can I find its heart?'

King Llud decided to go on a journey to find the heart of the land.

He walked away from London until he reached the sea.
Then he walked all the way around the land, always singing his song:

> *Listen to the heart,*
> *Listen to the heart,*
> *Listen to the heart of the land.*
> *Something's wrong*
> *Something's gone*
> *We need to understand.*

Every day he drew a map of the land he had seen. He drew all the hills and valleys, rivers and lakes, cliffs and beaches.

Every day: walking and singing and mapping.

After seven years he had a picture of the whole land, the first map of Britain.
'But I still haven't found the heart of the land,' he thought.

He walked back and forth across the middle of the country again and again, through forests and over mountains, always singing. In the evening he listened to the land as he drew his map, looking for the place where the screams were loudest. That would be the heart!

Finally after many years he came to the place where the screams were loudest. There, he dug down deep into the ground and found a cave. In the cave were two dragons screaming at one another, one red and the other white. They flew up into the air screaming and scratching and kicking and biting.

The king put out a great barrel of beer and when the dragons drunk it they fell asleep. He put them in a stone box and sent them away to a small island in Scotland.

Then he listened. The screaming had stopped.

When he went home his wife and son were happy and welcomed him. In the streets the people were friendly and listened to one another. The screaming land was quiet.

They built a church in the place where they found the dragons and soon a city grew up around it. This became the city of Oxford.

Some say, if you put your ear to the ground you can still hear the land screaming, very faintly. Can you hear? What do you think the land is saying?

Chapter 3

Year 3 Stories

The Marriage of Ganesh – India	142
Cap of Rushes – England	145
Lazy Jack – England	147
Baba Yaga's Black Geese – Russia	150
Three Brothers and the Polar Bear – India/Arctic	152
Three Dolls – India	154
The Lighthouse Keeper and the Selkie – Scotland	157
Death in a Nutshell – Scotland	159
The Fox and the Healer – Native American	162
Jack and the Dancing Trees – England	164
Little Burnt Face – Native American	167
The Monk and the Thieves – Chile	169
The Story Bag – Korea	171
How a Boy Learned to be Wise – Uganda	174
Persephone – Greece	178
The Wooden Horse – Greece	180

SHORTER STORIES:

Half a Blanket – Scotland	182
Fruit of Love – Native American	184
One Wish – Ireland	186
Birth of Athena – Greece	187
The Lode Stone – England	189
The Scorpion and the Frog – India	191
Three Wishes – Sweden	192

The Marriage of Ganesh

This story from India is great for all sorts of teaching. First, it's a conflict between two brothers and is great for practising dialogue and character development. Secondly, one brother travels all the way round the world so you can use it to teach about any country you like. Third, it's all about the imagination and how much we can learn from stories. Get the two characters clear and the story will work well. Practise telling the punch line for maximum impact. Traditionally, the story is used to show that there are always many valid points of view for any issue.

Elephant-headed Ganesh, the God of Success, was sitting in his library. In two of his hands he was holding a book and was thoughtfully turning the pages. In his other two hands he was carefully cutting and eating a mango.

Suddenly his brother Kartikeya burst into the room. 'Brother, brother!' he said, excitedly, 'I've got something to tell you.'

'Oh yes?' said Ganesh thoughtfully.' And what would that be?'

'I think it's time I got married. I'm old enough now and I've decided who to marry. You know those two princesses from the temple, Siddhi and Buddhi? I want to marry them. What do you think of that, brother?'

Ganesh stroked his long trunk and smirked. 'I'm older than you,' he said. 'Maybe I should marry them.'

Kartikeya stamped his foot and shook his head. 'But it's my idea!'

'And now it's my idea too,' said Ganesh.

'Maybe we should fight for it? The winner gets the girls,' said Kartikeya.

'I'm not that stupid!' purred Ganesh. 'You're the God of War! That's like me saying, 'Let's decide it with a quiz.' You'd have no chance!'

'Well, how about a race around the world?' asked Kartikeya enthusiastically. 'I love races.'

Ganesh thought about it, then said carefully, 'Do you mean that I can travel around the world in my own way, in any way I wish, and if I get around the world before you then I win the girls?'

'Yes, that's what I said!' snapped his brother.

'Agreed,' said Ganesh.

'Great! One, two, three – GO!'

Kartikeya ran out of the library, out of the palace and up the Himalayan mountains. At the top he stopped and looked around. There was snow at his feet and eagles circling below him. He saw the tracks of a snow leopard on the edge of the forest but there was no sign of his brother!

He slid down the mountains and was soon in the forests of China, running past panthers, tigers, even the odd panda or two.

He ran and he ran until he reached the rice fields and on through field after field until he reached the sea.

Then he swam from island to island, past dolphin, whale and shark.

He reached America and ran deep through the Amazon forest and up to the buffalo plains, running north with the buffalo, occasionally stopping to hear their stories, until again he was swimming in the sea.

Onwards, through blocks of ice, he swam to the frozen plains, passed polar bear and seal, over the top of the world and down the Russian Steppes beyond, until finally he was back where he started.

He looked for Ganesh and found him in the library. He was reading a book and eating a mango.
'Welcome back,' said Ganesh. 'Where have you been? I've been waiting for you, so you can be at my wedding.'
Kartikeya was astounded. 'What? How do I know you really did travel around the world? You don't look as if you've moved from that chair!'
'I could ask you the same thing,' said Ganesh. 'How do I know you went round the world?'
'Hmm. So tell me, brother. If you went round the world, tell me what it was like,' asked Kartikeya. 'Where did you go first?'
'It was very cold. There was snow on the ground. I saw eagles and snow leopards, and load of big woolly yaks.'
'Hmm. And what then?'
'Through the Chinese rainforests, full of so many animals: tigers, pandas, snakes – you name it!'
Kartikeya's face fell. 'And then?'
'Rice fields – all the way to the sea.'

Ganesh described his journey to his brother in great detail, noting all the things that Kartikeya remembered and more. In the end Kartikeya was persuaded. 'OK, brother,' Kartikeya said. 'You've won. Marry them then!'

And so Ganesh married the two princesses. After the wedding, Kartikeya came over to his brother. 'Brother, did you really travel the world? I'm still not really sure about that.'
'Well, yes and no,' said Ganesh. 'You travelled round the world your way and I travelled round the world my way.'
'How do you mean?' asked Kartikeya.
'While you were running and swimming, I was reading. I read book after book about every country on the journey. As I read I saw them all in my imagination. In that way, I travelled around the world.'
'Hmm....' said Kartikeya. 'Isn't that cheating?'

What do you think?

Cap of Rushes

This is a popular Traditional English story. To tell it you need a good strong character for the father (foolish) and the daughter (patient). The image of losing her royal clothes and dressing in reeds is powerful. In the end I like the way the father repents and she forgives him. Put strong feeling into that final scene.

Once, a rich man had three daughters. The first was tall and greedy, the second short and jealous, and the third young and thoughtful. One evening the king sat them all down and said, 'Tell me daughters. How much do you love me?'

'As much as a king loves gold,' said the eldest and he rewarded her with a bag of gold.

The second thought about how to get more than the first. 'As much as a queen loves diamonds,' she said and got a bag of diamonds.

The youngest thought about it for a while and then said, 'Father, I love you as much as food loves salt.'

The father frowned. Salt wasn't worth much, he thought.

'She insults you!' whispered the greedy daughter.

'She doesn't love you!' murmured the jealous daughter.

'Do you love me that little?' he shouted. 'After all I've done for you?'

'I love you as much as food loves salt,' she said firmly.

'How dare you!' he shouted. 'Get out of my house!'

There and then he pushed her out of the house. 'Never come back!' he shouted as she walked away, sobbing into the forest, with only the dress she was wearing on her back.

She walked and walked until she came to a marsh. She picked some reeds and platted them into a hood and dress and hid her other dress inside a tree.

Soon she came to a grand house and knocked on the door. A butler answered. 'I am looking for a job,' she said.

'Go round the back!' he shouted, 'To the servants' entrance!'

At the back door the cook gave her a job scrubbing pans and cleaning the floor until her hands were red and raw. The cook asked her her name but she was silent.

'Why are you wearing a dress of rushes?'
Again, no answer.
'Then we'll call you Cap of Rushes.'

In a house nearby, a prince was having three days of dancing and feasting so he could choose a wife. All the rich young girls were invited.
'Shall we watch them arrive?' said the servants to Cap of Rushes.
'No thanks,' she said. 'I have to clean the floor.'

When they were gone, Cap of Rushes slipped back into the forest, put on her lovely dress and went to the party. All night she danced with the prince.

The next morning the servants were chattering to Cap of Rushes. 'You should have seen the girl,' they said. 'She was lovely and had a fabulous dress. He danced with her all evening but nobody knows who she is!'
'Really!' said Cap of Rushes and smiled.
The second night the servants asked her to come and watch.
'No,' she said. 'I have to scrub the pans.'
When they had gone she slipped off again and put on her dress. She danced with the prince all night.
In the morning the servants said, 'Oh she's so lucky! He'll marry her for sure, but who is she??'
Cap of Rushes smiled.
On the third night the prince asked her to marry him and she accepted.

At the wedding feast her father was invited. Cap of Rushes wore a thick veil so he would not recognise her. She ordered that no salt be put in the food. The guests sat and chewed on the food but it tasted terrible. Her father sat there crying. From behind her veil she asked him why.
'I was a fool,' he said. 'I threw my daughter out even though now I see she loved me most of all. All I wish is to see her and beg her forgiveness.'
Cap of Rushes threw back her veil.
'Then your wish will come true. Here I am father and I love you still, you silly old man!'

From that day on, every time they put salt on their food, they remembered their love for one another.

Lazy Jack

Here's another popular English classic. This one is comedy all the way so you can tell it like a stand-up comedian. Jack can be enthusiastic but a bit foolish, his mum getting fed up with him. Then she can be delighted when it all turns out right!

Once upon a time there was a boy whose name was Jack. He lived with his mother in a little cottage next to the village common. They were very poor. Jack's mother made a little money spinning wool and selling it, but Jack never helped at all. He did nothing but lie in the sun in the summer, and sit by the fire in the winter, warming his hands. So they called him Lazy Jack.

One day his mum got angry. She said, 'Jack, it's time you helped around the house. If you don't start working and helping then you'll have to leave. It's up to you. Off you go!'
'OK, Mum. I'll try!'

The next day he went over to the neighbour's farm and worked all day building a fence. Hammering and sawing all day. The farmer paid him a penny. On the way home Jack stopped at a lake. He didn't really understand about money. 'I wonder what this penny is for?' he thought. 'It would be good to skim on the water.'
So he skimmed the penny on the lake. It jumped three times and then disappeared under the water. 'Not bad!' he thought and went home.

'How did you get on today?' said his mum.
'I did well!' said Jack. 'I worked all day sawing and hammering, got paid a penny, then I skimmed the penny on the lake and it jumped three times! Busy day!' He grinned and waited for his mum to praise him, but she frowned, 'Jack, that's not the way to do it. You should have put it in your pocket and brought it home, not skimmed it on the lake!'
'OK, Mum,' he said. 'I'll try again tomorrow.'

The next day, Jack went out and got a job milking cows. All day he sat and pulled on the udders filling bowl after bowl with rich creamy milk. At the end of the day he was paid a jar of milk. Jack was walking home with the milk when he remembered what his mum had said. He took the milk and poured it all into his pocket. It went everywhere! None was left by the time he got home.

Chapter 3 Year 3 Stories   147 Traditional Stories

'How did you get on today?' asked his mum.

'I did well!' said Jack. 'I worked all day milking the cows, got a jar of milk, and then I did what you told me. I poured it into my pocket and walked home, and here I am. Busy day!' He grinned and waited for his mum to praise him, but she frowned, 'Jack, that's not the way to do it. You should have carried it on your head, not put it in your pocket.'

'OK, Mum,' he said. 'I'll try again tomorrow.'

The next day, Jack worked in a dairy helping make cream cheese. They paid him with a bowl of soft cheese. Jack was walking home with the cheese when he remembered what his mum had said. He took the cheese and put in on his head. It went into his hair and ran down his head and shoulders. None was left by the time he got home.

'How did you get on today?' asked his mum.

'I did well!' said Jack. 'I worked all day making cheese, got paid a bowl of cheese and then I did what you told me. I put the cheese on my head and walked home, and here I am. Busy day!' He grinned and waited for his mum to praise him, but she frowned, 'Jack, that's not the way to do it! You should have put it in a bag and carried it home, not put it on your head.'

'OK, Mum,' he said. 'I'll try again tomorrow.'

The next day, Jack worked in a bakery making bread, mixing the dough, putting it in tins and baking it in the oven. They paid him with a big strong cat. Jack was walking home with the cat in his arms when he remembered what his mum had said. He'd brought a paper bag specially, and so he tried to stuff the cat into the bag. It scratched and bit and ran off.

'How did you get on today?' asked his mum, back home.

'I did well!' said Jack. 'I worked all day making bread, got paid a big tom cat, and then I did what you told me. I put the cat in the bag but it didn't like it and ran away. Then I walked home, and here I am. Busy day!' He grinned and waited for his mum to praise him, but she frowned, 'Jack, that's not the way to do it! You should have tied a string around its neck and pulled it home on a lead, not put it in a bag.'

'OK, Mum,' he said. 'I'll try again tomorrow.'

The next day Jack worked for a butcher, chopping and cleaning and weighing the meat. They paid him a large piece of meat – a leg of lamb. Jack was walking home with the lamb when he remembered what his mum had said. He took the leg of lamb and tied it to a piece of string, then pulled it along the ground. Soon dogs followed him and ate all the meat. None was left by the time he got home.

'How did you get on today?' asked his mum.

'I did well!' said Jack. 'I worked all day at the butcher's and got paid a leg of lamb. Then I did what you told me. I tied the meat with a piece of string and walked home. The dogs ate the meat, and now I'm home. Busy day!' He grinned and waited for his mum to praise him, but she frowned, 'Jack, that's not the way to do it! You should have carried it on your shoulders, not dragged it along the ground!'

'OK, Mum,' he said. 'I'll try again tomorrow.'

The next day Jack worked for a cattle farmer, looking after the cows, feeding them with straw and grain and cleaning their pens up. They paid him with a donkey.

Jack was walking home with the donkey when he remembered what his mum had said. He took the donkey and lifted it up onto his shoulders and tried to carry it home. He kept falling over and picking it up and doing his best to carry the donkey.

He was walking past the house of a rich man, and a rich man's daughter looked out of the window. She had never spoken since her mother died years before. The rich man had tried many cures but nothing had worked. Finally, he had promised that anyone who could make her speak would get twelve bags of gold. The rich man's daughter looked out the window, saw Jack trying to carry the donkey, and smiled. The smile became a grin. The grin became a snigger. The snigger became a laugh. 'Look, Dad!' she shouted. 'Look at that silly boy!'

The father was so happy. He walked out into the street and gave Jack a big hug!

'Well done!' he said. 'That was a brilliant idea what you did with the donkey!'

Jack grinned. 'Thanks! It was my mum's idea really. She's very clever!'

Jack took his twelve bags of gold and walked home with them.

'How did you get on today?' asked his mum.

'Good,' said Jack. 'I worked all day for the cattle farmer. Got paid a donkey. Carried it on my shoulders like you told me, and got paid twelve bags of gold by the rich man for carrying it, and now I'm home. Busy day!'

'Well done, Jack!' said his mum and took the gold inside. And they were never hungry again.

And that's why it's always good to do what your mother tells you…

Baba Yaga's Black Geese

Here's another Russian tale, this time with a heroic heroine. It's a witch story, so make her as horrible and nasty as possible. When the action starts, make sure the audience feels the danger. When the magic starts try and convey the wonder. I learned this one from storyteller Adam Guillain.

Once upon a time, on the edge of a forest in a little cottage there lived a family: a mother, a father, a daughter and a little baby boy. The daughter's name was Olga and the baby was called Sergei. Every morning when the parents went off to work in the fields, the mother would say to Olga, 'Don't forget to stay in the garden. Never go out into the forest, or the witch, Baba Yaga, will get you and eat you and your little brother up.'

One day Olga was feeling a bit bored looking after the baby all by herself so she picked him up and walked out of the garden, through the gate and off into a field by the forest. She laid her brother down in the grass and started picking flowers for her mum. Just then three huge black geese flew over the field, picked up Sergei in their beaks and carried him off into the forest. Olga chased after them.

She ran and she ran and she ran until she came to a fish lying on the path by a stream. 'Olga, Olga, Olga!' called the silver fish. 'Help me!' Olga threw the fish into the stream. It popped its head out of the water and swam towards Olga with a shell in its mouth. 'You have helped me and now I will help you,' it said. 'Take this shell and if you need help throw it over your shoulder. I will come and help.' Olga took the shell and continued along the path.

She ran and she ran and she ran until she came to a squirrel caught in a trap. 'Olga, Olga, Olga!' called the squirrel. 'Help me!' Olga pulled the squirrel free from the trap. It scurried off up a tree and came back with an acorn in its claws. 'You have helped me and now I will help you,' it said. 'Take this acorn and if you need help throw it over your shoulder. I will come and help.' Olga took the acorn and continued along the path.

She ran and she ran and she ran until she came to a mouse that couldn't get into his hole because it was blocked by a pile of earth. 'Olga, Olga, Olga!' called the mouse. 'Help me!'

Olga moved the pile of earth and the mouse scurried off into its nest. Moments later he came back with a tiny stone. 'You have helped me and now I will help you,' it said. 'Take this stone and if you need help throw it over your shoulder. I will come and help.' Olga took the stone and continued along the path.

She ran and she ran and she ran until she came to Baba Yaga's house. Peering in through the window she saw the old witch asleep in her rocking chair. Her face was green and grey, her nose was long and twisted and her lips were thin and mean. Sergei was playing happily on the floor with a pile of bones. Olga tiptoed in through the door, picked up Sergei, and, as quick as a flash, was out of the door running for her life. Baba Yaga woke and saw the baby was gone. 'Who's taken my dinner?' she screamed and went chasing after Olga.

Olga ran and she ran and she ran, but the witch was close behind ... just about to grab her when she remembered the shell. Olga threw the shell over her shoulder and a great lake appeared between her and the witch. Baba Yaga stopped, bent down and drank up all of the lake. Then she chased after Olga again.

Olga ran and she ran and she ran, but the witch was close behind ... just about to grab her when she remembered the nut. Olga took it from her pocket and threw it over her shoulder. A forest sprang up behind her, so thick that the witch could not get through. Baba Yaga opened her mouth and ate up the forest, then chased after Olga again.

Olga ran and she ran and she ran, but the witch was close behind ... just about to grab her when she remembered the stone, took it out of her pocket and threw it over her shoulder. It turned into a huge mountain. Baba Yaga stopped and stared at the mountain. She couldn't eat it; she couldn't climb it; she couldn't go round it and so she went back to her house.

Olga ran home, shut the gate behind her and put little Sergei to sleep in his crib. He was fast asleep when their parents came home from the fields.
'How was your day?' asked the mum.
'Fine,' said Olga.

And that was the end of that...

Three Brothers and the Polar Bear

This is a riddle story originally from India but reset in the Arctic. The story sets up a discussion at the end: a good story to lead into argument and persuasive writing. It's important to convey the showing off quality of the brothers as they demonstrate their skills, and then something of the horror of being hunted by the polar bear.

Once upon a time in the land of ice, seals hunted fish, polar bears hunted seals and man hunted polar bears (although sometimes man was hunted too, by the polar bears).

In the land of ice lived three brothers. When they finished school each travelled to study in their chosen subject.

The first brother studied skeletons and how to piece them back together from a pile of bones. He became a bone expert.

The second studied a kind of magic where he could conjure up blood, flesh and fur to reveal a dead corpse around a skeleton. He became a corpse maker.

The third brother studied the dark art of bringing life back to the dead. He became a life bringer.

One day, soon after they finished their training, the three brothers were walking home across the ice when they saw a pile of bones.

'Look what I can do!' said the first brother. He started to snap the bones together and had soon re-made the complete skeleton of a polar bear.

'Pretty good,' said the second brother. 'Look what I can do!'

The second brother poured a magic potion onto the bones, whispered a spell, and conjured organs, meat, veins, flesh and fur, leaving the body of a dead polar bear lying on the ice.

'Pretty good,' said the third brother, 'but look what I can do!'
The third brother closed his eyes and chanted the life-giving chant, then bent down and breathed life into the polar bear. The polar bear's heart started beating, its lungs started moving, and then its eyes opened.

Then its mouth opened and it ROARED!
It was hungry and saw breakfast.

The brothers ran across the ice.

The bear caught one brother and tore him limb from limb. The second died from the first bite, and the third was eaten bit by bit, scream by scream, till there was only his sealskin boots left in a pool of blood.

What a sad end for the brothers ... after all that study!

But here's my question for you.
Who was most to blame for their deaths?

Three Dolls

Here is a wonderful story explaining how stories help us learn language. It's also a great way to teach the class riddles and have them teach you some too. Maybe before you tell the story you can ask them to collect riddles from home and see what they bring. Riddles make great mini-stories. In this story the character of the teacher and daughter is important. Slow down when she explains about the dolls, so suspense can build. I developed this story from a lovely version by David Novak.

Once upon a time, when riddles were still the judge of character, there was a teacher. He was a good teacher, a fine teacher. When he walked down the street children would get excited and say, 'That's our teacher. He knows lots and lots of things!'

Parents would speak to the teacher with respect and almost reverence.
'We're so lucky to have such a clever teacher!'
They'd even bow sometimes to him in the street.

Can you tell that this is an old, old story?

In class he would talk, talk, talk, and the children would listen, listen, listen.
Some students remembered what they heard and wrote it down in the exams – they were considered good students. Some students couldn't remember what he said. It went in one ear and out the other – they were considered bad students.

One day he said to his class, 'Tomorrow is riddle day. Bring riddles to ask me. See if you can beat me. If there's one I can't guess then you can choose what we do in class for the rest of the term.'

So the children went home and they collected their riddles and they brought them back to class the next day.

'Teacher, teacher, what is it that has two hands and a face but no feet?'
'Why a clock, of course.'
'What runs all day yet stays in one place?'
'A river.'
'What has a head, a foot and four legs?'
'A bed.'
The teacher was pretty good and guessed all the riddles until the storyteller's daughter stood up with three dolls in her hands.
She asked, 'What is the difference between these three dolls?'

The teacher couldn't tell the difference. They all looked the same.

He sent the children out to play, saying that he would have the answer upon their return. First he asked the smartest student in the school to see if she could see any difference between the three dolls. She measured them, smelt them, examined them very closely and said, 'They're all the same.'
Then the teacher asked the most foolish student in the school the same question and he said, 'Of course they are different, look, this one is an aeroplane!' and the foolish child took one of the dolls and started to zoom it around the classroom. '...and the other two are in love!' and he made the two dolls kiss!

The children came in from play and the teacher said to the storyteller's daughter, 'There is no difference that I can see. So if you can show me a difference, you win.'
'The difference is on the inside,' she told him. 'Come here and I'll show you.'

He bent down toward the doll and looked. Quickly she plucked a long white hair from his beard.
'OW!' he said. 'Why did you do that?'
'Wait and see.'
Taking the hair she pushed it into the first doll's ear till it came out through the other ear, out the other side.
'This is what you call a bad student,' she said, 'because what goes in one ear comes out the other.'

She plucked a second hair and poked it into the ear of the second doll. It stayed in and didn't come out the other side.
'This is what you call a good student,' she said, 'because what goes in the ear stays in the mind.'

She took a third hair for the third doll. This time it went in one ear and out the mouth.
'But teacher, this is the best doll. This is a storytelling doll. In this one it goes in through the ear and then out the mouth. And look! It comes out differently, with a curl!'

'And why is that the best doll?' asked the teacher.

'Because that's what we need for life, teacher. Listening's fine but we need to be able to take the things we've heard and talk about them, explain them, storytell them. Everyone needs that to do well in the world.'

'So,' said the teacher smiling, 'You've won. What is your wish?'
'I want us all to learn to be storytellers.'
So the teacher taught his students to tell stories.

And that's how the first storytelling school began.

The Lighthouse Keeper and the Selkie

A selkie is a woman who is sometimes a seal and sometimes a woman. Britain's seal-rich coast is full of stories about selkies and their contacts with humans. Here's one example from Scotland. Emphasise the loneliness of the keeper, the wonder of seeing the seal women, his happiness during marriage and then his sorrow at the end.

Once there was an island. A small rock in the sea.
On the island was a lighthouse. Nothing else, just a lighthouse.

The lighthouse keeper lived there alone. Every night he lit the lamp so that the ships would stay clear of the rocks. In winter the seas were rough and no boat could reach the lighthouse. In summer it was warm and quiet. He was quite happy in this peaceful life, but sometimes he felt lonely and wished that he had a wife to keep him company.

One night he was sitting on a rock fishing in the sea, when he saw seven seals come ashore on the beach. As he watched in the moonlight they slipped off their sealskins and stood up as lovely young women. They were changelings! They were selkies – seals in the sea and women on land. He watched as they laughed and danced and played together, singing and clapping.

As they played he sneaked over to one of the skins and took it back to the lighthouse, locked it in a wooden chest then returned to the beach.

As the sun rose the selkies slipped on their skins and slid back into the sea. One woman stayed behind, looking for her skin.

The lighthouse keeper walked towards her with a blanket.

'It's OK,' he said quietly. 'I won't hurt you. Let me help.'

She let him cover her with a blanket and lead her to the lighthouse. She stayed there with him, living as his wife. She didn't cook or clean. She just spent her days staring out at the sea with tears in her eyes. When she saw seals she would call out to them in a strange language and they would call back.

Sometimes she'd sing to the sea:

> *Take me home, rolling sea,*
> *To the place I belong*
> *Take me home, rolling sea,*
> *Take me home.*

The lighthouse keeper was so happy to have such a beautiful wife. He loved to sit by her in the evening telling her stories and singing her songs.

Time passed and she gave birth to three lovely children. He was so happy.

Then one day the eldest was playing in the lighthouse store when he found a key. He looked and looked till he found the chest it fitted and inside was a smooth sleek pelt.

He took it to his mother. Her eyes lit up.

'Come, children!' she said and walked with the three children down to the sea. 'Hold my hands!' she said as she slipped on the sealskin.

The keeper saw them on the beach and walked down to join them but when he arrived all he could see was a mother seal with three baby seals swimming out from the rock.

He never saw his family again.

Death in a Nutshell

Here's another great story about death and dying. This time the focus is on why things must die and what would happen if they didn't: lots of talking points and personal relevance. The son is the key character who cannot stand the idea of his mother dying. Get into that role and the story will flow easily. You can tell it in a tender way, with as much crazy comedy as you like in the middle. Activist storyteller, Eric Maddern, has written a lovely picture book about this story.

Once there was a long straight beach of stone shingles. Behind the beach was a tiny cottage where a mother lived with her only son. The father, a fisherman, had been killed in a storm soon after the boy was born and his mother had raised him alone, living off the food from a small plot of land behind the cottage, and occasional work mending the fishermen's nets. Soon after the boy's eighteenth birthday his mother fell ill and took to her bed. He made her soup, but she wouldn't take any.

'I'm tired,' she said. 'I feel like my life will end soon.'
'Don't talk like that,' said the boy. 'You've many good years ahead of you. I'll take care of you.'
'No, son,' she said. 'I'm tired. I think my time is coming.'

The boy stepped out of the cottage for a breath of fresh air and walked down to the beach. Just then he saw Death walking along the beach toward the cottage with a grim grin on his face. He knew that Death had come for his mother.

'No!' he shouted, 'I won't let her die!'

He picked up a piece of driftwood, rushed at Death and started to pound him with the piece of wood. He pounded Death smaller and smaller until he was the size of a nut then, picking up two halves of a walnut shell from the beach he stuffed Death inside, tied the nut closed and threw it with all his might, out into the sea.

Pleased with himself, he went back to his mother's bedside.

'I'm feeling better,' she said. 'Can you make me some chicken soup?'

'Sure!' said the boy happily and went out to the chicken coop with his chopper. He picked out a fat chicken and took it squawking to the chopping block. Stretching out the neck he chopped through it with the axe, and was about to start collecting the blood when the chicken head flew up off the ground and stuck itself back on the chicken body. The boy looked on in disbelief as the chicken started squawking and clucking again.

'I must be dreaming,' he thought and chopped off the head a second time.

Immediately the head snapped back on again.

'Strange,' he thought. 'I'll try another chicken.'

But the same thing happened again. The chickens just would not die.

'I'll make some vegetable soup,' he thought and pulled up some onions and carrots but the moment he laid them on the kitchen table they flew through the air, out of the window and planted themselves back into the earth where they had been pulled.

The boy went down to the village to buy some food, but there was no meat in the butcher's and no vegetables at the grocer's. There was nothing to buy and nothing to eat! Everyone was talking about how nothing would die, so how could they live!

Perplexed, he went home and told his mother what had happened.

She gave him a piercing look. 'What have you done, son? Tell your old mum!'

So he explained about meeting Death and how he had tied him up in a nutshell and thrown him away, to save her life.

The old lady shook her head.

'That's no good,' she said. 'Things need to die so we can live. There'll be no food now, but also people need to die when they get old. Without death our bodies would fall apart but we'd still be alive, suffering in terrible pain. There's no life without death, my boy. Now off you go and set Death free!'

Easier said than done. The boy went back to the beach and looked out to sea but there was no sign of the nut. Then he felt the tide push something against his toes. He looked down and there was the nut.

'She's right,' he thought. 'There can be no life without death. When her time comes I must accept it.'

He opened the nut and Death jumped out, no worse for wear. He tipped his hat to the boy and walked up the path to his cottage. The boy sighed and followed Death inside to his mother's bed.

He held his mother's hand as she slept into a deep sleep and, with a relieved smile on her face, she died.

Her son spoke at the funeral. He said there could be no death without life and no life without death. His mother had led a good and kind life and he was proud to be her son. He loved her and missed her, but death comes to us all and this was her turn. After the funeral he sat outside the cottage and began to grieve.

The Fox and the Healer

Here's a mysterious shamanic-type tale from North America. I like it because it is not really clear what is going on and it gives the audience lots to think and talk about. At the same time it is set in snow and ice with all sorts of possibilities for imagination and descriptive work. Good for using all the senses. Hear Hugh Lupton's brilliant version on Tales of Wisdom and Wonder *from Barefoot Books.*

Once there was a village of tipi tents, camped on the edge of a plain. In one of the tents a young girl was sick, coughing and sweating with fever. Her parents sent for the old healer and she came right away, hobbling on her walking stick into the light of the tipi fire. The old lady knelt down and pressed her ear to the little girl's chest, and stayed there for a while.

'What are you doing?' said the mother.
'Shhhh!' said the woman. 'Patience!'
'What can you hear?' asked the father a little later.
'I hear the sound of a fox. She is running over snow, but she is sick. She is looking for a warm place but can find neither food nor shelter. I can hear the sound of her footsteps. They are too slow.'
The girl's father was a hunter. He said, 'Shall I go and find the fox and bring it back here?'
'Yes,' she said. 'That will help a lot!'

The girl's father pulled on his furs and set off into the night. After a while, by the moonlight, he found some fox tracks in the snow and started to follow, running through the deep thick drifts.

He ran and he ran and he ran as the old lady listened in the tent.
'Good!' she said. 'Now I can hear the footsteps of the hunter. He is running fast while the fox is slow. I can hear all that!'

The father ran and he ran till a day later he caught sight of the fox. The fox turned and stared at him.

Back in the tent the old lady smiled.
'Good! I can hear them both now, together. She has seen him. Soon he will help her.'

That night the hunter built a fire and took some rest while the fox watched from a distance. Back in the tipi the old lady said, 'Good! Now I can hear the flames of the fire. She will have a fever now to burn away the sickness.'
And the girl's face burned all through the night.

The next morning the fox was too tired to move and the hunter picked her up.
Back in the tent the old lady said, 'Now she is frightened. Now her heart is beating fast. Soon they will be home!'

The next morning they were home and the hunter laid the fox down next to his daughter. The old lady made a bed for the fox in the furs by the fire.
'Get me some meat!' she said and fed it to the fox, who ate hungrily. Then fox and daughter slept for a whole day.

When the fox woke up she jumped up and ran out of the tent.
'Shall I follow?' asked the father.
'No!' said the woman. 'No need now!'

The daughter stood up and walked towards the tent flap. She was well again. She stared out at the fox as it trotted away, fit and healthy,
The father looked at the old woman.
'Tell me,' he said, 'how did the fox cure the girl? How did the girl cure the fox?'

That's what he asked, but the old woman gave no answer.

What do you think?

Jack and the Dancing Trees

There's something about trees getting up and going for a dance that I find quite lovely. There are all sorts of artistic possibilities with dance and 3D art here. The story also notes the summer solstice, which is good to be reminded of. It's also a fine fable about greed and non-greed with a lovely love interest. Enjoy! You can find a version on the web in verbatim dialect told by Scottish storyteller, Stanley Robinson.

Once there was a shepherd boy called Jack. He worked for a rich farmer looking after his sheep as they grazed through the long summer months. Jack loved being outdoors, watching the birds fly and the salmon leap. He loved the oak woodland on the farmer's land, with its huge ancient trees. The farmer was rich and greedy and paid Jack almost nothing for his work, but Jack didn't mind. He was content.

One day Jack's mother brought him lunch of bread and cheese to the field where he was watching his sheep.

'Jack,' she said, 'last night I had a dream. I saw all the trees in this wood uproot themselves. They walked down to the river and started to dance. I saw sparkling jewels in the places where they had been rooted. Do you know what this means?'
'You had a nice dream?' said Jack.
'No, Jack! Don't you know the legend? They say that once every seventy years, on midsummer's night, all the trees of this forest go down to the river to dance and mate, and that in the holes they leave behind there is treasure. One they've finished the dancing they go back and reroot themselves but, on that night, if you're quick, you can find treasure there.'
'Really!' said Jack, wide-eyed.
'Yes!' said Jack's mum. 'So listen, Jack – tonight if you wait and watch, once the trees have gone off to their dancing, jump into one of the root holes and take one or two jewels. Not too many or you'll never get out. Just one or two. And take this rope. You'll need it to get out.'

She handed him a rope which he put in his pocket and she went off home.

Jack lay down on the grass and made up a song:

> *Once in a while, the trees go down,*
> *Down to the river to dance.*
> *Once in a while, the trees go down,*
> *And then I'll take my chance.*

As Jack was singing the farmer came over to Jack, checking up on his work.
'What are you doing, Jack?' asked the farmer. 'What's that about the trees dancing?'
'I'm thinking,' said Jack.
'I don't pay you to think!' snapped the farmer. 'What are you thinking about?'
'Tonight's the night, once in seventy years, when the trees go down to the river to dance. I'm thinking about that and if I can find some treasure tonight.'
'Really?' said the farmer. 'How interesting!'

Now Jack was very fond of Mary, who worked in the farmer's kitchen. A while later she came rushing over to Jack, flustered.
'Jack, Jack!' she said, 'I heard the farmer talking to his wife. He's coming tonight for the tree treasure, and he's taken a knife. I think he means you harm. He was saying the treasure belongs to him and not to you! Be careful!'
Jack gave her a hug and said he would be fine, she shouldn't worry.

As the sun set Jack was hiding behind a bush watching the trees. Once the sun was gone there was a creaking and a groaning and he watched the trees pull up their roots and walk off down to the river. Then he heard the sound of knocking and drumming as the trees began to play their music and dance their dance.

Once the trees were gone, Jack went over and stared into the hole left by a giant oak. It was full of jewels! He was just about to jump down when a voice shouted:
'Oi! Jack! You keep away for that hole! That treasure is for me!'
It was the farmer with a knife in one hand and a big sack in another.
Jack backed away and the farmer jumped into the hole, and started stuffing gold and jewels into the sack. Jack noticed that every time he picked up a jewel, the hole got a bit deeper. He watched the farmer going deeper and deeper into the ground as the sack filled with jewels till he was just a tiny speck in the distance.

Jack went to another tree hole and jumped in.

'Just a few jewels,' he said to himself.

He picked up three shining jewels, a diamond, an emerald and a ruby, and put them in his pocket. Jack looked up and saw that the hole was now three times as deep as he was tall. How could be get out?

Just then Mary appeared.

'Throw me the rope, Jack, and you can climb out.'

He threw up the rope and she tied it to a rock. As Jack climbed out he realised that the music had stopped and there was the sound of root steps coming up the hill.

'That was quick!' he thought. 'What about the farmer?'

They looked down the hole and he was almost out of sight, deep in the ground, still stuffing jewels into the sack.

'Come out!' shouted Jack. 'They're coming back!'

But the farmer only had eyes for the jewels. Moments later the oak stepped back into its hole.

The farmer was never seen again.

And as for Jack, he sold the jewels and bought a lovely little cottage next to the oak woods and lived there happily with Mary and his mum. Seventy years later, when Jack was 86, on midsummer's night, Jack's grandson went up to the woods with his granddad and waited...

But that's another story...

Little Burnt Face

Here's a First Nation story about honesty and integrity with a love interest, linked up with magic warrior powers. It's a sort of golden apple story but this time it works out well! You can play the start for comedy, the middle for tension, and the end for happiness. There are many versions on the web and in print. One good variant is in the Anthology of Children's Literature by Johnson and Scott.

Once there was a warrior called Strong Wind. He knew powerful magic and could make himself invisible at will. He could walk amongst his enemies and hear their plans. He could hunt and kill without being seen. Enemies were defeated without seeing him. In this way he became famous.

Many women wished to marry such a powerful man, and went to his tent to ask. Each one was given a test: they were taken down to the river by his sister and made to wait for a while, then she would ask:
'Here he comes along the road. Can you see him?'
'Oh yes!' they'd answer, although they could not.
'And how does he pull his sledge along?'
Now they had to guess.
One said with rope, another said with string, another said with leather straps.
No one ever guessed right. The sister knew they were liars, and sent them off home.

In a nearby village the chief had three daughters. As children the youngest was gentle of heart and beautiful of face. The other daughters were so jealous that they stole her clothes and jewellery and cut off her hair. When she still looked beautiful they took burning coals and pressed them into her face, and told her father she had done it herself. She was then known as Little Burnt Face.

One day the eldest daughter went to offer to marry Strong Wind. The sister took her down to the river.
'Do you see him?' asked his sister.

'Oh, yes!' she said.
'Then how does he pull his sledge?'
'Hmm ... with a wooden handle?'
'No!' said the sister and sent her home.

Next the middle daughter tried her luck.
'Do you see him?' asked his sister.
'Oh, yes!' she said.
'Then how does he pull his sledge?'
'Hmm ... with leather rope?'
'No!' said the sister and sent her home.

Then Little Burnt Face went to the tent, dressed in her rags.
'I would like to marry Strong Wind,' she said.
'Come,' said his sister.
They waited for a while down by the river.
'Can you see him?' asked the sister.
'No,' said Little Burnt Face, sadly.

Strong Wind heard her truthfulness and her kind heart, and revealed himself to her.

'Oh yes!' she said laughing. 'There he is!'
'So how does he pull his sledge?'
'It is wonderful! He pulls it with a rainbow!' and she smiled at the wonder of the sight.
'Yes! Now what is the bowstring made of?'
'Wow! It's made from the stars of the sky!'
'Yes!' said the sister.

She bathed the girl in the river, gave her fine new clothes and rubbed a healing balm on her burnt face so the scars were gone. She gave her necklaces and earrings and bracelets and sent her to Strong Wind's tent.

They were married and together practised magic for the good of all.

As for the sisters ... if you were Strong Wind, what would you do with them?

The Monk and the Thieves

Here's a trick tale from Chile: you might tell it with puzzlement and suspense as your audience tries to make sense of what is going on. Get the clever, tricky character of the monk and the gullible nature of the cattleman. Play out the ending and the foolish nastiness of the thieves.

Once a cattleman was walking along the path towards home when he heard a sound coming from a big brown sack.

'Let me out!' it shouted. 'Help!'

He untied the sack and out hopped a monk.

'Thank you, my son,' the monk said. 'I am saved!'

'What were you doing in there?'

'You'll never believe it. Four thieves told me about how they had stolen a pile of gold. I told them stealing was wrong and they wanted to give it to me. Then, when I refused – as monks should never own things, especially stolen things – they said they would kill me and put me in the sack. They're going to throw me in the river!'

'Well, I could have the gold,' said the cattleman. 'Let's swap clothes, sew me in the sack and when they come back I'll tell them.'

'Fine,' said the monk and sewed him up inside.

Minutes later the thieves came back.

'Let me out and I'll take all your gold!' the cattleman shouted.

The thieves shrugged and threw him in the river.

The cattleman was just about to drown when someone pulled the bag onto dry land and let him out. It was the monk.

'I'm not a monk,' he said. 'I was pretending to be a monk to collect money, but when I saw the thieves' gold I tried to steal it and they decided to kill me. But give me my clothes back and I'll get their gold – half for me and half for you! Just lend me your cattle for half an hour, that's all.'

The cattleman wasn't sure but in the end he agreed.

The monk went to the thieves followed by all the cows, and started singing.

'Aren't you dead?' they asked.

'No. I am alive and very rich. At the bottom of the river is a fairy kingdom. I went there and they rescued me and gave me all these cattle as a present. It's lovely down there.'

The thieves looked at the cows.

'Do you think they'd give us some if we went there?'

'Definitely,' said the monk.

'So please throw us in the river!'

'OK!'

The monk tied them in four sacks, loaded them on a boat and let it float off downriver, then collected up the thieves' gold and split it 50/50. The cattleman was rich!

The Story Bag

This is a much-told story about stories needing to be told and what happens if they get bottled up inside. I can't imagine why storytellers like it! It's a great theme to discuss and allows for lots of innovation – which stories would you find in your bag? Daniel Morden tells a brilliant version of this story if you ever get a chance to hear him. Practise doing different voices coming from the bag to bring the moment alive, and find a character feel for the servant as a loving and wise man. Build up suspense for the final scene – what will happen to the servant?

There once lived a very rich family. They had only one child, a boy, who loved to have stories told to him. Whenever he met a new person, he would say, 'Tell me a story. I'd love a new story.' Every time he heard a new story he'd store it away in a small bag, which he kept on his belt. Soon the bag was packed tight and he had to push the new ones in hard to fit them in. He kept it tightly tied so no stories would escape.

Time passed, the boy grew into a man, met a woman, and planned to get married. Everyone in that rich house was involved in planning the wedding and getting ready to welcome the bride to her new home.

In the house there was a faithful, old servant who had known the boy since he was a child. One evening before the wedding, he was working in the kitchen when he heard a strange voice coming from the corner of the room even though there was nobody else in the kitchen. He followed the sound and realised it was coming from a bag hanging on the kitchen wall. It was the story bag hanging on the wall, long forgotten by the young master of the house.

'Listen, everyone,' said a voice. 'The boy's wedding is to take place tomorrow. He has kept us this long while stuffed in this bag, never letting us out at all! Now's a good time to pay him back and get our revenge!'

'I agree,' said another voice. 'How about this? Why don't I change into bright red berries on the path to his bride's house? He'll eat a few and they'll be poison. That way he'll die and it serves him right for keeping us locked up like this.'

'Yes, and after that, if he's still alive,' squeaked a third voice, 'I shall become a clear spring by the path with a cup to drink from. He'll fill the cup, drink, and then I will poison him.'

A fourth voice than broke in, 'Good idea! And if he's still alive I'll become a red hot chunk of metal. When he gets off his horse at his bride's house he'll step on me and burn his feet terribly, then die a slow and horrible death. That'll sort him out!'

A fifth voice whispered, 'If that fails too, I shall become a poisonous snake, hide in the bed, and bite them both when they are asleep.'

The next day was the day of the wedding and the servant was ready to help his master. Early that morning, the groom came out of the house and mounted his horse. The servant came running out and grabbed the horse's bridle and asked to be allowed to lead the horse, but the young master said, 'You have other work to do. You had better stay behind.'
'But I must lead the horse today,' the servant said. 'I don't care what happens, but I insist that I take the bridle.'
He refused to listen to anyone and finally the master, surprised at the old man's obstinacy, allowed him to lead the horse to the bride's home.

All the family set off following the young master's horse in a long joyful procession. Berries grew all along the hedgerow. They looked sweet and lovely.
'Wait!' the bridegroom called out. 'Stop the horse and pick me some of those berries.'
The servant kept leading the horse as if he didn't hear. Then he said, 'Oh, those berries. You can find them anywhere. I can pick some for you later.' And he gave the horse a good crack of the whip.
The groom was surprised at this but said nothing.

Next they came to a spring with a lovely shining cup next to it.
'Bring me some of that water!' the bridegroom said to the servant. 'I have been thirsty for some time.'
But, again, the servant refused his order. 'Once we get into the shade of those trees, your thirst will soon disappear,' he said, and urged the horse on.
'Do what you are told, man!' shouted the groom, but the servant just ignored him.
The bridegroom was surprised at this unusual behaviour.

Soon they reached the bride's home. There, already gathered in the yard, was a large crowd of people. The servant led the horse into the compound and stopped it in the centre of the yard. As the groom stepped down from his horse, the servant pushed him over out of the way of the burning metal. Immediately the metal disappeared.

The bridegroom blushed with shame at his clumsy fall. However, he didn't want to scold his servant in front of all the people so he kept silent and entered the bride's house.

They were married in the house, and then the couple began their journey to the groom's home. They arrived surrounded by the family and danced and drank till late into the night.

Finally they went to their bedroom. The servant hid behind the curtain in the bedroom with a sword and waited. As soon as the bride and bridegroom were in bed, the servant jumped out from behind the curtain and onto the bed. He pushed them out of the way and turned over the mattress revealing a huge black snake under the bed. He killed it with one cut of his sword.

'How did you know?' asked the young master.
'Well, I was in the kitchen last night and I heard the stories in your bag talking…'

He told the whole story from start to finish and the master rewarded him with one hundred gold coins.

Soon the young master became a father. He made sure to tell his children all of the stories that he had heard as a child, opening the neck of his story bag so his stories were free to come and go as they pleased.

So the master and his family and all their stories lived happily ever after.

How a Boy Learned to be Wise

I love this little known story about coming of age and learning to live with others. It's from Uganda so you can set it in Africa if you like. The theme of the child who disappoints his parents is a great one to work with. Almost everyone can identify with this. Here the hare is the wise and trusted friend. Get in touch with your inner wise person and your sulky child when you tell it. Also it's good to explain about potters before you start.

Once upon a time, in a little village by the deep green forest, there lived a potter with his wife and one child, a little baby boy. The boy never played with his parents or with other children. He never laughed or sang. Mostly he just sat by himself, alone, and did very little. This made his parents worried.

One day the potter spoke to his wife:
'Wife,' he said, 'maybe our son will become a fool and maybe he will become wise, but let's not worry about it. Let's just wait and see what happens.'

The boy heard all this and he thought about it all night. In the morning he walked off into the forest to think some more. All day he wandered about, singing a song like this:

> *Foolish or wise, foolish or wise, what's the one for me?*
> *Foolish or wise, foolish or wise, what am I going to be?*
> *Thinking I am foolish fills me up with fear*
> *But how can I learn to be wise?*
> *I've really no idea.*

He walked and walked until he came to a little clearing and sat down for a rest, still singing his song:

> *Foolish or wise, foolish or wise ...*

A lion appeared from the trees and walked towards him. 'I heard your song. What are you doing here?' said the lion.

'I am sad because I don't know if I am wise or a fool,' he said.
'Is that what you are thinking about?' said the lion.
'Yes,' answered the boy, 'I think about it all the time.'
'Then you are a fool,' said the lion. 'Wise men think about things that benefit others.' The lion walked back to the forest.

The boy went back to his song:

> *Foolish or wise, foolish or wise, what's the one for me?*
> *Foolish or wise, foolish or wise, what am I going to be?*
> *Thinking I am foolish fills me up with fear*
> *But how can I learn to be wise?*
> *I've really no idea.*

An antelope came into the clearing and stopped to stare at the boy. 'I heard your song. What are you doing here?' it asked.

'I am sad,' said the boy, 'because I do not know whether I am wise or a fool.'
'When do you eat?' asked the antelope.
'I eat when my mother cooks for me,' said the boy.
'And when do you thank her?' said the antelope.
'Never,' said the boy. 'I just eat!'
'Then you are a fool,' said the antelope. 'Wise men say thank you!'
The antelope ambled off back to the forest.

The boy felt sadder and went back to his song: *Foolish or wise, foolish or wise ...*

Just then a leopard came up and looked at him.
'I heard your song. What are you doing here?' he asked.
'I am very miserable,' answered the boy. 'I don't know if I am a wise man or a fool.'
'Do you have good friends in your village?' asked the leopard.
'Not really,' said the boy. 'I don't get on well with the other boys. They don't like me.'
'Then you are a fool,' said the leopard. 'Wise men make friends and earn respect.'
The leopard walked back to the forest.

The boy went back to his song: *Foolish or wise, foolish or wise ...*

Just then an elephant came out into the clearing.

'I heard your song. What the matter?'

'I am sad,' said the boy. 'I don't know if I am a wise man or a fool.'
'What job do you do?' asked the elephant.
'I don't have a job,' said the boy.
'Then you are a fool,' said the elephant. 'All wise men have work to do.'

The elephant went back to the forest and the boy went back to his singing, sobbing as he sang.

Foolish or wise, foolish or wise ...

As he sang tears rolled down his cheek.

A hare came out of the forest.
'My little brother, do not cry so! Tell me your trouble,' said the hare.

'I am sad because I am a fool,' he said. 'All the animals say so.'

The hare said: 'It is true that you are a fool. It is true that the wise think of others, are thankful and friendly and work hard. All animals work hard, and you should do the same. Why waste your time doing nothing?'

'Maybe I shall be a potter like my father,' said the boy.

'If you are to be a potter,' said the hare, 'then be the best in the country. Wise men do the best they can.'

The boy went home. When he saw his mother he said:
'Thank you for all the food and care you have given me,' and she smiled.

He said to his father,
'I would like to be a potter. Will you teach me how?' and the father smiled.

The boy worked hard and studied hard and became a great potter. Everything he made was beautiful and sold for a good price.

Sometimes he would go to the edge of the forest and sing his song:

Foolish or wise, foolish or wise, what's the one for me?
Foolish or wise, foolish or wise, what am I going to be?
Thinking I am a little bit wise make me feel quite good.
I'd rather be wise than foolish, I really think I should.

The little hare would come running down the forest path, and the two friends would spend a long day together. The boy would tell all his heart to the hare, and the hare always listened and gave good advice.

And his parents were happy and proud of their son till the end of their days.

Persephone

Here's our first Greek myth. If the class don't know about these myths then start by explaining a bit about the gods and their qualities: Zeus – King of the Gods; Hades – God of Death; Demeter – Goddess of Life; and Persephone – daughter of Demeter. Too many new and unfamiliar names can lead to confusion with an audience so find an activity that gets them familiar with their names and attributes. This story is hugely popular. It's generally easy to identify with the fear of separation from parents and so children can connect well with the story. Of course there can also be the wish to separate from parents, so you can tell the story that way too if you like. It also provides a delightful way of explaining the seasons.

Demeter was Goddess of Life. Everything grew and lived on earth because of her.

Demeter had a daughter called Persephone, who she loved more than anything.

One day Persephone was picking poppies in a field of corn when Hades, God of Death, appeared in his chariot. He picked her up and took her down under the earth to his home.

When Demeter couldn't find her daughter she was sad. She looked everywhere but couldn't find Persephone, and became so sad that she stopped smiling, stopped speaking, and stopped making life on earth.

> *The world became cold.*
> *Nothing would grow.*
> *Nothing could be born.*
> *Everything began to die.*

Down under the earth, Persephone was sad too and missed her mother. Hades wanted her to stay and marry him but she said no and refused to eat or drink anything. After a few days she became hungry and ate just six seeds of a pomegranate fruit.

Up above the earth Zeus, King of the Gods, was worried. The earth grew cold and colder and nothing could grow. He asked Demeter to make life again but she shook her head, 'Not without my daughter!'

Zeus went to talk to Hades.
'You must let her go!' he said, 'Or everything on earth will die! You cannot make her stay unless she has eaten food from this place.'

Hades smiled.
'She has eaten six seeds from a pomegranate! So now she will stay.'

Zeus thought about it for a while.
'If she has eaten six seeds then she will stay with you for six months of the year. And for six months she will live above earth with her mother.'

So from that time to this, Persephone spends half the year under the earth. During this time Demeter is sad and the world grows cold, with nothing growing. This time we call winter. For the other half, Persephone returns to her mother, who happily makes new life for earth. The world grows warm and everything can grow again. This time we call summer.

The Wooden Horse

This must be one of the most famous trick tales in the world. It a good action-thriller story if you can spin it out a bit.

Long ago the kingdom of Troy was at war with Greece. A Trojan prince, Paris, had run away with the beautiful Greek queen, Helen. She was a married woman. When her husband found out he rounded up all the Greek kings and declared war on Troy. They would win back his wife and punish this insult to all Greeks.

A great fleet of Greek ships set sail for Troy, but when they arrived there they realised that they would have a long wait. Troy was surrounded by a high stone wall that no army could overcome by attacking.

So instead the Greeks laid siege to the city, letting nothing in or out for ten long years.

Ten year later the Trojans were still living fairly comfortably inside. They had their own stores of food and a water supply for drinking, and could wait for another ten years if need be.

But the Greek kings couldn't wait another ten years. They wanted to get home to their kingdoms and families.

Then one of the Greek kings, clever Odysseus, made a plan.

They made a huge wooden horse as high as ten men and mounted it on a cart with six giant wheels, so that it could be moved around. Then all of their ships set sail and left the shores of Troy, leaving only the wooden horse behind.

From the walls of Troy the Trojans were delighted, 'We've won! We've won!' they called as they ran down to the beach to celebrate, dancing and singing around the wooden horse which the Greeks had left behind.

The king of Troy looked carefully at the huge wooden horse.

'This is an offering to the gods,' he said. 'We will take it into our temple in the city and honour the gods with it too, and thank them for helping us win this war.'

So they tied long ropes to the wooden horse and one hundred men pulled it through the city gates and into the temple courtyard to the cheers of the Trojans inside the city.

That night, while the Trojans were drinking and dancing, the Greek ships sailed back in darkness to the shores of Troy. Not a single light was lit, so they would not be discovered. Then they sat and watched and waited...

Inside Troy a small secret door opened in the belly of the wooden horse and a rope snaked down to the ground. Odysseus silently slid down the rope and another ten men followed, with swords and daggers ready for fighting.

They hardly needed them. All of the city was busy celebrating and there was nobody to stop them as they crept through the streets towards the city gate. They spied out the four guards and at the same moment slit their throats without a sound being heard.

Then, as quietly as possible, they pushed open the great gates of the city.

Moments later the armies of Greece stormed through with swords drawn and blazing torches ready to burn and destroy. It was all over quickly. Soldiers rushed out of their homes; many were killed before they even found their swords. The palace of the king was unguarded and easily taken.

Soon the whole of the city was brimming with Trojans running for their lives.

Within a few hours the city was taken. The Greeks had won the war by the trick of the wooden horse.

SHORTER STORIES

Half a Blanket

I really like the way Traditional stories often teach about respect and care for elders. In cultures where youth is valued over age these provide great talking points. Here's a sharp little tale about that from Scotland, with lots of role-play options in the tale, replaying family narratives. Try and bring alive the depressed father, the ailing grandfather and the loving daughter.

Once there was a woodcutter. He lived with his wife, daughter and father in a little house on the edge of a forest. Every day he went off to work chopping wood in the forest, selling the wood in the town and bringing home whatever food he could buy for the family.

Sometimes there was enough food, but sometimes they all went hungry. This made him sad and frustrated. He hated to see his family suffering and felt like he was a failure.

His father had been a woodcutter like him and in the past had gone to the forest with him every day. Then they had collected more wood and more food, but as the old man got older his joints became stiff and his back became bent. It was all he could do to walk from his bed to his chair. He couldn't even help around the house. The old man felt bad about this. He spent more time by the fire chatting with his granddaughter, who loved spending time with her kind old granddad.

Time passed and the two men started to argue about one thing or another. The father felt criticised. The woodcutter felt taken for granted. The father felt unwanted. The woodcutter felt resentful.

One evening the whole thing blew up and the father said, 'Fine! If I'm not wanted here then I'll go and live somewhere else!' and walked off towards the door.

'That suits me just fine!' snapped the woodcutter.

It was midnight. There was snow on the ground and the nearest neighbour was half a mile away.

The woodcutter just sat there scowling as his father opened the door.
'Daughter!' he called out angrily. 'Go and get Granddad a blanket and give it to him, to keep him warm on the road.'

The girl looked carefully at the woodcutter and said, 'No Dad, I think we should only give him half a blanket.'

The woodcutter was surprised. He knew the girl was fond of her granddad. 'Why, Daughter?'

The girl looked her father straight in the eyes. 'I'll keep the other half to give you when you get old and have to leave.'

The two men stared at the girl, and then the woodcutter walked over to his father and led him back to the fire.

'Sorry, Dad!' he said. 'Please stay with us.'

Fruit of Love

I was taught this First Nation story by storyteller Michael Moran, when I was looking for a story on the theme of forgiveness. It's simple and can be told in many ways. The main thing is to stoke up the anger of the argument, the stubbornness of the person walking away (either wife or husband, up to you!), and then the tenderness of the ending. It can be retold between the first two friends if that's more suitable.

In the beginning when the world was new, First Man and First Woman were having their first argument. Whatever it was about, they shouted and got more and more angry. I wonder what they were arguing about? Finally First Woman walked off across the desert, her nose in the air, grumbling to herself.

'How dare he say that to me! How dare he! I'll never speak to him again! He's horrible. I hate him!'

First Man began to feel worried. 'I was angry,' he thought, 'but now I'll never see her again. Oh no! What have I done?'

He prayed up to the sky to the God of Love. 'Bring her back to me, please! I love her.'

The God of Love was watching the whole thing. He thought, 'She'll never come back while her nose is sticking up in the air like that. I'll have to get that nose down.'

And so the God of Love covered the desert in a blanket of lush green leaves. 'That ought to get her nose down!' he said.

But it didn't work. She didn't even notice. She carried on grumbling, with her nose in the air.

'I'll have to try harder,' thought the God of Love and created a sea of tiny white flowers blooming on top of the green leaves.

First Woman still didn't notice. She kept on striding away from her husband and grumbling. Her nose stayed stuck up in the air.

The God of Love thought about it some more. 'This is harder than I thought,' he said, and created a carpet of wonderful sweet-smelling red fruits.

Maybe it was the colour. Maybe it was the smell. First woman stopped and looked down.

She bent down and picked one, and tasted it, biting it in half. The fruit tasted sweet.

She looked at the half that remained. It was in the shape of a heart with a sweet tender inside.

'Hmm ... I suppose I do love my husband even though he's a fool,' she thought.

She picked up a handful of heart-shaped fruits and took them back to her husband.

And that's how the first strawberries came into the world.

One Wish

Here's an example of the popular 'one wish' story retold with a football interest. That makes it a bit more interesting for the football fans in your class. Obviously, just change the name of the place, river and the local team. When it has been learned the tellers can add any team they like. It's good practice for punchline telling.

Once, in the city of Oxford, there lived a man. He was a good man, a kind man, and a happy man, but three things made him sad.

First, he was a keen football fan and supported Oxford United. Unfortunately they kept losing. Second, his old mother had lost her sight and was finding life very difficult. And third, he had been married for ten years but had no children, and his wife really wanted children badly.

One day the man was walking down by the River Thames, right by a pub called The Isis, when he saw a fish flapping on the bank. He bent down, gently picked the fish up and returned it to the river. The fish popped its head up out of the water.

'Thank you,' it said. 'And as you've been kind to me, I shall be kind to you. I will give you one wish, but choose wisely – you only have one.'

The man thought, 'I could wish for Oxford United to do well ... or I could wish for my mother to have her eyesight back, which would make her really happy ... or I could wish that my wife and I finally have the son we've longed for.'

He thought very hard then had an idea. He looked down to the fish and spoke. 'I wish that one day my mother will see my son score the winning goal for Oxford United in the FA Cup Final.'

From that day his mother's sight started getting better until she could see again. A year later his wife gave birth to a little baby boy, and today he's playing centre forward for Oxford United's youth team. In a few years' time, who knows what will happen!

Snip snap
That's the end of that.

Birth of Athena

I like the way this story gives a positive spin to having a headache. Or to put it another way, sometimes learning things can be painful! Explain in advance that Athena was Goddess of Wisdom, talk a bit about what that means, and then tell this story about how she was born. It can be fun to make up new birth tales with the class. Also explain about Zeus, unless you have already done so.

Soon after Zeus became King of the Gods he got married to his first wife, Metis.

It wasn't long before she was pregnant. At first he was happy at the thought of being a dad, but then someone whispered in his ear, 'The child in your wife's womb will be greater and wiser than you.'

Zeus did not like the sound of that. There was a history of trouble between fathers and sons in his family!

'I am the King of the Gods,' he thought. 'No one should be greater and wiser than me.'

So he came up with a plan to stop his child being born.

'Wife,' he said, 'let's play a game. Let's see who can turn themselves into the biggest creature.'

She turned herself into an elephant and he into a giraffe.

'It's a draw,' he said. 'I am taller but you are heavier.'

'Now, let's see who can be the fastest creature.'

Metis became a greyhound and Zeus became a falcon.

'Still a draw,' he said.

'Let's see who can be the smallest.'

Metis turned herself into a fly and hovered in front of him.

Zeus grabbed the fly and swallowed it.

'That's the end of that child!' he thought with a smile.

But ... a few months later Zeus's head started to ache. The pain got worse and worse until it felt as if a spike was pressing hard into his brain from the inside of his skull. There was a voice too, inside his throbbing head.

'Let me out! Let me out!' it cried.

Zeus wasn't sure what to do, but the pain got worse and worse until he just had to do something.

He summoned Hephaestus, the blacksmith, who took out a hammer and chisel and cracked open Zeus's skull.

Out leapt a goddess with a roar, a helmet on her head and a spear in her hand. She was Athena, the Goddess of Wisdom.

And that is how Wisdom came into the world. So, if you ever find yourself with a really bad headache, or some other kind of ache, don't worry, it might just be Wisdom trying to come out.

The Lode Stone

Here's a lovely little tale about paying attention and noticing what is important. You can make the main character a bit wild and obsessive.

Once upon a time there was a pebbled beach ten miles long. Legend said that on that beach there was one stone that had the power to turn iron into gold – the Lode Stone.

A man decided that he would find the Lode Stone. He started at one end of the beach, picked up the first stone and held it against the iron buckle of his belt. When nothing happened, he tossed it over his shoulder and tried another one. He held the next stone against his belt and waited and when nothing happened, he threw it over his shoulder again. He touched, waited and threw, touched, waited and threw again and again and again and again.

In this way he moved across the beach. A day passed, then a week, then a month and then a whole year.

As time passed, the man became quicker and quicker with his actions. He touched, waited and threw, touched, waited and threw, faster and faster, keen to get to the end of the beach. After five years he had combed almost the entire beach without discovering that stone.

One day, a boy eating an ice-cream asked him what he was doing.
'I am searching for the Lode Stone,' he told the boy. 'The stone that has the power to turn iron into gold. I pick up each stone, touch it against my iron belt and wait. If nothing happens I throw the stone over my shoulder.'

The boy looked at the man's belt. 'But your buckle is gold,' he said.

The man looked down and, sure enough, his buckle was gold. Sometime over the last five years the man had stopped looking properly and along the way must have actually had his hands on the Lode Stone.

He let out a long, long sigh and trudged all the way back to his house to find another old belt. Then he made his way to the other end of the beach and started again, this time paying much more attention.

Many years later, a young girl playing in a rock-pool on that beach saw an old man with wobbly knees and a crooked back picking up stones and holding them to his belt.

'Your belt!' she called. 'It's so beautiful! Is the buckle gold?'
The old man sighed ... 'Here we go again!'

The Scorpion and the Frog

Here's a very popular little Asian fable that pops up all over the place. It is told by the main protagonist in the movie The Shawshank Redemption *as a fable for how life can be. It can be about the way we can all sow the seeds of our own destruction just by 'being ourselves'. Get two clear voices for the two animals and create tension as the frog tries to decide what to do.*

Once there was a scorpion, a creature with a deadly sting in his tail. One day he decided to travel to visit his relatives across the river. When he got to the riverbank he saw a frog.

'Brother Frog!' he called. 'Let me ride on your back across the river. I can't swim and I need to visit relatives on the other side.'

'Do you think I'm stupid?' croaked the frog. 'I know you scorpions. If I let you get near me then you'll sting me and kill me!'

'Why would I do that?' asked the scorpion. 'I need a ride over the river and if I sting you then you will die of the poison, but I will die from drowning. So of course I won't sting you.'

'Alright then, Brother Scorpion,' the frog agreed reluctantly. 'Climb on my back and I'll give you a ride.'

Halfway across the river the scorpion stung the frog on his back. The frog started to sink as the poison filled his body.

'Why did you do that, Scorpion? You promised not to!' cried the frog.

'I am a scorpion. It's in my nature to sting!' answered the scorpion, as the waters closed over his head and the two creatures sank to their deaths.

Three Wishes

I first heard this story from the inimitable TUUP at the Crick Crack Club in London, who told the 1001 Nights version. He was very funny! Here is the sausage version; there are many such tales featuring foolish wishes, including an old English version featuring a black pudding collected by Joseph Jacobs.

The story is all about foolishness and impatience so you have to evoke the foolish character in a funny, crazy way!

Once there was a fisherman. One day he was walking by the river when he came upon a silver fish, flapping on the riverbank. He felt sorry for the fish and threw it back into the river.

The fish popped its head out of the river and spoke.

'You have helped me so I will help you. You and your wife may have three wishes. Wish for anything you want and wish well.'

The fisherman went off home to tell his wife the good news. When he got home she was standing at the cottage door frowning.

'No fish for me to cook?' she said. 'What have you been doing all day? I am hungry and we have nothing to eat.'

'Wife, I have good news. I helped a fish and now we can have three wishes!'

'Mmmm,' she said, smiling. 'That's good. What I would like now is a lovely big sausage!'

Just then a long fat sausage appeared in her hand, cooked and ready to eat!

She smiled and prepared to take a bite.

'You foolish woman!' he shouted. 'You have wasted our wish on a sausage when we could have had anything. You don't deserve to eat it. I wish it was stuck to your nose!'

Just then the sausage stuck to her nose.

She pulled and pulled but it would not come off. He tried but she just wailed.

'It won't come off,' she wailed. 'It is stuck there forever. What shall we do with the last wish?'

The fisherman began thinking about all the things he wanted. A new house, money, power …. But then he looked at his wife sobbing with the sausage on her nose, and felt sorry for her.

'Wife,' he said, 'You can't go through life with a sausage on your nose. I wish the sausage were gone!'

And just like that the sausage disappeared.

'Oh well,' said the fisherman. 'If I ever get three wishes again I will be more careful.'

'Me too,' said his wife.

If you had three wishes, what would you choose?

Chapter 4

Year 4 Stories

The Blind Man and the Hunter – West Africa	196
The Birth of Osiris – Egypt	200
Prometheus – Greece	202
The Eagle Who Thought He Was a Chicken – Native American	204
How Butterflies Came to Be – Native America	206
Icarus – Greece	208
The Shepherd's Dream – Ireland	211
The Piper's Boots – Scotland	213
Midas's Wish – Greece	216
Midas and Apollo – Greece	218
Theseus and the Minotaur – Greece	220
The Woman of the Sea – Scotland	224
How Jerusalem Began – Palestine and Jewish	226
Odysseus and the Cyclops – Greece	228
The Four Dragons – China	230
The Land of the Deep Ocean – Japan	233
Rama and Sita – India	236

SHORTER STORIES:

The Building of St Paul's Cathedral – England	238
Feathers in the Wind – Jewish	239
Heaven and Hell (1) – Japan	240
Heaven and Hell (2) – European	241

The Blind Man and the Hunter

This is a much-loved and commonly told story from West Africa. There is a lovely text version in McCall Smith's The Girl Who Married a Lion. *Here there are two main characters to develop – the wise brother and the arrogant hunter who learns to be more humble. There are lots of chances to describe an imagined African jungle and lots of talking points about world affairs and what to do.*

Once there was a forest and in the forest was a village and in that village there were huts woven from branch and earth. In one of these huts there lived a blind man. The man was greatly respected in the village. It was said that even though he could not see with his eyes, he could see with his ears. People came to him with their problems and found his listening satisfying. He shared his hut with his sister, who looked after their home and looked after a small piece of land where they grew vegetables and kept a few goats for milk.

They lived happily together.

In another hut there lived a hunter. He was a skilled hunter, proud of his ability with the bow and trap. He considered himself the best hunter in the village and, after a few cups of palm wine, he'd sing a little song to himself:

> *A hunting I will go.*
> *A hunting I will go.*
> *There's nothing so fine*
> *As a man in his prime.*
> *A hunting I will go.*

One morning he noticed the blind man's sister working on her land and fell in love with her quiet simple beauty. He courted her and within a month they were married. Sister and brother moved in with the hunter.

Every day the hunter would go out to the forest, trapping and tracking, and every evening he'd come back with his kill and hand it over to his wife for cooking. He'd lie in his hammock and sing himself his song: *A hunting I will go…*

He'd sing himself to sleep till the food was ready. He never once thanked his wife for her work in the home.

One day the family was eating supper. The hunter was chatting away about his adventures in the forest when the blind brother interrupted, 'Let me go hunting with you tomorrow. I can help you.'

The hunter laughed. 'What! You? What possible use could a blind man be to me?'

He went back to his story.

The blind man shrugged and went back to his supper.

The next day the blind man asked again. 'Let me go hunting with you tomorrow. I can help.'

'Look, I've told you. You can't help. I am fine. I go hunting. I bring the food. She cooks it and you eat it. That's it. You can't come.'

Every day for one hundred days the brother asked to go hunting, but was always dismissed as being of no use until finally the hunter relented. 'OK brother, tomorrow you can come. Just once. Then maybe you'll stop bothering me.'

The next day the two men set off into the forest. For a while the hunter sang his hunting song as they walked, the blind man followed him easily along the path without help. After a while the blind man said, 'Shhh! Careful! There's a lion with her cubs nearby, over there that way.'

The hunter stopped singing. 'How do you know?' he asked doubtfully.

'I can hear them playing.'

The hunter listened but could only hear the wind in the trees. He peeped around the corner and sure enough, there was a lioness with a handful of suckling cubs, lying in the sun. Very dangerous! The two men tiptoed away and the hunter went back to singing again: *A hunting I will go...*

After a while the brother said, 'Shhh! Careful! There's a mamba snake on the branch above your head. Move away slowly or he may strike.'

The hunter looked up and saw the snake poised ready to strike. He moved away quickly. 'How did you know?' he asked, impressed.

'I smelled its scent,' answered the brother.

The hunter went back to his song, but soon the brother stopped for a third time. 'There's a family of elephants down by the river. Should we go the other way?'

The hunter listened but couldn't hear the river, let alone the elephants. They walked for a good ten minutes before coming to the river where a family of elephants were playing and washing. Now the hunter was really impressed.

'Maybe a blind man can be of use after all,' he thought, but did not say it.

They came to a clearing and the hunter showed the brother how to set a bird trap. The hunter set one trap and the blind man another, and then they went on their way. Then they went hunting with bow and arrow. The brother listened out for prey and the hunter watched. The blind man was really useful, the hunter realised.

That evening at supper the hunter said, 'Brother, come hunting with me tomorrow. Let's see what we have caught in our traps.'
The brother nodded and smiled.

The next morning they came to the clearing where they had set the traps. There was a bird in each. In the hunter's trap was a plump brown bird and in the blind man's trap a bird about the same size but covered in the most beautiful feathers, all the colours of the rainbow.

The hunter liked the coloured bird more. He felt a little jealous. 'Well done!' he said to the brother as he took the birds out. 'You have caught a bird on your first try. Here, take it.' He handed him the brown bird.

The blind man nodded and said nothing.

The hunter took the rainbow bird as his kill and together they walked home.

Somehow the hunter felt uneasy all the way home. As they approached the village he stopped. 'Brother,' he said, 'you are said to be wise so tell me. Why is there so much trouble in the world?'

The brother replied quietly, 'It is because of people like you, who do what they should not!'

The hunter flushed with shame. 'I am sorry, brother. I was selfish. I thought you wouldn't know or wouldn't care but it was wrong. Here – take the rainbow bird.'

The brother nodded and they exchanged birds.

They walked for a while longer and the hunter stopped again. 'So tell me. So many people take what is not theirs. Is there any hope for the world then?'

'Oh, yes!' he said smiling. 'There is hope. Because there are people like you who can admit their mistakes and learn from them.'

The next day they went off into the forest together:

A hunting we will go.
A hunting we will go.
There's nothing so fine
As men in their prime
A hunting we will go.

The Birth of Osiris

This is our first creation myth. Find a voice to tell it in that conveys the enormity of creating everything! Maybe explain at the beginning that it is from Ancient Egypt and tells the story of Ra the Sun God and his children, Osiris and Isis. Get them used to these names before you start. There is a love interest here and how you handle it depends partly on the maturity of your class and partly on how confident you are. Creation by alphabet can be fun if you want to play it with your class. These kinds of stories have a huge and different atmosphere that children love to experience and create. Try using a drum in parts of the story for atmosphere. I like the treatment of these and other stories in Morley's Egyptian Myths.

In the beginning there was only water. Water in all directions, into infinity. Nothing else.
Then the creator spoke his own name from inside the water. 'I am Ra.'
He rose up above the water, a blazing sun disk, and looked down on it.
He began to name the world he would make.
He said, 'Earth!' and there was earth.
He said, 'Sky!' and there was sky.
He said, 'Mountain!' and there was mountain.
He said, 'Forest!' and there was forest.
He said, 'Desert!' and there was desert.

Next he named trees and bushes, flowers and grasses.
Then he named all the creatures of the earth – ant, bear, cat, dog, elephant, fox, giraffe, horse, iguana, jaguar, koala, lion, mouse, newt ... he named them all.

Ra looked down on the earth and saw the animals playing and feeding, mothers feeding their young. He smiled and tears of joy fell from his eye.

Then he saw death and tears of pain fell from his other eye.

Those tears dropped from his eyes down into the ground and mixed with soil to become humans – humans made from the tears of the Sun God. Tears of joy and tears of pain. That is why we all have both joy and pain inside us.

Time passed. The Sky looked down at the Earth and the Earth looked up at the Sky. Each gazed at the other and liked what they saw. Sky admired Earth's mountains and valleys. Earth admired Sky's white clouds and dark twinkling night. They were in love. So Sky came down and wrapped herself around Earth.

Ra was watching and was jealous. 'No!' he commanded. 'You will not be married! Why should you be together when I am alone? Wind – push them apart, and keep them apart!'

Wind came between them and blew, pushed Sky up away from Earth, up so only the tips of Sky and Earth were still touching out on the horizon.

Soon Sky's belly began to swell. She was going to have babies.

Ra saw this and was furious. 'I am the creator!' he yelled. 'Not you! You will not give birth in any day of any year!'

Sky grew heavier and heavier with her babies but could not give birth. She moaned and groaned. Thunder roared and lighting flashed. 'Help! Someone, help!' she cried.

The God of Wisdom, Thoth, heard her cries and made a plan. He challenged the Moon to a game of chess.

'Listen,' said Thoth, 'let's play for something to make it interesting. Every time you win I'll give you some of my wisdom. And every time I win you give me some of your moonlight. Deal?'

'Deal!' said the Moon, and they started to play.

They played game after game, Thoth winning easily until he had enough light for five new days. Then he slipped those new days in between the old and new year. Ra knew nothing about the new days, and so his curse did not apply.

In each of those five days Sky puffed and pushed and gave birth to her five children. Among them was Osiris, who was to become ruler of the world, and Isis, who would become his queen.

Prometheus

This is another lovely creation myth, this time from Ancient Greece. I like the quality in this one of imagining physically moulding clay into men and women before giving them life. Get some modelling clay for a follow-up activity! A nice gory ending of unbearable torture – that's the joy of the Greeks!

When the world was new, Prometheus was given the job of starting life on earth. He lived in a high walled garden with a workshop where he made all sorts of creatures, keeping them all inside the high walls.

He made trees and flowers, bushes and grasses, fish and birds, lions and leopards, cats and cougars. On and on he worked making life after life and letting it out into the garden to see how each plant and animal would fit with the others. As the garden filled with amazing creatures he began to love them as if they were his children.

'They are good. They are beautiful,' he thought, 'but who will look after them once I have let them out into the world? Who will be their protector?'

One night he had an idea.

He took some river clay, mixed it with that-which-gives-life, and began to work.

He moulded a head, with two eyes, two ears, a nose and a mouth. He moulded a neck, shoulders and two arms, each with a five-fingered hand on the end. He moulded a chest and a belly. He moulded hips and legs, knees and ankles, and two five-toed feet.

In this way he created something that looked rather like the gods themselves.

When he'd finished he made another, and another, all through the night until the table was covered in a crowd of what looked like gods and goddesses. When they were finished he waited, and when the first rays of sun came up over the garden wall, the creatures came to life. Lungs filled with air. Hearts pumped blood around their veins. Their eyes opened and they climbed down from the table and walked out into the garden.

'Yes!' thought Prometheus. 'Now there are creatures that can protect and look after the life I have made. These humans are a little like gods. They can look after the earth and its life.'

He opened the doors of his garden and all the life he had made rushed out and into the empty world, which was soon covered with forests and jungles, plains and deserts – all filled with the life he had made and we humans with the job to protect it all.

Prometheus watched over his creatures out in the world, and soon noticed that humans were a little cold in winter. They needed something to keep them warm or they would die.

He sneaked up to Mount Olympus and took some of the gods' fire down to earth. He showed the humans how to use it to cook and keep warm.

But Zeus looked down from Olympus and was angry. 'How could Prometheus steal from us, the gods!' he thundered. 'For this he will be punished!'

They chained Prometheus to a cliff over the sea. Every morning an eagle would come and eat out his liver, slowly, bite by bite, agony by agony. Every night his liver would grow back again.

This was his punishment for bringing us fire.

The Eagle Who Thought He Was a Chicken

Here's a lighter tale after those heavy myths – a First Nation story about learning who you are. Some schools change it to 'The Red Kite Who Thought He Was a Chicken' so it can be connected to local fauna. You can play this for comedy as the powerful bird acts like a chicken, and then for celebration as he learns what he can really do. May we all follow in the story's wingbeats!

Once ... there was a farmer. One day he was walking through a forest when he heard two gunshots up ahead on the path. A few minutes later he came to the bodies of two huge golden eagles lying on the ground, both stone cold dead.

'What a pity,' he thought, 'to kill such beautiful birds! They help keep down the numbers of rats and mice and rabbits and do little harm to us humans. They are the kings of the sky. Who would do such a thing?'

He looked up and saw an eagle's nest above his head in the highest branches of a tall pine. 'I wonder...' he thought.

Carefully he climbed up the tree and looked into the nest. There were two eagle eggs there, still warm. He slipped them into his pocket and climbed down.

Back at the farm, he wondered how to take care of them. He slipped the eggs under a hen who was hatching a clutch of her own eggs, and waited to see what would happen.

The eggs all hatched and the eaglets were accepted as part of the mother hen's family, one brother and one sister. She treated them as her children and they thought she was their mother. They learned how to live like chickens – how to cluck and scratch in the dirt, eat seeds and grubs, and how to hide when eagles flew overhead.

Time passed and the eaglets grew. Soon they were bigger than the other chicks. Their beaks were longer, their wings wider and their claws sharper. Still they continued clucking and pecking and scratching in the soil, running for cover when an eagle flew by.

One day, as the sun was going down, the brother eagle heard the sound of a huge owl hooting from the tree above the farmyard, except the owl seemed to be laughing. 'Hoot, Hoot, ha, ha, ha, hoot, hoot!'
'What are you laughing at?' asked the brother.
'I'm laughing because you are an eagle, but you walk and talk like a chicken!'
'No, I'm not!' shouted the brother, annoyed. 'I am a chicken.'
'Really?' said the owl. 'Then why are you so big? Why is your beak so long?'
'I'm an unusual chicken, that's all.'

The owl swooped down and landed next to the brother. 'Jump on my back and I'll prove it to you.'
The brother jumped on the owl's back. The owl took off and soon was flying high above the earth.
'I don't like it up here!' shouted the frightened brother. 'I might fall! Put me down! Take me back!'
'Sorry about this,' said the owl, 'but you'll thank me later!'

The owl turned upside down in the air and the brother fell off his back and started to plummet down towards earth.
'Heeeeelp!' he cried as he fell.
'The owl dived down through the air next to the falling bird, shouting, 'Open your wings! Open your wings!'
The brother opened his long brown wings and in a moment, he stopped falling and started to climb through the air, with the owl laughing next to him.
'You see!' the owl hooted. 'You are an eagle! You can fly!'

The next day the brother went to his sister. 'Jump on my back!' he said. 'I want to show you something.'

Soon brother and sister were circling above the chicken coop. Proud eagles. They felt like king and queen of the sky.

'Thank you, owl,' they called, 'for showing us who we really are.'

How Butterflies Came to Be

This is another First Nation tale, this time about joy and beauty. Tell it with tenderness. Find the things you love and put them in the story, then get your class to do the same.

In the beginning the Creator made all things: birds and bees, fish and fowl, plants and porcupines, horses and humans. He made it all, then had a long sleep.

When he woke up he went for a walk to see how his creatures were getting on.

Fish were swimming, birds were flying, snakes were slithering. It all seemed to be going to plan, till he came to a human village.

He noticed the children playing, laughing, singing and was pleased, but then he saw their parents working and worrying about themselves and their families. They had no joy, only hard work and worry.

'That's not right,' he thought. 'But what shall I do?'

He went off to the wise woman of the forest and asked her advice. She was sitting in her hut smoking a pipe.

'The parents are all so serious!' he said. 'They have no joy, just duty! That wasn't my plan. I made the world so they will have joy.'

'So,' she said, 'you have to make something to give them a little joy. Take the best things from what you have made, the things that give you most joy, and mix them together into something new. See what happens.'

He went out into the world and collected his favourite things:

Moonlight shining on the water
A flower's delicate petals
Pollen from a flower
The pattern of a snakeskin...

He collected them all and then mixed them all up in a bag, breathed in the breath of life, and out came...

Butterflies. Beautiful butterflies of every colour in the rainbow, delicate and beautiful.

As he watched they flew into the village. The children laughed and chased them around the streets.

Then the parents looked up, just for a moment from their work and worry, to see what was going on.

Each time they saw a butterfly they smiled, just for a moment before going back to work.

And that's why, when you see butterflies, just for a moment, you find yourself smiling.

Icarus

Icarus is a useful story for so many reasons. On the one hand it is about foolish risk-taking and on the other about listening to others and taking advice when needed. This boundary between safety and thrills, obedience and autonomy, is important for us all. This simple tale is great to explore for these reasons, not to mention the science topics of flight and wings. There are lots of great role play options between parent and child. You might explain, before starting, a little about the Minotaur story as background and the Ancient Greeks in general.

When Theseus killed the Minotaur, King Minos was furious. Theseus had killed his son and stolen his daughter away from right under his nose! Someone was to blame! Someone had to pay! And that someone was Daedalus the Smith, the man who had made the labyrinth. Minos summoned Daedalus.

'How can I help your majesty?' Daedalus smiled, confident as usual.

'All this is your fault!' snapped the king. 'You were told to build a maze so tangled that all who entered would never leave. Weren't you?'

'Yes, your majesty,' he argued, still calm. 'But you saw the thread, no maze can defeat a thread, however perfect.'

'I don't want excuses, and anyway I hear you were mixed up somehow with the queen in making that bull-headed child in the first place! What do you have to say about THAT?' Daedalus hung his head. 'Nothing, your majesty. I only do what I am told to do. I cannot be responsible for what my superiors do with my creations...'

Minos shook his head. 'No, blacksmith! You make them, you are responsible, and this time you will pay! You and your son can spend some time in my prison while I think about what to do with you. Guards!'

Daedalus and Icarus were taken to the prison tower which the blacksmith himself had designed and built, and were locked inside the highest cell with a lock that Daedalus himself had made.

His son didn't like it there. 'Dad,' he whined, 'I want to go home.'

Daedalus patted the boy on his shoulder. 'Don't worry son, give me a week and I'll solve the problem.'

Every day Daedalus took half of the bread the guards gave them to eat, and scattered it on the window sill of the cell.

Icarus was curious. 'Dad, what are you doing? I'm hungry.'

'Wait and see,' came the reply.

When the birds came to feed on the bread, Daedalus would crouch like a cat by the window and every now and then pounce on a bird, pull out its longest feathers, let it go and wait for the next bird. After a week he had a great pile of feathers.

In the evenings he saved half of the wax from the candles the guards gave them, and when he had saved enough, he started working, sticking the feathers together with the wax, making two huge pairs of wings.

As ever, he was proud of his creation. 'Look son, these wings will take us away from here, to a new land with a new king to serve. But you have to be careful.'

'Don't worry, Dad!'

'No! Listen, Icarus! This is important! The wings are made from wax and feathers. They are weak! You have to be careful! Fly straight and steady next to me and you'll be fine, but don't do anything else. Fly too high and the wax will melt in the sun's heat. Fly too low and the sea will wet the feathers and you will fall. Stay with me and we'll both be fine.'

'Don't worry, Dad, I'll be alright.'

With the wings strapped to their arms and shoulders they stood, perched for a moment on the window ledge. Below them a bull bellowed, above them an eagle hovered.

'Now!'

Together they fell into space, their wings catching the updraft of their falling. Their falling slowed and then, meeting a pocket of rising air, they climbed with it, above the tower and glided, wingtip to wingtip, north over the cliffs, out over the ocean.

Icarus was delighted and excited. 'Look, Dad! Look what I can see! Look down there, dolphins! This is great!'

'Just stay straight and steady.'

For some time they flew together, till Icarus grew restless.
'Dad, look what I can do!'

Icarus turned a somersault in mid-air.

'No, son! It's dangerous. The wings aren't strong enough. Stay by me!'

'Dad, you worry too much! Look! Watch me climb!'

Icarus began to spiral up above his father, ignoring the pleas to return. He climbed higher and higher into the heat of the sun until he felt the drip of liquid wax on his shoulder and, in an instant, the feathers were gone. He plummeted like a falling anvil, down past his father, smashing into the sea with such force that his spine snapped.

Daedalus hovered and watched his son's lifeless body floating in the water below, adding his own tears to the sea's stock of salt, as he felt, for the first time, the suffering which his own creations had caused.

The Shepherd's Dream

This mysterious Irish story allows the audience to puzzle and try to make sense of its meanings. It takes us into the world of dreams where one thing can stand for another. Tell it with wonder. I like Crossley-Holland's telling in Folktales of the British Isles. *You can also hear Hugh Lupton tell the story on his* Tales of Wisdom and Wonder *CD.*

Once there were two shepherds who lay down to rest under a tree while their sheep grazed the long green grass of the field. The shepherds had a lovely view down over the field, over a sparkling stream and a bed of long golden reeds. The sun shone down and all was well.

They smiled and sang a little song:

> *Life is a mystery.*
> *It's very hard to see*
> *What is real and what is true,*
> *What is me and what is you.*

Then the older shepherd puffed on his pipe and admired the view, while the younger shepherd fell into a deep sleep.

Then something started crawling out of the young man's mouth. The elder watched in amazement. It was a butterfly! How could that be?

The butterfly hopped out of the mouth, crawled down the young man's chin, neck and belly and down onto the path. It fluttered down the path through the field towards the stream. The old shepherd followed behind it, trying to make sense of what he was seeing.

At the stream there were some stepping stones over the river and the butterfly hopped from one to the next till it got to the other side, with the old shepherd close behind.

Next, it followed the path through a clump of bulrushes and out into a green field. The old shepherd watched as it flew to a bleached white horse's skull in the centre of the field.

He watched the butterfly fly into the eye-socket of the skull and disappear. He waited and a while later if flew out of the mouth and back towards him, over the field, through the rushes, over the stepping stones and up the path back to the young shepherd. There it crawled up his chin and disappeared back into the young man's mouth.

Moments later the young shepherd woke up. 'I've just had the most amazing dream!' he said. 'I dreamed I was walking down a road lined with tall green trees. I walked till I came to the ocean, and there I started flying, out over the sea from island to island, till I came to a new land where the trees where tall and thin and golden. I travelled through the forest of giant trees until I came to a white palace. I went inside but it was empty. Nothing there at all. So I came back home, through the forest of giant trees, over the ocean, island to island, then up the road surrounded by a green, green forest. Then I got home and woke up. What does it mean?'

'I'll show you,' said the elder shepherd.

He led the young shepherd down the pathway that led through the long green grass.

'In your dream, this was the road through the green forest,' he told him.

He pointed to the stream and stepping stones. 'This was the ocean and the islands.'

He led the young shepherd through the clump of bulrushes. 'And this was the giant forest,' he said and then pointed out the skull. 'And that was the palace.'

'This is amazing!' exclaimed the young shepherd. 'But what do you think it means?'

'I don't know,' said the elder shepherd. 'But it must be something wonderful.'

They sang their song again as they walked back to their sheep:

> *Life is a mystery.*
> *It's very hard to see*
> *What is real and what is true,*
> *What is me and what is you.*

So here's a question for you:
What do you think the story means?

The Piper's Boots

Here's a great gritty and somewhat gory story from Scotland with a brilliant twist at the end. Conjure up the main character of the travelling piper, his poverty and hunger and how he feels about being treated like dirt. Then enjoy his revenge. If you can play an instrument you can put that into the story, too. There are lots of talking points about poverty and generosity.

Once there was a piper who travelled from town to town playing his pipes in the street for anyone who would listen. People would give him a coin or two or some food, and in that way he kept body and soul together. In summer he was fine, playing to the people working in the fields and sleeping out at night in the woods and on the haystacks. But winter was tough for the piper, especially when there was snow. In winter he worked as a carpenter doing odd jobs around people's houses in return for food and a warm bed for the night.

It was on one such winter evening that the piper was trudging along a snow-covered path. His boots were old and full of holes and his feet were wet and frozen. His belly was empty – he hadn't eaten for two days. 'Oh! What I'd give for a new pair of boots and a plate of porridge!' he thought to himself.

Just then he tripped on something under the snow and fell flat on his face. Curious as to what had tripped him, he felt under the snow and found a boot, but when he tried to pull it out of the snow it wouldn't move. Scooping away the snow he found a leg connected to the boot, and a body connected to the leg, then a head and arms connected to the body. It was a dead body frozen solid in the snow!

The piper looked at the glistening face and frowned. 'That'll be me soon,' he thought, 'if I don't get some food inside me.'

Then the piper noticed the man's boots – they were almost new and made of fine soft leather. 'These will suit me just fine!' he said. 'He won't need them now!' He tried to pull one of the boots off. He pulled and pulled but it was stuck fast, frozen solid. 'Just one thing for it then!' he thought, took out his saw and sawed through the legs of the corpse just above the boots. He put the boots with the feet in them into his bag and walked off down the road imagining how good his feet would feel in the new boots once they has defrosted.

A mile down the road the piper came to a farmhouse. He looked through the window and saw a table piled high with food: meat, fish, potatoes and gravy. His mouth watered at the sight of so much food even before he could smell the delicious aromas from under the door.

He knocked on the door and a farmer answered with a scowl on his face. 'Beggars are not welcome here!' he snapped and slammed the door shut in the piper's face.

'I'm not a beggar, I'm a piper!' he shouted at the closed door and knocked again.

When the door swung open again he said, 'Please sir, it's a freezing night. I have nowhere to sleep and nothing to eat. Please spare me a crust and a place out of the cold.'

The farmer was about to slam the door a second time when the farmer's wife came over to the door. 'Let the piper sleep in the barn!' she said. 'It's freezing out. Off you go to the barn and be off with you first thing in the morning. It's safe in the barn but keep away from the black cow. She sometimes bites strangers!'

The door shut a second time and the piper went off to the barn. Keeping his distance from the black cow who was fast asleep by the door, he settled down on a bed of straw. Just then he remembered the frozen boots and feet and went over to the cow and slipped them under the sleeping cow so they would thaw out by morning.

Before dawn he woke up, pulled out the boots from under the cow, and slipped them easily off the feet and onto his own feet. They fitted just right.

But what to do with the sawn-off feet? Just then he remembered how the farmer's wife had said that the black cow was a biter, and he decided to play a little trick on them.

He slipped the sawn-off feet into his old boots and put them next to the cow's head with the bloody cut stumps pointing towards its mouth and then hid up in the hayloft above the cow and waited.

Soon after this the crock crowed and the farmer's wife came into the barn with a bucket to milk the cow. When she saw the boots in front of the cow she shrieked, 'Husband! Husband! Come quickly! Come and see!'
The farmer rushed over to the barn. 'What is it, wife?'
'Look!' she said. 'The cow has eaten the piper! There's only his boots left!'
'Oh dear,' he said. 'There'll be trouble if the police hear about that. What'll we do?'
'Let's bury the boots next to the barn. Then nobody will ever know!'

They went out behind the barn, dug a hole, threw in the boots and feet, filled in the earth again and piled the snow back on top, then went back to the farmhouse for a glass of whisky.

As they were drinking they heard the sound of bagpipes being played. Looking out the window they saw the piper standing exactly at the place where they had buried the boots, staring at them with cold angry eyes.

'GHOST!' he shouted.
'GHOST!' she shouted.

They shot out of the door and down the lane as fast as their legs could carry them, with the piper walking behind still playing. When they were out of sight he walked back to the farmhouse, sat down at the kitchen table and helped himself to a full and hearty breakfast.

The piper had just finished his breakfast when there was a knock at the door. He opened it and saw an old man, cold and shivering.

'Come in!' said the piper, and warm your feet at the fire.

The old man shook his head. 'I'll come in, but I can't warm my feet. Someone has cut them off!'

Midas's Wish

This is the first of two Midas stories from Ancient Greece, where the king gets the Midas touch. It's a powerful story. Conjure up the greedy and foolish king, and then how wonder and joy turns to horror as he realises what his wish means. You might explain about Dionysus first and what the God of Wine might be like. Talking points: booze and gold.

Once ... there was a king who loved gold. One day he was walking through his forest when he saw a creature with a goat's body and a human head sleeping under a bush. 'I know this creature,' said the king, 'This is a friend of Dionysus, God of Wine. Let us take him to the god's temple.'

So the servants picked up the creature and carried him to the temple of Dionysus, deep in the forest. When they arrived the god appeared, with his little horns poking through his curly hair.

King Midas bowed. 'Great God, we found your friend sleeping in the forest and returned him to you.'
'Why thank you!' said Dionysus. 'That is good. Last night he drank so much wine he just fell asleep. We lost him in the forest. Thank you. Now, what would you like as a reward?'

Midas thought for a moment. 'I just love gold. What I'd really like is to have more gold than anyone in the world. I'd like it that whatever I touch turns to gold. Can you arrange that for me?'
Dionysus grinned. 'Do you really want that?'
'Oh yes please!'
'Then it shall be done.'

The god disappeared with his goat-friend, and Midas set off for the palace. 'I wonder if this will work?' he said to himself. He reached down and touched a flower. To his delight it turned to gold – gold petals, gold stem and gold leaves. He was so happy he started to sing:

Gold! Gold! I love gold! It makes me feel so fine.
Whatever I touch it'll turn to gold
And it will all be MINE!

He walked a bit further, singing his song, then reached out and touched a tree.
A wave of gold rippled out from his finger, along the branches, down the twigs and into every leaf. It was a solid gold tree!
'Wow!' he thought. 'I'm the richest in the world.'
He skipped back to the palace singing his song.

Back home he opened the gate. It turned to gold! He opened the door – it turned to gold!

'I'm hungry,' he said. 'Bring me food!' He sat at a table and waited. They brought him a plate of meat. He picked up a piece and popped it in his mouth, but his teeth broke against the solid metal. 'OWW!' he shouted.

He picked up a cup to drink away the taste. It turned to gold. He poured the wine in his mouth and it turned to thick wet gold. He spat it out on the table – gold mixed with blood!

Then his daughter rushed in. 'What is it, Dad? What's the matter?'
'Get away from me!' he roared.
But it was too late! She reached out to hug him and froze, turned from flesh and blood to a solid metal statue.
'OH NO!' he groaned. 'I love her more than gold! More than anything! Please Dionysus, take my wish back! Can it all be reversed? Please take back my power, and turn all those things back the way they were!'

Dionysus heard and smiled. 'As you wish,' he said.

The daughter and the meat and the wine and the door, the gate and the tree and the flower all returned to normal.

The king smiled at his daughter as she hugged him.
'Why are you crying, Dad?' she asked, puzzled.
'I'm just happy to see you,' he said.

Midas and Apollo

Here's the second half of the Midas story, where foolish Midas shares his bad taste with a god and bears the consequences. Lots of follow-up options on music, taste, points of view and dealing with shame. It works well as a comedy. I love Ted Hughes's treatment in his retelling of Ovid's Metamorphoses.

After his trouble with gold, Midas spent a lot of time in the forest. He made friends with Pan and loved to dance to his pipes. Midas would dance and dance with Pan's half-men, half-goat friends. He was happy there.

Pan was very proud of his music. 'I play the best music in the world!' he boasted one day. 'Better even that Apollo himself.'
Apollo appeared immediately with his cosmic lyre. 'Really!' he said. 'Do you think that?'
'Oh yes,' said Pan, 'definitely!'
'Fine!' snapped Apollo. 'Then we will have a competition! Let the mountain be the judge!'

Midas and the goat men sat and watched. First Pan played his jigs and dance songs. They loved it and jumped up and danced to the tunes. At the end they clapped. 'Very good!' shouted Midas. Apollo looked at him darkly.
'Next!' said the mountain. Apollo picked up his lyre and began to play. He played everything. He played joy and sorrow, light and dark, creation and destruction, love and hate, war and peace, beauty and ugliness. He played it all – everything in the universe. It was so powerful nobody could breathe. It was the most incredible thing ever played before or since. At the end the goat men sat in silence.
'Apollo wins!' said the mountain.
'Oh no!' said Midas, 'I liked Pan's music better. Apollo was so boring…'
'Really?' said Apollo. 'You listen like a donkey, so now you will look like a donkey too.'

Two donkey's ears sprouted where Midas's human ears had been. All the goat men laughed. Midas borrowed a big hat and put it over his ears so no one could see.

From that day he wore the hat all the time. Nobody in the palace knew why, except the barber. One a month he came to cut the king's hair and saw the donkey's ears sprouting from his head. 'Tell anyone,' said the king, 'and you'll be sorry!'

The barber so wanted to tell someone the secret. Everyone in the city was talking about the king and why he always wore a hat. Was he going bald? Was he getting sick? Was it the new fashion? The barber heard all this and was BURSTING with his story but was too frightened to tell, so one day he went deep into the forest, dug a hole, and sang into the hole:

Donkey's ears! Donkey's ears! The king's got donkey's ears!
They're big and hairy. It's just as clear as that!
The king's got donkey's ears. That's why he wears a hat!

He sang it for a while till he felt better then filled in the hole and went home.
Soon reeds grew where he had dug the hole. Sometimes the reeds seemed to be singing:

Donkey's ears! Donkey's ears! The king's got donkey's ears!...

One day some musicians were travelling thought the wood and they cut some reeds to make new flutes. The next day they played in Midas's palace. But when the musicians started to play, they found that all the reed flutes were singing a song of their own. As they blew the flutes they seemed to sing a song:

Donkey's ears! Donkey's ears! The king's got donkey's ears!...

Everybody listened in silence, staring at the king and his hat. Midas stood frozen to the spot, his heart beating like a drum. What should he do? Then he smiled. 'It's true!' he said. 'Look!'
Midas whipped off his hat and everyone gaped at the donkey's ears. There were a few sniggers but then everyone clapped.
'Bravo!' they called.
'Such courage!' said another.
'Long live the king!' said the third.

Midas took a bow, smiled and then started to sing along with the flutes:

Donkey's ears, donkey's ears, I've got donkey's ears!
They're big and hairy. It's just as clear as that!
I've got donkey's ears. That's why I wear a hat!

And that's the end of that!

Theseus and the Minotaur

This killing-the-monster story remains a favourite, combining heroism and horror and a love interest in a powerful mix. Here's a more extended text for you to take ideas from for your telling.

A very long time ago a war broke out between Crete and Greece. The war lasted for ten years – ten years of killing, ten years of looting, of burning and all manner of terror. After ten years Minos, the king of Crete, went down to the sea and he prayed to his father, Zeus. Minos called up to the sky, 'Father, help me! End this war and punish the Greeks for what they have done!' The sky rumbled and flashed, and Minos knew he'd been heard.

In Greece the ground began to shake and as it shook the houses began to topple one on top of another and people inside were squashed by the falling rubble. The place where the water came from – the springs – closed up and there was no more water to drink. The people of Athens were desperate, their city was being destroyed, and they knew that they should go to Minos to seek peace.

When they asked Minos if he had a price for peace, he said, 'You have hurt me. You have hurt my sons and daughters. You have hurt my people. My price is that you will remember that pain, and this is the way – once every nine years, send me a boat with fifteen young men and women on it. I will take those young people and place them in the Labyrinth under my palace. They may enter but they will never leave, for down there, there is the Minotaur, half-bull, half-man. He will devour them! Send them once every nine years and you will have peace. Refuse and it will be war – this time with my father Zeus fighting with me!'

The Greeks agreed, feeling they had no choice, and so it began. Once every nine years a black-sailed ship set off from Athens and sailed through the islands to Crete. Fifteen young men and women were wined and dined by Minos, and then locked inside the Labyrinth never to leave. It was a great weight and a great sorrow for the people of Greece, and one for which they saw no end.

Then a hero came to Greece. His name was Theseus, adopted son to the king. He was a man who liked to fight and who liked to win, and he liked to brag about his victory. The Greeks saw him as a hero, a great hero, and he was worshiped as if he was a king. His strength was famous.

They say the first time Theseus came into Athens, with his long hair down to his shoulders, two workmen on the roof of a house looked down thinking him a woman and said, 'Oh! There's a pretty young girl!' It happened that a cow was walking past him in the street, and they say that Theseus took hold of the cow with one hand and threw it higher than the building where the men were working. After that the men kept quiet. The story spread around the city and around the country, and everyone was pleased that Greece had such a hero.

Well, the year came round, the ninth year, when the black-sailed ship was to sail for Crete. Theseus went to the king and said, 'Father, let me go as one of the fifteen. I will kill this creature and finish with this problem once and for all.'
'No,' said the king, 'it is too dangerous. Anyone who goes there never returns.'
'Father,' said Theseus, 'I have not been defeated by any of the tasks that you have set me, what makes you think that I will fail now?'

So Theseus joined the young men and women and together they sailed down to the island of Crete. Minos welcomed them on the shore and said, 'Welcome, my friends! It is our last night together before you go to the Labyrinth. Let us eat and dance.' And Minos laid on a great banquet. All of his relatives were there, his wife, his sons and his daughters, and they all listened in amazement to Theseus as he bragged about his adventures and his battles and the things that he had done. They were surprised because he wasn't frightened – he was full of confidence. But one of Minos's daughters, Ariadne, looked at him in a different way. She looked at his long hair, his eyes, his nose, his chin. She found it all quite lovely.

When everyone had gone to sleep, she sneaked into Theseus's room, sat on the edge of his bed and gave his leg a little shake.
'Oh, what is it?' he said.
'Theseus!' she said. 'Theseus! Do you think I'm pretty?'
'Yeah, you're quite pretty,' he said.
'Theseus, if you like me, I like you too. Maybe I can help you?'
'Well, what kind of help do you want to give me?'
'Well, I know how to get into the Labyrinth and how to get out, and if you take me with you when you go I'll tell you.'
'Alright then, I promise.'
'This is it, you see – I've got a ball of silver thread and I tie it to the door when I go in, and I just unwind the thread as I go deeper and deeper into the Labyrinth and then, when I want to leave, I just follow the thread back. It's easy really, I'll show you. We can go now if you like.'
'Alright then,' he said. 'Let's go now! Let's do it now!'

Theseus took the ball of thread and went to the entrance of the Labyrinth. He tied the thread around the door lintel and walked down into the passage. Deeper and deeper into the earth, darker and danker, until he could hear nothing but the beating of his own heart and the drip, drip of water from the ceiling to the stone floor.

What happened in the Labyrinth no one knows exactly but later Theseus emerged from the Labyrinth winding back that thread, with blood on his sword and a smile on his face. Ariadne was there. She said, 'Theseus, is it done? Can we go now?'
'Yes,' he said, 'it's done. Let's leave.'

So Theseus took Ariadne and the other young people who'd come with him. They went to the harbour and they took that black-sailed boat and started sailing back towards Athens.

Ariadne was so happy, this was her first boyfriend, and she really liked him. She really loved him! That first night she snuggled up next to Theseus in the boat looking at the stars thinking how romantic it all was, how lovely everything was, how she was going to live happily ever after with Theseus. But Theseus had other ideas. As Ariadne lay next to him in the boat he fell asleep and in his dream he dreamt of the God of Wine – the God Dionysus. In the dream, Dionysus spoke. 'Theseus, this girl, Ariadne, she's very lovely but you don't need her now. You've got what you want and she's what I want, so do me a favour. Tomorrow as you go pass the island of Naxos, drop her off there. I'm having a party there and I'd really like her to come. Do it for me, Theseus, and I won't forget you. Do it for me.'

In the morning Theseus woke and said to his men, 'Sail for Naxos! We'll rest there.' When the boat landed he said to Ariadne, 'My dear, why don't you pick some shells on the beach for a while? We've got things to do and then we'll leave.'
Ariadne said, 'OK, darling, I'll go and collect those shells with the holes in the middle and I'll make you a necklace because I love you so much.'
'Yeah,' he said. 'Great. You do that.'

But when Ariadne had got to the edge of the beach Theseus and his men and the young people got back into the boat and it sailed away. Ariadne couldn't believe her eyes! She called out, 'Theseus, wait! Wait for me!' But he didn't even turn his head. She understood she'd been betrayed. She grew angry and clenched her fist at him, and then called to the sky, 'Grandfather Zeus! Grandfather Zeus! This man! Look what he's done to me! He's taken me from my family! He's promised me and then he's betrayed me! Let his ambition turn bitter in his mouth! Do that for me, Grandfather Zeus, let his pride turn bitter!' And the sky rumbled and she knew that she had been heard and she watched as the black-sailed ship disappeared over the horizon.

As the black-sailed ship carried Theseus back to Greece, he was imagining his welcome. Imagining the crowds in the streets calling his name, shouting his praises. He was thinking how the stories would be passed from place to place, from storyteller to storyteller, until he would be the greatest hero of all Greece. He was so busy with these thoughts that he forgot to change the colour of the sails. Now, the king was waiting for his stepson up on the cliffs above the port, and when he saw the black-sailed ship returning he thought his stepson dead. Such was his grief that he fell from the cliff, twisting and turning through the air and then breaking his back on the rocks below.

In this way Theseus was welcomed home, not with a banquet, but with a funeral. The city was in mourning for their king and he joined the mourners. In this way the taste of victory turned bitter in his own mouth. Zeus had taken revenge for his betrayal of Ariadne.

The Woman of the Sea

This is another selkie story from Scotland, where seals turn to women and back again. As well as the magic of the transformation, there are the resonances of separation and reunion in the family: lots of strong feelings to evoke with the divided family.

One summer evening a young man was walking along a long, wide sandy beach, under a full moon, next to a quiet shining sea. He had been working all day in the fields cutting and binding the hay. Hot and sweaty, he thought to go for a swim. In front of him in the moonlight he heard the sound of strange music and saw a group of women dancing on the beach. He stopped and hid behind a rock as they danced to strange flowing music. It seemed to come from instruments made of shells and seaweed. The women rose and fell together like crashing waves. He had never seen anything so beautiful. Beside the dancers he saw a pile of sealskins, glistening in the moonlight.

'These must be seal-women,' he thought. 'I have heard about them. Sometimes they are seals and sometimes they are human.'

He crept closer and saw that they had no shadows in the bright moonlight. When his own shadow touched the circle they turned as one and stared, like a shoal of startled fish, then rushed for their sealskins, ran into the waves and, slipping on the skins, became seals once more. But one of the seal-women could not find her skin and ran up and down the beach looking for it. The man realised it was next to his feet and, quickly, he picked it up and hid it behind a rock.

'Come here!' he said. 'Let me help you!'
She ran to him, out of breath. 'I've lost my skin! Help me find it!'
'Alright,' he said, and walked up and down the beach with her till morning.
'It's gone!' he said. 'Come home with me instead. Be my wife!'
'But I cannot come. My family is there in the sea! I cannot leave my children!'
'Maybe one day you will find your skin,' he said, 'but till then, come and live with me. Be my human wife.'
She was frightened and nodded, waving out to the cluster of seals bobbing around in the waves as she walked away.

For seven years she cared for his house – cleaning and cooking and looking after the three young children she gave birth to. The man was happy to have such a beautiful wife. Every evening after work it was a delight to come home. Even if she was always a little sad, she never complained and, after a while, he stopped noticing.

Every evening she'd go down to the sea and stare out over the waves. Sometimes a seal head would appear and call out to her from the waves.

Then she would sing to them:

> *Take me home, Mother Sea! Take me home!*
> *Take me home, Mother Sea! Take me home!*
> *Let me be in the waves of your sweet flowing heart.*
> *Take me home, Mother Sea! Take me home!*

In the day, when he was at work, she'd cook and clean, singing that same song to herself as she worked. And in the evening she sang her children to sleep with it in their beds.

> *Take me home, Mother Sea! Take me home!...*

Then, one winter day, she was playing hide and seek with her children on the beach when one of them found a dark skin under a rock.
'Mum, what's this? It's so soft and dark!'
She looked at her home. She looked at her children. She looked at the sea. She hugged each child and ran to the water, slipping on her skin. The next moment there was just a seal head bobbing in the waves. The children ran to the waves and called, 'Mother, come back! Don't leave us!' They watched as a group of seals swam to her and then they all disappeared under the waves.

From that day on the home was sad. The children helped to cook and clean and every evening they'd go down to the sea and sing:

> *Take me home, Mother Sea! Take me home!...*

One day she came for them, with three small skins, and they were gone, leaving the husband alone with only his memories for the rest of his days. On clear nights he'd go to the beach and wait and hope, but the seal-woman never returned.

How Jerusalem Began

I love this version of how Jerusalem began. It is claimed variously by Palestinian, Jewish and Christian communities around the world. You can read another version penned by myself in One City, Two Brothers *from Barefoot Books. It's a fable of love, generosity and sacred place. It is quite a tricky tale to tell. Pay attention to the detail of what happens when and make the physical description really clear. Build up suspense in the first half – what is going on?*

Once, on opposite sides of a hill, were two villages. Between the villages was a field where two brothers farmed together. The elder lived in one with his wife and children. The younger lived in the other village. He was single and lived alone.

Every spring the brothers ploughed the land and sowed it with wheat, then watered and weeded till the grain was golden. Then they cut and threshed the crop, pouring the grain into bags and tying up the straw into sheaves of hay for the animals. Every year they divided it all half and half.

One summer they had just divided the harvest, fifteen sacks of grain each, and had carted off the sacks to their own villages. The elder brother thought, 'My little brother needs this grain more than me. When he's old he won't have any children to look after him. I know what I'll do. I'll sneak these extra bags into his grain store tonight and he'll get a surprise in the morning.'

That night the elder brother loaded three sacks onto the top of his donkey, climbed up over the top of the hill and down to his brother's village, and sneaked the bags into his brother's store.

The next morning the elder brother said to his wife, 'We have just twelve sacks to last us for the year. That's one sack every month. That will be plenty!'
'Hmmm...' she said, 'I thought there was more than that?' She went into her husband's store and came back a while later, puzzled. 'Husband, there are fifteen sacks in there, not twelve. You must be tired after all that work!'

He went and counted and sure enough there were fifteen. 'How strange!' he thought. 'I must have dreamt it. I'll give him the bags tonight.'

So that night he loaded up his donkey and walked to his little brother's house, slipped the three sacks in the store and came home.

The next morning he told his wife what he had done, but when she looked into the store she saw there were still fifteen sacks. 'What are you up to?' she asked, 'Is this a trick?' The elder brother was confused now, but was determined to give away the sacks. That evening he set off down the hill for the third time, towards his brother's home.

Two nights earlier the younger brother was just unloading his sacks of grain when he thought, 'My elder brother needs this more than me. He has a family to feed and I'm by myself. I know what I'll do. I'll give him a surprise!' That night he loaded three sacks of grain onto his donkey and led it quietly up and over the hill to his brother's home, slipped the sacks into the store and came home, smiling.

The next day he noticed that there were still fifteen sacks in his store. 'Strange!' he thought. 'I'll give them to him tonight anyway.'

So the next night he led his donkey up and over the hill to his brother's village and put three more sacks into his store. But the next day there was still fifteen sacks in his own grain store.

'What's going on?' he thought. 'Is this some magic trick, or am I just imagining that I give the sacks away every night? Anyway, third time lucky!'

He loaded up his donkey that night with three more sacks and set off up the hillside. As he climbed he saw someone coming towards him, looking just like his own reflection – a man with a donkey and three sacks on top. As the brothers came closer they recognised each other and understood the puzzle of the sacks, and they were filled with joy at the love they had given and received.

That holy spot where the two brothers met is the holy place where the city of Jerusalem began.

Odysseus and the Cyclops

Here's another popular monster tale from the Ancient Greeks. It's gritty and gory and great for action drama. Tellers can build on all their knowledge of monsters and heroes from digital sources. It's a delightful mixture of comedy and horror and of course a link into The Odyssey.

Once there was a war between the city of Troy and the armies of Greece. For ten long years the Greeks laid siege to Troy, which was finally defeated by the Greeks thanks to the cleverness of one of their kings, Odysseus.

When the war was over, Odysseus set off for home sailing from island to island on the way back to Ithaca where his wife waited for him. On one such island, Odysseus had anchored his boat offshore and rowed to the beach with a party of twelve men in order to look around for food. After a while they came to a cave packed full with sheep and goats. Odysseus and his men waited in the cave for the owner of the sheep to arrive so they could offer to buy a few for their journey.

Around nightfall a huge one-eyed giant, Polyphemus, returned to the cave to check on his sheep and immediately smelled the presence of humans inside. 'Who's in there?' he roared. 'Come out and show yourself or, when I catch you, I will stick you on a spit and roast you for supper!'

Nobody came out, and the cave was too small for the giant to get in, but he reached into the cave, grabbed two of the men and ate them, there and then, as the others listened to their screams. Then Polyphemus blocked the entrance to the cave with a huge stone, impossible for the men to move, and went away to sleep.

The next morning he returned, rolled away the stone, reached inside, grabbed two more of the men and devoured them. Then one by one he let the sheep and goats out of the cave, looking closely at each, one by one, to check there were no men trying to escape.

All day Odysseus thought about the situation and came up with a plan. He took a long wooden club of the giant's and sharpened one end to a fine point. Then, when the giant came back for his evening meal, Odysseus offered him some wine. 'It's good,' he said.

'The best wine in Troy. Try it!'
'I will,' said the giant. 'But tell me, what is your name?'
'Nobody,' said Odysseus. 'My name is Nobody.'
'That's a strange name,' said the giant, and started drinking.

Polyphemus drank and soon became sleepy and fell asleep in the entrance to the cave, blocking it. Odysseus and his men carried the club up to his snoring head and plunged it hard into the giant's single eye. Polyphemus screamed and bellowed and tried to find the men who had done it but they scurried back to the corner of the cave out of reach, where the giant could not get them!

So Polyphemus rolled the stone back over the cave entrance and then ran around the island in a blind drunken rage calling out, 'Nobody has blinded me! Nobody has blinded me!' and all the other giants laughed, thinking he was just being foolish. So no one came to help him.

The next morning the giant came back to the cave, rolled away the stone and started to lead the sheep out one by one. Odysseus and his men had tied themselves to the bellies of the sheep in the cave with their belts. As the sheep were led out the giant felt the coat of each, one by one, to make sure there were no men hiding, but didn't notice the men hanging underneath the sheep.

The men rushed down to their boat and rowed out to the ship. As Odysseus sailed away he shouted out to Polyphemus, 'You think I am Nobody – but I am somebody. I am Odysseus, the great warrior, remember me!'

Polyphemus did remember him. He told the story to his father, God of the Sea, Poseidon, who from that day became Odysseus's enemy, creating storms and trouble for Odysseus on his long journey home.

And that's how Odysseus escaped from the cave of the one-eyed giant, Polyphemus.

The Four Dragons

Here's a Chinese story about how its four main rivers began: the Heilongjiang, the Huang He in central China, the Yangtze, and the Zhujiang. You might show your class a map of China with these four rivers on it as an introduction. Dragons create huge enthusiasms. I like this one because the dragons are helpful and compassionate, as is often the case in that part of the world. It's also a way into discussions about the environment and the importance of water for life.

Once, long ago, there were no rivers or lakes on the earth. The rain came and watered the land, but then disappeared underground.

In those days there were four great dragons who lived in the eastern sky – the Long Dragon, the Yellow Dragon, the Black Dragon and the Pearl Dragon. They were great friends and would spend their days flying and playing together above the earth. One day they were playing in the sky as usual when they noticed people down on earth praying.

'Please send us rain! Let the gods send us rain! If not our crops will die and then we will die of hunger. Please send rain to us so our children will have rice to eat!'

The dragons looked down and saw that the earth was as dry as a bone. Nothing could grow in such soil and all the fields were bare and dry. The people were thin and dying. The dragons could see the ribs of the children and their swollen hungry bellies.
'How poor the people are!' said the Yellow Dragon. 'They will die if it doesn't rain soon.'
The Long Dragon nodded, 'Let's go and beg the Emperor for rain.'

The Emperor was chief of the gods. If anyone could help, he could. The dragons flew off to the Heavenly Palace to see the Emperor but he was not pleased to see them.
'What are you doing here without an invitation?' he said. 'Go back to the eastern sky and leave me in peace!'

The Long Dragon stepped forward and said, 'Please, your majesty, we have seen the sufferings of people on earth. Without rain they will all die. Have pity and send them rain. We come to ask for that.'

'You go away,' the Emperor said, 'and I'll send some rain down soon.'

The four dragons went happily back. But ten days passed, and not a drop of rain came down. The people suffered more, some eating bark, some grass roots, some forced to eat white clay when they ran out of bark and grass roots. Seeing all this, the four dragons felt very sorry, and realised that the Emperor only cared about pleasure, and never thought about the troubles of the people.

'So what shall we do?' said the Long Dragon.
'We have to do something ourselves. He will never help,' said the Yellow Dragon.
'How can we make it rain?' said the Pearl Dragon.
'Is there not plenty of water in the sea where we live? We should scoop it up and spray it towards the sky. The water will be like raindrops and come down to save the people and their crops,' suggested the Black Dragon.
'Good idea!' said the others as they clapped their hands.
'But,' said the Long Dragon after thinking a bit, 'we will be blamed if the Emperor learns of this.'
'I will do anything to save the people,' the Yellow Dragon said.
'Then let's begin. We will never regret it,' said Long Dragon.

The dragons flew to the sea, scooped up water in their mouths and on their wings, and then flew back into the sky, where they sprayed the water out over the earth. The four dragons flew back and forth, making the sky dark all around. Before long the sea water became rain pouring down from the sky.

'It's raining! It's raining! The crops will be saved!' the people cried and leaped with joy.

On the ground the wheat stalks raised their heads and the rice stalks straightened up. The people were happy, but then the Sea God reported what had happened to the Emperor.

'How dare the four dragons bring rain without my permission!' he fumed.

The Emperor ordered his armies to arrest the four dragons. Being far outnumbered, the four dragons could not defend themselves, and they were soon arrested and brought back to the Heavenly Palace.

'Go and get four mountains to lay upon them so that they can never escape!' the Emperor ordered the Mountain God.

The Mountain God used his magic power to make four mountains fly there, and pressed them down on top of the four dragons. Imprisoned as they were, they did not for one moment regret what they had done. Instead they worked some dragon magic, and turned themselves into four rivers, which flowed from the four high mountains down the mountain valleys, crossing the whole land from the west to the east and finally emptying into the sea.

This is how China's four great rivers were formed – the Heilongjiang (Black Dragon) in the far north, the Huang He (Yellow River) in central China, the Changjiang (Yangtze, or Long River) farther south, and the Zhujiang (Pearl) in the south.

So when the rain stops for a while, people can take water from the rivers to make their crops grow. All thanks to those four dragons.

The Land of the Deep Ocean

Here's another careful-what-you-wish-for story, this time from Japan, which plays with the idea of time being different in different places. Our kind hero travels to a wonderful undersea world and lives happily for a while, until restlessness is his undoing. Try and conjure the wonder and wonderfulness of the other world, and then the growing horror as he returns home to his doom! Hear Rafe Martin tell this one on his Yellow Moon *CD.*

Once, on the edge of the great ocean, there was a beach. Next to the beach was a village and in the village was a wooden house. Inside the house there lived a fisherman. He was single, but happy enough and loved spending the evenings with his brothers and sisters and parents, all of whom lived close by in the same village. Every morning he'd row his boat out into the sea, cast his nets, pull them in and sell whatever he caught at the village market. In this way time passed happily.

Then one day he was walking down the beach when he saw a group of children crowded around something, jeering and throwing stones. Coming closer he saw that they had surrounded a huge turtle, which was as long as the fisherman was tall. It was trying to get back to the sea but the children were blocking its way.
The fisherman called out, 'Why do you hurt this innocent creature?'
'Why not?' said their leader. 'There's nothing else to do here.'
'Leave him,' he said. 'Let me give you a few coins and you can go and spend them in the market.'
The children grinned, pocketed the coins and ran off down the beach, while the turtle waddled down to the sea and swam out through the waves. He turned and stared intently at the fisherman before he dived underwater and was gone.

The next morning the fisherman rowed out into the ocean, dropped his nets and waited. It was a gentle, warm day and he fell asleep in the boat, fell into a deep and lovely dream. He dreamt of a beautiful young woman with eyes as green as seaweed, skin as fair as beach sand and hair as black as a seagull's eye. In the dream she rose up out of the water, walked towards him in his boat and touched him on the shoulder. At that moment he woke up and there she was with him in the boat!

'Who are you?' he asked, astonished.

'I am the daughter of the Sea King who lives in the land of the deep ocean. He was that turtle. You helped him and now he will help you. He has sent me to be your bride. If you wish, you can come home with me to live in the Kingdom of the Deep. Would you like that? But if you come you may never return.'

He nodded. He had never seen anything so beautiful. She leaned over and kissed him softly on the lips and he felt his world explode.

Together they dived into the water and, taking his hand, she swam with him down to the deep ocean, down through a tunnel and up unto a vast cave filled with all the creatures of the sea.

'Welcome, Good Man!' the sea creatures called to him. 'Welcome to our kingdom!'

The fisherman and the Sea King's daughter were married and lived happily for a while in the king's palace, playing with the fish and dolphins, swimming out into the deep ocean and exploring the tunnels and caves of the sea bed. The fisherman had never been so full of joy and life.

In this way the years passed and he began to think of his family and friends in the village. He wanted to see them. The more he thought about it the bigger this want became until he could bear it no longer.

'Let me go back home,' he said to his wife. 'Let me see my family again.'

'I told you there was no way back!' she said softly.

'Please! There must be a way. I cannot live here as a prisoner!'

She nodded sadly. 'If you must go then take this box with you – it will protect you as long as you never open it. But believe me, you'd be happier here.'

It was a tiny black box the size of a matchbox.

They swam up to the surface of the sea and the Sea King's daughter led the fisherman to the beach by his village, waving sadly goodbye as he clutched the black box in his hand. He was so excited at the thought of seeing his family and friends he rushed up the beach and into the village.

Then he stopped. It all looked very different. 'I suppose it's because I've been away,' he thought. He looked up at the mountains behind the house. They were covered with tall thick trees! He remembered the mountains as being bare. He looked at the wall around his village. It was made of stone! He remembered it as being of wood. He went to the place where his own house had stood, but there was nothing there. Just an empty field!

An old man walked by.

'Excuse me,' said the fisherman, 'but what has happened to my house? I used to live here but the house has gone. What has happened?'

The old man shook his head. 'I've lived here all my life and I've never seen a house here. You must be lost. What's your name?'

The fisherman told him, 'Taro. My name is Urashimo Taro.'

The old, man looked at him, puzzled. 'Is this a joke?'

'No!' said the fisherman. 'That's my name.'

'There's a story here that long ago there was a man by that name who went out to sea and never returned. His family searched for him but only found an empty boat. They say he was taken by a mermaid, but that's just stories. Anyway, that was long ago but if you don't believe me you can go to the graveyard. His family are all buried there.'

As if in a dream the fisherman walked to the graveyard on the edge of the village and looked from grave to grave. It was true – there was the gravestone of his father covered in moss and lichen. There was his mother's stone. Also his brothers and sisters and the graves of their children and grandchildren and great-grandchildren.

How was it possible? It was as if he had been away not just for three years but for three hundred years. How could it be?

He walked back to the beach and stared out at the sea. He had no home, no family here. Just the little back box in his hand. Maybe that had the clue.

The fishermen carefully slid open the box and as he did so a white light spiralled up out of the box and away over the ocean.

The next moment he felt tired, then there was pain all over his body. It was hard to breathe. He felt his skin shrivel and his hair turn white. Then his skin and flesh was gone, leaving only white bone. As the skeleton fell to the ground it crumbled into dust mixing with the sand on the beach. There was no trace of the man who had once been … Urashimo Taro.

Rama and Sita

This is one of the best-known stories from India from the epic Ramayana tales and works well as a killing-the-monster tale. Conjure up the horror of the demon and the courage of the Monkey God. If you've got a drum, try using it to create atmosphere.

Once there was a great prince, Rama, who lived with his good wife, Sita, in their father's kingdom. But when the king announced that Prince Rama should become king, one of the palace queens plotted against him.

She went to the king and said, 'Your majesty, do you remember your promise to grant me a wish once we were married? Well, I have thought of my wish.'
'What is that?' said the king.
'I wish that Rama be banished from this kingdom forever and never allowed to return. I would rather that my son becomes king and not him.'

The king was sad but he had given his word and so Rama was banished. He left the city and his wife, Sita, went with him, determined to support her husband in this time of need. They lived together happily with Rama's brother, Laksman, deep in a beautiful forest. Rama was skilled with the bow, providing food and protection for Sita and his brother.

Then one day Demon King Ravana of Sri Lanka decided to kidnap the lovely Sita. He sent a golden deer into the forest. When Sita saw it she asked her husband to catch it for her so Rama ran off leaving her alone with his brother.

When Rama shot the deer it called out, 'Help me! Help me!' in a way that sounded just like Rama. When his brother heard this he thought Rama was in trouble. He told Sita to stay inside a magic circle, which he drew on the ground, so she would be safe and then he ran off into the forest, leaving Sita alone.

Moments later an old man appeared in front of Sita asking for help. 'I am tired and hungry,' he said. 'Help me!'

Sita stepped towards him – out of the circle – and at that moment he turned into an eight-headed demon. The Demon King grabbed Sita and flew up into the air, taking her away to his island.

As the Demon King Ravana travelled with Sita, the King of the Birds saw what was happening and flew up into the air and fought with Ravana, but the demon was too strong and, wounded by the many claws of the Demon King, the King of the Birds fell down to earth, dying.

At that moment Rama and his brother, Laksman, came across the bird who told them what had happened to Sita.

Rama and Laksman set off to rescue Sita. On their journey they were joined by many warriors and a race of huge monkeys. Rama sent the chief of the monkeys, Hanuman, to Sri Lanka to look for signs of Sita and to give her his ring.

Hanuman travelled to Sri Lanka, leapt across the sea to the island and found Sita, trapped in prison. When he gave her Rama's ring she knew he was alive and coming to find her.

After that, huge Hanuman started to rampage in the city, destroying many buildings with a huge club until he was shot with an arrow, captured and sentenced to death by burning. But, as the fire was lit it burned the city, not Hanuman. He leapt away from the island and returned to Rama to tell his story.

When Rama and his armies arrived at the shore near Sri Lanka they could not get across the sea but the giant monkeys threw huge stones into the sea, building a causeway from the land to the island.

When Rama and his armies finally reached Sri Lanka the two armies faced each other in battle.

Rama was victorious, and when Demon King Ravana tried to run away he was caught and crushed by two rocks. Inside the rocks were the souls of his daughters who he had murdered. In this way they took their revenge.

Sita was freed and reunited with her husband. After fourteen years away, they returned home to their city and Rama finally ruled as king.

The Building of St Paul's Cathedral

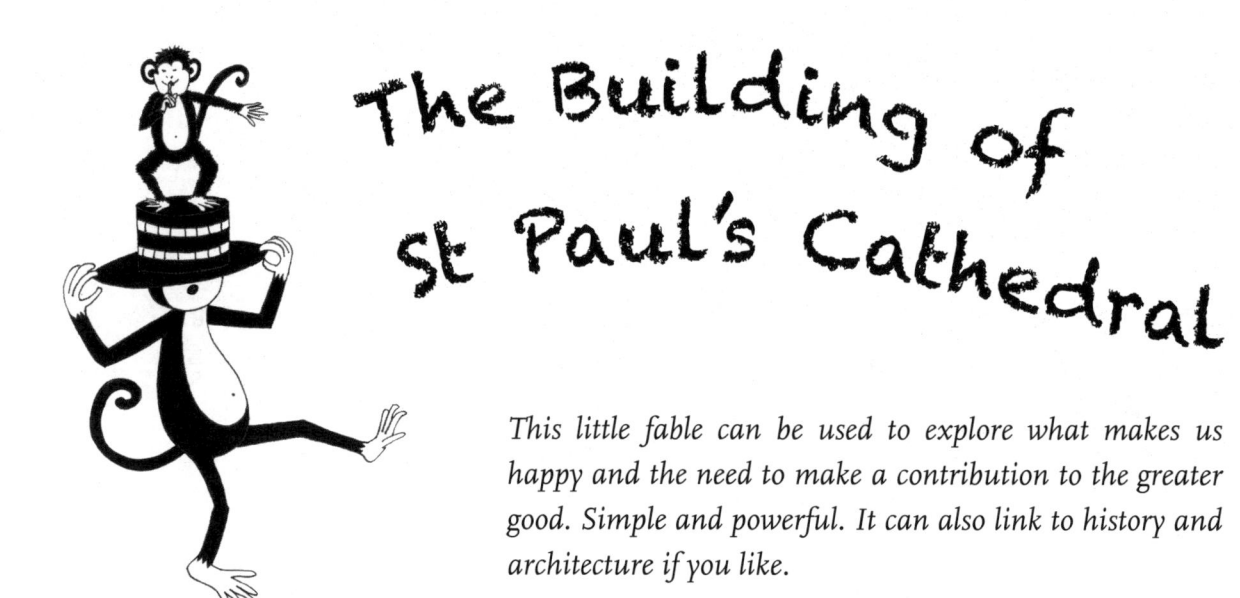

This little fable can be used to explore what makes us happy and the need to make a contribution to the greater good. Simple and powerful. It can also link to history and architecture if you like.

In 1666 London was burned to the ground in the Great Fire of London. Afterwards the architect, Sir Christopher Wren, designed a new building for the heart of the city. It was to be an enormous cathedral, dedicated to St Paul, with a huge domed roof, bigger than any that had been built before. It was to be a place for prayer and meditation.

During the building of the Cathedral, Christopher Wren went to visit the site.
He noticed three men working building a wall – bricklayers – lifting and setting the stone blocks in cement. Two of them were frowning and a third was smiling.

Curious, Sir Christopher went over to the men for a chat. He asked the first frowning builder, 'What are you doing?'
'I'm doing what I'm told,' the builder answered, crossly. 'Building a wall. Isn't that obvious? If I didn't I wouldn't get paid.'

He asked the second frowning builder the same question.
'I'm earning money so that I can feed my family!' he snapped.

Finally, Sir Christopher asked the man who worked with a smile on his face, 'What are you doing?'
'I am building the most beautiful building in London,' he replied with a smile. 'For hundreds of years to come people from all over the world will visit this magnificent building and admire its beauty. They will feel inspired, uplifted and find peace here. I am playing my part in making all that happen.'

If you go to London and visit St Paul's Cathedral you will see that it is still there, still a beautiful place for prayer and meditation.

Which builder would you rather be?

Feathers in the Wind

I heard this story first from the wonderful Doug Lipman. It's from the Jewish tradition and offers a chance to reflect on unwise speech and the spreading ripples of consequences. Evoke the gossiper in a way appropriate to your class.

Once upon a time there was a village. In that village, like most villages, there was a woman who loved to gossip. Every day she would sit with her friends gossiping about the bad things she said others had done. 'Can you believe he did that?' 'Can you believe she said that?' and 'Did you see what he was wearing? A man of his age!' On and on and on she would gossip.

The stories spread around the village and caused much trouble. Friends became enemies, husband and wife became separate, parents grew angry with their children, and all because of the gossip that came from this one lady.

One day the Rabbi asked to see her.
'Will you do something for me?' he asked.
'Of course, Rabbi. What can I do?'
'Please take this cushion, go outside, cut it open and release all the feathers, and then come back in.'
'But why?' she asked.
'Just do as I ask,' he told her.

The woman went outside, slit the cushion open and released all the feathers into the wind. She watched them billow up into the air and away into the distance. She made sure all the feathers were gone and then walked back inside to the Rabbi.
'Job done!' she said. 'Anything else I can help with?'
'Yes please. Just one more thing. I would like you to go out and bring back all the feathers.'
'What? But I can't!' she said. 'They've been blown all over the place – down the street, over the hill and far away. I'll never be able to bring them back.'
'True!' said the Rabbi. 'And so it is with words and idle gossip. Words once spoken can never be taken back. There is no telling how far they will travel and what harm they will do. From now on, I want you to think before you speak.'

And so she did.

Heaven and Hell (1)

This is a well-known Japanese story often found in many Zen collections. I love its simplicity and hopefulness. For the story to work you have to evoke the outrage and anger of the warrior so the audience is drawn into his fury, then the shift to silence and respect as he understands the lesson. May we all learn it!

A samurai warrior, famous for his courage and skill, went to see a wise monk.

'Teach me about Heaven and Hell!' commanded the warrior.

The holy man frowned.
'Certainly not, you are a violent and stupid man. You would not understand!'

The warrior flushed with anger.
'How dare you talk to me like that!' he said.

'You think you are so important!' retorted the monk. 'But you are nothing but a pathetic worm! Go away and leave me alone.'

'Nobody talks to me like that and gets away with it,' said the warrior. 'One more word out of you and this sword will slice through your neck!'

'You dog,' laughed the holy man. 'You wouldn't dare!'

Furious, the warrior drew back his sword and was about to strike, when the wise monk raised a finger and smiled:
'That, my friend, is hell.'

The warrior dropped his sword and bowed.

'Thank you,' he said. 'You are indeed wise, and have shown me my weakness. Thank you!'

'And that,' said the monk, 'is heaven.'

Heaven and Hell (2)

This one is often told within the Christian tradition. Again, it is a simple and enduring image, so work on clarity of description when you tell it.

Once there was a man who, having lived a good life, died and was met at the gates of heaven by St Peter.

'Where would you like to live?' asked St Peter. 'Heaven or Hell?'

'I don't know,' said the man. 'What's the difference?'

'Let me show you,' said St Peter.

They flew down for a while until they came to Hell.

'Look!' said St Peter. 'It's nearly time to eat.'

People were sitting at long wooden tables piled high with wonderful food. But there was something strange about it. Each person had two long wooden spoons strapped to their arms, so that their arms where effectively twice as long.

When the food bell ran they started trying to eat with the spoons, but however hard they tried they could not get a single mouthful of food into their mouth. All the food ended up on the floor as the people wailed with frustration and hunger.

'Those are the spoons of hell,' said St Peter. 'Now let's go to heaven.'

They flew up to heaven and went inside.

'This is heaven,' said St Peter.

The man was puzzled. It looked exactly the same as the last room.

People were sitting at long tables piled high with wonderful food. Each person had long spoons strapped to their arms just as before.

Then the food bell rang.

Everyone picked up up some food in their spoon and then fed the food to the person opposite. Slowly and playfully they fed each other till they were full and satisfied.

'These are the spoons of heaven,' said St Peter.

Chapter 5

Year 5 Stories

The Hunter and the Leopard – West Africa	244
The Boots of Abu Kassim – Iraq	246
Who is the Thief? – Japan	248
Beowolf – England	251
The Tiger's Whisker – Indonesia	253
The Apple Tree Man – England	255
Godmother Death – Mexico	258
The Weaver's Dream – China	261
The Prince and the Birds – Spain	264
Jumping Mouse – Native American	269
Jack and Jackie – Ireland	272
The House That Has Never Known Death – Germany	274
Why the Seagull Cries – Native American	276

SHORTER STORIES:
Luckily Unluckily – China	279
Language Lesson – England	281

NASSERADEEN TALES – Iran
Looking on the Bright Side	283
Stop Eating Sweets	284
Hitting the Target	285
Nasseradeen and the Perfect Wife	286
The Neighbour's Cockerel	288
Nasseradeen's Nail	289
Nasseradeen and the King's Hunting Party	291
Nasseradeen Speaks Truth	292
Nasseradeen and the Light	293
Nasseradeen Teaches Justice	294
Who Do You Trust?	295
Nasseradeen and the Turnips	296
Cause and Effect	297
Nasseradeen Teaches Empathy	297

The Hunter and the Leopard

This is a brilliant African story about cruelty and payback. There's a great text version in McCall Smith's The Girl Who Married a Lion. *I once heard Jan Blake tell this story – it was unforgettable. Here we conjure the environment of the African jungle, the hubris of the hunter and the fierce predator power of the leopard woman.*

Once there was a hunter. He was a proud hunter. He loved to kill the fiercest wild animals – lions, tigers and pumas. The thrill of the danger was like a drug for him. He'd carry the bodies of his kill through the village and show them to everyone.
'Am I not the best hunter?' he'd ask with a smile.
'Oh yes, you are the best!' they'd reply.

One springtime the hunter took time off from his hunting to find himself a wife. Soon he was married and soon his wife's belly began to swell with child. After nine moons a healthy baby boy was born. The hunter was delighted.
'We will celebrate!' he shouted to his visitors. 'At the naming ceremony I will bring a leopard cub and sacrifice it to the gods.'

The people were impressed – to steal a live leopard cub was dangerous, very dangerous. If the mother leopard caught you she would kill you for sure.
'Are you sure?' they said.
'Oh yes,' he said. 'I will do it!'

He trekked off to the deepest, darkest part of the forest and searched for leopard tracks. After a week he found the tracks of a mother and two cubs and followed them, silent as night, till be reached their cave. Hiding downwind he waited for the mother to go out hunting then ran into the cave, scooped up the sleeping cubs, popped them in his sack and ran back to the village where he put them in a cage in his hut.
'Tomorrow,' he said to himself, 'they will die. The naming ceremony of my boy will be remembered for ever.'

Deep in the forest the mother leopard returned to an empty cave. She smelt the smell of the hunter.

'Man!' she growled. 'Are my children still alive?'

She found the hunter's tracks and followed them to the door of his hut. There she stood up on hind legs and peeled off her leopard skin. Inside, was the body of a beautiful young woman with a leopard skin wrapped around her hips. Her hair was long and dark and her eyes black and fierce. Hiding the peeled skin behind a tree, she knocked on the hunter's door.

The hunter opened the door and smiled at her.

'Hello,' he said. 'Who are you?'

'I am lost,' she said, smiling at the hunter. 'I have nowhere to stay tonight. I am frightened, can you help me?'

'Oh yes,' said the hunter, 'you can spend the night in my hut if you like!'

'Oh thank you,' she said, fluttering her long dark lashes. 'How can I ever thank you?'

'Oh, I'll think of something!' he said, grinning. 'Come on in!'

They sat together in the hut and drank some palm wine. In the next room the cubs were whining.

'What's that noise?' she asked.

'I caught two leopard cubs,' he said proudly. 'Tomorrow, at my son's naming ceremony, I will sacrifice them. It will be remembered for ever.'

Suddenly she began to cry. 'Please don't!' she said. 'Please spare their lives! I'll do anything for you if you let them live!'

The hunter was angry.

'Get out of my hut!' he shouted. 'And don't come back till you stop crying. I have promised to kill the cubs and I will kill them!'

She stepped outside for a moment, slipped into her leopard skin and leaped back onto the hunter as a leopard, ripping out his throat before he could reach for his knife. She went to her children, smashed the cage with a blow of her paw and led them back to the cave.

The next morning the whole village waited for the hunter to come, but he could not. They found his body ripped and torn on the floor of the hut.

So it was that the ceremony was remembered in the village for many years. Indeed it is even told by storytellers to this very day!

The Boots of Abu Kassim

This story is hugely popular in the Middle East as a much-loved parable about generosity. Mean old Abu Kassim sees his fortune disappear as his meanness bears fruit. The plot is fairly absurd and can be played for comedy. Let Abu Kassim get more and more animated as his doom deepens.

Once there was a rich man called Abu Kassim. He was a rich merchant but was mean and just saved and never spent. His old boots were full of holes and covered in patches, but he was too mean to buy himself some new ones. They were famous boots. If something needed replacing people would say, 'Now that's just like Abu Kassim's boots!' and everyone would understand.

Abu Kassim was so mean that he only took a bath once a year at the public baths in the centre of town. More than once was too expensive, he thought. One time he was taking his annual bath when, for a joke, someone swapped his old boots for the fine shoes of the Chief Judge, which were left in the next cubicle.

When Abu Kassim had finished his bath he went back to change and saw the fine new shoes. He smiled, thinking the new shoes were a gift, and wore them home happily, thinking how by waiting with the old boots he had saved quite a few pennies.

But when the Judge had finished bathing he saw the old boots with his clothes and knew immediately who the owner was. Abu Kassim was summoned to the court wearing the Judge's shoes.

'You stole my boots!' the Judge thundered. 'So you must pay a fine of 100 dinars, or spend a month in prison.'

It was very painful for Abu Kassim to pay the fine but he couldn't afford to go to jail. He paid the 100 dinars and walked home with his old boots, fuming.

Walking by the river he cursed the boots and threw them in the river.

'I never want to see you again!' he said.

Some fishermen were fishing downstream, and the old boots caught in their nets. The nails in the boots cut the nets to shreds. When the fisherman saw the boots they recognised them immediately.

'Abu Kassim!' they shouted. They went round to his house and threw the boots in through his window.

Abu Kassim had just bought a crate of glass bottles and a case of expensive perfume and had just finished filling the bottles. He was set to make 1,000 dinars from the sale of the perfume in the fancy bottles. Just then his boots flew in through the window and smashed all the bottles to pieces.

'Oh no!' he shouted at the boots. 'How could you do that to me? You have cost me 1,000 dinars!'

He put his wet boots up on the roof to dry but a dog on the roof started playing with the boots and knocked them down onto the head of a woman walking in the street below. She was pregnant and the boots hit her so hard that she lost the baby.

Abu Kassim was summoned to the court and ordered to pay 10,000 dinars to the family of the woman in compensation. That was all of his wealth.

He sold his house and business and paid the fine, cursing his boots as he did it.

Then he went to the Judge and handed over the boots, saying that from this day, whatever the boots did was not his responsibility.

Instead he opened a shoe shop in the market and would stand in the doorway, telling this story when people walked past wearing worn-out boots. In this way his business thrived. From then on he always wore a nice clean pair of shoes.

Who is the Thief?

Many schools have used this Japanese story in conjunction with a 'Crime Scene Investigation' topic for the term. It's a great way of introducing crime-solving plots, and shows how this can be done in an unexpected and interesting way. You can find a lovely text version of this by Susan Klein in Holt's Ready-To-Tell Tales. *Pay attention to the wording of the Judge's lines as you tell this. You have to get it fairly precise for the desired effect. Linger with the moment when the stone is accused and the people protest. Let the audience be puzzled for a while.*

Once there was a city. In that city was a bakery, and in the bakery – a baker.

Every day he'd get up in the middle of the night, mix up the flour, salt, yeast and sugar, knead it into smooth dough and wait for it to rise. When the dough was ready he'd cut it into small pieces and fry them in hot oil to make oilbread. At dawn he'd put the oily breads in a basket and carry it to the market where he would always sell out – they were delicious and a real treat!

One morning he had sold all the bread, and had a pile of crisp yen notes in his basket. He walked up the hill behind the market, sat next to a large stone and counted his money before putting it back in the basket. Then, a little weary, he closed his eyes and fell asleep.

When he woke up the money was gone. Furious, he ran back down to the market calling out, 'There's a thief! There's a thief in the market! Someone has stolen my money! Beware!'

The shopkeepers crowded around him clutching their money pouches tight to their bellies.

'I sold my breads, put the money in my breadbasket and went to sleep by the stone up the hill. When I woke up the money was gone!'

The shopkeepers were frightened now – what if it happened to them? They started arguing and shouting about what to do and even eyed each other suspiciously, wondering if one of the shopkeepers was the thief.

'Let's ask the Judge,' said the baker. 'He'll know what to do.'

The baker went off to the Judge's house and was soon sitting in his front room drinking tea.

'Please listen to my story and see if you can help. I was in the marketplace today selling fried dough. I sold everything and climbed the hill for a rest. I put my basket on the stone there, counted the money, put it back in the basket and fell asleep, and when I woke up the money had gone. There's a thief in the market!'

The judge stroked his chin. 'Tell me again,' he said.

The baker repeated his story.

'Again.'

'So!' said the Judge. 'You sold your dough, climbed the hill, counted the money, put it in the basket on the stone and fell asleep, and when you woke up the money was gone.'

'Yes!' said the baker, feeling a little impatient.

'Let's go to the place where you slept.'

The baker and Judge walked through the market and up the hill to the stone, followed by a crowd of excited shopkeepers. When they were all there, the shopkeepers were chattering excitedly.

'Quiet!' thundered the Judge. 'This is the situation. The baker sold his dough, he climbed the hill, counted the money, went to sleep and when he woke up the money was gone. There is a thief in the market!'

Everyone started talking excitedly at once.
'SILENCE!' shouted the Judge. 'I have thought it all through and the answer is simple. If the baker put the money in the basket and the basket on the stone and then fell asleep, then the stone must have taken the money. The stone did it! That is the solution. Let us arrest the stone.'

All the shopkeepers were shouting at once, unable to believe that the Judge would talk such rubbish.
'QUIET!' he bellowed. 'How dare you disrespect me? I am the Judge. How dare you! You must all be punished!'

The shopkeepers fell to their knees and apologised, all at the same time.

'QUIET!' he shouted. 'Each of you will spend three days in jail for your impertinence!'

'Please, NO!' they all wailed. 'We need to feed our families! Have mercy!'

'Very well,' said the Judge. 'I will show mercy, but each of you must pay a twenty yen fine for your rudeness.'

He shouted at the baker. 'Go and get me a bucketful of hot water. Now!'

The baker brought back a steaming bucket and placed it in front of the Judge.

'Now, each of you put twenty yen into the bucket.'

One by one, as the judge watched, each shopkeeper threw a twenty yen note into the bucket and then went on his way. One by one until ... a young man tossed a note into the bucket. Immediately the judge roared out, 'YOU! You are the thief! Arrest him!'

The judge was right, but how did he know?

(Hint: oil floats on water)

Beowulf

Beowulf is one of the classics of early English literature. The original text is a huge epic poem about killing first the monster and then its mother. It is a hero story about monster-killing, so you have to get into that kind of world. Below are the bare bones: expand it any way you like.

Once, a great Danish king built a great hall so that all of his vast army could eat and drink under one roof. His men were singing and drinking long into the night, which disturbed a ferocious monster that lived nearby – Grendel.

The monster waited until the men were sleeping and then, creeping into the hall, he killed thirty men where they lay. After that the Danes lived in fear of this monster that would come from time to time and take a few lives. No one could think of a way to defeat the monster.

Then Prince Beowulf, strongest of warriors, decided he would fight the monster. He set sail with twelve men and arriving at the Danish king's hall he was warmly welcomed. That evening they held a feast in his honour. Beowulf promised he would kill the monster or be killed trying.

Later that night, when the men were falling asleep, Grendel appeared ready to kill a few men, but Beowulf, not even bothering with a sword, leapt on the monster and started to wrestle him. The fight went on for hours until Beowulf got a firm grip and ripped off the monster's arm and claw. Grendel ran away back to his lake, leaving his bloody arm in Beowulf's hand.

The Danes were delighted with their new hero and sang his praises long into the night, feasting again till morning.

The next night, when all were sleeping, a stronger monster, the mother of Grendel, came to the hall and took away one of the Danes together with her son's claw.

When Beowulf woke up he followed the monster's tracks to the lake. Above the lake on a rock was the bloody head of the kidnapped Dane.

This time, taking a sword, Beowulf dived down to the mother's home under the lake. There was a long and terrible battle. Both were fearsome and fought to the death. In the end Beowulf killed her with his sword and then chopped off the head of her son for good measure.

After this battle Beowulf returned to the Danish court and told his story, and after another feast and gifts of great treasures Beowulf returned home with his men, leaving Denmark free from the fear of Grendel and his terrible mother.

And that's how Beowulf saved the Danes from not one, but two monsters.

The Tiger's Whisker

This gentle and surprising story about patience and understanding comes from Indonesia, and is often told as a parable for parents giving their kids a bit of space. There's a fine telling in Courlander's book of the same name. You need to evoke the pain of the mother, then her skill and patience with the tiger. Pause when the whisker goes in the fire and keep the tension there before delivering the punchline. It's a chance to evoke the mountains and tigers of Indonesia.

Once there was a mother and a daughter. They loved each other and delighted in each other's company, telling each other stories and secrets like two sisters. But, one day when the daughter reached that age when she was no longer a little girl, she stopped speaking to her mother. It happened after an argument about something or other, and the girl just stopped speaking.

'Talk to me!' said the mother. 'Let me help you! Tell me what the matter is. I am your mother.'
But the girl said nothing.
The mother grew angry. 'Don't be so rude. Talk! Say something!'
But the girl said nothing.
The mother started to cry. 'How can you treat me like this after all I have done for you?'
The girl left the room.

Desperate, the mother went off to the wise woman of the forest to ask her advice. Inside her hut, the old lady was sitting on a three-legged stool smoking a long black pipe.

'My daughter won't talk to me! What shall I do?'

The old lady stared long and hard at the tearful mother. 'Bring me a whisker from the angry tiger who lives at the top of the mountain.'

So the mother went home, had a think, made a plan, packed a sack full of meat and climbed up the mountain. She dropped a piece of meat about a hundred paces from the entrance to the tiger's cave, hid behind a rock, and waited. A while later the tiger came out, huge and fierce, sniffing the air nervously. He padded over to the meat, picked it up in his razor teeth, and padded back into the cave.

The mother waited all day and all night behind the rock, then the next morning she put out another piece of meat, this time fifty paces from the cave. Again the tiger padded out, picked up the meat and went back into the cave.

She waited another day and put the meat twenty-five paces from the cave. The next day ten paces.

This time when the tiger came out she showed herself standing and watching in the distance as the tiger took the meat. The tiger eyed her curiously.

The next day she was a little closer and the next closer still until after two weeks she stood outside the cave with the meat at her feet.

As the tiger bent down to pick up his food she stroked his neck and purred to him. He waited for a while before returning to the cave.

The next day she held the meat. The tiger came and ate from her hand as she sang to him. As he ate she reached out slowly and pulled out one of his white whiskers. He was so busy eating the meat he hardly noticed.

That afternoon she returned to the hut of the wise woman brandishing her whisker.
'Here's the whisker,' she said triumphant. 'Take it!'
The wise woman took the whisker and threw it onto the fire.
'Why did you do that?' asked the mother.
'Now you are ready. It took great skill and patience to get that whisker,' replied the wise woman. 'Now use those same skills at home.'

The mother went home and for a week she said nothing to her daughter, keeping busy with other things, just sharing a silent meal every evening. The she started to sing to her at bedtime asking for nothing in return. Slowly the daughter softened and relaxed and with time, in her time, they began to talk again.

The Apple Tree Man

This story is popular among English storytellers, especially in autumn for the apple harvest and in winter during the New Year period. You can find it told in various Traditional folk songs, too. The climax of the story is the final scene when the animals make a fool of the greedy brother. Get the animals and mean brother well into character to make that moment work.

Once there was a farm where a farmer lived with his two sons. The eldest, Jack, was a quiet boy who didn't talk much, but worked hard and well. The youngest, John, was always talking and joking and worked when he wished and not when he didn't. The father loved the youngest most, enjoying his charm and style, and somehow found the elder son a disappointment. The farmer was prudent and careful and saved a great deal of money, which he kept hidden in a secret place. He told no one about it.

In the evenings, when the boys were young, he'd tell them stories around the fire. Their favourite was a tale about talking animals in which all the farm animals talked to each other about this and that.

Sometimes he'd say to his boys, 'If you want to know where my treasure is hidden, listen to the donkey and cow talking at midnight on Christmas Eve. That's the one time when you can hear them talk. They know everything about the farm. Maybe they'll tell you where the treasure is.'

When the farmer died he left the farm and land to John, the younger son. John promptly hired a manager to run the business and lived a life of ease. Jack inherited nothing, and John rented him a small piece of land for the rent of one silver shilling a year. Jack's piece of land was just ten paces square, with a tumbledown cottage, an apple tree, an old cow and an even older donkey. Jack lived there, tending to the tree, making cider from its apples, milking the cow, making cheese from its milk, and growing vegetables to make ends meet as best he could. He cared for the cow and donkey with love, finding them the best food and straw and rubbing oils and herbs into their hides to make them well.

Every year in midwinter, when the cider was almost finished, Jack would pour the cider dregs onto the tree's roots and sing it a song:

Apple tree, apple tree,
I give to you just as you give to me.
Apple tree, apple tree,
Blessings on your harvest!

Every Christmas Day Jack would pay his silver shilling to his brother, who had grown fat and greedy with the passing years.

One Christmas Eve John came to visit his brother's cottage. 'You owe me a shilling for rent,' he said, impatiently.
Jack shook his head. 'Sorry, I don't have any money. Can you wait till I sell the next set of cheeses in a couple of weeks?'
'No!' snapped John. 'Pay up tomorrow or you're out!'

Just then, John remembered his father's story about the donkey and cow talking.
'Wait a minute,' he said. 'I'll tell you what, Jack, you wake me up at midnight and I'll come and listen to your animals. Maybe they'll tell me where my treasure is buried.'

That evening Jack fed the animals, bedded them down in the hut and took the last of the year's cider and poured it over the roots of the apple tree singing to the tree:
Apple tree, apple tree...

Just then the trunk of the tree seemed to shimmer and shift in front of his eyes. One moment there was a tree trunk, the next a man stepped out of the trunk. He was as worn and wrinkled and knobbly as the old apple tree, with skin like tree bark, rosy red cheeks and long green hair. Jack wanted to run, but the apple tree man said, 'Wait, my friend! All these years you have looked after me as if I was your child with love and care. Now it's my turn to look after you. Your father's treasure is buried under my roots. Dig it up and you will be rich. But keep it quiet – your brother is greedy and jealous and he would try and steal it.'

Jack took a shovel and sure enough, down under the roots where he had poured the cider, there was a chest filled with gold. Jack took it and hid it in his cottage and waited.

At midnight he went to his brother's mansion and woke him up. 'It's midnight, brother!'
'Good. Now go away! I want to listen to these animals by myself!'

John went over to the animal hut and peeped in at the window. The two animals were awake. One moment they were mooing and braying, the next he could hear the meanings of their sounds. They were speaking! The story was true!

The cow said, 'Hey, Donkey. Happy Christmas!'
'Thanks, Cow. Happy Christmas to you!'
'What's new with you?'
'Nothing, what's new with you?'
They chatted about straw and grass and the weather for ages while John listened impatiently.
'What about the treasure? What about the treasure?' he thought.
Finally the donkey laughed. 'You know the old man's treasure?'
'Yup!' laughed the cow.
'You know where it is?' asked the donkey.
'Yup!' laughed the cow.
'Are you going to tell me?'
John was excited now. Finally he'd get his hands on the treasure.
'Nope!' said the cow, chuckling.
'Why's that then?'
'Because that selfish so and so, John, is listening at the window and he doesn't deserve it. All his life he's just helped himself and never anyone else. So I think I'll just keep quiet!'
'Good plan!' laughed the donkey.
John jumped up and shouted out, 'Tell me!' but after that all he could hear were moos and brays.

Christmas Day came and Jack went round to visit his brother. 'Happy Christmas, John,' he said smiling. 'Here's your shilling!'
'Where did you get that?' John asked suspiciously, but Jack just smiled.

Within the year Jack had bought his brother's farm from him, and he looked after the land with care and love. And every Christmas Eve he'd go to that old apple tree, pour some cider on the roots and sing to the tree:

Apple tree, apple tree...

Godmother Death

This is a story about trying to trick Death, and learning to accept it. It comes from Mexico and is associated there with the Mexican Day of the Dead. It speaks of issues of poverty and injustice and has a powerful twist at the end. Develop the characters of Death and the son.

Riddle: What has one head, one foot, and four legs? Answer: A bed.

Once, on the edge of a capital city, there was a sprawling shanty of huts and tents where the poorest of the city lived. In one of those huts there lived a husband and his pregnant wife. As her belly grew and grew the worries of the father grew with it.
'How can I look after this child and offer him a good life? How can I give him power, when the poor are powerless? How can I give him justice when all the poor know is injustice? The poor children starve while the rich play with golden toys. How can I give him mercy? For the poor the world is brutal and unmerciful.'

The man's son was born on the Day of the Dead, the luckiest day of the year to be born in Mexico. That same day, the father went off to look for a godmother for him, walking around the streets of the shanty town. 'I want someone,' he thought, 'who can give him those three things: mercy, justice and power.' He put his wish in a song:

> *Who will be godmother for my son?*
> *Who will do that for me?*
> *Who can give him what he needs,*
> *Power, justice and mercy?*

He walked and walked, singing his song. A rich carriage rolled by pulled by four fine horses. It stopped by the father and a rich lady looked out with gold around her neck and furs on her shoulders. 'That's a lovely song,' she said. 'Why do you sing it?'
'I'm looking for a godmother for my son. He was born today, the Day of the Dead!'
'Oh! Well, I could be his godmother. I can give him riches and power.'
'No thanks,' said the father. 'You rich people have power, but know little of justice or mercy. You eat while we starve. That is not suitable for a boy born on the Day of the Dead.'

The father continued on his way, singing the song: **_Who will be godmother..._**
He walked past a woman dressed in rags. 'That's a lovely song,' she said. 'Why do you sing it?'
'I'm looking for a godmother for my son, born today, the Day of the Dead!'
'Oh! Well, I could be his godmother. I can teach him mercy and justice.'
'No thanks,' said the father. 'You are poor so you know much about justice and mercy, but you are powerless. We starve and there is little you can do. That is not suitable for a boy born on the Day of the Dead.'

The father continued on his way, singing the song: **_Who will be godmother..._**
He came across a tall thin woman wrapped up in a dark cloak. He could not see her face.
'Let me be the godmother,' she said in a dark, even voice.
'Who are you?' said the man, with a chill in his belly.
'I am Death!'
He brightened up immediately. 'Death! Mmm.... Death has mercy – when suffering is too much you bring relief. Death shows justice – coming to all whether rich or poor. And Death has power – no one is stronger than Death. Yes, you can be my son's godmother.'

The baby grew into a child and the child into a man. One day his godmother visited him and took him into the woods. 'You see this herb?' she said. 'It is called the herb of life. Take it and crush it and you will heal the sick. Use it unless you see me at the head of the bed.'
The young man nodded.

With this gift the young man became a healer, using his power for good for the rich and poor alike. He became well known and well respected for his powers.

One day the king's daughter fell sick. No healer could help her. Her father was desperate and offered half his kingdom to anyone who could heal her, so the young man turned up at the palace with his herb. When he got to the princess's room he was disappointed – Death was standing at the head of the bed. What should he do?
Then he had an idea. 'Turn the bed around quickly!' he called. 'The princess must face the window!'

They twisted the bed around so that Death was at the foot of the bed and he slipped in a drop of herb before Death could move. Death glowered at the young man and disappeared.

The princess was soon healed and the young man became wealthy beyond dreams. He spent his time in the palace and soon won the love of the princess. They planned to marry but a week before the wedding she fell sick again. He went to her bed with his herb, and again saw Death at the head of the bed. Again he turned the bed around and healed her as Death looked on.

The day after the wedding Death came to visit the young man. 'Come with me!' she said.

The young man followed Death out of town and down a tunnel into the deep earth. They entered a grave filled with flickering lights – some going out and some bursting into life. 'These are the lives of people,' said Death. 'When the light goes out, the life has ended… This is yours.' She pointed to a candle that had almost finished – just a liquid pool of wax was left on the rock.
'No! Godmother! Please show me mercy. I am just married!'
'I have shown you mercy. Twice you disobeyed me and I did not punish you. I have given you power, I have given you mercy. Now it is time for justice!'

Death bent down and blew out the candle.

The Weaver's Dream

I love the way this Chinese story plays with the idea of stories and imagination making dreams come true. It can link into all sorts of art projects, creating the images in the story. Make sure your class knows all about weaving before you tell it. It switches into wonder in the final scene. Tell that with amazement.

Once there was a poor widow who lived with her three sons in a little shack on the edge of town. Every day she sat at her loom weaving – threading the shuttle back and forth between the threads. As she wove she sang:

> *I'm weaving the warp and weaving the thread.*
> *I'll weave and weave until I am dead.*
> *I weave and weave with fingers swift.*
> *My life is weaving – that's my gift.*

Every day she'd weave from dawn to dusk until her fingers were so tired she could work no more. In this way she made just enough money to feed her three sons. Two of her sons thought little of this. Their mother was just the way she was – they had never known any different. The youngest, however, saw how hard she worked and wished he could help.

One night the weaver-mother had a dream. In the dream there was a fine house, a wonderful garden, a glimmering lake and a golden shining sun above high white mountains. When she woke she was delighted by its beauty and resolved to weave it into her next cloth.

Every day she sat at her loom pushing and pulling the threads until, after a year and a day, the cloth was ready. It was the finest thing she had ever made and she was proud as she showed her sons. 'We'll keep it!' she said. 'This is my dream home. When I look at it I will be at peace.'

Just then a wind picked up the cloth and lifted it up out of the window and into the sky, high away onto the hills. The widow cried and cried as her sons clustered around. 'Bring me the cloth,' she said, 'or I will die!'

She took to her bed and refused to eat, just staring at the wall.

The eldest son set off on the path into the hills and after three days he came to an old lady sitting under a peach tree heavy with fruit. Next to her was an old stone horse.

'Where are you going?' the old lady asked.

'To find my mother's cloth,' he said.

'It's been taken by the mountain goddess,' the old lady said. 'But I'll tell you how to get it back – knock out your two front teeth and put them in the stone horse's mouth. Then he will come alive and fly you through the Land of Fire and then the Land of Ice. It's very hot and very cold, but if you live you'll get to the goddess's palace. Then you can ask her for the cloth back.'

The son said he didn't really want to knock out his teeth and asked if there was some other way to get his mother's cloth back.

'Fine!' the old lady said, 'Take this box of gold home and your mother will no longer be poor.'

The eldest walked down the hill with the box of gold, but, ashamed to admit his failure, and rather fond of the gold, he bought a house in a village elsewhere and never went home.

After a while the middle son went off to look for the cloth. He met the old lady and got the same speech.

'I'm not sure about the Lands of Fire and Ice,' he said. 'Isn't there another way?'

The old lady smiled and gave him a box of gold for his mother, and he set off for home. Full of shame and greed, he settled in the same village as his brother.

By this time the mother was as thin as a needle and never smiled at all. The youngest went off in search of the cloth and met the same old lady on the road. She gave the same speech and without hesitation he knocked out his teeth with a rock and stuck them into the stone horse's mouth. As it came alive the youngest son jumped on the horse's back and flew off to the east. They passed through fire and passed through ice, and then came to the palace of the mountain goddess.

The son walked into the palace and saw a beautiful woman standing next to a loom where a weaver was working. Next to the loom was his mother's cloth. He wasn't sure which was more beautiful, the cloth or the woman, but he said, 'Please may I take back the cloth? If not my mother will die.'

'Just a few more hours,' said the goddess. 'I love the picture so much. When we have finished copying it you may take it home.'

The son waited and watched until he fell asleep. While he slept the copy was finished but the goddess could not bear to lose the original. She told the weaver to put it back on the loom and weave her picture into it. The weaver did so and then the goddess rolled up the cloth, woke up the son and gave it back to him.

He flew back to the old lady, took the teeth out of the horse and walked home with the cloth. The mother was delighted. 'Thank you, son,' she said, smiling. 'Oh look! There's a lovely lady there now. I wonder who she is?'

At that moment the wind picked up the cloth and it flew out the window.
'Oh, no! Not again!' said the son.
Mother and son rushed outside, but this time the cloth hung in the air as if held by invisible hands.

As they watched the cloth began to grow – larger and larger until it stretched from the earth to the sky. One minute it was a cloth and then the next minute it was gone. In its place was a golden sun, white mountains, a beautiful garden and, behind them, a wonderful house. Sitting on a seat by the lake was the goddess.

The son was delighted and married the goddess on the spot. The three lived happily in their lovely dream home.

As for the brothers, they lived until they died, never returning to their family home.

Too bad for them!

The Prince and the Birds

Here's a charming Spanish wondertale, with a chance to practise your poetry. It's set in the amazing Alhambra in Granada, so lots of background research is possible here. The prince travels around Spain so you can map out his journeys later. There are lots of twists and turns in this one. Enjoy.

If you were ever to travel from where you are right now, north, south, east and west, until you come to a country called Spain, and if you continued with your journey to a town called Granada and if you climbed the hill in the city you would come to the Palace of Al Hambra, one of the most wonderful buildings on the Earth. If you were to enter its gates and explore its gardens and pools and beautifully decorated chambers, you might enter the Jannat al Arife – also known as the Summer Palace.

You might wander through the water garden with its water channels and fountains, surrounded by blossoms and fruit and vines, or explore the empty rooms of the palace, a labyrinth of arches and wonderful decorated ceilings. Each view breathtaking. Each view a celebration of life and God.

If you were to meet the storyteller who still sells his stories in the palace, and were to ask him for a story, and if he understood that your heart was searching for happiness, you might just be lucky enough to hear this story...

Once, in the city of Granada, at the time of Muslim rule, there lived a king who liked to hold on tight to the things that he loved. He loved his palace, he loved his kingdom and he dealt firmly with anyone who challenged his rule. Heads rolled from those bodies which displeased him.

When his first son, Ahmed, was born, the Royal Astrologer read the patterns in the stars and in the entrails of three eagles and reported the results to the king. 'One day,' he predicted, 'your son will fall in love with a foreign girl from a distant land and leave the palace to win her hand.'

This thought took root in the king's mind. He imagined his son as a young man leaving him and never coming back. He imagined being without an heir to his throne. He imagined a lonely old age. Year by year these thoughts grew and grew until, on Ahmed's third birthday, he ordered that his son should live in the Summer Palace behind closed walls and that he should know nothing of the world of women.

So Ahmed grew up behind closed walls, in a palace of unsurpassed beauty. He spent his time wandering the gardens of the palace, bathing in its pools and gazing from its windows. All he knew was the world of men. They tilled his garden, brought him his food. And they taught him. An old whitebeard was his tutor-teacher and friend. Anyone who entered the palace was sworn to secrecy about the existence of women on pain of death.

When Ahmed reached the age when he was no longer a child, but not yet a man, he became restless. In his dreams he saw images from his early years, the sights and touch and scent of the women who had cared for him. He did not know what they were but he woke every morning with an ache in his belly and a longing for something other than the flowers and fountains and beautiful views. With this longing he became ill and thin and pale.

When news of his sadness reached the king the old tutor was summoned.
'What's the matter with my son?' asked the king, as the whole court listened.
'He is unhappy,' answered the whitebeard, carefully.
'Yes! But why?' snapped the king.
The old man thought for a minute and frowned. 'He wants to marry a dragon and kill a beautiful princess.'
Everyone laughed at the old man's stupidity. Then the king scowled and everyone held their breath.
'You are dismissed!' he shouted.
The old man thanked the king and left the palace with a grin on his face, leaving the prince without his friend and mentor.

From that day Ahmed grew sadder and sadder. He spent his time wandering the gardens and writing poems, which no one ever read. One day a white dove perched on his window sill. Ahmed left corn on the sill for the bird to eat and soon it was feeding out of his hands. Wanting to keep the bird as a friend he popped it in a golden cage, but that evening he saw that there were tears in the dove's eyes.

'What's the matter?' Prince Ahmed asked. 'Don't you like your cage?'

'I miss my Love,' said the bird.

'What's Love?' asked the prince.

'Misery for one and happiness for two,' answered the bird. 'Good when together and sad when apart. Please let me go!'

The prince opened the cage and the dove flew away, leaving the prince deep in thought. 'Maybe that's why I am sad,' he thought. 'Maybe I need Love too?'

A few days later the dove returned to the palace. 'Now I can help you,' it said. 'In a castle to the north there is a sad and lonely princess, as fair as a field of ripe wheat, with eyes as bright as cornflowers. Why don't you write her a letter?'

The Prince sat and, putting pen to paper, he wrote her a poem. The dove took it and flew off.

A while later the dove returned at dusk, but as it approached the window a huntsman's arrow flew up from the field below and pierced its heart. It fell onto the sill, a bundle of white feathers and red blood, and died in the prince's hands. Around its neck the prince saw a necklace and locket. When he opened the locket there was the face of a woman as fair as a field of golden wheat, with eyes like cornflowers.

That evening he slipped out of the window, down the drainpipe and out into the garden to the old hollow oak where the wise old owl lived. Prince Ahmed showed the owl the locket and asked for help.

'I will take you to my aunt in Seville,' said the owl. 'She is the wisest old bird I know.'

Together they left the garden and climbed the mountains until after weeks of journeying they reached Seville. The owl aunt was perched in the attic of a fine palace when they arrived. The prince explained his problem.

'Go and see my uncle, the crow, in the mosque minaret,' she said. 'He knows everything.'

They went to the top of the Seville minaret. The prince explained the problem again – about the princess and the wheat and the eyes like cornflowers. He showed the crow the locket.

'What's her name?' asked the crow.

'I don't know,' said the prince.

'You are in love but you don't know her name?'

'Yes. Is that unusual?'

'Most unusual!' said the crow.

'But if you know everything,' said the prince, 'then you must know what to do.'

'I do know almost everything,' said the crow, 'but I haven't thought about Love for years.

Better go to the bird at the foot of the minarets of Cordoba. He knows even more than me. He'll know what to do.'

They travelled to Cordoba and at the foot of the mosque was a parrot. A thousand people were listening to the parrot speak.
'A parrot!' said the prince to the owl. 'Can this be the one?'
'Shh!!' said the parrot's assistant. 'This is Professor Parrot, who is a thousand years old.'
The prince waited and waited till the talk was over, then he explained the problem to the parrot.
'Oh!' said the parrot, 'that must be Princess Algeduna. She is locked up by her father and he lets no one see her because he wants to choose her husband when the time is right.'

The parrot flew off to the castle where the princess was held. He perched on a window sill and watched. She was reading a letter and crying.

'I bring you good news,' said the parrot. 'A message from the Prince of Granada.'
'Ahmed!' she cried. 'I have his poems here. They are lovely. How terrible that we shall never meet!'
'Look down there, princess!' said the parrot, pointing with his claw to the street.
'You see that young man with his headscarf on? That's Prince Ahmed.'
She smiled from head to toe.
'Tell Ahmed to get ready. Tomorrow I will be seventeen and all my suitors will do battle for me. Give him my scarf and ask him to fight for me.'

How could he fight in the tournament? He had no armour and no horse, no sword!
At that moment a large white bird appeared.
'This is Cousin Stork,' said the parrot. 'He will help you.'

Prince Ahmed climbed on the stork's back and they flew to a cave. Inside the cave were a horse and armour and lance and sword. Soon he was ready and rode to the tournament with the princess's scarf around his shoulders. His armour and sword were from a magician and had great power.
'Only until midday,' said the stork, 'will the armour's spell protect you, then you are on your own.'

All morning Ahmed fought and none could defeat him. But the king was unhappy with the thought of a Muslim husband for his daughter and rushed at the prince himself, shouting. The horse shied and knocked the king to the ground.
'Oh no!' thought Ahmed. 'Now I've lost any chance of marrying her!'

He ran back to his cave and returned the next day dressed in rags and sneaked under the princess's window. The princess was sobbing her heart out, thinking she had lost her prince.

Prince Ahmed sang to her – all the poems he had written in his first letter and all those he had imagined since. She sat up and called out for him – 'Where are you?'
'At your feet forever,' he said.
'What's going on?' demanded the king, hearing the noise.
'Only the beginning,' said Ahmed. 'This is a happy beginning which never ends, always coming back from time to time.'

Two birds flew down, picked up the prince and princess and carried them off to the Summer Palace. And there they lived, husband and wife, king and queen, mother and father, delighting in each other's love until the day they died.

Jumping Mouse

This is one of the most popular First Nation stories among British storytellers. It has a marvellous, surprising plot, and a challenging set of learnings. It can be told quite gently with attention to the voices of the various animals.

Once there was a mouse. He was a busy mouse, doing this and doing that. But every now and then he'd stop and listen. There was a roaring sound somewhere. He wasn't sure if it was in his head or out there in the world.

He asked another mouse, 'Do you hear a roaring in your ears, my brother?'

'No, no,' answered the other mouse, 'I hear nothing. I am busy now. Talk to me later.'

He asked another mouse the same question and the mouse looked at him strangely, 'Are you foolish, mouse? What sound are you on about?'

After that Little Mouse stopped asking but he didn't stop wondering and every now and then he'd stop and listen to the wonderful roaring, always there, quietly as if in the distance.

One day he decided to go off and find where the noise came from. He went off through the long grass in the direction of the sound. It got louder and louder but he still couldn't see what it was. Then someone said, 'Hello!' It was a raccoon. The mouse had never seen one before. Little Mouse was about to scamper off when the raccoon said, 'Don't be frightened. I mean you no harm. Tell me, Little Mouse, what are you doing here all alone?' Little Mouse said, 'I hear a roaring in my ears and I am trying to find out where it comes from.'

'That roaring in your ears,' replied the raccoon, 'is the river.'

'The river?' said the mouse. 'What is a river?'

'Walk with me and I will show you the river,' Raccoon said.

Little Mouse was scared, but he was determined to find out once and for all about the roaring. 'All right, Raccoon, my brother,' said the mouse. 'Lead on to the river. I will walk with you.'

Little Mouse walked with Raccoon. His heart was pounding in his breast. The raccoon took him along many new paths and Little Mouse smelled the scent of many things that he had never smelt before. Finally, they came to the river. It was huge and for the mouse it was amazing. He'd never seen a river before. 'Wow!' Little Mouse said, 'I never imagined anything like this!'

'It is a great thing,' answered the raccoon, 'but here – come and meet my friend.'

In a smoother, shallower place was a lily pad, bright and green. Sitting upon it was a frog – almost as green as the pad it sat on. 'Hello, little brother,' said the frog. 'Welcome to the river.'

'I must leave you now,' said the raccoon, 'but do not fear, little brother. Frog will care for you now.'

'Who are you?' Mouse asked. 'Are you not afraid of being that far out into the great river?'

'No,' answered the frog, 'I am not afraid. I have been given the gift from birth to live both above and in the river. This is my home.'

'Amazing!' said Little Mouse.

'Would you like to know more?' Frog asked.

'Yes please!' said Little Mouse.

'Then try jumping. Jump as high as possible and see what happens.'

Little Mouse started jumping. Every time he jumped he saw the peaks of some beautiful mountains in the distance. He had never seen mountains before but he thought they looked wonderful. 'What are those things up in the sky?' he asked Frog.

'Those are the sacred mountains. Now you have seen them. That is good. Now you can go back to your people with a new name and tell them what you have learned. You are Jumping Mouse.'

Jumping Mouse returned to the world of the mice and tried to tell everyone about his journey and his new name and the river. But no one would listen to him at all. They were busy with food and families and thought him a bit strange. In his mind, Jumping Mouse kept thinking of the beautiful mountains.

The images were deep in his mind and one day he decided to go and climb them. He walked and walked under the cover of the long grass till he came to the foot of the mountains. Here there was no long grass and no bushes for cover. He looked up in the sky and saw eagles circling. He knew they were dangerous. He knew he would be safer hidden in the long grass, but he was determined and he ran off across the bare ground. He ran and he ran, ready at any moment to be caught by an eagle, till he came to a tree. Under the tree the eagles could not see him, so he sat and rested.

He must have fallen asleep because when he woke up there was a buffalo next to him lying on the ground in the shade.

'Hello, my brother,' said the buffalo. 'Thank you for visiting me.'

'Hello, Great Being,' said Jumping Mouse. 'Why are you lying here?'

'I am sick and I am dying,' Buffalo said, 'my eyes are weak and I can see little. Only the eye of a mouse can help me. But I don't know what a mouse is. Do you know?'

Jumping Mouse thought about it. 'He will die,' thought Jumping Mouse, 'if I do not give him my eye. He is too great a being to let die.'

So Jumping Mouse went back to where the buffalo lay and said, 'You, brother, are a great being. I cannot let you die. I am a mouse and I have two eyes, so you may have one of them.' The minute he said it, Jumping Mouse's eye flew out of his head and the buffalo was healed and could see. He jumped to his feet. 'Thank you, my little brother,' said Buffalo. 'I know of your quest for the sacred mountains and your visit to the river. Now I will protect you. Run under my body as you climb the mountain and you will be safe from the eagles.' They climbed and they climbed with Little Mouse safe under the buffalo's shelter, then the buffalo said, 'Now you must go alone. Goodbye, little friend!'

Jumping Mouse was just looking around when he saw a wolf lying sick on the ground. 'Hello, Brother Wolf,' Jumping Mouse said.

The wolf's ears pricked up and he looked about. 'Oh yes, I am wolf. But not for long. Soon I will die without a mouse's eye.'

Jumping Mouse thought carefully. Could he lose another eye? How would be continue with no eyes? But something inside him said that it was the right thing to do so he said, 'Please take my eye so you can be healed.' As he spoke his eye flew out of his head and the wolf was made whole.

Tears fell down the cheeks of Wolf, but Jumping Mouse could not see them, for now he was blind. 'Thank you, little one,' said the wolf. 'Now let me take you further on your journey. My eyes can be your eyes.'

The wolf guided Jumping Mouse through a pine forest till he came to a lake.

'I must leave you here,' said Wolf.

'Thank you, my brother,' said Jumping Mouse. 'But although I am frightened to be alone, I know you must go.'

Jumping Mouse sat alone there trembling in fear. It was no use running, for he was blind. He knew an eagle could easily catch him now. He felt a shadow on his back and heard the call of an eagle. The next moment he blacked out. Then he found himself up in the air. He opened his eyes and he could see again. He saw the view from high above the earth.

'I can see! I can see!' said Jumping Mouse.

Something flew toward him and said, 'Let the wind carry you, Jumping Mouse. Let it carry you!'

He flew higher and higher, looking down over the mountains and the lake and the wolf, the buffalo, the frog by the river and the mice down in the long grass.

In his mind Jumping Mouse heard Frog's voice saying, 'You have a new name now. You are Eagle.'

Jack and Jackie

This Scottish story has the power to get your audience's attention where other stories fail. The shock and curiousness of gender-changing makes the story work easily. If you get a chance, hear the great Ben Haggarty tell this delightful parable about storytelling. It works well if told with glee. It's always fun to imagine gender-swapping – lots of talking points.

Once there was a boy called Jack. Once a month in his town the Lord of the Manor would organise a feast and everyone would be invited. The only thing was, once you were sixteen you had to tell a story or sing a song.

The day after his sixteenth birthday Jack went off to the feast and listened to all the stories as usual, but when it was his turn to tell a story he just went blank.
'I don't know any stories,' he said.
'Well sing us a song!' said the Lord.
'I don't know any songs.'
'Poems?'
'No.'
'Then go down to the river and get us some water to drink.'

Jack slunk out of the room with a bucket and went down to the river. It was icy down there and he slipped on the ice. His feet went up and his head went clunk on the ice. Everything went dark.

When he woke up he felt strange. His body felt different. Rounder. Softer. He felt around under his shirt and ... he was a girl! He had all the things that girls had!
'Gosh, what shall I do?' he thought, panicking.

Just then a young man came along and asked Jack if she was OK.
'Yes ... er ... no,' said Jack, 'I'm a bit cold and lost, can you help?'
'Sure,' said the man, a little flustered. 'What's your name?'
'Er ... I don't know. Maybe Jack ... or ... Jackie!'
'And what are you doing here, Jackie? This is no place for a young woman.'

'I don't know.'
'You don't know? Are you sick?'
'I don't know.'
'So come back to my house. My mum will look after you.'

Jackie walked back, shivering, with the young man and his mum put her to bed with a hot drink. When she woke up they dressed her in a dress and gave her a meal.
Jackie stayed there helping around the house and in the kitchen and was soon like one of the family.

A couple of years went by and the man asked her to marry her.
'Yes!' she said, and so they wed.

Soon there was a son and then a daughter and then another son and Jackie loved them more that her own life, cooking and cleaning and taking care of them when they were sick.

Then, one winter evening, she went for a walk with them by the river. One moment she was admiring the view, the next minute she slipped and her feet went up over her head and her head went clunk on the ice. Everything went black.

When she woke up she felt different – stronger, younger. She felt inside her dress and ...
!!! She was a young man again down by the river with that old bucket.

Jack rushed back to the banqueting hall.

'You'll never guess what happened to me!' said Jack as he rushed in.
'Where's the bucket?' asked the Lord of the Manor. 'You had to bring water instead of your story.'
'Forget about that!' said Jack. 'Listen to what happened to me!' And he explained about the ice and everything that happened. Everyone listened, amazed and incredulous.

At the end of the story the Lord laughed. 'Wonderful story, Jack!' he said, patting him on the back. 'You can tell that one as often as you like.'
'But it's true!' said Jack.
'It is truly a great story!' said the Lord. 'And you are a great storyteller!'

And that's how Jack started telling stories.

The House That Has Never Known Death

Here's another story about death. There are many versions of this around the world, including the famous Mustard Seed parable of the Buddha. I came across this Saudi version in the amazing Arab Folktales *by Inea Bushnaq.*

Once there was a forest. On the edge of the forest was a village. In the village was a hut and in the hut lived a young couple and their little boy.

Every day the husband would go out hunting in the forest. Every day the little boy would say, 'Daddy! Daddy! Let me come with you!' and every day his mother would say, 'No! He's too young. It's too dangerous.'

Then one time the mother was away and the hunter said, 'OK, son. This time you can come with me.'

They walked into the forest and soon were on the tracks of a gazelle. They came closer and closer until the hunter could see his prey between the trees.
'Just wait here, son, and I'll shoot the gazelle. Then I'll be back.'
'OK, Dad.'

As the little boy waited for his father to return a snake slid out of a tree and bit him on the neck. By the time the father had returned the little boy was dead. The hunter wrapped his son's body in a blanket and carried him home to the village.

When he got back his wife was waiting for him.
'What have you got there?' she asked.
'This is a gazelle that I caught today.'
'Really?' she said. 'Show it to me!'

'There's something I need you to do first, Wife, before I show it to you. I want you to get a cooking pot from another house. A good big one. But it must be from a house that has never known Death. Go around the village and see if you can find me the pot.'

She went to the first house and knocked on the door. A young woman answered. 'Has your house ever known Death?' asked the hunter's wife.
'Yes,' replied the woman. 'About a year ago my father died in this house. I still miss him.'
She went to the second house and again a woman answered.
'Has your house ever known Death?' asked the hunter's wife.
'Yes,' replied the woman. 'My husband died here last year and I am a widow.'

She went to the third house and yet another woman answered the door.
'Has your house ever known Death?'
'Yes,' replied the young woman. 'My baby son died here. It was painful. Even now I grieve.'

The hunter's wife went from house to house and every household had a story of Death. Finally she returned home, her heart full of the tears of every house she had visited.
'I'm sorry, husband. I've been to every house in the village and in every one I heard a story of Death. Death has come to every house.'
'I know,' said the hunter. 'And now you are ready to see what I have in my blanket. Now it is our turn.'

He showed her their son's body and quietly, together, they prepared for his funeral.

Why the Seagull Cries

This is a curious little Raven story from First Nation America. It's full of learnings and levels of meaning. What do we cling to? Why do we suffer? What does it take to let go? All this and more can be found in this tale. Tell it with clarity to the characters of Raven and Seagull, and if you can, practise making a cry like a gull!

In the beginning when the world was new, each animal was given a job. One was in charge of the earth, another in charge of the wind, another in charge of the sea. There was one for clouds and one for rain. The job of looking after light was given to Seagull.

Seagull was so pleased about his job. 'I have the most important job!' he'd brag to the others. 'Without light nothing else can work.'

All of the light in the world was kept in a little box which Seagull looked after, keeping it tightly closed under his wing. He kept it so tightly closed that no light at all could get out. He felt important. He felt good. He felt in control.

The other animals were less happy with the situation. Without light they bumped into each other all the time. Predators couldn't see who to hunt and their prey didn't know who to run from. It was very confusing. There was no light for plants to grow so vegetarians were hungry. Birds flew into trees by mistake. Rabbits went down the wrong rabbit holes. The whole thing was a big mess!

So the animals got together and tried to figure out what to do.
'We have to get Seagull to let out a bit of light from that box!' said Fox.
'I'll talk to him,' said Mouse, who went over and asked very nicely, 'Please, Mr Seagull, would you let some light out of your box? We can't see anything and it's much too dark. Pleeeease!'
Seagull shook his head. 'I'm in charge and I decide what happens to the light. Not you, little mouse!'
Mouse went back and told them what had happened.

Bear got cross. He went over and shouted at Seagull, 'You are not doing your job right! We need the light! Open the box, you foolish bird!'
'If I was so foolish then why have I got such an important job,' pouted Seagull. 'You mind your own business!'

Hyena had a go. He went over and started howling and crying. 'Please, Mr Gull, please give us some light! My family is so hungry. Awww! Awww!'
'Too bad!' said Seagull. 'I'll give you some light when I'm good and ready and not a moment before.'

Animal after animal tried but Seagull would not listen and left them all in the dark. It was looking bad for the world. Life wouldn't last long without light.

Then tricky old Raven croaked up and said, 'I'll sort it out. You leave it to me. Just get me a thorn and I'll sort it.'

Crow bought a long sharp thorn and gave it to Raven, then Raven walked over to Seagull who was strutting on the beach. Raven crept up as silent as a shadow and stuck the thorn into Seagull's foot.
'Aww! Aww! Aww!' cried Seagull. 'Help! Help! My foot hurts!'
'Oh you poor thing!' croaked Raven. 'Let me help you.'
He pushed the thorn further into the foot.
'AWW! AWW! AWW! That hurts even more! Why did you do that?'
'Sorry,' said Raven. 'But I couldn't see properly. Could you open your box just a tiny little chink so I can see, then I'll be able to see what I'm doing.'
'OK,' cried Seagull and opened the box so that just a tiny line of light could come out. Raven pushed the thorn in even further.
'AWWWWW! AWWWW! AWWWW! That's even worse! You are hurting me too much!'
'So sorry,' croaked Raven. 'I just need a bit more light. That wasn't enough.'
Seagull opened the box a bit more and Raven pushed the thorn really hard.
Seagull was crying now. 'It hurts! It hurts! Please make it stop! Now! Please! Now!'
'Open up the lid so I can see and it'll be fine.'

Seagull was in such pain that he threw the lid right open and out came all the light in a fiery ball and went up into the sky. There was light everywhere but his box was empty.

Raven chuckled, went back to the animals and took a bow.

Seagull called after him, 'What about me? What about me?'

'What about you, you stupid bird?' he said and flew off back to the forest.

And that is how light came into the world.

Now, even today, you can still hear Seagull cry, because of the pain in his foot, as the thorn is still there.

Seagull also cries with sadness at the loss of his most important job: he was once keeper of the light.

Luckily Unluckily

By the sixth year of school, children are getting old enough for a little philosophical distance, and here is a great story for that about things not being quite what they seem. Tell it slowly with attention to the character of gossip and the wise granddad. Ensure a knowing narrator's voice.

There was once a village and near that village was a farm. On that farm there lived a farmer, his wife, his mother and father, and his son. One day, the son was out in the fields when he caught a fantastic, wild, white horse. He took it home and all the villagers crowded around.

'Lucky you,' said the villagers, 'to catch such a fantastic horse!'

The son grinned, but his grandfather went over and put his hand on his grandson's shoulder. 'This is maybe not so lucky,' he said. 'Maybe not so lucky.'

The next day the son tried to ride the horse. It jumped and jerked until the son was thrown from its back, breaking the boy's leg in several places. The villagers crowded around as they carried the boy off to the hospital.

'I see what you mean,' said the boy to his granddad, who was walking by the stretcher. 'If I hadn't caught the horse I wouldn't have broken my leg.'

'That was so unlucky,' said the villagers, 'breaking your leg!'

'Maybe not so unlucky. Maybe not unlucky at all,' said Granddad.

A few weeks later war broke out. Soldiers came to the village and rounded up all those who could fight. They did not take the boy with the broken leg.

'I see what you mean,' said the boy to his granddad. 'If my leg wasn't broken I would be sent off to war.'

'Lucky you, not to get taken to war!' said the villagers.

His grandfather stroked his beard. 'Maybe not so lucky,' he said.

A few weeks later a terrible sickness came to the village and many died. The boy was taken to his bed very ill while his granddad watched.

'I see what you mean!' said the boy. 'If I was away at war I wouldn't be sick.'

'Unlucky you, to get sick!' said the villagers.

'Maybe not so unlucky,' said his grandfather.

A nurse came to the house to nurse the boy. They fell in love and in time were married.

At the wedding the boy said to his granddad, 'I see what you mean. If I hadn't been sick I wouldn't have met her.'

'How lucky you were!' everyone said.

And this time his grandfather smiled happily and said nothing.

In time the couple had a baby boy. The baby grew into a fine man. One day, that man was in his field when he caught a fantastic, wild, white horse.

'Lucky you!' said the villagers.

His father stroked his long, white beard. 'Maybe not so lucky,' he thought. 'Maybe not...'

Language Lesson

Tell this story if you think your class will get the joke! Build up the tension as the cat approaches and we imagine the worst, then the jump and then the joke.

Once upon a time there was a family of mice living in a nest in a hedge by a field of grass. Every morning they went off to mouse school and studied. They learned about cheese and seeds and nits and nests and all sorts of things that mice need to know. There were lots of lessons about cats and how cruel they were – how they'd play with little mice for hours just for fun before killing them.

'Keep away from cats!' said their teacher, again and again. 'They are your worst nightmare.'

They also had to learn new languages, but they didn't like that much. They'd come back home and moan about the French lessons and the German lessons.

'It's so boring, Mum!' they'd say. 'And what's the point? We just want to live in this little hedge, not travel the world. Why would we want to travel the world? We might meet a cat!'

The mother mouse shook her head. 'It's always good to learn a second language. You never know when it'll come in handy.'

Every afternoon they went out foraging for food, collecting seeds and grains from the fields and woods nearby.

Every evening they heard stories from their gran about the Big Cat who sometimes caught little mice and ate them up.

'If you ever see a cat, or smell a cat, then hide!' she said. 'And if you can't hide then run! And if you can't run then burrow! A cat will eat you up slowly. They are cruel and terrible. There's nothing worse than a cat.'

One such afternoon one of the little mice was eating grain from the top of a stalk of wheat when it saw a big, black cat come slinking across the field towards their nest.

Oh n-n-n-no!' he squeaked. 'It's a big cat coming this way. It's a cat!'

All the little mice rushed back to their nest deep in the hedge and snuggled up together with their mum, trembling with fear. They imagined being eaten, slowly one by one, bit by bit. Little mouse tears dripped from their eyes.

'Quiet!' whispered their mum. 'He's coming!'

The cat was close.

He sniffed around the hedge.

He sniffed around the entrance to the nest.

He pushed his nose into the hedge, slowly, until it was an inch away from their nest with the terrified little mice inside.

He knew there was something there.

He wasn't sure what it was.

Maybe a snake that would hurt him?

Maybe a rat that would bite him?

Maybe something for him to eat?

Cautiously, he waited and watched to see what would happen.

Inside the nest, the mice hearts were beating. They were shaking. They were dead meat.

Just then the mother mouse took a deep breath and went, 'WOOOF WOOF WOOOF WOOF!' as loud as she could.

The cat jumped up and ran off across the field to the other side.

'Wow!' said the little mice. 'Mum! That was amazing!'

'You see, children,' said the mother mouse. 'It is really important to learn a second language. You never know when it might come in handy!'

NASSERADEEN TALES

Nasseradeen is a much loved foolish/wise folk hero from Iran. His character and stories are popular throughout the Arab world too, where he usually goes by the name of Juha, and Hodja in Turkey. Here are a few samples. Barefoot Books have a good collection of Nasseradeen stories if you want more. You could divide the class into groups of three, give each group a story and then spend the morning swapping stories and talking about their puzzling meanings.

Looking on the Bright Side

Once there was a spate of burglaries in Nasseradeen's street, so Nasseradeen went to bed with a bow and arrow next to his bed, just in case.

One night a noise in the garden disturbed him. He jumped up with his bow and arrow in his hand and looked out of the window. In the garden was a white shape. He couldn't quite see what it was but, just in case it was the burglar, he took a shot at it with his bow and it disappeared. Then he went back to sleep.

The next morning Nasseradeen got up and went out into the garden to see if there was any sign of the burglar. There in the mud, under the washing line, he saw his white nightshirt pinned to the ground with his arrow. He picked them up and started to laugh.

His wife looked out from the window and saw her husband holding his torn gown and the arrow.

'What are you laughing for, you stupid old fool?' she called. 'You've torn your nightgown and it's covered in mud.'

'But wife,' he said, grinning from ear to ear, 'I'm so fortunate. This is such good luck!'

'Why's that?' she asked, curious.

'I'm lucky to have escaped with my life. Imagine what would have happened if I'd been in the nightshirt at the time!'

Stop Eating Sweets

Mullah Nasseradeen was known to be good with children. Parents would come to him at the mosque when they had trouble with their kids, and ask for his help.

One day a mother came to him with her young son.

'Tell him to stop eating sweets,' she told Nasseradeen. 'He eats them all the time and they're so bad for his teeth.'

Nasseradeen looked at the boy and was about to speak, when he hesitated.

'Come back in three months,' he said.

The mother obediently took the boy away.

Three months later to the day she came back with her son.

Nasseradeen stared severely at the boy. 'Stop eating sweets!' he said.

The mother looked puzzled. 'Why couldn't you have said that three months ago?' she asked.

Nasseradeen smiled sheepishly, 'I had to give up sweets myself first.'

Hitting the Target

Once there was a man who wanted to be the best. He didn't mind what he would be the best at, but he wanted to be the best. He chose archery. All day, every day he practised, until every time he shot his arrow he'd hit the bull's-eye. Soon he was champion of his village, then champion of his county and in time he became champion of the country.

Often he'd say to young people, 'If you want to succeed in life then you have to work hard. Practise and practise and that makes perfect. You can do it too. With hard work you can succeed just like me.'

One day, after a competition, a young man approached the archery champion. 'You're very good at archery,' said the man, 'but I know someone who is better than you.'
'Impossible!' said the archer. 'I am the best! On a good day nobody can beat me!'
'I don't agree,' said the young man. 'The one who is better lives over there in that farm. His name is Nasseradeen. If you don't believe me you can go and meet him.'

Together they walked over to the farmhouse, through the gate and into the farmyard. On one side of the yard was a high wooden barn. Painted onto the side of the barn were about a hundred archery targets, circles within circles. Each target had a single arrow stuck exactly at the centre of the bull's-eye.

The archer was impressed. 'Wow!' he thought, 'I can hit the bull's-eye, but he can hit the exact centre of the bull's-eye. That's amazing!'

Nasseradeen came out to say hello.

'Tell me,' said the archer, 'I've practised my whole life to be as good as I can. I can hit the bull's-eye every time, but you not only hit the bull's-eye, you get it right in the very, very centre. How do you do that?'

Nasseradeen smiled. 'Well, you do things your way,' he said, 'and I do things my way. You see, me, first I shoot the arrow, then I paint the target around it!'

Nasseradeen and the Perfect Wife

One New Year's Eve Nasseradeen was sitting with a friend drinking coffee and mulling over their plans for the coming year.

'Friend,' Nasseradeen said. 'I think it's time I found a wife. This single life is getting tiresome. It's time I found a good woman to share my life with.'

'Good idea!' said his friend. 'But a good woman is hard to find. What kind of wife would you like?'

'Oh I know exactly what kind of woman I want,' he said. 'She will have to be beautiful, cultured and spiritually developed. That would make her the perfect wife.'

'Good luck, my friend.'

The year went by and on New Year's Eve the two friends met again.

'So tell me, how did you get on with your search for your perfect wife?'

'Not too well,' said Nasseradeen. 'I found someone who was really beautiful. She had a lovely face, lovely hair, lovely skin, lovely everything ... the most beautiful woman I've ever seen. I think she liked me, but the trouble was that she had never read a book and knew nothing about music or poetry, so she just wasn't for me. She had no culture. Next year I'll look further afield.'

'Good luck, my friend.'

The year went by and on New Year's Eve the two friends met again.

'So tell me, how did you get on with your search for your perfect wife?'

'I looked in all the towns in this part of the country till I found this gorgeous woman, as lovely as I could have dreamed of, and so cultured. We had read all the same books and poets and we talked for hours about music and poetry. She was perfect, except ... well, she never went to the mosque and knew nothing of the holy books. So of course she wasn't for me. Next year I'll have to try even further afield.'

The year went by and on New Year's Eve the two friends met again.

'And how did you get on this year?' asked his friend. 'Did you finally find your perfect wife?'

'I did,' replied Nasseradeen, smiling. 'She was absolutely perfect. She was drop-dead gorgeous, totally cultured and passionate about religion. She went to the mosque every day and knew all the Koran by heart. She was perfect.'

'Congratulations,' said his friend. 'So have you got married yet?'

'No,' said Nasseradeen shaking his head. 'There was just one problem ... she was looking for the perfect husband!'

The Neighbour's Cockerel

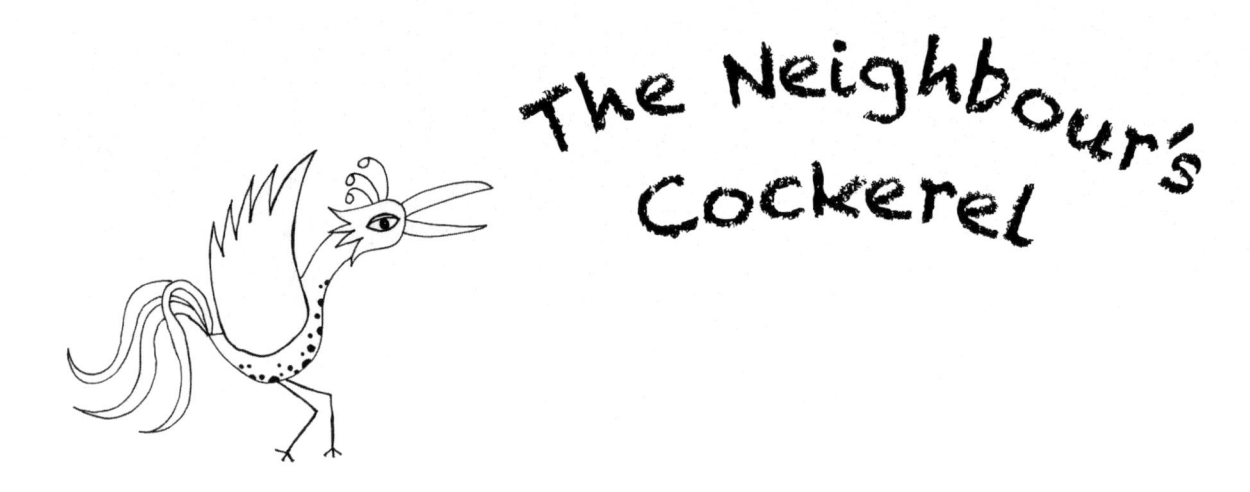

Nasseradeen lived next to a farm. One time his neighbour got a new cockerel which liked to crow in the middle of the night.

Nasseradeen would be fast asleep when the animal would call:
COCKADOODDLE DOO!

After that Nasseradeen couldn't get back to sleep. He'd lie awake fuming.

Every day he moaned to his wife over breakfast.

'That cockerel is so annoying. That farmer is such a bad neighbour. He should keep that animal quiet!'

'Oh you poor thing!' she'd say. 'But what can you do? Our neighbours are farmers and they need a cockerel.'

After a few weeks Nasseradeen had had enough.

'Wife!' he fumed. 'I'm going round to our neighbours to sort out this cockerel thing once and for all.'

He stormed off to the neighbour's house while his wife waited worrying in case there would be trouble.

An hour later Nasseradeen came back holding the offending cockerel.

'What have you done?' she asked.

'I bought the cockerel off the farmer,' he told her. 'Now we'll see how he likes it when my cockerel wakes him up in the middle of the night!'

Nasseradeen's Nail

Nasseradeen lived in a fine big house while his neighbour lived in a smaller one. The neighbour was jealous. One day he decided to try and persuade Nasseradeen to sell his house by making his life miserable.

First he got up every night and made as much noise as possible, banging pots and pans and singing at the top of his voice. When Nasseradeen asked him to stop he said, 'No, I can't stop, but if you would like to sell your house then I'd be happy to buy it.'
'Really?' said Nasseradeen. 'I'll think about it.'

Next, as well as the noise every night, rubbish started appearing in Nasseradeen's garden every morning. He knew it was from his neighbour.
'Do you know anything about all that rubbish in my front garden?' Nasseradeen asked his neighbour.
'Oh, the neighbourhood is going downhill, I suppose. It's a good time to sell up and leave, don't you think?'

The last straw came when Nasseradeen was walking past his neighbour's house one day. His neighbour threw a bucket of dirty water out of the doorway, right onto Nasseradeen's head.
'Oops,' said the neighbour. 'Didn't see you there!'
Nasseradeen said nothing and went home to change.

The next day he went to visit his neighbour and told him he was ready to sell.
'How much will you give me for my house?' asked Nasseradeen.
'Twenty thousand dinars,' replied the neighbour, very pleased that his plan had worked.
'Fine,' replied Nasseradeen, 'I'll sell it to you for half, for ten thousand dinars.'
'Why?' asked the astonished neighbour.
'Well, the thing is, there is the matter of my nail. You see in the house there is a nail. It belonged to my father and before that to his father and I am very fond of it. I am willing to sell you my house, but on the condition that I keep the nail. It's stuck in the wall in the front room. I want to be able to visit the nail whenever I want, and hang whatever I want on it, to honour the memory of my father and grandfather. Agree to that and I'll give you the house for half price.'

The neighbour couldn't believe his luck, getting the house and for half price! So he readily agreed. Lawyers were brought in, signing over the house, but giving Nasseradeen rights to his nail.

The next evening, the neighbour was fast asleep in his new home, when a knock came on the door. It was Nasseradeen, come to visit his nail. Well, it was a nuisance, but for 10,000 dinars saved, it was worth it. The neighbour went back to bed, and Nasseradeen went to his nail.

In the morning the neighbour woke to a disgusting smell. He and his wife went downstairs and found, hanging on the nail, a pair of rotten old boots, smelling like a rubbish dump and teeming with maggots and slugs. The smell was terrible throughout the house, but well, for 10,000 dinars they would put up with it.

A few nights later there was another midnight knock on the door – Nasseradeen again.
'Oh thank God you're back!' said the neighbour. 'Please take away the boots!'
'Yes, I'm planning to take them away,' said Nasseradeen, shuffling towards his nail.
'Good!' said the neighbour and went back to bed.

The next morning the neighbour woke up itching all over. His body was covered in little insect bites which itched like mad. His wife and kids were also covered in bites. They looked around for the source and found an old jacket hanging up on Nasseradeen's nail. The jacket was actually light green, but it was covered in so many fleas that from a distance it seemed black. The fleas were hungry and jumped at any warm-blooded creature they could find. Nasseradeen's neighbour washed and scrubbed the house all day, but more and more fleas kept jumping off the coat, keeping his whole family awake every night for a week.

Finally a knock on the door came in the middle of the night. 'Please! Please!' begged the neighbour, 'Please take away that jacket! It's driving me mad!'
'Oh, I am sorry to hear that,' replied Nasseradeen with a smile. 'You'll be pleased to hear I'm going to take it away.'

Nasseradeen went to his nail and replaced the coat with two rotten old fish. If the boots had smelt bad, the fish were a hundred times worse. Everything in the house smelt of rotten fish, the kids smelt so bad they were sent home from school, and the neighbour smelt so bad nobody would buy from his shop…

The neighbour had had enough – he went off to find Nasseradeen.
'Please,' he begged. 'Buy your house back. It's unbearable for us to live there with that nail of yours. Please take it back!'

And so Nasseradeen bought his house back for half the price he had been paid for it, and his neighbour never tried to get rid of him again…

Nasseradeen and the King's Hunting Party

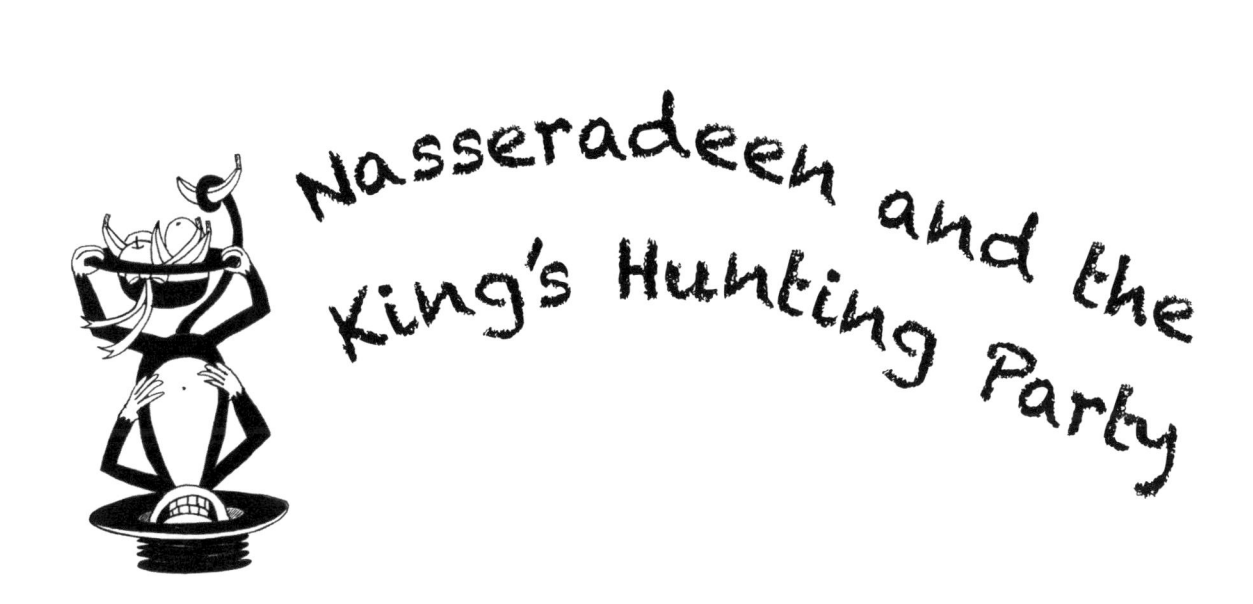

Once, the king was out hunting in the forest when he saw Nasseradeen by the side of the road.

'Not you!' shouted the king. 'You always bring me bad luck. If I see you before hunting then I won't catch anything. Guards! Beat this man severely and order him to keep out of my way!'

So the king's soldiers whipped, punched and kicked Nasseradeen, and left him lying unconscious in a pool of blood.

It turned out that the hunting went well and the king rode triumphant back towards the palace.

On the road he met Nasseradeen, hobbling back home with several broken ribs, two black eyes and aching limbs.

'Ah, Nasseradeen,' said the king magnanimously, 'How are you doing?'

'Aching, your majesty, aching.'

'Oh yes,' said the king generously, 'Sorry about that! The thing is, when I saw you I thought you were bad luck'.

'Really, your majesty? YOU thought I was bad luck!'...

Nasseradeen Speaks Truth

Once Nasseradeen was advisor to the king.

One day Nasseradeen advised the king that truth was the highest good that all should seek with vigilance and determination. The king was persuaded, and was determined to do something about it. He issued a declaration that all his people must tell the truth from now on. Anyone caught lying would be hanged. He told his guards at the gates of the city that they should question everyone entering the gates. Those that told the truth should be allowed to pass, those that lied should be taken and hanged.

The next day Nasseradeen was entering the city when a guard stopped him.
'Where are you going?' asked the guard.
'To be hanged!' replied Nasseradeen grimly.
'Is that the truth?' asked the guard.
'You tell me,' replied Nasseradeen.

Well the guard tried to puzzle it out. He thought, 'If I take him and hang him then he will have told the truth so I can't hang him, but if I do hang him then he will have told the truth so I can't hang him ... what shall I do?'

The guard couldn't decide so he took Nasseradeen to see the king. The king looked displeased. 'What are you up to?' he said.
'Are you going to hang me or not?'
'If I hang you then you would have been telling the truth. If I don't hang you then you would have been lying.'

'Do you now see, your majesty, what you mean when you talk about truth? You mean your truth. Here there are three truths, yours, mine and the guard's.'

The king laughed and cancelled his decree.

Nasseradeen and the Light

One time Nasseradeen was kneeling on the ground under a street light. His friend came over and Nasseradeen told him he was looking for his keys, so his friend knelt down under the light and helped with the search.

After a while the friend asked, 'Where did you drop the keys, Nasseradeen?'

'I dropped them over there,' replied Nasseradeen, pointing to a dark corner away from the light.

'So why are we searching over here?' asked the friend.

'It's much too dark to see anything over there,' replied Nasseradeen. 'Over here there's plenty of light so I'm searching here!'

Nasseradeen Teaches Justice

Nasseradeen was asked to solve a dispute between two brothers who had inherited their family's land and gold, amounting to more than 1,000 gold dinars. They couldn't agree on how it should be divided. Nasseradeen agreed to mediate, on the condition that his decision was binding on both sides. The brothers agreed, trusting in his wisdom.

'The main question,' said Nasseradeen, 'is whether you want human justice or divine justice.'

The brothers were devout believers and agreed that they wanted divine justice.

'OK,' said Nasseradeen. 'The older brother gets two chickens and a donkey, the younger gets the land, the gold and everything else.'

'Why!' complained the older. 'That's not fair!'

'Do you think it is more fair, the way that God has organised the world?' replied Nasseradeen.

Who Do You Trust?

Nasseradeen's neighbour was always trying to borrow things from Nasseradeen. One time he came round and knocked on Nasseradeen's door.

'I need to borrow your donkey,' he announced. 'Mine is too tired for ploughing, so will you lend me yours?'

'I'm sorry, neighbour,' said Nasseradeen, 'I would lend you my donkey, but he's not here.'

As chance would have it, as Nasseradeen was speaking a loud EE-AWW came from behind the house where Nasseradeen's stables were. Obviously it was his donkey.

'But Nasseradeen,' complained his neighbour, 'Your donkey is in the stables, I just heard him.'

'Impossible!' said Nasseradeen confidently. 'The donkey is not there. I told you.'

But again, as he was speaking the sound of a braying donkey was heard from behind the house.

'Nasseradeen, I just heard the donkey!' argued the neighbour, firmly.

'No, you didn't. It must have been a dog barking.'

Just then the EE-AAW came for a third time from behind the house.

'There it is again, Nasseradeen. You can't deny that was your donkey!'

Nasseradeen paused for thought and gave his beard a stroke.

'It seems to me,' he said, 'that this is a question of trust. Who do you trust? Do you trust me, or do you trust the donkey?'

Nasseradeen and the Turnips

One time Nasseradeen had a good crop of turnips, each one the size of a large watermelon. He decided to give a sack of his turnips to the king to celebrate the fine harvest. Walking along the road to the palace a friend asked him where he was going, and Nasseradeen explained he was taking the turnips as a gift for the king.

'You can't give the king turnips!' protested the friend. 'They are not suitable at all. You should give him a fine, sweet fruit. Here, give me the turnips and take this plate of figs!'

So Nasseradeen took the figs to the king and handed him the plate. Now it happened that the king was in a bad mood that day, and as soon as he got the plate he started throwing the figs at Nasseradeen. To the king's surprise, Nasseradeen waved his hands towards the sky, laughing and shouting, 'Thanks to God for the figs! Thanks to God for the figs!'

The king was curious. 'Nasseradeen, why are you laughing and shouting?'

'Well you see, your majesty, I was going to bring turnips but my friend told me to bring figs. If you had thrown turnips at me, I would be dead by now!'

Cause and Effect

Nasseradeen was sprinkling sawdust in his garden when his neighbour poked his nose over the fence and asked Nasseradeen why he was sprinkling sawdust.

'I'm sprinkling sawdust to keep away the tigers!' replied Nasseradeen.

'But there aren't any tigers in this country!' answered the puzzled neighbour.

Nasseradeen smiled: 'Well, that just proves how well it's working!'

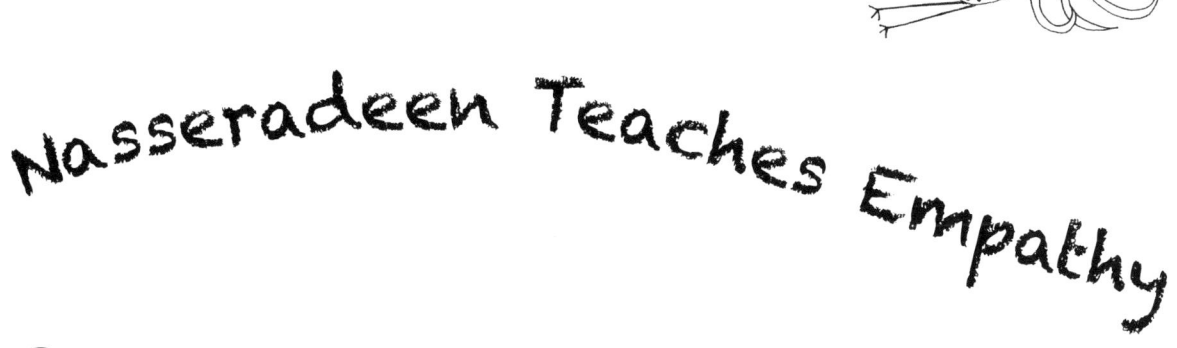

Nasseradeen Teaches Empathy

One time Nasseradeen was walking along a long road with his disciple beside him. Suddenly a great wagon came roaring along the road drawn by six great horses. The driver was in a terrific hurry, and shouted at Nasseradeen and his companion to get out of the way. Unfortunately they didn't move in time, and both men were knocked into a rather muddy drainage ditch by the side of the road.

Nasseradeen stood up and waved his fist at the departing wagon.

'May all your needs be satisfied!' he shouted after the wagon.

His disciple was puzzled. 'Why did you say that, Nasseradeen? He could have killed us!'

'That's true,' answered Nasseradeen. 'But do you think that he would have knocked us into the ditch if all his needs had been satisfied?'

Chapter 6

Year 6 Stories

Children of Wax – Africa	300
Warrior – Egypt	302
Baldur – Norway	309
Ericython – Roman	312
Quetzalcoatl Brings Chocolate to Earth – Aztec	314
Skeleton Woman – Inuit	318
The Boy who Learned to Shudder – Germany	320
The Woodcutter and the Snake – Serbia	325
Three Questions – Russia	328
Gawain and the Green Knight – Britain	331
Mother Sun and Her Daughters – Argentina	334
Five Wise Trainings – India	336
Gawain Gets Married – Britain	340
Everything You Need – Iraq	344
Gilgamesh – Iraq	348
A Drop of Honey – Iraq	352
SHORTER STORIES:	
Who is the Husband? – India	356
What Happens When You Really Listen! – India	357
The Power of Stories – India	358
The Diamond Dream – India	359
Bird in Hand – India	361
Traveller at the Gates of a City – USA	362

Children of Wax

This is a frequently told African story about children made out of wax who can't go out in the day. Evoke the worry of the parents and the trapped feel of the child who wants to explore. Let the tragedy of the melting sink in before moving to the final transformation scene. As students prepare to leave for a new school this can be a great transition story.

Once there was a forest where the sun blazed fiery and hot every day of the year. In the middle of the forest was a village of thatched huts, where the hunters hunted and the farmers farmed and the children played in the sun. Some played football, some played tag, and some went exploring in the forest.

One day a hunter got married and built a hut from wood and leaves on the edge of the village where he lived with his wife. Soon her belly swelled and she gave birth to a lovely baby boy.

The midwife was there at the birth. She looked at the baby boy and frowned. 'This is no ordinary child,' she said. 'He is not made of flesh, he is made of wax. You will have to keep him indoors. If he goes into the sun then he will melt.'

Two other children were born, a boy and a girl, and they too were made of wax. All three were kept indoors until night-time when they were allowed out – but not far. It was dangerous to go out of the village at night so they had to stay close to the hut in case lions or tigers were out hunting, or in case they trod on a snake.

In the day their mother would sit with them and tell them stories about the wide world. Mountains, oceans, deserts and forests. Tales of adventure and amazing creatures.

The eldest son was restless. Every day he'd peep through the cracks in the wall at the world outside. He wanted so badly to go out and explore the forest, travel to the ocean, climb the mountain. He looked up at the birds in the sky and envied them.

As we watched, he sang this song:

> *I want to break free*
> *Go out of these walls*
> *To climb many mountains and sail seven seas.*
> *I want to be free*
> *To go my own way*
> *Not stuck inside*
> *These old cold walls.*

'No!' said his mother. 'You cannot leave! You will melt in a moment.'

One day he'd had enough. He pushed open the door and ran out into the sunlight. His brothers watched as he stood there in the sun, staring up at the sky. He sang his song and danced in the dust. In a few moments his head began to melt, then his arms and his chest, and finally his legs, till there was just a puddle of wax on the ground. When night fell the children went outside and scooped up all the wax.

'He loved birds,' said his sister, 'let's make him into a bird.'

They moulded the wax into the shape of a bird and covered it in cool green leaves to protect it from the sun, then left it perching on the fence outside their hut.

The next morning at dawn they watched through the window, wondering if the bird would melt. But something else happened. As they watched the leaves seemed to turn into feathers, the wax eyes turned into living beady eyes, the waxy beak into a sharp black beak. The bird opened its wings and glided up on an updraft high above the hut, circling and calling down. His brother and sister thought they could hear the same song:

> *Now I've broken free*
> *Gone out of these walls*
> *Now I'll climb many mountains and see seven seas.*
> *I will be free*
> *To go my own way*
> *Not stuck inside*
> *These old cold walls.*

They watched, delighted, as he flew away toward the mountain, which rose high and mighty above the forest.

Warrior

This story, sometimes called the Black Prince, is both memorable and powerful, evoking the tragedy of a young man who feels he is not good enough, not likeable, and so misses his chance for happiness. This story works well with upper KS2, encouraging the idea of taking the opportunities which life offers, and overcoming the fears which hold us back. If you can play a flute or recorder, even just a little, use it in the story. It's one of my favourites. For a change here's a long text with lots of things you can include. For a shorter text you can use Laura Simm's version in Holt's Ready-To-Tell Tales.

Once there was a desert. In the centre of the desert was a city built from river clay. Every road, roof and wall was the same blood-red hue. They called it the Red City. From a distance it looked like a red jewel nestling in a swathe of yellow silk.

The poor lived in shack shanties around the edge of the city, finding work when they could, and living off favours and friends when they could not. In one of these shacks there lived a boy called Qassim, the seventh child in a family of nine children. On the day that he was born his mother looked at him and felt, somehow, that Qassim was a little strange, a little different from the other babies. There was something about his face that unsettled her. Something not quite right. To her eyes the face lacked symmetry, the two sides a little unequal, and so she named him Qassim, which means the divider.

As Qassim grew up, his brothers and sister sensed strangeness in him, and left him to himself in the home, reluctant to include him in their games. In the streets the children were less kind. They would chase and taunt him:

> *'Qassim, Qassim*
> *Face like a dog*
> *Your mother's a bat*
> *And your father's a frog.'*

Under such conditions Qassim grew up as a solitary boy, keeping himself to himself and expecting the worst from whoever he met. There was, however, one thing which Qassim loved. When he was six years old his father had given him a wooden flute. Qassim loved to play it. When he was feeling sad he would find a quiet corner and close his eyes, and play and play. Through the music he found a place of happiness and freedom. In this way the years passed.

Our story begins with Qassim as a young man, wandering through the blood-red streets of the city. In the distance, at the end of a long straight road, Qassim saw something white. 'Strange,' he thought and walked, intrigued, towards it.

As he came closer he saw that it was a white wall. Closer still, and he saw that the white stone was smooth and finely cut. Closer still and he touched the cool, smooth stone, each block perfectly fitting on the next without any gap or imperfection. Qassim was delighted by its beauty but puzzled by its purpose. What was it doing here? What might such a wall enclose? He climbed up a date palm growing next to the wall and, hidden behind the palm leaves, he peeped over the top of the wall.

The sight took Qassim's breath away. It was a garden, more lovely than anything that Qassim had seen or even imagined. There were flower beds packed with blossoms and blooms of every imaginable colour, trees in flower, trees in fruit, huge spreading canopies and tiny delicate miniatures. There were vines and climbers, bushes and shrubs, lawns and rockeries. Humming birds and butterflies were everywhere. Qassim had never seen so many colours packed into one place, or smelt such wonderful scents.

After a while he noticed a white fountain made from the same stone which had first caught his attention. Sitting by the fountain was a young woman, smiling as a small yellow bird splashed its wings in the fountain pool.

'The garden is lovely,' he thought, 'but it's nothing compared to that smile.'

Who can say how long he sat there between the fronds of the palm, watching her. Maybe a moment; maybe a whole morning. Certainly Qassim had no idea how long he had been sitting there, the bright colours of the garden framing the edge of his vision while his focus remained centred on her face.

When a fly landed on his nose he slipped back into himself and started thinking: what if I were to call out and say hello? What if we were to become friends? What if we were to become more than friends?

His mind started spinning schemes about her – love, marriage, children – until another inner voice stopped him in his tracks. 'She wouldn't want to talk to you!' it said. 'She wouldn't even want to look at you. You are ugly. No one wants to look!'

The thought brought with it a cascade of memories – past moments of teasing and shunning – and his heart closed like a clam. He climbed wearily down the tree, sat in its shade with his back to the trunk and took out his flute. He closed his eyes, firmly shutting out the world, and began to play. Soon he was lost in the tangled meanderings of rhythm and phrase that his heart conjured.

Sometime later Qassim re-opened his eyes to the world and mooched off home, determined to forget all about the garden and any absurd dreams it might have spawned. That evening though, try as he might, he found himself unable to do so. Again and again he told himself the facts about himself and all the reasons he should forget her but, just like child on a swing, the harder he pushed those thoughts away, the more forcefully they returned.

The next day, against all the advice he could give himself, he returned to the white wall, climbed up the rough and jagged trunk and nestled between its prickly fronds, contemplating the garden once again, hidden in the heart of the canopy. While part of him was hoping to find the garden empty, his heart jumped when he saw her sitting, as before, staring at the water.

Again he watched from his hiding place. He imagined calling out, or jumping down from the tree, or throwing her a gift ... anything to attract her attention. But every idea met with the same inner answer. 'You know she will not want to see you. Better keep quiet and hidden.'

Later he slipped down the trunk, rested his back against the cool smooth wall, took out his flute and closed his eyes, playing all the longing and regrets to an audience of crickets and sparrows.
Every day Qassim returned to the garden; every day he climbed and watched her from his leafy hide; every day he longed to speak to her and yet kept silent; every day he shut out the world with closed eyes and escaped into his flute's song.

This was repeated for one hundred days until one day Qassim was strolling through the city after his daily visit to the garden when he happened to be walking through the vegetable market, and he happened to pass by two old peasant women who were squatting on the ground behind their piles of produce. As he stood there the two women started to talk. 'You know, he spoils her,' crowed the one behind the tomatoes, 'that's the problem. A father should give his daughter direction but he just lets her do what she wants.'
'Oh, I know,' echoed the other, 'but fathers are always like that with daughters, especially when there's only one.'

'Oh, I know! But he's our king. He has responsibilities. The princess needs to find a husband. She should be going to feasts and banquets where she can be seen. Instead she seems to spend all her time alone in that garden.'

'Oh, I know! They say she goes there every day, but no one knows why. He should put a stop to it if you ask me!'

As Qassim followed their chatter, he felt as though a shell around him was cracking open, as the outside world flooded in. She was the princess! At that moment the dream of what-might-just-be crumbled; that unfulfilled yet imaginable possibility became unimaginable, hopeless. She was the princess. She would only meet the rich and royal. She would never, ever, befriend a pauper like him, whatever he looked like. As for love, ridiculous!

For the rest of the day Qassim slouched around in the red dust of the city streets, filled with a bitter gloom. How could he have been so stupid? He wandered, aimless, without knowing where he was going, wishing to be anywhere else but in his own threadbare shoes.

Around sunset he found himself outside the city walls walking towards a fire. Its flames were surrounded by a circle of men, squatting and sipping coffee, wearing the dark headscarves and thick robes of desert nomads. Behind the fire was a cluster of tents and camels. Behind the tents there was nothing but the ripples of dunes from there to the blood-red skyline. Qassim slipped into the circle and listened as the men spun stories. There were stories of war, stories of love, but mainly stories of camels!

For a while Qassim lost himself in the nomads' world, but when, as was the custom, he was asked to share a story of his own, he took his heart in his hands and told his own story. His home – his family – the flute – the garden. When he had finished he said, 'I just wish I could be someone else, then there might me a chance for me and her. But we are who we are, and this world had proved me a fool.'

At that moment the atmosphere changed around the circle. The men looked at one another, raising eyebrows and nodding.

'What?' demanded Qassim. 'What is it?'

Across the fire from Qassim a man spoke through the flames, his face in shadow.

'Welcome, friend.'

The voice had a firm authority, perhaps, Qassim thought, the voice of their chief. There was something unsettling about it: a hint of mockery, or perhaps a threat. But what he said next grabbed Qassim's full attention.

'Our people have a magician skilled in the arts of change. He can change a man from one thing to another with his power. He might change you if you want, but once changed no man will be able to change you back. Your old self will be gone forever. Would you like to be introduced?'

Qassim nodded.

'Come tomorrow then.'

The next morning a guide led Qassim through the desert. After three nights they approached a cluster of palm trees around a small pool of water. Standing between the trees was a thin old man in a pristine white robe and headscarf, staring towards them with the white eyes of a blind man.

'Come closer,' he called, beckoning. 'Come closer and tell me why you have travelled here.'

'I've come because you have the power to change a man from one thing to another. Will you change me?'

'What would you like to be, young man?' he replied evenly.

Qassim didn't hesitate. He'd had plenty of time to plan this moment.

'I want to be strong, handsome, a warrior and a champion fighter. Can you do it? Will you do it?'

'Hmm. A strong, handsome warrior. What will you give me in payment?' he asked bluntly.

Qassim felt panic rising in his throat. He hadn't realised there would be payment. He had no money. His clothes were worth nothing. Perhaps the flute? He held it out for the man to feel.

'Would you take this?' he asked.

The blind man nodded and the deal was sealed.

Three months later war broke out in the kingdom of the Red City. A hoard of tribes came out of the western mountains and rode across the desert towards the city. They were seasoned fighters, skilled in the use of sword and bow from the saddle.

The soldiers of the Red City were no match for their power and speed. In every encounter the king's forces were routed, either killed or driven back towards the city. Within just one week the invaders were within two days' ride from the palace. That day, the king was contemplating his fate. He imagined his head on a spike over the city gates. He imagined his family being sold as slaves. He imagined life for his people under the new rulers.

As he pondered this, a stranger entered the city. He walked with the poise of an athlete, all muscle and power. He wore the sword and clothes of a warrior. As he strode towards the palace men moved out of his way sensing danger, while from a distance the women admired his striking features.

The warrior went to the palace and asked to see the king, offering help. When the king received him he bowed and said, simply, 'Let me lead your men into battle, your majesty. With me leading them we will send the invaders back to the mountains. Let me try. You have nothing to lose and everything to gain.'

The next morning the king's cavalry rode out against the invaders, the warrior leading the charge, striking into the mountain tribes with a ferocity that rallied his men and terrified his enemies. Within the hour the invaders turned tail and returned to their mountains leaving the city and kingdom intact.

The next week was filled with celebrations in the Red City, as the stranger was honoured again and again as their new hero. At the final banquet the king sat at the table of honour with his daughter and the stranger, while all around the guests feasted. When the time for speeches came the king stood and spoke, 'We are here today to honour this man who has saved us all from a terrible fate. Today, before you all, I thank him, and ask him to name his reward. If it is in my power to grant it then I will not refuse him.'

The warrior stood and bowed. 'Thank you, your majesty. I have only one wish, and that is for me to marry your daughter. Will you grant me that?'

A silence swept through the hall. Everyone, shocked but curious, waited to see how the king would react to such an idea. Who was this man to ask such a thing? He claimed no royal blood, no position that would sanction such a marriage, and yet the king had promised and a king's word could not be lightly broken.

All were surprised when the princess herself stood, stared calmly into the eyes of the warrior and bowed in a gesture of obedience. 'Honoured guest,' she began. 'You are most welcome and we are deep in your debt for your service to our country. My father has promised and, with his blessing, I do agree to marry you.'

As she spoke the warrior's body seemed to soften, his eyes moist as he opened his mouth to reply, but the princess held up her hand and continued. 'But I am not sure if you really wish to be married to me. First, let me tell you something about myself. When you have heard it, if you still wish to marry me then I will freely consent. If you change your mind then so be it.'

The warrior nodded and waited.

'I have a garden, a wonderful place surrounded by a wall of white marble. I love to go there. It is a place of great peace and beauty. I can happily sit there watching the birds and flowers for hours without tiring of them. A few months ago I was sitting in the garden when I heard the sound of a flute being played somewhere nearby. The music was so beautiful! I had never heard anything like it. Just hearing it I wanted to cry and laugh at the same time. I listened for a while and then, curious, decided to find out who was playing, so I climbed up the vine on the wall and peeped over the other side. There I saw a young man, with his eyes closed, playing a wooden flute. He had the most extraordinary face I have ever seen. It was like – how can I explain – like summer and winter ... no, happiness and sadness, fused together in one face. I found him quite beautiful and watched him for a while, lost in his music.

'I started to imagine calling out, saying hello, to find out about him, but a voice inside me said, "No, that would not be proper for a girl, let alone a princess." So I kept quiet and returned to my seat by the fountain, hoping he would say something or climb up and say hello. But when the music stopped he must have gone away, because when I looked up again he was gone.

'That night, all I could think of was his music and that lovely face, and then next day I returned to the garden and waited, hoping he would come back. Again I heard the flute being played. Again I climbed the vine and watched him for a while but couldn't quite find the courage to speak.

'For one hundred sweet days I went there every day. Every day I heard his music and watched him, but kept silent. Then one day he didn't come, and he hasn't been back since. Every day I go there and wait but he hasn't been back. I don't know what has happened, if he is dead, or if one day I will see him again, but the thing you have to know is this: in my heart it is him that I love. I long to see his face and hear his music. If you marry me then you will do so knowing my heart waits for another.'

The princess sat and the room waited for the warrior's reply. For a while he just stared at the floor then, resolved, turned to her. 'My lady,' he said quietly. 'I once had a dream like your dream. Mine is gone now. I would not take yours away from you.'

Without another word he walked out of the hall, out of the palace and into the desert, and was never seen in the Red City again.

It is said that he asked that these words be written on his tombstone:

Three things in life may never be taken back –
Words from the mouth,
An arrow from the bow,
Or a missed opportunity.

Baldur

This is a great story from the Norse myths. Before you start, explain the main gods (Odin, Frigga, Baldur, Hodur and Loki) so the class gets used to their names. Evoke the beauty of Baldur and how loved he is, the jealous trickiness of Loki, and the grief of his mother.

Once, Odin's wife, Frigga, gave birth to a son called Baldur. Baldur was the most lovely and handsome of all the gods and the best loved. He ruled over light and spring, all things right and good and he was loved by all, or almost all.

Then one night his mother had a dream. Baldur was in the underworld with the Goddess Hel, its ruler. Baldur was dead. His mother was troubled by the dream and told it to her husband.

Odin went to the grave of Wala, one who could see the future, and summoned her from her grave. 'Tell me,' he said, 'who will be the next to go to the realm of Hel.'
'It will be Baldur,' she crooned. 'And the cause will be his blind brother, Hodur.'

Immediately the gods all met to decide what to do. They agreed that every creature on earth would swear an oath never to harm Baldur. In this way he could not be killed. This was their plan.

Frigga, his mother, organised the swearing. The sky, the earth, fire, water, giants, dwarves, elves and men as well as every plant and animal in the world swore their oath never to hurt Baldur.

From that moment on nothing could hurt the beautiful young god. Rocks did not bother him, arrows could not pierce him, swords just bounced from his skin. The beautiful young god was invincible. The gods were so happy that they started playing a game. Who could kill Baldur? Nobody! Baldur stood and they would all attack him, laughing, with spears, arrows, swords and knives. Nothing could hurt him. Everyone was delighted with the game.

Well, almost everyone. Loki, the trickster, had other ideas. Loki knew that on an old oak tree there was a plant – mistletoe – which had not sworn the oath to protect Baldur. It seemed so harmless that Frigga had not bothered with the oath. Loki cut a twig from the mistletoe, then he returned to the circle of the gods. They were still playing their weapons game with Baldur. The only one standing aside was the blind Hodur.

'How can I play when I can't see what I'm doing?' he complained to Loki.

'Take your bow and get ready to shoot,' replied Loki, 'and here is your arrow.' He handed Hodur the twig. 'I'll help you aim,' he said.

Hodur shot the mistletoe twig and it pierced Baldur's side. He fell to the ground and, as his parents held him in their arms, he died.

So the gods set about burying the body of their beloved Baldur. They erected a funeral pyre on Baldur's own ship, *Ringhorn*. At the sight of her much loved husband, dead upon the pyre, Nanna, his widow, died of a broken heart. Her body was laid at the side of her husband's.

The giants pushed the burning ship out into the open waters and wild flames accompanied the god on his last journey. When the ship finally sank into the depth of the ocean, it seemed as if the whole world went into a grieving twilight.

No one was grieving more than Frigga, his mother. Was Baldur, the God of Light and Springtime, lost forever? Was there a way she could persuade Hel, the goddess who ruled in the land of the dead, to let Baldur return to the daylight?

Touched deeply by Frigga's grief, Hermodur, the messenger god, decided to try and free his brother. For nine nights, Hermodur rode his father's eight-legged horse down to the underworld until he reached Bifröst, the bridge that separates the world of the dead from the world of the living. He crossed over the bridge and found Baldur, pale and dazed. He called to Hel, asking her to release him but she shook her head. 'The dead are for my realm alone, Baldur belongs to me.'
'But all the world is grieving. Every creature in the world is crying for him.'
'I don't think so!' replied Hel scoffing.
'It is so,' said Hermodur.
'If all creatures will cry for him, then I will let him go!' she said.

Hermodur returned to the gods and told his story.

Frigga sent out the elves to ask that all things in the world should cry for Baldur.

The stones cried, the sky cried, the earth cried, the sea cried, animals wept and plants sobbed. Things were looking quite good for Baldur until the elves found a cave with a giantess in it.
'Cry for Baldur!' they asked, but she shook her head.

'Please!' they begged but she would not.

Some say that she was Loki in disguise. Who knows?

What is known is that, without her tears, Baldur was stuck in the underworld with Hel, which suited her just fine.

As for clever tricky Loki, the gods sent the giants to catch him.

He had just finished making a net for fishing. When the giants came he threw the net in the fire, burning it, jumped into a stream and swam away to the sea. But the gods saw the shape of the net in the ashes and made a net just like it. They waited by the river for their chance. When he swam upstream they caught him and punished him.

He was taken to an island in the realm of Hel and bound to a sharp-edged rock. Above his head they hung a huge black snake, who continuously dripped acid poison into his face, burning him horribly. Sigyn, his wife, came to him and held the bowl above his head to catch the acid, but every time she went away to empty the bowl he was burned again by the poison. He screamed and trembled and the earth shook. This is the true source of earthquakes.

So it is and so it will remain until the end of all things.

Ericython

This story, from Ancient Rome, is all about respect for a forest. When a king cuts it down he is cursed by its guardian and pays a terrible price. It can be seen as a story about what happens if we do not respect the environment. It's quite a gory and shocking tale, which is usually popular with this age group. I like Ted Hughes's version in his Tales from Ovid.

Once there was a greedy king called Ericython.
He loved money more than anything, more even than the gods.

One day he decided that a grove of oak trees should be cut down for wood and sold. These trees belonged to Ceres, Goddess of Life. It was forbidden to cut any of her trees, but Ericython didn't care.

He took his woodcutters to the grove and ordered them to chop the trees down, but nobody moved.

'We dare not!' said the chief woodcutter. 'These are sacred trees. The gods will punish us if we harm them.'

'If you don't,' snarled the king, 'then I will punish you! These trees are worth good money. Cut them down or I will cut you down.'

Reluctantly, the men began to work. As their axes cut into the trees, red sap sprayed out, as if the trees were bleeding.

They chopped down every tree and loaded the wood on carts for sale in the town.

From the heavens, Ceres was watching.

Cold and furious, she pondered a suitable punishment for this greedy stupid king.

She called to the God of Hunger, who lived in the land of ice and snow in the far north. When Hunger heard the call she was scratching lichen and moss from a rock to eat. Her head was like a skull, her skin so thin that the bones beneath could all be seen. Her teeth were broken and bloody. Her organs could be seen through her skin – tiny belly and guts, heart and lungs. No fat, no meat, just skin and bone.

She jumped onto the wind and floated easily south until she came to Ericython's house, floating in through the window of the bedroom where he slept.

For a while she crouched over his snoring body and then clamped her bony mouth to his fat lips. She breathed ice cold hunger into his mouth then floated away.

In the morning he woke, ready for breakfast. He ate and ate but the more he ate the more he wanted. All morning he ate breakfasts, then lunches and dinners, but seemed to ache with hunger all the time. He couldn't sleep. His hunger was too much. He just sat in the kitchen eating and eating, day and night.

Soon the food in the house was all gone, and he ordered his servants to sell whatever they needed so they could keep buying food. Within a month his savings were gone. Within a year everything in the palace was sold. It was empty, with all the servants gone: just him and his daughter.

He took her to the slave market and sold her as a slave to buy food.

Finally, when he had nothing left to sell, he sat in the street and started to feed on his own fingers. When they were gone he ate his toes, then started biting and swallowing the flesh from his own arms and legs, until there was nothing left but a head and limbless body, dead in a pool of blood.

This was the revenge of Ceres.

Quetzalcoatl Brings Chocolate to Earth

This is an Aztec story of creation, the fall from grace of the creator, and his parting gift to the world: chocolate! It is an extraordinary tale with echoes of Prometheus and Osiris, featuring drunkenness as a route to doom. It is a creation story, so tell it with atmosphere and spaciousness.

In the beginning there was no life on this earth. Just rock and sky. Black, bare rock. Clear wide sky. Just that…

Then the Dragon God Quetzalcoatl woke up. Up in the heavens in his cloud cave, the Dragon God stretched, yawned and looked over the edge of the earth down onto the bare black rock of earth.
'I can do better,' he thought. 'This place needs some life.'

He filled his dragon lungs and breathed down onto the earth:
Sea … he breathed and the sea became.
Forest … he breathed and forest became.
Moorland …
Desert …
Lion … etc.

All day he breathed life onto the earth and then, pleased with his work, he slept.

The next day he woke and looked down again at the earth now teeming with life.
'Hmm,' he thought, 'just one more thing.'
He slipped out of his cave, stretched his wings and flew up to perch on the morning star. He waited until a ray of light shone down onto the earth and hooking his tail around the light he slid down towards earth.

As his claws touched the ground, he transformed into a man with thick strong fingers, a smile on his face and a jaunty hat on his head. He walked over to a field of corn, picked some cobs, and then ground the corn into flour between two stones. Next, he mixed in water and shaped the dough into two figures, one man and one woman. When that was done he leaned down over the figures and breathed on them... Live ... and they transformed into four men and women. Breathing and hearts pumping.

He turned to the ray of starlight – as his hand touched the light he returned to his dragon form, hooked his tail around the light, opened his wings and followed the light back up to the morning star.

The people watched.
'Who was that?' said one.
'That was our father, our maker, our God,' said another.
'Then we must worship him every day,' said a third.
'Let's start now,' said a fourth.
They sang and danced for the dragon, and he heard the sound and was pleased.

Time passed and every day Quetzalcoatl worked in the heavens to the sound of their singing and their praises. Every morning he smiled, yawned and purred as he watched his people honour him before starting their day.
'It is good,' he purred.

Then one day there was silence when he woke. He looked down and saw that the people had made statues of all kind of creatures and were worshiping them instead.
'Time I paid them a visit,' he thought, perched on the morning star, and slid down the starlight ray to earth.

As he came down people stopped and stared – 'Who's that?'
'It's a dragon,' said one.
'I remember the story,' said another.
'It's our father, our maker, come back to visit,' said a third.

When Quetzalcoatl's claws touched the ground he turned into a man with thick hands, a big smile and a jaunty hat.
'Do you know me?' he asked.
'Yes. You are our father,' they said.
'Good!' he said.
'Wait!' they said.
They took sticks and broke apart the clay gods they had made.
'Now we will worship you!'
They built him a temple with four stone pillars in the shape of men, holding up the roof with their hands. Outside were carvings of tigers and butterflies. Inside was a throne for Quetzalcoatl.

Every day he sat and the people came and sang him their song of praise, dancing for their father. Every day he smiled and said, 'Now, let me teach you something.'

On the first day he taught them fire.
On the second how to plough and sow, and water and harvest.
On the third day he taught them to grind and bake.
On the fourth day he taught them to build.
On the fifth day to play music.
On the sixth day to count and multiply.
On the sixth day to write and read.

Week by week they listened and learned and soon their city was growing into a great and happy place – food, shelter, arts flourished under Quetzalcoatl's guidance. Quetzalcoatl sat happily on this throne and watched, pleased that his people were happy. Then he thought, 'We need just one more thing to make like even sweeter. Then this would be perfect.'

He went to the morning starlight, turned into a dragon and flew up to the heavens.

There he saw a crowd of gods drinking from golden goblets and behind them the fields of bushes where they grew the beans to make the drink. As the gods chatted and sipped he sneaked over to the field, gently pulled up one of the bushes, slipped it under his feathered wing, and went back unseen to earth.

There he went to a farmer and planted a field of cuttings from the bush. He helped the farmer water them, and watched as they flowered in spring, gave red fruits in summer, which dried to dry brown beans in autumn. Then he showed the farmer how to pick and roast and grind the beans, then mix them with water to drink.

The farmer added some honey and chilli and gave the drink to the king. He sipped it and felt his body fill with happiness.

'Good!' he said. 'This is a drink fit for the gods. Now it will be the drink of kings.'

Every day the royal family supped at the sweet drink and were content. Then one day the God of Darkness looked down from the heavens and saw the kings drinking.
He called out to the other gods, 'Look! See what Quetzalcoatl has done. He has given our drink to them. He is a thief. I will punish him!'
'Yes!' they said. 'Punish him well!'

Turning into a huge spider he hooked his thread onto the edge of heaven and lowered himself down to earth. As he touched the ground he turned into the form of a thin man with long thin hands, a bitter smile and a thin dark hat on his very thin head.

He went to Quetzalcoatl in the temple with a large pot of something.
'Quetzalcoatl,' he said, 'I come from heaven. I have something for you that all the gods are drinking all the time. It's the best drink there is. Better than that old drink of the gods. Its happiness is stronger. Try it!'

Quetzalcoatl was curious and drank from the pot. It was curious. A bit bitter, but he felt himself relax as he drank. It was beer.

Soon his head was spinning. He tried to walk but kept on falling over.
'What's happening?' said the people.
He started to laugh and laugh in a strange way.
'What's going on?' said the people.
He jumped around singing and doing a drunken dance.
'This is not right!' said the people.
He got angry and started shouting and smashing things.
'This is not worthy of respect!' said the people.
'Who wants to fight?' he shouted, and the people turned their backs on him.
'We will not worship you anymore,' they said.

In the morning he had a headache. He saw the people looking for new gods and he felt shame. He walked away from his people and he saw that the fields where the beans had been grown had changed. Now the bushes grew the fruit for the beer he had drunk. The place was no longer perfect.

He walked away until he came to the sea. By the beach was a field. He reached into his pocket and pressed three beans into the soil, then, touching a ray of sunlight he turned into a dragon and flew away from the earth forever.

When the seeds sprouted to bushes and flowers become fruits and dry beans, a farmer took the beans and made them into a drink.

'This is good!' said his wife as she sipped. 'What is it?'

'This is the drink of the gods,' said the farmer. 'Chocolate!'

Skeleton Woman

Skeleton Woman is a very popular Inuit story made famous by the landmark book, Women Who Run with the Wolves *by C.P. Estes. I have found that this story works well with Year 6, mixing the spookiness of a weird ghost story with the mythology of rebirth as a skeleton reclaims her body and her life. Create an atmosphere of mystery and fear for the fisherman, then tenderness in the final scene.*

Father and daughter stand on the top of the cliff. Beneath them the water breaks on the rocks. The father's eyes are angry. He holds his daughter's neck. Her eyes wide with fear. Shouting at her. She screams.

Maybe she was pushed, who knows? Maybe she slipped. Whatever the cause, she fell, her body twisting and turning as she fell through the air, crashing and cracking against the rocks like a limp, lifeless puppet, breaking her neck on the rocks below.

The sea came and drew her in, out into the bay and down to the bottom of the ocean where she lay. The fish came and feasted on her flesh until there was nothing left but her bones, swaying back and forth on a bed of seaweed. From that day fishermen avoided that place. They believed it to be haunted. Cursed. They kept away.

Then one day a fisherman, new to that part of the coast, came to find work, build himself a home and maybe find himself a wife. He rowed out to that haunted bay, hooked on his bait and cast out his line. He waited all day but no fish took his bait, until, as the sun went down, the line suddenly tightened. His rod bent under the weight of his catch.

What kind of fish was it? Something heavy? He imagined the locals at the market when he carried in the fish to sell. Maybe he'd find a wife there.

He was so busy in his imagination he didn't notice as the skeleton rose out of the water as if dancing on the surface, caught in his line. Then he looked up and saw her.

Terrified, he turned, grabbed the oars and began to row away to the shore, away from the skeleton. Every now and then he looked over his shoulder and saw she was still there dancing on the water behind him. 'It's following me!' he thought.

At the shore he grabbed his rod, jumped onto the beach and ran up the beach towards his tent up on the hill above the beach.

Every now and then he looked over his shoulder and saw the skeleton twisting and bouncing against the rocks, all the time following him.
He reached the door of his tent, threw it open, jumped inside and closed the door behind him. He sat there in the dark and waited and listened.

He sat in the darkness, his heart beating like a drum, but nothing happened. Reassured he got up and lit a candle. As the light filled the tent he saw her, a tangled mess of bones on the floor by the door, blocking his escape.

He saw the clutter of bones and staggered backwards until his back was against the wall, frozen with fright. He waited but nothing happened.

Then he saw the line tangled in the bones. He stood and walked over to them and started to rearrange them, untangling the line and snapping each bone back in its right place until her skeleton was complete and whole.

Then he slipped into bed, pulled his sealskin blanket over his body and fell asleep. As he slept he dreamed – who knows of what? And as he did so a tear ran down his face. As the tear appeared Skeleton Woman moved her head, turning to watch the tear.

Slowly, carefully, she stood and walked over to the bed, bent down and touched the tear with her bony lip. Then she started to sway over him, singing her song. She sang for her flesh to return, for legs so that she could dance, arms to cook, hair so that she might be beautiful once more, lips so that she could speak and kiss – a belly so that she might give birth. In this way, she sang and sang herself back onto her bones. And when she was done, she lay down next to the fisherman and slept.

In the morning, when they awoke, he took her for his wife.

The Boy Who Learned to Shudder

This is a ghost story and a comedy, following the narrative collected by the brothers Grimm. Create suspense when you tell it, and pay attention to the descriptions of the various ghouls and monsters. Evoke the character of the son: fearless and matter-of-fact about all his experiences.

A father had two sons. The oldest one was clever and intelligent, and knew how to manage everything, but the youngest one was foolish and could neither understand nor learn anything. When people saw him, they said, 'He will be a burden on his father!'

Now when something had to be done, it was always the oldest son who had to do it. However, if the father asked the eldest to fetch anything when it was late, or even worse, at night, and if the way led through the churchyard or some other spooky place, he would always answer, 'Oh, no, father, I won't go there. It makes me shudder!'

The younger son was quite different. He was never afraid. When scary stories were told round the fire at night, he felt no fear at all. Others said, 'That makes me shudder,' but the younger son was puzzled. What could they mean?

One day his father said to him, 'Listen, you there in the corner. You are getting big and strong. You too will have to learn something by which you can earn your living.'

'Well, father,' he answered, 'I do want to learn something. Indeed, if possible I would like to learn how to shudder. I don't understand that at all.'

The oldest son laughed when he heard that, and thought to himself, 'Dear God, what a dimwit that brother of mine is. Nothing will come of him as long as he lives. As the twig is bent, so grows the tree.'

The father sighed, and answered him, 'You may well learn to shudder, but you will not earn your bread by shuddering.'

So the boy went out into the wide world to learn how to shudder with fear.

After some time he arrived at an inn.

'Where are you going?' said the innkeeper.

'I want to learn fear,' he said. 'I want to be able to shudder!'

Hearing this, the innkeeper laughed and said, 'If that's what you want, you've come to the right place.'

'Oh, be quiet,' said the innkeeper's wife. 'Too many people have already lost their lives. It would be a pity and a shame if his beautiful eyes would never again see the light of day.' But the boy said, 'I want to learn to shudder, however difficult it may be. That is why I left home.'

The innkeeper explained that there was a haunted castle not far away where a person could very easily learn how to shudder, if he would just keep watch there for three nights. The king had promised that whoever would dare to do this could have his daughter in marriage, and she was the most beautiful maiden under the sun. Further, in the castle there were great treasures, guarded by evil spirits. These treasures would then be freed, and would make a poor man rich. Many had entered the castle, but no one had come out again alive.

The next morning the boy went to the king and said, 'If it be allowed, I will keep watch three nights in the haunted castle.'
The king looked at him, and because the boy pleased him, he said, 'You may ask for three things to take into the castle with you, but they must be things that are not alive.'
To this the boy replied, 'Then I ask for a fire, a lathe, and a woodcarver's bench with a knife.'
The king had all these things carried into the castle for him during the day. When night was approaching, the boy went inside and made himself a bright fire in one of the rooms, placed the woodcarver's bench and knife beside it, and sat down at the lathe.
'Oh, if only I could shudder!' he said. 'But I doubt if I'll learn it here either.'

Towards midnight he decided to stir up his fire. He was just blowing into it when a cry suddenly came from a corner of the room, 'Au, meow! How cold we are!'
'You fools!' he shouted. 'What are you crying about? If you are cold, come and sit down by the fire and warm yourselves.'
When he had said that, two large black cats came and sat down on either side of him, looking at him savagely with their fiery eyes.
A little while later, after warming themselves, they said, 'Comrade, shall we play a game of cards?'
'Why not?' he replied. 'But first show me your paws.'
So they stretched out their claws.
'Oh,' he said, 'what long nails you have. Wait. First I will have to trim them for you.'
With that he seized them by their necks, put them on the woodcarver's bench, and tightened them into the vice by their feet. 'I have been looking at your fingers,' he said, 'and my desire to play cards has disappeared,' and he struck them dead and threw them out through the window into the pond.

He was about to sit down again by his fire, when from every side and every corner there came black cats and black dogs connected by red-hot chains. More and more of them appeared until he could no longer move. They shouted horribly, then jumped into his fire and pulled it apart, trying to put it out.

He quietly watched them for a little while, but finally it was too much for him, and he seized his carving-knife, and cried, 'Away with you, you villains!' and hacked away at them. Some of them ran away, the others he killed and threw out into the pond. When he came back he blew into the embers of his fire until they flamed up again, and warmed himself.

As he sat there, his eyes would no longer stay open, and he wanted to fall asleep. Looking around, he saw a large bed in the corner. 'That is just what I wanted,' he said, and lay down in it. However, as he was about to shut his eyes, the bed began to move by itself, going throughout the whole castle.
'Good,' he said, 'but let's go faster.'
Then the bed rolled on as if six horses were harnessed to it, over thresholds and stairways, up and down. But then suddenly, hop, hop, it tipped upside down and lay on him like a mountain. But he threw the covers and pillows into the air, climbed out, and said, 'Now anyone who wants to may drive.' Then he lay down by his fire, and slept until it was day.

In the morning the king came, and when he saw him lying there on the ground, he thought that the ghosts had killed him and that he was dead. Then said he, 'It is indeed a pity to lose such a handsome person.'
The boy heard this, got up, and said, 'It hasn't come to that yet.'
The king was astonished, but glad, and asked how he had fared.
'Very well,' he replied. 'One night is past. The two others will pass as well.'
When he returned to the innkeeper, the latter looked astonished and said, 'I did not think that I'd see you alive again. Did you learn how to shudder?'
'No,' he said, 'it is all in vain. If someone could only tell me how.'

The second night he again went up to the old castle, sat down by the fire, and began his old song once more, 'If only I could shudder!'
As midnight was approaching he heard a noise and commotion. At first it was soft, but then louder and louder. Then it was a little quiet, and finally, with a loud scream, half of a man came down the chimney and fell in front of him.
'Hey!' he shouted. 'Another half belongs here. This is too little.'
Then the noise began again. With roaring and howling the other half fell down as well.
'Wait,' he said. 'Let me blow on the fire and make it burn a little warmer for you.'
When he had done that and looked around again. The two pieces had come together, and a hideous man was sitting in his place.
'That wasn't part of the wager,' said the boy. 'That bench is mine.'

The man wanted to force him aside, but the boy would not let him, instead pushing him away with force, and then sitting down again in his own place.

Then still more men fell down, one after the other. They brought nine bones from dead men and two skulls, then set them up and bowled with them.

The boy wanted to play too and said, 'Listen, can I bowl with you?'

'Yes, if you have money.'

'Money enough,' he answered, 'but your bowling balls are not quite round.' Then he took the skulls, put them in the lathe and turned them round.

'There, now they will roll better,' he said. 'Hey! This will be fun!'

He played with them and lost some of his money, but when the clock struck twelve, everything disappeared before his eyes. He lay down and peacefully fell asleep.

The next morning the king came to learn what had happened. 'How did you do this time?' he asked.

'I went bowling,' he answered, 'and lost a few pennies.'

'Did you shudder?'

'How?' he said. 'I had great fun, but if I only knew how to shudder.'

On the third night he sat down again on his bench and said quite sadly, 'If only I could shudder!'

When it was late, six large men came in carrying a coffin. At this he said, 'Aha, for certain that is my little cousin, who died a few days ago.' Then he motioned with his finger and cried out, 'Come, little cousin, come.'

They put the coffin on the ground. He went up to it and took the lid off. A dead man lay inside. He felt his face, and it was cold as ice.

'Wait,' he said, 'I will warm you up a little.' He went to the fire and warmed his own hand, then laid it on the dead man's face, but the dead man remained cold. Then he took him out, sat down by the fire, and laid him on his lap, rubbing the dead man's arms to get the blood circulating again.

When that did not help either, he thought to himself, 'When two people lie in bed together, they keep each other warm.' So he carried the dead man to the bed, put him under the covers, and lay down next to him. A little while later the dead man became warm too and began to move.

The boy said, 'See, little cousin, I got you warm, didn't I?'

But the dead man cried out, 'I am going to strangle you.'

'What?' he said. 'Is that my thanks? Get back into your coffin!' Then he picked him up, threw him inside, and shut the lid. Then the six men came and carried him away again.

'I cannot shudder,' he said. 'I won't learn it here as long as I live.'

Then a man came in. He was larger than all others, and looked frightful. But he was old and had a long white beard.

'You wretch,' he shouted, 'you shall soon learn what it is to shudder, for you are about to die.'

'Not so fast,' answered the boy. 'If I am to die, I will have to be there.'

'I've got you,' said the old man.

'Now, now, don't boast. I am just as strong as you are, and probably even stronger.'

'We shall see,' said the old man. 'If you are stronger than I am, I shall let you go. Come, let's put it to the test.'

Then the old man led him through dark passageways to a blacksmith's forge, took an axe, and with one blow drove one of the anvils into the ground.

'I can do better than that,' said the boy, and went to the other anvil. The old man stood nearby, wanting to look on. His white beard hung down. The boy seized the axe and split the anvil with one blow, wedging the old man's beard in the crack.

'Now I have you,' said the boy. 'Now it is your turn to die.' Then he seized an iron bar and beat the old man until he moaned and begged him to stop, promising that he would give him great riches. The boy pulled out the axe and released him.

The old man led him back into the castle, and showed him three chests full of gold in a cellar.

'Of these,' he said, 'one is for the poor, the second one is for the king, and the third one is yours.'

Meanwhile it struck twelve, and the spirit disappeared, leaving the boy standing in the dark. 'I can find my own way out,' he said. Feeling around, he found his way to the bedroom, and fell asleep by his fire.

The next morning the king came and said, 'By now you must have learned how to shudder.'

'No,' he answered. 'What is it? My dead cousin was here, and a bearded man came and showed me a large amount of money down below, but no one showed me how to shudder.'

Then the king said, 'You have redeemed the castle, and shall marry my daughter.'

'That is all very well,' said the boy, 'but I still do not know how to shudder.'

Then the gold was brought up, and the wedding celebrated, but however much the young king loved his wife, and however happy he was, he still was always saying, 'If only I could shudder.'

Then, one morning he imagined what would happen if his wife left him. He started to shake and cry.

'I have learned it,' he cried. 'I have learned fear. Look, I am shaking!'

And that's how he finally learned to shudder.

The Woodcutter and the Snake

Here's a Serbian story about thinking for yourself, not just going along with the crowd. The nice thing about it is it seems to be about something else and has a great dramatic ending. On the way there are three dreams, which you can develop with atmosphere and description, and a repeating story about giving bad advice to the king where you and your audience can make sections up. I first heard this from Ben Haggarty, who told it right after the 9/11 bombings. A good story to take with you into secondary school life.

Once there was a king who had a dream. He dreamed he was walking through a dark forest. Foxes jumped out, biting and barking, and we woke in a cold sweat.

In the morning he asked his advisors what the dream meant.
'You are as smart as a fox,' said one.
'We should chop down the forest,' said another.
'We should hunt all the foxes,' said a third.
'No,' said the king, 'none of those answers feel right.'

He announced that anyone who could interpret his dream in a way that seemed right would receive three bags of gold.

A woodcutter sitting by a wall in the wood was thinking about this when a snake popped out.
'I am the snake who knows everything,' it said.
'Then do you know the meaning of the king's dream? Tell me and we can share the gold.'
'OK,' said the snake, who told him the meaning of the king's dream.

The woodcutter went off to the king and said, 'The dream means that now is a time of trickery. Be on your guard.'
The king felt that was right and gave him the gold.

The woodcutter went home and kept it all.

A year passed and the king had another dream. He was in the same wood. This time arrows were being fired. He was wounded in the leg and shoulder when he woke up shaking.

In the morning the advisers gave their interpretations:
'You are as sharp as an arrow.'
'We need to train more archers.'
'Kill all the outlaws in the woods.'
'No,' said the king, 'not right.' This time he offered five bags of gold to anyone who could tell him its meaning.

The woodcutter saw an opportunity and returned to the snake burrow and knocked on the wall.
'What do you want?' said the snake who knows everything.
'Sorry about the gold. But would you tell me the meaning of this dream. We'll share the five bags and also I'll pay you what I owe you.'
The snake agreed and explained the dream.

Later at the palace the woodcutter said, 'It means that this will be a time of killing. Your life is in danger and many will die. Be on your guard.'
'That's feels right,' said the king and handed over the gold.

The woodcutter went back to the burrow and knocked on the wall. Out came the snake.
'I've got something for you,' said the woodcutter and he whipped out a knife and tried to stab the snake, but it slipped back into the hole faster that the woodcutter could stab.

A year passed and the king had a third dream. He was in the wood looking at a light at the end of the path. He walked out into a green field full of butterflies and sheep, lay down and looked up at the blue sky with a smile on his face.

In the morning he asked the advisers the meaning:
'We need more sheep.'
'You will lead our nation to happiness.'
'The weather will be fine.'
'No,' said the king, 'that's not it!'

He offered seven bags of gold for a good interpretation and the woodcutter saw another opportunity. He went to the burrow and knocked on the wall.
'Sorry,' he said when the snake appeared. 'I was wrong to try and kill you, but now I am truly sorry. Forgive me. If you tell me the meaning of the last dream I'll pay you everything I owe you.' (That's 1.5 plus 2.5 plus 3.5 = 7.5 bags.)

The snake agreed and told him.

At the palace he said, 'Your dream means that we are in a time of harmony and happiness. No more danger. Now you can relax and enjoy good times.'
The king was pleased and handed over the gold.

The woodcutter went back to the snake's burrow and knocked.
'Here's the gold,' he said. 'Is that OK? Does that make everything right?'

The snake slithered out of the hole and stood up on tail tip, towering above the man like some great dragon. He hissed and snarled, 'Do you think I care about that!' he said. 'I am the snake who knows everything. I can have anything I want! You are pathetic! You are like some parrot that only copies and never thinks for himself. Look! When it was a time of trickery you tried to trick me; when everyone was killing you tried to kill me; when everyone was being peaceful and loving you were peaceful and loving. What about YOU? You're a unique human being but you behave just like everyone else. Think about that!'

The snake went back to his burrow and the woodcutter went back to his home and thought for a long time about what the snake said.

Three Questions

This Russian folktale was made famous in its retelling by Tolstoy himself. It asks the big questions about life and comes up with a clear-cut answer to ponder. It is used by various spiritual teachers as a 'perfect parable'. It's a great story to take with you on your journey through life. The telling is quite straightforward, but make sure the sequence of actions by the enemy of the king is clear, so that we understand how the king saved his own life.

It once occurred to a certain king, that if he always knew the right time to begin everything; if he knew who were the right people to do things with; and, above all, if he always knew what was the most important thing to do, he would guarantee success in all his works.

So he declared that he would give a great reward to anyone who would teach him those three things: what was the right time for every action, the most important people to deal with, and how he might know what was the most important thing to do.

Learned men came to the king and offered their answers. In reply to the question of right timing, some said that to know the right time for every action, one must draw up in advance a table of days, months and years, and must live strictly according to it. Only in this way could everything be done at its proper time.

Others declared that it was impossible to decide beforehand the right time for every action but that one should always attend to all that was going on, and then do what was most needful.

Others, again, said that however attentive the king might be to what was going on, it was impossible for one man to decide correctly the right time for every action, but that he should have a council of wise men, who would help him to fix the proper time for everything.

But then others said there were some things which could not wait to be laid before a council, but about which one had at once to decide whether to undertake them or not. But in order to decide that, one must know beforehand what was going to happen. It is only magicians who know that; and, therefore, in order to know the right time for every action, one must consult magicians.

There were equally varied answers to the second question. Some said, the people the king most needed were his councillors; others, the priests; others, the doctors; while some said the warriors were the most necessary.

To the third question, as to the most important thing to do: some replied that the most important thing in the world was science. Others said it was skill in warfare; and others, again, that it was religious worship.

The king was not satisfied with any of the answers. Indeed, he noticed a certain self-interest in most of the replies. Doctors promoted doctoring. Priests promoted religion. Magicians promoted magic.

He knew of a wise hermit who lived in solitude deep in the forest, and decided to visit him and ask for his advice. It was known that the hermit would only receive commoners, so the king dressed in simple clothes and set off with his bodyguards for the forest. At the forest's edge he left his horse and asked them to wait for him, and continued alone towards the hermit's hut.

When the king approached, the frail old hermit was digging the ground in front of his hut. When he saw the king he gave him a brief smile and then carried on digging.

The king watched the old man digging: he was obviously tired but he kept on going.
After a while the king said: 'I have come to you, to ask you three questions: How can I learn to do the right thing at the right time? Who are the people I most need to do it, and what is the thing that should be done?'
The hermit listened to the king, but said nothing. He just spat on his hand and recommenced digging.
'You are tired,' said the king, 'let me take the spade and help.'
The hermit gave the spade to the king, and sat down on the ground.
When he had dug two rows, the king stopped and repeated his questions, but the hermit again gave no answer, but rose, stretched out his hand for the spade, and said, 'Now rest and let me work a bit.'

But the king did not give him the spade, and continued to dig. One hour passed, and another. The sun began to sink behind the trees, and the king at last stuck the spade into the ground, and said, 'I came to you, wise man, for an answer to my questions. If you can give me none, tell me so, and I will return home.'

'Here comes someone running,' said the hermit, 'let us see who it is.'
The king turned round, and saw a bearded man come running out of the wood. The man held his hands pressed against his stomach. Blood was flowing from a wound in his belly. When he reached the king, he fell fainting on the ground moaning feebly. The king and the hermit unfastened the man's clothing. There was a large wound in his stomach. The king washed it as best he could, and bandaged it with his handkerchief and with a towel the hermit had. But the blood would not stop flowing.

Again and again the king washed and re-bandaged the wound. Finally the bleeding stopped and the man opened his eyes. The king gave him a drink of water, carried him into the hermit's hut and laid him on a bed where he slept till morning. The king fell asleep too, exhausted from his day's exertions.

When the king woke it was morning and the bearded man was staring at him with tears in his eyes.
'Forgive me!' said the bearded man.
'I do not know you, and have nothing to forgive you for,' said the king.
'You do not know me, but I know you. I am your enemy. Once you had my brother executed and confiscated our family lands. I swore revenge. I came here to kill you: I was waiting to ambush you when you left this place but your bodyguards caught me and I was wounded. Still I got away and came here, where you saved my life. So please, forgive me. I am in your debt and will serve you in any way I can.'
The king smiled, 'Let us now be friends,' he said, 'and both forgive the past. I will restore your family lands when I return to the city.'

The king left his new friend to rest and went outside to look for the hermit, who he found, on his knees, sowing seeds in the beds that had been dug the day before.
The king approached him, and said, 'For the last time, I pray you to answer my questions, wise man.'
'You have already been answered!' said the hermit with a grin.
'How answered? What do you mean?' asked the king.
'Do you not see?' replied the hermit. 'If you had not pitied my weakness yesterday, and had not dug those beds for me, but had gone your way, that man would have attacked and killed you. So the most important time was when you were digging the beds; and I was the most important man; and to do me good was your most important business. Afterwards when that man ran to us, the most important time was when you were attending to him, for if you had not bound up his wounds he would have died without having made peace with you. So he was the most important man, and what you did for him was your most important business.

'Remember then: there is only one time that is important – now! It is the most important time because it is the only time when we have any power.

'The most important person is the one right in front of you; and the most important thing is to do him good, because for that purpose alone we are sent into this life!'

The king was filled with joy at the hermit's words. They guided his rule as king till the end of his days.

Gawain and the Green Knight

This is one of the classics of medieval British literature, evoking the world of Arthurian chivalry. The beginning is shocking and gory, the middle can be funny and a bit weird, and the ending is puzzling and surprising.

Long ago, in the castle of Camelot, King Arthur was at table with his knights. It was New Year's Eve and all the knights were there sharing stories and swilling their mead. Just then the door swung opened and in rode a huge man, almost a giant, riding a huge horse. It was strange to see a rider in the banquet hall, but stranger still was the colour of this man. He was green from head to toe – green hair, green face, green hands, green teeth – everything was green. He had fearsome flaming eyes and carried a huge axe in one hand.
'You are welcome,' said Arthur from his throne. 'Tell me friend, what brings you here? Will you eat with us tonight?'
'NO!' he growled, 'I am not here to eat. I'm here to challenge you. Do any of your knights dare this challenge? Tonight chop into my neck with this axe, and then in a year's time if I am able, I will do the same to whoever tries his luck with me.'
Sir Gawain, Arthur's most perfect knight, quickly stepped forward.
'I will do it!' he said.
The Green Knight dismounted, knelt down in front of Gawain, handed him the axe, and bent down so Gawain could swing the axe at his neck. Gawain lifted the heavy axe up in to the air, let it swing down and ... whhhhsh ... it sliced clean through the green man's neck. His head rolled down over the floor and under the table. Gawain was just about to raise his hand in a salute of victory when he noticed that the Green Knight's body was still kneeling and headless. As he watched, the body stood, walked over to the table, reached underneath it and took hold of its own head by the hair. Then the head spoke, 'See you in a year, Gawain. Ask for the Green Lodge. You can meet me there.'

Winter turned to spring, spring to summer and summer to autumn and when the first snows of winter began to fall Gawain set off in search of the Green Lodge.
Everywhere he asked about the Green Lodge, but nobody knew where to find it.

Then on Christmas Eve he was riding down a valley when he saw a large manor house on the road. He rode up the drive and was greeted by a huge man with a big bushy beard and bright staring eyes.

'I am the Baron,' he said. 'This is my home. What brings you here?'

'I seek the Green Lodge,' he said.

'You are near your journey's end. It is one hour's ride from here. Stay for a few days, rest and then be on your way.'

Gawain was tired and happily agreed.

That evening Gawain sat at the table between the Baron and his beautiful young wife. All evening she talked with him, smiling and laughing as they talked.

Before bed the Baron said, 'Tomorrow I will go hunting. You stay here and rest. Whatever I catch I will give to you. Whatever you win while I am away you must give to me. Do you agree?'

Gawain nodded.

The next morning Gawain was resting in bed when there was a knock on the door and the young wife slipped in and sat on the edge of his bed.

'Hello,' she said, smiling.

'What are you doing here?' said Gawain. 'You shouldn't come into my bedroom!'

'Oh, I just want a kiss!' she said giggling, leant over and kissed him on the cheek, then left.

That evening the Baron came back from hunting and Gawain was there to welcome him. He threw a brace of rabbits at Gawain's feet.

'That's what I won. What did you get?'

Gawain walked over to the Baron and kissed him on the cheek!

'I see,' said the Baron. 'Then let's do the same thing tomorrow. I'll hunt and you rest. Whatever each of us wins in the day we will give to the other.'

The next morning the Baron's wife came into his bedroom again and sat on the bed.

'Out!' shouted Gawain.

'In a minute,' she said, leaned down and kissed Gawain on both cheeks.

'Bye!' and she giggled her way out of the room.

That evening the Baron came back with a wild boar.

'This is for you,' he said to Gawain. 'What have you got for me?'

Gawain walked over to the Baron and kissed both of his cheeks.

'Good man!' said the Baron. 'Same again tomorrow?'

'Fine!' said Gawain.

The next morning, with the Baron off hunting, she came into his room again.

This time she took off a green garter from her leg and gave it to him.

'Keep this for me!' she said and kissed him straight on the lips!

That evening when the Baron came back he gave Gawain a wild deer. In return Gawain went up to the Baron and kissed him on the lips. But he didn't give him the garter...

The next day, following the Baron's directions, Gawain arrived at the Green Lodge, and saw the Green Knight outside sharpening his axe.
'Good,' said the Knight. 'Just in time. Come over here!'
Gawain dismounted and knelt down ready to face death. The Green Knight stood above him, swung back the axe and then swung it down at Gawain's neck ... but stopped the swing just before it touched him.
'That's for the first day, when you kissed me once!' he said, laughing.
Gawain was puzzled and glanced up at the Knight. He looked familiar but... The axe swung down again, and again stopped just short of his neck.
'That was for the second day, when you kissed me twice.' Gawain looked again. The Green Knight looked just like the Baron. Could it be the same person? The axe swung a third time and this time just nicked Gawain's neck so that three drops of blood fell onto his tunic.
'And that's for the third time. You kept your word with the kiss but kept the garter for yourself. That cut is for the garter.'
Gawain was confused. 'So ... you are the Baron?'
'Yes,' he said. 'You passed the test of honesty well enough. Now you can go home. Happy New Year!'

So Gawain, relieved, went home and told the story to the Knights of the Round Table.
At the end of the story he said, '...and I feel so bad. I kept the garter and broke my word. I have failed you all.'
'Not at all,' said Arthur. 'On the contrary, we all honour you and your courage. You have been brave and honest and also you have been human. Nobody is perfect, not even you, Gawain, and that's just fine. From now on let us all wear a green garter to remind us all that nobody is perfect, not even a Knight of the Round Table. In the end we are all imperfect and *human*.'
Everyone cheered, the music played and the mead flowed and they danced and danced and danced.

Mother Sun and Her Daughters

This story, from Argentina, evokes cycles of having children and leaving home. It provides a mythical and magical take on the subject. I love the way it cycles and that in this story the mother is the sun. Anyone who has ever had or been a parent can connect with this story.

Once.

Mother Sun would dance across the sky every day surrounded by her twelve daughters. She loved them and they loved her and she shined with happiness.

As they danced across the sky they sang an ancient song.

> *Dawn to dusk, dusk to dawn*
> *The sun will shine, the moon will dance*
> *Dusk to dawn, dawn to dusk*
> *We feel the mountains call*

In the evenings the daughters would look down over the edge of the sky down to earth. They saw fires, they saw men, and they saw dancing, heard singing.

They said, 'Mama, can we go down there?'

'Why would you want that?' she said, nervously. 'Everything is perfect up here.'

Then one night, under their mother's bed, they found a rope made from their mother's dreams. They hooked it to the edge of the sky and climbed down to the earth, singing their song.

The men stopped dancing and watched as the girls slipped down the rope, singing:

> *Dawn to dusk, dusk to dawn*
> *The sun will shine, the moon will dance*
> *Dusk to dawn, dawn to dusk*
> *We feel the mountains call*

They led them over to the fire. The drummers drummed, the players played and the daughters danced and danced with their new friends.

Raven was watching.
'Time for a change!' he croaked to himself.

He flew to the rope of dreams
He flew up to the place it met the sky.
He cut though the rope with his sharp beak and it fell to the ground.

At dawn the daughters looked for the rope to climb back to their mother but it was gone, so they returned to the fires and stayed with their men. Soon they were all married. In a way they were happy to be married but there was also a feeling of having been tricked into it – an unspoken resentment towards their husbands.

Now Mother Sun was sad. She gazed down at her daughters and cried. Her light was weak and her journey across the sky was swift. It was winter. She missed them so much. There was no more singing and dancing. Only grieving.

Then one evening she looked over the edge of the sky into a cave, down into the eyes of Jaguar Man. She wove a rope of her dreams, hooked it to the edge of the sky and climbed down into his cave.
Now she was happier.
She visited him every night.
Then one day she felt her belly swelling.
She no longer visited Jaguar Man.
She waited as her belly grew round and huge.
She gave birth to twelve new daughters and hid that rope of dreams under her bed.
Soon they all danced and shone across the sky, singing and smiling.

> *Dawn to dusk, dusk to dawn*
> *The sun will shine, the moon will dance*
> *Dusk to dawn, dawn to dusk*
> *We feel the mountains call*

Time passed and in the evenings the daughters peered down towards earth…

Five Wise Trainings

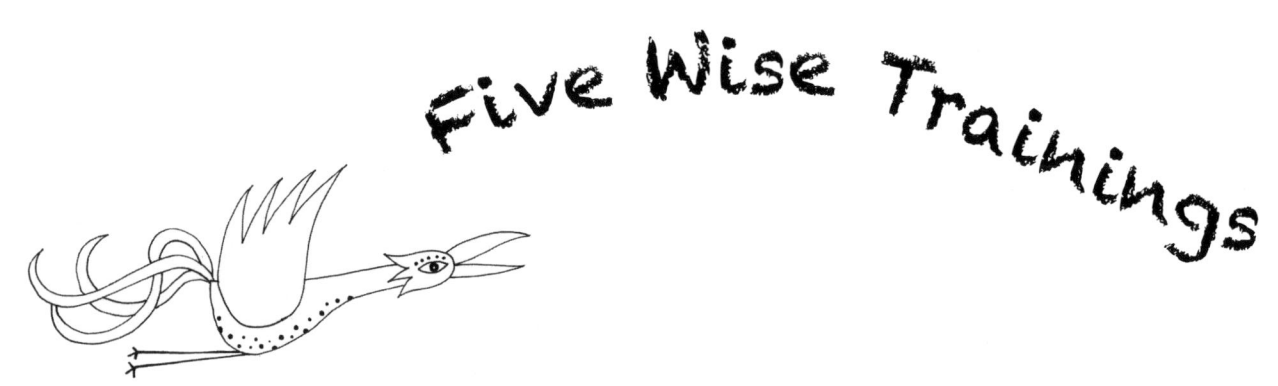

Here's an Indian story about finding rules and principles from which to live your life. It has all sorts of plot variety within it. Pay attention to the ending: make sure it is clear how and why the king's brother was killed.

Once there was a boy called Ram Sing, who lived in a little village on the edge of a wide shimmering desert. His family was very poor and often they went to bed hungry.

One day his father told him he should leave home, leave school and travel to the city to find work as there was not enough food to go round. Ram Sing agreed. He packed a small sack with food and a few clothes and went off to the temple to speak to the wise old monk who lived there. The old man had been a friend to Ram Sing since he was a baby. Ram was going to miss him.

'I have to leave now,' said Ram Sing. 'Tell me how I should behave in the wide world. What is it like? I have never left this village!'

The old man smiled, 'You are a good young man,' he said. 'Behave in the world as you do in this village, with kindness and courtesy, and you will do well. Here are five rules – try and keep them and they will protect you from harm.
First, work hard: this will lead to success.
Second, be kind: this will lead to safety.
Third, be truthful: this will lead to trust.
Fourth, be humble: this will lead to friendship.
Fifth, listen to those wiser than you: this will lead to wisdom.

Ram Sing bowed, left the temple and started off across the desert. As he walked he replayed the conversation over and over in his mind, trying hard to remember the five things he should do.

After three days and nights he came to a city and, hungry and tired, he went to the marketplace. He looked around, saw a man dressed in fine expensive robes, and went up to him.

'Excuse me, sir,' he said, 'I am new in this town and need a job. I am young and strong and will do whatever work is needed. Can you help me?'

The man looked Ram up and down and smiled.

'As it happens the chief minister needs a personal servant. You look honest and trustworthy. Would you like the job?'

Ram Sing nodded and smiled and within the hour he was working for the minister.

A few weeks later the minister and the king were travelling across the desert with a caravan of servants and soldiers, on the way to the neighbouring kingdom. Halfway across they ran out of water. They stopped at the next village and asked for water but the villager said they had none to spare, there was just a little for themselves.

The king was not pleased and shouted at the minister to find water. The minister bowed and told Ram Sing to solve the problem. Ram Sing remembered the monk's advice to work hard. He bowed to the minister. 'I will do my best,' he said.

He walked off into the village asking everyone he saw if there was a way to find water. At first everyone just shook their heads but finally a very old little man said, 'There is an old well on the edge of town, but we don't use it. Everyone who goes there never comes back!'

Ram Sing took two buckets and set off for the well. When he got there he saw a staircase leading deep down into the ground. He went deeper and deeper into the ground until it was completely dark. Finally his toes touched water and he started to fill the buckets. Just then he saw a light coming down the staircase. As it came closer he saw a huge giant carrying a flaming torch in one hand and clutching a pile of bones to his chest with the other. The giant looked angry. Ram Sing kept quiet.

The giant stared down at him, growled and looked at the bones.

'What do you think of my wife then?' he said.

Ram thought about it. The bones must have been his wife. He must have loved her. What should he say? Maybe he thinks she's still alive!

Just then he remembered the monk's second piece of advice: to be kind. But also he should speak the truth. What should he say?

'I am sure,' he said, 'there is no other like her in all the world.'

The giant smiled.

'You answer well,' he said. 'Others have said she is just a pile of bones and I have killed them for that. But you were kind. How can I reward you?'

'Well,' said Ram. 'I'd like you to stop haunting this well please and let people drink from it again.'

'OK!' said the giant, and disappeared.

An hour later Ram returned to the king with buckets brimming with sweet cold water and told them where to get more. He then went and told the villagers that the well was safe and they were delighted.

The king was impressed too. 'Now you can work for me!' he said.

Back in the city, Ram Sing worked as a clerk in the king's office, working hard and always trying to speak the truth. Soon he became trusted by all and rose through the ranks till he was the chief treasurer.

This made the king's brother jealous. The brother liked to steal money from the king's treasury but with Ram Sing in charge it was difficult. One day he came to Ram and said, 'My friend. You are now one of the most important persons in the kingdom. We should be friends. Let me offer you my daughter as your bride and then you will be like a royal family member. Better than ordinary people. Marry her!'

Ram Sing was tempted, but it didn't feel right. He remembered the words of the old monk (be humble) and politely declined.

This made the brother angry and he decided to plot against him. He went to the king and said, 'Brother, that Ram Sing is speaking against you. He says he would make a better king than you. He wants to be king. You must do something!'

The king believed his brother and hatched a plan.

There was a building project by the western gate that Ram had been supervising. The king sent two guards there saying, 'When someone comes and asks when the project will be finished, chop off his head and bring it to me in a bag.'

The guards went off and Ram Sing was summoned. 'Go to the building project by the western gate,' the king said, 'and ask them when it will be finished.'

Ram set off toward the gate but on the way he heard the sound of teaching coming from a temple. Remembering the monk's advice about listening to those wiser than oneself, he went into the temple to listen to the talk. He became so absorbed in the teaching he lost all sense of time.

Meanwhile the king's brother was impatient. He went to the king and asked what had happened.
'I have sent Ram Sing to the western gate where he will be killed. I am just waiting for his head to be delivered.'

They waited for a while and then the brother left and rode out to the gate. He stopped at the building project and asked the guards, 'Well! Has it been done? When will it be done?'

The guard swung his sword and the brother's head rolled. They put it in a sack and set off back for the palace.

Meanwhile, the king had lost patience and was riding out to the gate to see what had happened. As he passed by the temple Ram Sing heard the clatter of hooves, turned and saw the king and ran out to him.

At the same moment the guards met the king in the street.
'We have done as you asked,' said the guards and handed the king the bag.
The king looked at Ram Sing, puzzled. Then he looked in the bag and was shocked.

He kept quiet and made an investigation, which revealed his brother's treachery. Ram Sing remained treasurer and lived long and happily in the king's palace.

When he had children of his own he taught them the five trainings to protect you in life:

Work hard, be kind, be truthful, by humble, and listen to the wise.

With such good advice they did well when it was their turn to go out into the wide world, avoiding harm and finding happiness.

Gawain Gets Married

Here's another Arthurian tale about Gawain. This one provides a chance to look at differences between men and women, and gives a tip or two for successful relationships. Milk the ugliness of the old crone for maximum impact. Get lots of audience suggestions about what Arthur found on his research trip.

One summer's evening at the court of King Arthur, the knights were feasting and drinking and telling their stories when the door of the hall was flung open and in ran a woman. Her clothes were those of a noble woman, but were torn and dirty. She had a tear-streaked face and cuts on her arms and feet.

She ran to the throne of the king and knelt before him. 'Your majesty, I come to you for justice. The Black Knight came to my castle and burned it to the ground. He killed my husband and my three children and took others away as slaves. He is evil and must be stopped. Please, will you help me?'

Arthur nodded. 'I have heard of this Black Knight. Tomorrow I will ride to his castle and challenge him.'

The next day Arthur rode off through the English wildwood to the Black Knight's castle. When he arrived he stopped. It was a huge dark building surrounded by a wide moat with the smell of death. No way in. He rode around the castle three times. On the third circle a drawbridge appeared where there had been none before and he rode inside.

The courtyard was empty and silent as death. Arthur dismounted and was about to shout out his challenge, when he found himself frozen to the spot. He couldn't move anything from the neck down. Some enchantment was working on him so he just stood there and waited.

A while later a knight appeared wearing black armour over the whole of the body and a black helmet with a visor down over the face. No skin showed anywhere. The knight walked over to Arthur, drew a sword and pressed it against Arthur's neck.
'Welcome, Arthur,' hissed a voice from behind the visor. 'Now you are here, I think I will kill you.'

'I challenge you to a duel,' said Arthur. 'A fair duel. Will you fight?'
'Why should I bother with that stuff?' hissed the voice. 'I can just kill you now ... no, maybe I'll set you a challenge. You can either accept the challenge or I'll kill you now. What's it going to be?'
'Ummm ... I'll take the challenge.'
'Good, so here's your task. Find the answer to this question: what is it that the women of the world really want? You have a year to get the right answer. Come back here in a year's time and if you don't get it right then I'll chop off your head. Do you agree?'
'OK,' said Arthur.

The knight disappeared and moments later Arthur found he could move his body. He rode out of the castle and off to find the answer. Arthur travelled from place to place, asking everyone he met what they thought women really wanted. Men said one thing, women said other things, but Arthur was never really sure if he had the right answer.

After a year of travel he was riding back to the Black Knight's castle, preparing to lose his head, when he saw an old lady sitting by a bush. She was the ugliest lady he had ever seen. Matted hair, corkscrew nose and twisted chin. Her teeth were black and her skin had a greenish hue. 'Hello,' she said.
'Hello,' said Arthur.
'I know the answer to your riddle,' she said.
'Really?' said Arthur.
'Yes,' she said, 'but if I tell you I need something from you. Find me a young handsome knight to marry me. Do that and I'll tell you the answer.'
'OK,' said Arthur, 'I'll do my best.'
She told him the answer to the riddle.

Back in the castle Arthur returned to the courtyard and again found himself frozen to the spot. Out came the Black Knight, covered from head to toe in black armour.
'Well,' said the knight. 'What do women really want?'
'Handbags?' said Arthur.
'No!'
'Husbands?'
'NO!'
'Diamonds?'
'NO!'
This went on for a while, then the knight said, 'If you can't do better than that, Arthur, you don't deserve to live.'

'OK,' Arthur said, 'then I'll tell you. This is the true answer. Women want sovereignty: to be able to choose their own path. Just as a king rules over his kingdom, so women want to be able to rule over themselves.'
The knight hissed, 'How did you know that? How could you get that right?'
'Who are you?' said Arthur.
The knight took off the helmet and Arthur gasped. Long hair as black as a raven's back flowed out. Fair white skin and blood red lips. It was his half-sister, Morgana.
'Why?' he said. 'Why did you do this? Why did you kill that poor woman's family?'
'Oh, you silly man!' she said. 'That was all just a story. I made it up to get you here. You are so busy with dragons and rescuing maidens I thought you needed some education. That's all. Now you can go.'

She disappeared and Arthur returned to his castle, where he told the story to his knights. When he had finished his story he said, 'So now I need a volunteer, to keep my promise.'
The room went quiet. Knights were looking at the floor.
'I need a husband for the old woman. Who will marry her?'
He waited for a while and then young, handsome Gawain stood up.
'I will do it, your majesty. I will marry her, for you.'
The other knights clapped and breathed a sigh of relief. 'He's really brave!' they thought.

The next day Gawain rode to the bush where he found the old lady.
'Hello,' she said, grinning through her few blackened teeth. 'You must be my husband. Will you marry me?'
Gawain stared at her wrinkled twisted old face and her gummy mouth. Then he took a deep breath.
'I will,' he said.
'Oh goodie! Let's go back to the castle.'
She jumped up behind him on the horse and they rose back to Camelot.

They were married the same day. There was a small feast, but Gawain was not feeling very cheerful. Every time he looked at the old lady his heart sank.
'All my life I dreamed I would marry a perfect, beautiful woman, and instead I marry an old hag!'

After the feast they went to their bedroom. The old lady slipped under the covers and waited for Gawain to join her. He came a while later and lay in the bed, right on the edge, as far away from the old lady as possible.

'What's the matter, husband?' she cried. 'Don't you like me?'
He turned towards her and caught a blast of her foul, rotting breath.
'Kiss me!' she said, giggling.
With his mind firmly on duty Gawain closed his eyes, leaned over and kissed the old lady firmly on the lips. It was odd. They seemed strangely soft. He opened his eyes and in front of him was a lovely young woman with clear skin, ruby lips and long silky hair.
'Who are you?' he said.
'I am your wife,' she said. 'I was cursed to have the form of an old woman till I found a husband who could accept me the way I am. With your kiss you broke the spell.'
'Wow!' said Gawain. 'That's great news!'
'Yes,' she said. 'Now I can be young like this half the time and old the other half. It's up to you, husband. Would you like me young in the day and old at night, or the other way round?'
Gawain thought about it. He remembered Arthur's story about what women want.
'What would you like?' he asked.
She shrieked with delight.
'Oh Gawain, now you have broken the other half of the spell. I was to stay half and half, old and young, till I found a husband who wanted what was best for me. Now there is no spell and I can be cute like this all the time. Hooray. You are my hero!'

They delighted in each other's company and in the morning they went down to breakfast to the admiration of the court. When Gawain told his story the knights clapped.
'You deserve her,' they said. 'You are the bravest of knights.'

And so they lived as husband and wife happily until the end of their days.

Everything You Need

Here's a powerful and somewhat gruesome story from Iraq. It's full of tension and descriptive power – not for the faint-hearted, but certainly memorable and replete with learnings. The main thing is to evoke the character of Abdul and his desperation, and then the shock and horror of the various catastrophes. You can find more like this in a wonderful collection called Tales from the Arab Tribes *by C.G. Campbell, who collected the stories in southern Iraq about 100 years ago.*

Once in the ancient city of Basra there was a poor carpenter, Abdul, who lived with his wife in a tumbled down shack on the edge of town. When it rained the rain poured through holes in the roof, soaking husband and wife alike as they shivered in the cold.

On one such day a damp Abdul was sitting in an inn sipping coffee when he overheard a stranger talking at the next table. He was eating fine food and sipping sweet drinks. Abdul watched with jealously and felt his empty tummy rumble.

He listened to the stranger talking about his life in the desert and how there was buried wealth there.

'Under the desert I know of a tunnel that will lead a man to great wealth. Few dare enter the tunnel. There is talk of the ghosts and spirits that guard it but I say that is just old superstition. Anyone who has the courage to travel this tunnel will find more gold than they can ever count. Those who had the courage to travel to those treasure houses will find great wealth. Those who are frightened of superstitions and ghosts will remain poor. Do any of you have such courage? If so I can promise you more gold than you can hold in your hands, more jewels than you can count on your fingers, and more knowledge than you can ever speak of. Do any of you have the courage?'

The group around the table murmured the name of God and said that no, they would not go near the spirits of the desert, but Abdul, damp and cold, called out:
'I will do it! I have no such fear. Take me to the tunnel!'

The man smiled and nodded. The next day they took two camels out into the desert and travelled deep into the golden sand. They stopped by a ruined stone hut and stepped inside the walls. The man got down on his knees and started digging in the sand with his hands, revealing a brass door underneath.

Written on the door were the words:

HE WHO ENTERS HERE WILL HAVE MORE GOLD THAN HE CAN CARRY, MORE JEWELS THAN HE CAN COUNT AND MORE KNOWLEDGE THAN HE CAN SPEAK OF. KISS THE DOOR TO ENTER.

Thinking of his leaky roof and his unhappy wife, Abdul kissed the door. It slid open revealing a stone staircase going deep down under the earth.

'You're on your own from here,' said the man and settled down in the shade of the wall.

Abdul walked down the stairs thinking of all the money he would soon own, the house he would buy and the wonderful things he would fill it with.

The steps went deeper and deeper into the cold clammy depths of the desert. He stopped at a tunnel lit by flaming torches and he walked for what seemed like hours till he came to a second door with the same words on it.
HE WHO ENTERS HERE WILL HAVE MORE GOLD THAN HE CAN CARRY, MORE JEWELS THAN HE CAN COUNT AND MORE KNOWLEDGE THAN HE CAN SPEAK OF. KISS THE DOOR TO ENTER.

Abdul kissed the door and it swung open and he stepped inside.

At first he saw only darkness, but as his eyes adjusted to the dark he realised he was in a huge cavern. Skeletons hung from the cave walls, staring at him from their boney sockets. In the centre of the cave was a huge pile of gold. Abdul was just about to fill his pockets when a voice boomed down from the top of the golden hoard.

'Come!' she said. 'Kiss me and the treasure you seek will be yours.'

On top of the gold a woman sat with long black hair, covered in golden jewellery.

'Kiss me!' she repeated.

Abdul scrambled up the pile of coins and at the top he leaned over and kissed her.

Immediately he knew something was wrong. He couldn't pull away. Something was pulling on his tongue harder and harder. Blood filled his mouth as his tongue was ripped out of his mouth. Then something else, another tongue, entered his mouth and took its place. Then the woman was gone, dissolving into mist and he was alone with a strange tongue in his mouth.

Abdul was terrified. He tried to pray but the tongue pressed into his throat and choked him till he stopped the prayer.

'You do as I say!' it commanded, speaking through Abdul's own mouth.

The tongue ordered Abdul to go back to Basra and, terrified, Abdul obeyed.

He walked alone through the desert till he came to the city and the tongue ordered him to go to an inn where his friends were drinking coffee.

Then the tongue began to speak.

He said to one of his friends 'Do you know that your brother has been stealing from your shop? Every day he takes money and hides it under his bed. If you don't believe me go and see.'

The brother rushed home, found the gold and soon the two brothers were fighting. Soon one was stabbed in the belly.

To another friend he said, 'Do you know that your wife no longer loves you? Soon she will ask for a divorce.'

The friend believed the tongue and went home in tears.

One by one the tongue whispered poison to Abdul's friends until every face in the inn was black with anger.

Then the tongue ordered Abdul to go home.

Abdul's wife came out to greet him, but as she approached the tongue called out: 'I divorce you, I divorce you, and I divorce you.'

The wife could not believe her ears and ran away in tears.

Then Abdul's only son came out of the house.

'Go to the well!' ordered the tongue, 'and stand on its edge.'

The boy was frightened at the strange sound of his father's voice but he did as he was told and stood on the well's edge. Then the tongue gave a horrible shriek, giving the son such a fright that he slipped and fell down to the bottom of the well.

Abdul ran away into the streets of Basra trying to think of a way to get rid of the tongue, keeping away from anybody in case the tongue should do any more harm.
He left the city and wandered through the desert till he came to a deep wide river. As he approached for a drink he saw a holy man reciting prayers by the river.

The man stared at Abdul and pointed a staff at his mouth. He felt the tongue being pulled away, pulled out of his mouth, out and away. As it left his mouth he saw that it was a thick black snake.

At that moment Abdul fell into the water with blood pouring from his mouth. Four huge shark-like fish swam towards him and began to eat him alive, one feeding on each limb.

By the time the holy man had pulled him from the water his arms and legs were gone.

The holy man brought a doctor and cared for Abdul till his wounds had healed. He could not speak or write or tell his story to others, but the holy man arranged a place for him to beg in the market. In this way he lived for many years, fed by the good people of Basra city. Every day other beggars helped him to eat and drink, and when coins were dropped in his begging cup they took them for him as he could not do anything for himself.

In this way Abdul lived until he died.

On his grave they left a plaque:

Here is a man who found more gold that he could hold in his hands, more jewels than he could count on his fingers and more knowledge than he could ever speak of.

Gilgamesh

This is one of the first stories to be written down (on clay tablets) and is one of the most wonderful in the storytelling repertoire. It's a huge, many-layered epic of the king of Uruk, moving through friendship, adventure and finally the facing of mortality as the king learns to be a king. This is a short text with some of its best bits.

Once, in the city of Uruk, King Gilgamesh was out of control. He took what he wanted, whenever he wanted it, from anybody. If he wanted food, he took it. If he wanted a wife, he took her. If he wanted a house, he took it. If anyone stood in his way he crushed them with his brute power. He was the king and he did what he wanted. No one could match him in strength. No one could stand against him.

The people of Uruk prayed to the gods.
'Help us!' they said. 'King Gilgamesh does what he wants. He does nothing for the good of his people. He is out of control!'

The gods and goddesses agreed that Gilgamesh needed a friend, an equal, someone to match his power, so they took a ball of clay and threw it down from the heavens to a wasteland outside Uruk. As it hit the ground it turned into a wild man, Enkido.

Enkido lived there for some time as an animal grazing with a herd of deer, protecting them from danger and breaking up the traps the hunters set for them. One hunter saw Enkido, went to Uruk and reported him to Gilgamesh.
'He is a giant, your majesty. As tall and as wide as you. He lives like an animal, covered only in thick long hair.'
'Send him a wife!' said Gilgamesh. 'She will make him into a man.'

They sent a woman from the temple to civilise the wild man. She waited for him in the wasteland, silent and still. When his herd came grazing he scented her. She called to him and he came, sniffing and snorting, not understanding what she was at all. Soon her scent was in him and the herd ran from the smell, leaving Enkido alone with his new wife.

She took him to the city.
She taught him to eat from a plate.

She taught him to drink from a cup.
She taught him to speak.
She taught him all this and more.
Then she took him to the streets of Uruk and waited there.

Gilgamesh was walking to the house of a newly married couple, when Enkido stood in his way. Gilgamesh pushed him but he stood as solid as a tree. Gilgamesh hit him but he would not budge. Then the two giant men clashed, wrestling together for hours with such force that the walls of the city itself shook as they fought. Finally Gilgamesh forced Enkido down on one knee. 'It is over!' he said. The two men embraced and vowed to be friends forever.

From that day Gilgamesh and Enkido were inseparable. They ate together, swam together, wrestled together, played together. Gilgamesh no longer roamed the city taking what he should not. He had a friend.

The Gilgamesh decided that he needed an adventure.
'Come, my brother. Let us go to the Cedar Forest and kill the monster, Humbaba, who lives there. Let's do that now, so our names will be known forever for such a great deed.'

Enkido was not sure. 'Brother, Humbaba is a terrible and huge creature. Are you sure?'
'I will go. I must go. And you with me?'

In order to protect him, Enkido went along. They walked to the forest, covering in a day what would take most men a year. They were huge and marvellous. They walked and walked for three days and three nights until they came to the forest, and in the forest they followed the huge footsteps of Humbaba till they came to his den.

He was as tall as the tallest cedar. As vast as a mountain. He opened his cavern-mouth, showed his sword teeth, and roared.
'Prepare to die!' he cried and rushed out towards them.
Gilgamesh and Enkido drew their swords and rushed towards the great monster, roaring like two wild bulls.
The sun god, friend of Gilgamesh, saw their courage and threw a wind down at Humbaba, pinning him to the ground. Humbaba could not move. Gilgamesh put his axe to the monster's throat. In three strokes of the axe he was dead.

Then they chopped down mighty cedars and made a raft, floated it down the river back to Uruk. Gilgamesh carried Humbaba's head as his trophy.

Back in Uruk, one goddess was in love with Gilgamesh.
She went to him. 'Be my husband,' she said.
Gilgamesh refused. She felt insulted. She was angry.
Furious, she plotted revenge. She went to the gods and complained about Gilgamesh. 'They have broken the law. They have killed the forest guardian. They must pay. Let us send them the great bull of heaven. He will kill them.'

The great bull attacked the two friends but they killed it easily. But that night Enkido had a dream that the gods were meeting to decide his fate. In his dream the angry goddess spoke to the others: 'They have killed Humbaba, cut down the sacred trees and killed the bull of heaven. One of them must die!'
The gods debated and decided that Enkido must die.

When Enkido woke he said to Gilgamesh, 'I dreamed that I will die. I feel it will be soon.'
'NO!' Gilgamesh roared and strutted but could do nothing. His friend died and Gilgamesh laid his body out on a table, refusing to believe his friend had gone.
Then a maggot crawled out of Enkido's nostril.

Gilgamesh tore off his clothes and wearing only a lion skin he marched out of Uruk wild with confusion and grief.
'I will go to the man who has won everlasting life,' he said. 'He will teach me the secret, then I will not be defeated by death. Then perhaps I can save my friend.'

He walked to the tunnel to the other worlds, where the sun races under the earth between dusk to dawn. He waited till sunrise and began to run, running and running to get to the end of the tunnel before sunset when the tunnel would fill with the sun and burn him alive. He ran and ran and made it just in time.

He came to a man on the shore of a lake: a ferryman, surrounded by his stone oarsmen. Gilgamesh ran at them, wild and crazy, and smashed every stone man to pieces. Then he said to the ferryman, 'Take me across the lake to the one who is immortal. Take me!'
'You have smashed my crew!' said the ferryman. 'But cut me one hundred long straight poles from the forest, and I can take you there.'

Gilgamesh rushed at the forest, cutting and cleaning the poles till they were ready, then they boarded the raft. Each pole was used to punt the raft once, and then was dropped into the Sea of Death. To touch that sea means death. In this way they travelled to the opposite shore.

Gilgamesh stepped onto the shore and stared at a thin old man sitting on the beach.
'I seek the one who won immortality,' he said. 'Tell me where to find him.'
'You have found him,' said the man. 'I am he!'
'Then tell me your secret. How may I win immortality?'
'First stay awake for one week, then I will tell you!'
'Fine!' said Gilgamesh. He sat by the shore and immediately fell asleep.
The immortal looked at Gilgamesh and thought, 'When he wakes he will deny that he slept. I shall give him proof.'

Every day his wife baked a loaf of bread and left it in front of Gilgamesh. When he woke after seven days he saw seven loaves, one fresh that day, one covered in mould after the full week, and the others somewhere in between.

'You slept,' said the immortal. 'You have failed. Now go home! But before you go I will tell you this. In the deep ocean there is a green spiny plant. It holds the secret of youth.'

Gilgamesh tied great stones onto his legs and jumped into the great deep. He took the plant in his hand and set off with it back to Uruk. On the way he came to a lake. Leaving the plant by the lake he bathed in the water. While he was bathing a snake came and took the plant away, leaving only a snakeskin behind.

So Gilgamesh returned to Uruk empty-handed, without the secret of eternal life. Without the herb of eternal youth. Yet somehow now he was ready to rule.
He no longer just took what he wanted, whenever he wanted it.
If he wanted food, he asked for it.
If he wanted a wife, he asked the family.
If he wanted a house, he bought it.
If anyone stood in his way, he reasoned with them.

He ruled wisely, doing his best for Uruk and its people.
He was now a great king.
He remained great till his dying day.

That is the tale of Great King Gilgamesh, whose stories were written on clay tablets – the oldest written story in the human world.

A Drop of Honey

This is a great story for talking about conflict and escalation. It is found in the Arabian Nights collection and has also been collected in Iran, Burma and Thailand. Evoke the indifference of the king and the progressive escalation of violence step by step.

Once there was a shepherd from the Western Land. Every spring he took his goats across the river and up into the mountains of the Eastern Land, fattening his flock on the rich mountain grass until autumn, when the snows drove him back west to his village. For half the year he lived on milk, cheese and mutton from his flock, his only companion his beloved sheepdog. For the rest of the year he rested in the comfort of his family home. In this way the years passed.

One autumn the old shepherd, with his flock and dog, was making his way, as usual, down a mountain pass in the Eastern Land, when he passed a village with a large wooden sign advertising an inn and store just around the corner. The shepherd felt a longing for something sweet after nothing but milk and meat for so long. He left his goats grazing on the verge and stepped into the store with his beloved collie at his heels. The shopkeeper welcomed him in the Eastern tongue and, speaking a little himself, the shepherd asked whether he might buy a single spoonful of honey, as he had tasted nothing sweet for months. Although a little disappointed by the paltry scale of the transaction, the shopkeeper nodded his agreement politely and walked over to a large wooden barrel in the corner of the shop with a small metal spoon in his hand while the shepherd stood and waited.

Now, the king of the Eastern Land and his chief minister were in the habit of dressing up in disguise and wandering around the country. On that day the king and minister were sitting drinking coffee in the same shop where the shepherd was waiting for his honey.

The king was pleased that the owner had shown such courtesy to this Westerner by agreeing to his request. He watched as the innkeeper walked towards the barrel. He watched as the spoon was dipped into the honey. He watched as the shopkeeper walked carefully back across the room, the spoon brimming with golden amber.

The minister noticed that, as the shopkeeper walked, the honey on the underside of the spoon was collecting together into a single drop which hung tenuously from the centre of the spoon's base, growing larger moment by moment. He whispered playfully to the king.

'Look! In a moment some honey is going to drip onto the floor. Should we tell him?'

'Not our problem!' laughed the king.

They watched as the weight of the honey drop pulled against its attachment to the spoon and followed its fall down onto the stone slab next to the shepherd's worn old boots. Meanwhile the shepherd gratefully accepted the spoon, placed it in his mouth, and with eyes closed he let the sweetness dissolve onto his taste buds, savouring every sweet moment. While this was going on a large green bluebottle flew past the shepherd's legs and, catching the scent of the drop of honey on the stone floor, immediately changed course and began to descend towards the sweet mound.

The keen-eyed minister noticed this.

'Look, your majesty,' he whispered. 'The bluebottle is going for the honey on the floor. Should we do anything?'

'Definitely not our problem!' said the king.

The shopkeeper had a cat who hated bluebottles. She was sitting by the shepherd, warming herself on a sunlit patch of the floor when she saw the bluebottle veering in her direction. In an instant her muscles were tensed and she was ready to pounce. The minster was watching all this, and pointed it out to the king, who just shrugged and watched.

When the insect was within range the cat jumped, claws stretched, teeth bared, soaring through the air and catching it between her teeth, killing it instantly. However, the momentum of the cat continued to carry her horizontally through the air in the direction of the shepherd's dog who was sitting uneasily by his master, a little confused by the hustle and bustle of the shop after six months of clear mountain quiet.

The dog saw the cat flying towards him and, believing himself to be under attack, he readied himself for a fight, keenly observed by the king and minister. When the cat landed just in front of the dog he jumped on her, sinking his teeth into her neck, killing her with one bite of his strong jaws.

'There'll be trouble now!' whispered the minister. 'Shouldn't we do something?'

'No need,' replied the king. 'It's not our problem. Let's just watch and see what happens.' The shopkeeper was furious. The cat was his only mouser. She had kept his shop free from mice and rats for more than ten years. Seeing the cat limp and lifeless in the dog's mouth, he cursed and kicked out at the dog with all his strength, connecting his boot with the dog's head. There was a crunching of bone as the dog's neck snapped.

The minister looked at the king, but he just shrugged back. 'Not our problem,' he mouthed.

Now the shepherd loved that dog like an only child, his only companion during the long summer months. When he saw its neck snap he pushed the shopkeeper hard in the chest with his strong arms. The shopkeeper fell backwards, tripped over a box behind him, cracked his skull hard against the stone wall, and fell lifeless to the ground. Fearing for what would happen next the shepherd rushed out of the shop and away towards his flock.

The shopkeeper's son, a patriotic young man, was standing in the doorway of the store as his father slumped to the ground. As the shepherd rushed by, he imagined that his father was dead and called to his friends outside.

'Boys! Catch him! That Westerner just killed my dad!'

Inside the store the minster was getting agitated.

'Your majesty, we must do something. The youths are bringing sticks and knives. We should stop this now!'

But the king shook his head.

'Too dangerous,' he said. 'Let's wait till they've calmed down.'

Outside, a crowd of youths pushed the shepherd to the ground, laying into him with their clubs and boots until there was no more life in his bruised and bloody body. When they had finished they turned back towards the shop and saw the shopkeeper standing in the doorway, calling, too late, for them to stop.

News travels fast in the mountains, especially bad news, and it wasn't long before word reached the shepherd's village that he had been killed by a mob of Easterners. Intent on justice, the young men of his village gathered whatever weapons they could muster, crossed over the river and marched up the pass to the nearest Eastern village. When they arrived they found the village empty, its inhabitants fled. The mob eagerly began smashing and burning whatever they could find. Soon the whole village was in flames.

Eastern soldiers were sent to arrest the youths, but when they arrived one of the youths, the cousin of the shepherd, pulled out a pistol and started firing. The soldiers panicked and, in the confused melee that followed, seventeen Westerners were killed by Eastern bullets.

News got back to the Western rulers that there had been a massacre of their people, and the western army was sent to the border on full alert with instructions to repel any attacks with full force. The Eastern king sent his own army to the same border with the same instructions, believing the Westerners were preparing for war. For three tense days the armies faced one another across the river, until a young Westerner whose brother had been killed in the melee took a pot shot across the river at some soldiers who had been taunting them. The Eastern platoon fired back and soon both armies were engaged, shooting across the river and fighting hand to hand at the bridges and fords.

In this way a war began which neither king was able to win, yet neither felt able to stop. Each side blamed the other. Each side wanted revenge or compensation. Both peoples rallied around the thought of their victory over evil, convinced that God was on their side. The war raged for ten years until, with both peoples weary of grieving for their lost sons, a truce was finally declared.

When the two kings met to discuss their truce, the Eastern king told the story of what he had seen at the shop.

'If only I had done something about the honey, or the cat or the dog, or the shepherd,' he said, 'then maybe things would have been different.'

The kings declared that the truce day would be named Honey Day and ordered each country to remembered this story as a reminder that peace is a precious and fragile thing, that we should all, in our own way, protect.

Who is the Husband?

This riddle story is from India. It opens up discussions about who we are, body and mind and heart.

There were once two brothers, one tall and slim, the other short and tubby. The tall, slim brother was happily married. He loved his wife and she loved him just as much. The other brother was single.

One day the two brothers were walking through a forest when they were attacked by a bandit, who chopped off their heads before stealing their goods.

The tall brother's wife waited and waited, and when her husband didn't turn up she went out into the forest to see what had happened.

She found the two bodies and two heads lying on the ground, and collapsed in shock.

She wept and prayed to the goddess Kali, Goddess of Life and Death.
'Mother Kali,' she prayed. 'Please bring my husband back to life. Please!'

The air in front of the wife thickened and swam in front of her eyes as the great goddess appeared in front of her.

'I will grant your request,' she said. 'Replace the heads and I will do the rest.'

And so the wife put back the heads and then waited and watched as the wounds healed and the two men came back to life.

But when the two brothers stood up, the wife noticed something strange. She'd accidentally put the heads onto the wrong bodies. She looked at her husband's head on top of his brother's short, tubby body.
She looked to the brother's head, now on a tall, slim body.

'Oh no!' she thought. 'What have I done? Which one is my husband?'

Who do you think is her husband now?

What Happens When You Really Listen!

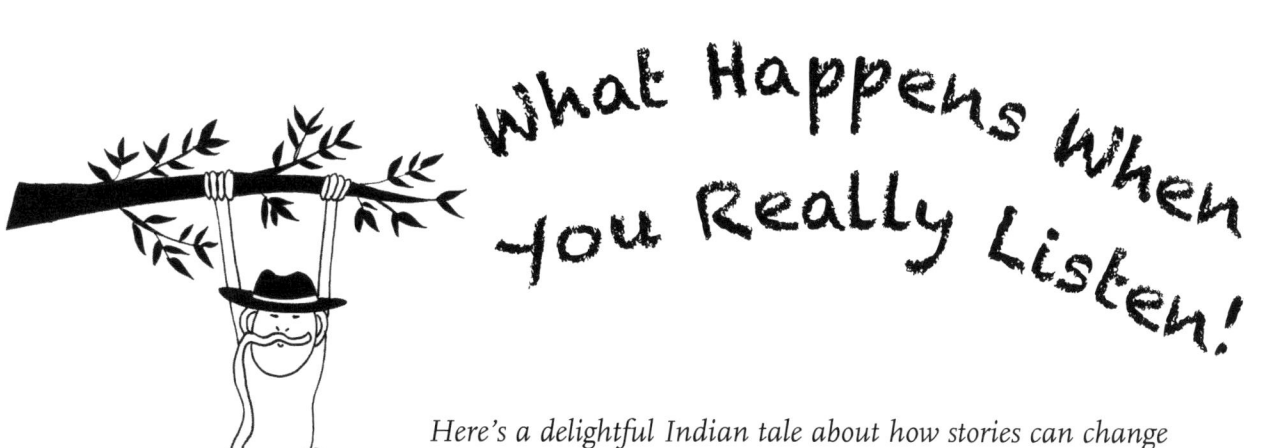

Here's a delightful Indian tale about how stories can change us. Evoke the character of the frustrated wife and maybe the dopey husband, who is somehow energised and transformed by his contact with a story. You can find a version of this and many other similar parables in Pantheon's Indian Folktales.

Once there was a wife who found her husband really dull. She decided to do something about it, so she sent him into town to hear a storyteller. The husband sat down in the crowd and began to listen to the stories but was soon fast asleep. While he slept, a dog came by and peed in his mouth. He woke up when the storyteller finished his telling and went home.
'How was that?' asked his wife.
The husband smacked his lips thoughtfully. 'It was a bit salty,' he said. 'Not to my taste.'

His wife thought that didn't sound quite right so she sent him back to see the storyteller again the next night. This time the crowd was even bigger and when the husband fell asleep a man stood on his shoulders to get a better view.
'How was that?' asked his wife when he got home.
'It was a bit heavy for my taste,' he told her.

Again, his wife sent him back. This time the husband stayed awake and listened, enthralled with a story about King Arthur. The storyteller came to the part of the story where King Arthur rode his horse out of the castle and across the drawbridge and dropped his sword, Excalibur, into the moat. The husband was completely absorbed in the story.
He called out, 'Don't worry! I'll help!'
He dived into the moat, swam to the bottom, collected the sword and gave it back to the king then returned to the audience.

When he got home that night his wife asked him, 'How was that?'
'It was great!' he cried. 'I was part of it and I loved it!'
And from that day on, the wife never found her husband dull ever again.
That's what happens when you really listen to stories.

The Power of Stories

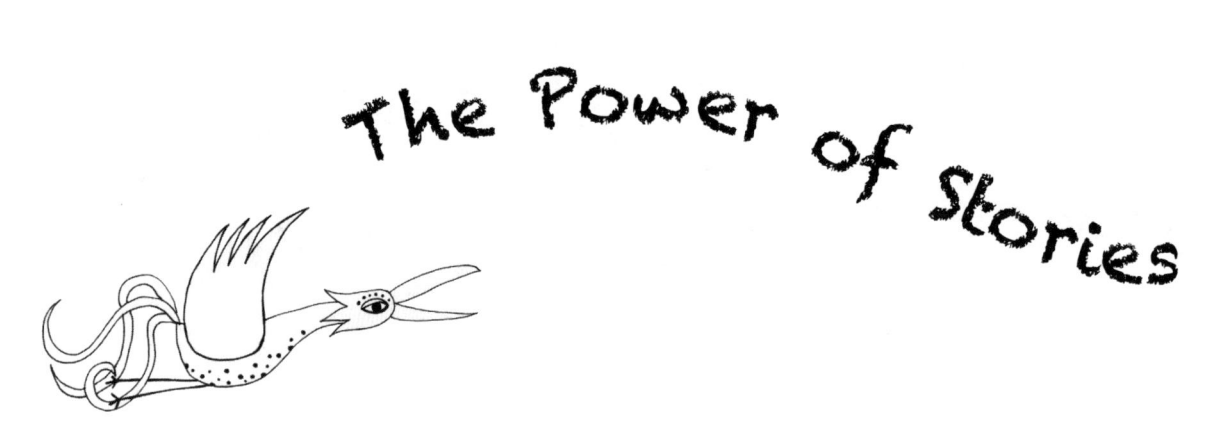

Here's another one from India from the Pantheon collection. It explores stories and healing and why speaking stories out can be important.

Once there was a woman who lived in a house with her father, her husband and her son.

Every day these three men would tell her to do this, do that, do that, do this, and usually she would do it in sullen silence without ever telling them what she thought.

She kept it all bottled up inside.

One day she went for a walk and came across a ruined cottage without a roof, with just the four walls standing. First, she turned to the north wall and started to shout at it, talking about her father, about all the things he had done, all the things he had said and how she had felt about them but had never said. The power of her words was such that the wall crumbled to the ground.

Then she turned to the east wall and started telling it all about her husband, about all the things he had said, how she felt and so on and so on. The power of her words reduced the wall to rubble.

Then she turned to the south wall and started telling it about her son, about all the things he had said to her in his life and how it had made her feel, and how she had never once said anything. Again the power of her words was so great, the wall collapsed into a pile of bricks.

Finally she turned to the east wall and started to tell it all about herself, about all the things she had never said, all the things she wished for and how she felt about everything. The force of her words collapsed this final wall.

Then she turned around and headed home.
'I feel much better now,' she thought.

The Diamond Dream

This is a challenging fable about letting go things that cause us pain – lots to talk about around what is important in life and what makes us happy. I found this story in David Holt's More Ready-To-Tell Tales. *It's from India.*

There was once a poor young man who loved diamonds, even though he could never afford one. He loved the way they sparkled, he loved the way they felt, and he loved how much money they were worth.

One night, he dreamed of a forest. In the forest was a hut. In the hut was a hermit and the hermit had a huge and wonderful diamond.

When he woke he recognised the forest and set off to find the hut and perhaps the diamond.

He walked and he walked till he came to the forest and then to the hut. He knocked and walked in, and saw a man sitting by the window gazing out at the moon, smiling.

On the floor of that hut was the diamond the man had dreamed about. The diamond was huge and sparkled in the moonlight.

'I'd love to have a diamond like that,' he said.
'Take it, it's yours,' said the man by the window.

The man couldn't believe his luck. He took the diamond home and hid it under the bed. He sat there all night checking that no one was going to steal it. The next day he started to worry about the diamond. Where was he going to put the diamond to keep it safe but where he could also look at it? He bought himself a safe and a gun and kept on worrying about what he was going to do to keep the diamond. His worries grew and grew. He became paler and paler and thinner and thinner.

Finally, weak and ill, he dragged himself back to that forest and that hut, the place he had first found in his dream. He walked in, clutching the diamond to his chest. There at the window was the man who had given him the diamond, still smiling up at the moon.

'I've come back,' said the man.
The man at the window turned to him.
'Why?' he asked.
'There is something I want to learn from you,' said the man, his hands tight around his precious diamond. 'I want you to teach me how to give this diamond away just as you did to me.'
And so he stayed in that hut with that man and studied. In time, the old man died, but the young man remained in the hut with that diamond, gazing happily out at the moon and stars every night.

One day a man walked into his hut and saw the diamond.
'I'd love to have a diamond like that,' he said.
The man at the window turned to the visitor and smiled.
'Take it,' he said.

Bird in Hand

I heard this story from storyteller, Eric Maddern. It's a lovely way of saying, 'Now it's up to you. Take responsibility!'

There was once a son who didn't like his father. He found him proud and pompous and stupid. His father was the village chief and was considered wise and important by the villagers. The son would fume and fume about how annoying his father was and planned to show him up.

At the next village council meeting, he thought, 'I'll catch a bird, hold it between the palms of my hands and walk up to my dad with everyone watching. Then I'll say, "Father, what have I got between my hands?"

'If my dad says, "A bird", then I'll squish the bird between my hands and say, "No, Father. Blood, feathers and bones – see you don't know everything!" and show him the dead bird.

'If my dad says, "Blood, feathers and bones", then I'll open up my hands and show the living bird and say, "Look Father! You are wrong!"'

Either way, the son thought, he would be able to show his father up.

The son waited until there was a very important meeting, found a bird and cupped it between his hands.

In front of all of the assembly he said, 'Father, what have I got between my hands?'

His father looked at him sadly.

'Son,' he said. 'The answer is in *your* hands.'

Traveller at the Gates of a City

Here's a wonderful little story about transitions and expectations – a good one for students to take with them to their next school! Evoke the enigmatic and wise character of the gatekeeper.

A traveller came to the gates of a city. He asked the gatekeeper:

'What are the people like in this place? What's it like to live here?'
The gatekeeper replied, 'What was it like in the last place you lived?'

The travelled thought for a moment.
'People were angry and selfish,' he said.
'It will be the same here if you stay,' said the gatekeeper.
Disappointed, the traveller turned around and set off for another town.

A while later a second traveller came to the same gates. He asked the gatekeeper:
'What are the people like in this place? What's it like to live here?'
The gatekeeper replied: 'What was it like in the last place you lived?'

The traveller thought for a moment.
'People were happy and kind,' said the traveller.
'It will be the same here if you stay,' said the gatekeeper.

The traveller smiled and walked through the gates, looking for a bed for the night.

Appendices

Classification of Stories

Topic	365
Value	368
Plot Type	371
Story Genre	374
Country or Region of Origin	377
Story Titles in Alphabetical Order	380

Topic

Stories arranged in school year order within each category.

Main Topic	Second Topic	Third Topic	Story Title	Year
Animals			The Fox's Sack	1
Animals	Food		The Lion's Roar	1
Animals	Forest		Skinny Old Lady	1
Animals	Forest	Family	How a Boy Learned to be Wise	3
Animals	Hunting	Forest	The Hunter and the Leopard	5
Apples	Festivals	Music	The Apple Tree Man	5
Arrows	Philosophy		Looking on the Bright Side	5
Arthurian	Winter		Gawain and the Green Knight	6
Arthurian	Growing Up	Gender	Gawain Gets Married	6
Beach			The Lode Stone	3
Beach	Other Worlds	Cleverness	The Monk and the Thieves	3
Beach	Sea	Birds	Why the Seagull Cries	5
Bees	Home	Journeys	The Bee's Treasure	2
Bridge	Goats	Troll	Three Billy Goats Gruff	1
Buddhist	Elephant		The Elephant's Fury	2
Buildings	Jobs	Happiness	The Building of St Paul's Cathedral	4
Butterflies	Environment	Play	How Butterflies Came to Be	4
Change	Transitions	Expectations	Traveller at the Gates of a City	6
Chickens			The King and Cockerel	2
Chocolate	Drugs		Quetzacoatl Brings Chocolate to Earth	6
Christian			The Birth of Jesus	1
Christmas			More!	1
Cockerel	Farm Animals	Philosophy	The Neighbour's Cockerel	5
Cold Hands	Danger	Bears	Three Brothers and the Polar Bear	3
Community	Death		The House That has Never Known Death	5
Community	Heaven	Hell	Heaven and Hell (2)	4
Community	Forest		Three Questions	6
Conflict	Philosophy		Nasseradeen's Nail	5
Creation	Sky	Moon	The Birth of Osiris	4
Crime Scene	Crime and Punishment	Bread	Who is the Thief?	5
Dance	Cave	Bats	Bat Learns to Dance	1
Death			Death in a Nutshell	3
Desert	Community	Friendship	Everything You Need	6
Dragons	Maps	Where I Live	The Two Dragons	2
Dreams	Growing Up	Free Thinking	The Woodcutter and the Snake	6
Elders	Age	Family	Half a Blanket	3
Environment	Water	Solid/Liquid/Gas	The Stonecutter	2
Environment	Life	Animals	Prometheus	4
Environment	Death	Viking	Baldur	6
Environment	Trees	Food	Ericython	6
Equality	Philosophy		Nasseradeen Teaches Justice	5
Family	Salt	Forest	Cap of Rushes	3
Family			Lazy Jack	3
Family	River	Fish	One Wish	3
Festivals	Death		Godmother Death	5
Fire	Trees	Coyote	How Coyote Brought Fire to Earth	2
Flight	Family	Death	Icarus	4
Fly	Family		Birth of Athena	3
Food	Farm	Turnip	The Giant Turnip	1
Food	Animals		The Gingerbread Man	1

Appendices 147 Traditional Stories

Main Topic	Second Topic	Third Topic	Story Title	Year
Food	Forest		The Magic Porridge Pot	1
Food			The Sweet-Talking Potato	1
Food			Stone Soup	1
Food	Animals	Helping	Three Wishes	3
Food	Farming	Buildings	How Jerusalem Began	4
Forest	Home	Family	Bandits and Berries	1
Forest	Princess	Prince	Sleeping Beauty	2
Forest	Princess		Snow White	2
Forest	Animals		Strength	2
Forest	Hunter		Little Burnt Face	3
Fortune			Luckily Unluckily	5
Friendship	Marriage	Community	Nasseradeen and the Perfect Wife	5
Giant	Father		Jack and the Beanstalk	1
Gold	Spinning		Rumplestiltskin	2
Gold	Family		Midas's Wish	4
Growing	Food	Cooking	The Little Red Hen	1
Growing Up	Birds	Family	Bird in Hand	6
Growing Up	Leaving Home	Freedom	Children of Wax	6
Growing Up	Forest	Death	Gilgamesh	6
Growing Up	Sun	Love	Mother Sun and Her Daughters	6
Homes	Food		Goldilocks and the Three Bears	1
Homes	Animals	Journeys	The Noisy House	1
Homes	Materials	Wolf	Three Little Pigs	1
Homes	Journey		The Pedlar of Swaffham	2
Hot and Cold	Music		The Piper's Boots	4
Induction	Philosophy		Cause and Effect	5
Islam	Spider	Journeys	The Nest and the Web	1
Islands	Fairies		The Island of Fairies	2
Jewel	Forest		The Diamond Dream	6
Kings	Philosophy		Nasseradeen and the King's Hunting Party	5
Kings	Philosophy		Nasseradeen and the Turnips	5
Kings	Justice	Philosophy	Who do you Trust?	5
Lake	Growing Up	My Body	Skeleton Woman	6
Languages	Animals	Philosophy	Language Lesson	5
Light	Philosophy		Nasseradeen and the Light	5
Lighthouse	Seal	Family	The Lighthouse Keeper and the Selkie	3
Love	Ghosts		The Boy who Learned to Shudder	6
Making a Difference	Forest	Fire	The Bird and the Forest Fire	2
Marriage	Body and Mind	Faith	Who is the Husband?	6
Migration	Flight	Helping	The Talkative Turtle	1
Monkey	Honey	Forest	Honey and Trouble	2
Monsters	Sight	Who am I?	Odysseus and the Cyclops	4
Monsters	Dragons	Rivers	The Four Dragons	4
Monsters	Mazes	Battle	Theseus and the Minotaur	4
Monsters	Hinduism	Islands	Rama and Sita	4
Monsters	King	Battle	Beowolf	5
Moon	Tower		The King and the Moon	1
Mountain	Animals		The Unlucky Man	2
Mountain	Tiger	Growing Up	The Tiger's Whisker	5
Music	Dance		The Dancing Harmonica	1

Main Topic	Second Topic	Third Topic	Story Title	Year
Music	Home	Rats	The Pied Piper of Hamlyn	2
Music	Who am I?	Shame	Midas and Apollo	4
Mystery	Dreams		The Shepherd's Dream	4
Nature	Water	Animals	Awongalema	1
Nature	Animals		A Husband for Miss Mouse	1
Ocean	Magical World	Time	The Land of the Deep Ocean	4
Peace	Philosophy		Nasseradeen Teaches Empathy	5
Pictures	Gold		The Magic Paintbrush	2
Poetry	Journeys	Birds	The Prince and the Birds	5
Points of View	Truth	Philosophy	Nasseradeen Speaks Truth	5
Prince	Shoes		Cinderella	2
Princess	Pea		The Princess and the Pea	1
Rules	Work	Journeys	Five Wise Trainings	6
Sea	Beach	Changeling	The Woman of the Sea	4
Seasons	Changes	Growing Up	Persephone	3
Shoes	Islam		The Boots of Abu Kassim	5
Sight	Sound	Forest	The Blind Man and the Hunter	4
Size	Forest		Mouse and Lion	1
Skull	Desert		The Talking Skull	2
Snake	Frog		The Snake and the Frog	2
Snow	Fox	Healing	The Fox and the Healer	3
Speech	Forest	Bird	The Freedom Bird	1
Speech	Judaism		Feathers in the Wind	4
Speech	Growing Up	Catharsis	The Power of Stories	6
Spring	Animals		Goose Girl's Wings	1
Stories	Death	Recycling	Snip-Snip	1
Stories	Who am I?	Gender	Jack and Jackie	5
Stories	Storytelling	Listening	What Happens When you Really Listen!	6
Storytelling	Animals	Forest	Monkeys and Hats	1
Storytelling	Stories		The Story Bag	3
Storytelling	Riddles	Toys	Three Dolls	3
Strawberry	Food	Fruit	Fruit of Love	3
Sweets	Learning	Philosophy	Strop Eating Sweets	5
Targets	Philosophy		Hitting the Target	5
Toys	Dolls	Monsters	The Wooden Baby	1
Transcendence	Changelings	Journeys	Jumping Mouse	5
Travel	Sport	Hinduism	The Marriage of Ganesh	3
Trees	Dancing	Treasure	Jack and the Dancing Trees	3
War	Weapons		The Wooden Horse	3
War	Conflict	Peace	A Drop of Honey	6
Warriors	Heaven	Hell	Heaven and Hell (1)	4
Water	Habitat	Environment	The Thirsty Frog	1
Weaving	Cloth	Stories	The Weaver's Dream	5
Who am I?	Animals	River	The Scorpion and Frog	3
Who am I?	Birds	Flight	The Eagle Who Thought He Was a Chicken	4
Who am I?	Music	Desert	Warrior	6
Witch	Forest		Baba Yaga's Black Geese	3
Wolf	Forest		Little Red Riding Hood	1

Value

Stories arranged in school year order within each category.

Main Value	Second Value	Third Value	Story Title	Year
Acceptance			The Noisy House	1
Acceptance	Freedom	Free Speech	The Freedom Bird	1
Acceptance	Interdependence	Self-Confidence	The Stonecutter	2
Acceptance			Death in a Nutshell	3
Acceptance	Confidence	Free Speech	Jack and Jackie	5
Acceptance	Realism		Nasseradeen and the Perfect Wife	5
Advice-Taking	Risk-Judging		The Land of the Deep Ocean	4
Anger	Speech	Choices	Three Wishes	3
Anger			Heaven and Hell (1)	4
Being in Control	Comedy		The Neighbour's Cockerel	5
Betrayal	Secrets		The Woman of the Sea	4
Bravery	Cleverness	Helping	Baba Yaga's Black Geese	3
Catharsis	Speech	Rebirth	The Power of Stories	6
Caution	Modesty	Thoughtfulness	Three Brothers and the Polar Bear	3
Clever Contracts	Comedy		Nasseradeen's Nail	5
Cleverness	Greed		Fox's Sack	1
Cleverness	Justice		Jack and the Beanstalk	1
Cleverness	Obedience		Little Red Riding Hood	1
Cleverness			The Thirsty Frog	1
Cleverness			Stone Soup	1
Cleverness	Cooperation		How Coyote Brought Fire to Earth	2
Cleverness	Love	Family	One Wish	3
Cleverness	Fairness	Comedy	The Monk and the Thieves	3
Cleverness	Tricks	Revenge	The Wooden Horse	3
Cleverness	Listening	Speech	Three Dolls	3
Cleverness	Carefulness	Courage	Odysseus and the Cyclops	4
Cleverness	Justice		Who is the Thief?	5
Confidence	Persuasiveness	Quest	The Bird and the Forest Fire	2
Cooperation			The Giant Turnip	1
Courage	Cleverness	Cooperation	Three Billy Goats Gruff	1
Courage	Strength		Beowolf	5
Courage	Bravery		Language Lesson	5
Courage	Determination	Friendship	Gilgamesh	6
Courage	Determination	Quest	The Boy who Learned to Shudder	6
Danger	Cleverness		Skinny Old Lady	1
Determination	Truthfulness	Quest	The Prince and the Birds	5
Determination	Honesty	Purpose	The Weaver's Dream	5
Empathy	Consequences	Pride	The Hunter and the Leopard	5
Empathy			Nasseradeen Teaches Empathy	5
Empathy	Respect	Autonomy	Gawain Gets Married	6
Equanimity	Change	Acceptance	Luckily Unluckily	5
Faith			The Nest and the Web	1
Faith	Appreciation	Unpredictability	The Bee's Treasure	2
Faith			The Pedlar of Swaffham	2
Faith	Loyalty	Comedy	Who is the Husband?	6
Faithfulness	Trust	Courage	Rama and Sita	4
False Logic			Cause and Effect	5
Flexibility			Hitting the Target	5
Foolishness	Intelligence		The King and the Moon	1
Forgiveness	Friendship		Fruit of Love	3

368   147 Traditional Stories   **Appendices**

Main Value	Second Value	Third Value	Story Title	Year
Freedom			The Lighthouse Keeper and the Selkie	3
Freedom	Rebirth		Children of Wax	6
Friendship	Helping		Mouse and Lion	1
Giving	Helping		Half a Blanket	3
Giving	Cleverness	Selfishness	The Piper's Boots	4
Giving	Courage	Purpose	Jumping Mouse	5
Giving	Consequences	Punishment	The Boots of Abu Kassim	5
Gratitude	Intelligence		The Unlucky Man	2
Greed	Stealing		Goldilocks and the Three Bears	1
Greed	Gifts		More!	1
Greed			The Wooden Baby	1
Greed	Kindness		The Magic Paintbrush	2
Greed			Jack and the Dancing Trees	3
Greed	Love		Midas's Wish	4
Greed	Pride		Ericython	6
Greed	Speech		Everything You Need	6
Greed	Letting Go		The Diamond Dream	6
Grief	Acceptance	Compromise	Persephone	3
Grieving	Interconnectedness	Empathy	The House That Has Never Known Death	5
Hard Work	Helping	Humility	Five Wise Trainings	6
Healing			The Fox and the Healer	3
Helpers	Boasting		Rumplestiltskin	2
Helping	Giving		Bandits and Berries	1
Helping	Friendship		The Little Red Hen	1
Helping	Restraint	Self-Harm	The Scorpion and the Frog	3
Helping	Self-Respect	Community	How a Boy Learned to be Wise	3
Helping	Generosity	Compassion	Three Questions	6
Honesty			Little Burnt Face	3
Honesty	Promises	Death	Godmother Death	5
Honesty	Independence	Rebirth	The Woodcutter and the Snake	6
Hope			Sleeping Beauty	2
Hope	Kindness	Fairness	The Blind Man and the Hunter	4
Hubris	Advice	Recklessness	Icarus	4
Humility			A Husband for Miss Mouse	1
Humility	Simplicity		Goose Girl's Wings	1
Humour in Adversity	Comedy		Nasseradeen & the King's Hunting Party	5
Humour in Adversity	Comedy		Nasseradeen and the Turnips	5
Inner Beauty	Kindness	Patience	Cap of Rushes	3
Intoxication	Care		Quetzcoatl Brings Chocolate to Earth	6
Investigation	Determination	Listening	The Two Dragons	2
Jealousy	Pride	Cleverness	The Birth of Osiris	4
Justice	Sharing		Nasseradeen Teaches Justice	5
Justice	Kindness	Gratitude	The Apple Tree Man	5
Kindness	Listening		The Magic Porridge Pot	1
Kindness	Goodness		Cinderella	2
Kindness	Goodness	Friendship	Snow White	2
Kindness	Helping	Wisdom	Heaven and Hell (2)	4
Kindness	Sharing	Giving	How Jerusalem Began	4
Kindness	Advocacy	Compassion	The Four Dragons	4
Learning			Bat Learns to Dance	1

Main Value	Second Value	Third Value	Story Title	Year
Learning	Listening		Monkeys and Hats	1
Learning	Assumptions	Comedy	Honey and Trouble	2
Letting Go	Change		Mother Sun and Her Daughters	6
Listening	Change	Rebirth	What Happens When you Really Listen!	6
Love	Care	Sacrifice	Prometheus	4
Luck	Charm	Helping	The Dancing Harmonica	1
Luck	Faith		Lazy Jack	3
Minfulness	Slowness		The Lode Stone	3
Optimism			Looking on the Bright Side	5
Patience	Empathy		The Tiger's Whisker	5
Perfectionism	Honesty	Temptation	Gawain and the Green Knight	6
Persistence	Justice		The King and the Cockerel	2
Play	Fairness	Quest	How Butterflies Came to Be	4
Points of View	Competition	Diversity	The Marriage of Ganesh	3
Points of View	Investigation		The Shepherds Dream	4
Pride	Selfishness	Consequences	Why the Seagull Cries	5
Pride	Hubris		Baldur	6
Responsibility	Rebellion		Bird in Hand	6
Re-use	Love	Letting Go	Snip-Snip	1
Safety	Caution		The Gingerbread Man	1
Safety	Protection		Three Little Pigs	1
Searching for Truth	Comedy		Nasseradeen and the Light	5
Self Confidence	Helping	Fear	The Eagle Who Thought he Was a Chicken	4
Self Confidence	Courage		Warrior	6
Self Knowledge	Positive Thinking		Traveller at the Gates of a City	6
Senses	Valuing Body	Healing	Skeleton Woman	6
Sensitivity			The Princess and the Pea	1
Shame	Fairness	Rebirth	Midas and Apollo	4
Shame	Thoughtlessness	Bravery	Theseus and the Minotaur	4
Silence			The Island of Fairies	2
Slowness			Awongalema	1
Speech	Silence	Helping	The Story Bag	3
Speech	Kindness		Feathers in the Wind	4
Subjective Truth			Nasseradeen Speaks Truth	5
Teach by Example	Comedy		Stop Eating Sweets	5
Thoughtfulness	Responsibility		A Drop of Honey	6
Trust	Truthfulness	Tragedy	The Pied Piper of Hamlyn	2
Trust			Who do you Trust?	5
Truth	Trust		The Sweet-Talking Potato	1
Violence	Killing		Strength	2
Vision	Happiness	Points of View	The Building of St Paul's Cathedral	4
Wisdom	Worry		The Lion's Roar	1
Wisdom	Freedom		Birth of Athena	3
Wise speech	Caution		The Talkative Turtle	1
Wise Speech	Friendship		The Elephant's Fury	2
Wise Speech	Caution		The Talking Skull	2

Plot Type

Stories arranged in school year order within each category.

Plot Type	Story Title	Year
Comedy	Monkeys and Hats	1
Comedy	The Noisy House	1
Comedy	The Sweet-Talking Potato	1
Comedy	Honey and Trouble	2
Comedy	Lazy Jack	3
Comedy	The Monk and the Thieves	3
Comedy	Three Wishes	3
Comedy	Cause and Effect	5
Comedy	Hitting the Target	5
Comedy	Looking on the Bright Side	5
Comedy	Nasseradeen and the King's Hunting Party	5
Comedy	Nasseradeen and the Light	5
Comedy	Nasseradeen and the Perfect Wife	5
Comedy	Nasseradeen and the Turnips	5
Comedy	Nasseradeen's Nail	5
Comedy	Nasseradeen Speaks Truth	5
Comedy	Nasseradeen Teaches Empathy	5
Comedy	Nasseradeen Teaches Justice	5
Comedy	Stop Eating Sweets	5
Comedy	The Neighbour's Cockerel	5
Comedy	Who do You Trust?	5
Comedy	Who is the Husband?	6
Monster	The Wooden Baby	1
Monster	Baba Yaga's Black Geese	3
Monster	The Birth of Osiris	4
Monster	Odysseus and the Cyclops	4
Monster	Rama and Sita	4
Monster	Beowolf	5
Monster	Language Lesson	5
Quest	Awongalema	1
Quest	Bat Learns to Dance	1
Quest	Jack and the Beanstalk	1
Quest	Stone Soup	1
Quest	The Dancing Harmonica	1
Quest	The Giant Turnip	1
Quest	The Nest and the Web	1
Quest	The Princess and the Pea	1
Quest	The Thirsty Frog	1
Quest	Three Billy Goats Gruff	1
Quest	How Coyote Brought Fire to Earth	2
Quest	The Bird and the Forest Fire	2
Quest	The Elephant's Fury	2
Quest	The King and Cockerel	2
Quest	The Two Dragons	2
Quest	One Wish	3
Quest	Persephone	3
Quest	The Marriage of Ganesh	3
Quest	The Wooden Horse	3
Quest	How Butterflies Came to Be	4
Quest	The Four Dragons	4

Plot Type	Story Title	Year
Quest	Theseus and the Minotaur	4
Quest	The Prince and the Birds	5
Quest	The Tiger's Whisker	5
Quest	The Weavers Dream	5
Quest	Who is the Thief?	5
Quest	Five Wise Trainings	6
Quest	Gawain and the Green Knight	6
Quest	Gawain Gets Married	6
Quest	Gilgamesh	6
Quest	The Boy who Learned to Shudder	6
Quest	The Diamond Dream	6
Rags to Riches	The Magic Porridge Pot	1
Rags to Riches	Cinderella	2
Rags to Riches	Rumplestiltskin	2
Rags to Riches	Cap of Rushes	3
Rags to Riches	Jack and the Dancing Trees	3
Rags to Riches	Little Burnt Face	3
Rags to Riches	Heaven and Hell (2)	4
Rags to Riches	The Piper's Boots	4
Rags to Riches	The Apple Tree Man	5
Rags to Riches	Traveller at the Gates of a City	6
Rebirth	A Husband for Miss Mouse	1
Rebirth	Bandits and Berries	1
Rebirth	Goose Girls Wings	1
Rebirth	The Birth of Jesus	1
Rebirth	The Freedom Bird	1
Rebirth	The Lion's Roar	1
Rebirth	Mouse and Lion	1
Rebirth	Snip-Snip	1
Rebirth	Sleeping Beauty	2
Rebirth	Snow White	2
Rebirth	The Snake and the Frog	2
Rebirth	The Stonecutter	2
Rebirth	Birth of Athena	3
Rebirth	Death in a Nutshell	3
Rebirth	Fruit of Love	3
Rebirth	Half a Blanket	3
Rebirth	How a Boy Learned to be Wise	3
Rebirth	The Fox and the Healer	3
Rebirth	The Story Bag	3
Rebirth	Three Dolls	3
Rebirth	Feathers in the Wind	4
Rebirth	Heaven and Hell (1)	4
Rebirth	How Jerusalem Began	4
Rebirth	Midas and Apollo	4
Rebirth	Midas's Wish	4
Rebirth	The Blind Man and the Hunter	4
Rebirth	The Building of St Paul's Cathedral	4
Rebirth	The Eagle Who Thought He Was a Chicken	4
Rebirth	Jumping Mouse	5

Plot Type	Story Title	Year
Rebirth	Luckily Unluckily	5
Rebirth	The Boots of Abu Kassim	5
Rebirth	Bird in Hand	6
Rebirth	Children of Wax	6
Rebirth	Mother Sun and her Daughters	6
Rebirth	Quetzacoatl Brings Chocolate to Earth	6
Rebirth	Skeleton Woman	6
Rebirth	The Power of Stories	6
Rebirth	The Woodcutter and the Snake	6
Rebirth	Three Questions	6
Rebirth	What Happens When You Really Listen!	6
Tragedy	Little Red Riding Hood	1
Tragedy	More!	1
Tragedy	The Fox's Sack	1
Tragedy	The Gingerbread Man	1
Tragedy	The King and the Moon	1
Tragedy	The Little Red Hen	1
Tragedy	The Talkative Turtle	1
Tragedy	Three Little Pigs	1
Tragedy	The Magic Paintbrush	2
Tragedy	The Pied Piper of Hamlyn	2
Tragedy	The Talking Skull	2
Tragedy	The Unlucky Man	2
Tragedy	Strength	2
Tragedy	The Lighthouse Keeper and the Selkie	3
Tragedy	The Lode Stone	3
Tragedy	The Scorpion and the Frog	3
Tragedy	Three Brothers and the Polar Bear	3
Tragedy	Icarus	4
Tragedy	Prometheus	4
Tragedy	The Land of the Deep Ocean	4
Tragedy	The Woman of the Sea	4
Tragedy	Godmother Death	5
Tragedy	The Hunter and the Leopard	5
Tragedy	Why the Seagull Cries	5
Tragedy	A Drop of Honey	6
Tragedy	Baldur	6
Tragedy	Ericython	6
Tragedy	Everything You Need	6
Tragedy	Warrior	6
Voyage and Return	Goldilocks and the Three Bears	1
Voyage and Return	Skinny Old Lady	1
Voyage and Return	The Bee's Treasure	2
Voyage and Return	The Island of Fairies	2
Voyage and Return	The Pedlar of Swaffham	2
Voyage and Return	The Shepherd's Dream	4
Voyage and Return	Jack and Jackie	5
Voyage and Return	The House That has Never Known Death	5

Story Genre

Stories arranged in school year order within each category.

Genre	Story Title	Year
Anecdote	More!	1
Anecdote	The Snake and the Frog	2
Creation	How Butterflies Came to Be	4
Creation	Prometheus	4
Creation	The Birth of Osiris	4
Fable	Awongalema	1
Fable	Bat Learns to Dance	1
Fable	Goldilocks and the Three Bears	1
Fable	Little Red Riding Hood	1
Fable	Monkeys and Hats	1
Fable	Mouse and Lion	1
Fable	The Fox's Sack	1
Fable	The Gingerbread Man	1
Fable	The Lion's Roar	1
Fable	The Little Red Hen	1
Fable	The Talkative Turtle	1
Fable	The Thirsty Frog	1
Fable	Three Little Pigs	1
Fable	Skinny Old Lady	1
Fable	Honey and Trouble	2
Fable	The King and Cockerel	2
Fable	The Stonecutter	2
Fable	Strength	2
Fable	How a Boy Learned to be Wise	3
Fable	The Scorpion and the Frog	3
Fable	Feathers in the Wind	4
Fable	Heaven and Hell (1)	4
Fable	Heaven and Hell (2)	4
Fable	The Eagle Who Thought He was a Chicken	4
Fable	Cause and Effect	5
Fable	Hitting the Target	5
Fable	Language Lesson	5
Fable	Looking on the Bright Side	5
Fable	Luckily Unluckily	5
Fable	Nasseradeen and the King's Hunting Party	5
Fable	Nasseradeen and the Light	5
Fable	Nasseradeen and the Turnips	5
Fable	Nasseradeen Speaks Truth	5
Fable	Nasseradeen Teaches Empathy	5
Fable	Nasseradeen Teaches Justice	5
Fable	Nasseradeen's Nail	5
Fable	Stop Eating Sweets	5
Fable	The Neighbour's Cockerel	5
Fable	Who do you Trust?	5
Fable	Why the Seagull Cries	5
Fable	Traveller at the Gates of a City	6
Folk	Bandits and Berries	1
Folk	The Freedom Bird	1
Folk	The Giant Turnip	1
Folk	The King and the Moon	1

Genre	Story Title	Year
Folk	The Noisy House	1
Folk	The Princess and the Pea	1
Folk	Snip-Snip	1
Folk	Stone Soup	1
Folk	The Bee's Treasure	2
Folk	The Elephant's Fury	2
Folk	The Pedlar of Swaffham	2
Folk	Half a Blanket	3
Folk	The Fox and the Healer	3
Folk	The Monk and the Thieves	3
Folk	Three Brothers and the Polar Bear	3
Folk	Three Dolls	3
Folk	How Jerusalem Began	4
Folk	The Blind Man and the Hunter	4
Folk	The Piper's Boots	4
Folk	Nasseradeen and the Perfect Wife	5
Folk	The Boots of Abu Kassim	5
Folk	The House That has Never Known Death	5
Folk	The Tiger's Whisker	5
Folk	Who is the Thief?	5
Folk	A Drop of Honey	6
Folk	Bird in Hand	6
Folk	The Diamond Dream	6
Folk	The Power of Stories	6
Folk	Three Questions	6
Folk	What Happens When you Really Listen!	6
Legend	The Two Dragons	2
Legend	The Building St Paul's Cathedral	4
Myth	The Birth of Jesus	1
Myth	The Nest and the Web	1
Myth	The Bird and Forest Fire	2
Myth	Birth of Athena	3
Myth	Fruit of Love	3
Myth	Marriage of Ganesh	3
Myth	Persephone	3
Myth	The Wooden Horse	3
Myth	Odysseus and the Cyclops	4
Myth	The Four Dragons	4
Myth	Midas and Apollo	4
Myth	Midas's Wish	4
Myth	Theseus and the Minotaur	4
Myth	Rama and Sita	4
Myth	Godmother Death	5
Myth	Baldur	6
Myth	Ericython	6
Myth	Gilgamesh	6
Myth	Mother Sun and her Daughters	6
Myth	Quetzacoatl Brings Chocolate to Earth	6
Myth	Who is the husband?	6
Wonder	A Husband for Miss Mouse	1

Genre	Story Title	Year
Wonder	Goose Girls Wings	1
Wonder	Jack and the Beanstalk	1
Wonder	The Dancing Harmonica	1
Wonder	The Magic Porridge Pot	1
Wonder	The Sweet-Talking Potato	1
Wonder	The Wooden Baby	1
Wonder	Three Billy Goats Gruff	1
Wonder	Cinderella	2
Wonder	How Coyote Brought Fire to Earth	2
Wonder	The Island of Fairies	2
Wonder	The Magic Paintbrush	2
Wonder	The Pied Piper of Hamlyn	2
Wonder	The Talking Skull	2
Wonder	The Unlucky Man	2
Wonder	Rumplestiltskin	2
Wonder	Sleeping Beauty	2
Wonder	Snow White	2
Wonder	Baba Yaga's Black Geese	3
Wonder	Cap of Rushes	3
Wonder	Death in a Nutshell	3
Wonder	Jack and the Dancing Trees	3
Wonder	Lazy Jack	3
Wonder	Little Burnt Face	3
Wonder	One Wish	3
Wonder	The Lighthouse Keeper and the Selkie	3
Wonder	The Lode Stone	3
Wonder	The Story Bag	3
Wonder	Three Wishes	3
Wonder	Icarus	4
Wonder	The Land of the Deep Ocean	4
Wonder	The Shepherd's Dream	4
Wonder	The Woman of the Sea	4
Wonder	Beowolf	5
Wonder	Jack and Jackie	5
Wonder	Jumping Mouse	5
Wonder	The Apple Tree Man	5
Wonder	The Hunter and the Leopard	5
Wonder	The Prince and the Birds	5
Wonder	The Weaver's Dream	5
Wonder	Children of Wax	6
Wonder	Everything You Need	6
Wonder	Five Wise Trainings	6
Wonder	Gawain and the Green Knight	6
Wonder	Gawain Gets Married	6
Wonder	The Boy who Learned to Shudder	6
Wonder	The Woodcutter and Snake	6
Wonder	Skeleton Woman	6
Wonder	Warrior	6

Country or Region of Origin

Stories arranged in school year order within each category.

Country	Story Title	Year
Africa	Awongalema	1
Africa	Skinny Old Lady	1
Africa	Honey and Trouble	2
Africa	The Talking Skull	2
Argentina	Mother Sun and Her Daughters	6
Australia	The Thirsty Frog	1
Aztec	Quetzacoatl Brings Chocolate to Earth	6
Britain	The Noisy House	1
Britain	Jack and the Beanstalk	1
Britain	Gawain and the Green Knight	6
Britain	Gawain Gets Married	6
Burma	A Husband for Miss Mouse	1
Chile	The Monk and the Thieves	3
China	Bandits and Berries	1
China	Goose Girls Wings	1
China	The Bee's Treasure	2
China	The Magic Paintbrush	2
China	The Stonecutter	2
China	The Four Dragons	4
China	Luckily Unluckily	5
China	The Weaver's Dream	5
Czech Republic	The Wooden Baby	1
Denmark	The Princess and the Pea	1
Dominican Republic	The King and the Moon	1
Egypt	The Birth of Osiris	4
Egypt	Warrior	6
England	Goldilocks and the Three Bears	1
England	The Fox's Sack	1
England	The Gingerbread Man	1
England	The Little Red Hen	1
England	Three Little Pigs	1
England	The Pedlar of Swaffham	2
England	The Unlucky Man	2
England	Cap of Rushes	3
England	Jack and the Dancing Trees	3
England	Lazy Jack	3
England	The Lode Stone	3
England	The Building of St Paul's Cathedral	4
England	Beowolf	5
England	Language Lesson	5
England	The Apple Tree Man	5
Europe	Heaven and Hell (2)	4
France	Little Red Riding Hood	1
Germany	The Magic Porridge Pot	1
Germany	Cinderella	2
Germany	The Pied Piper of Hamlyn	2
Germany	Rumplestiltskin	2
Germany	Sleeping Beauty	2
Germany	Snow White	2
Germany	The Boy who Learned to Shudder	6

Country	Story Title	Year
Greece	Mouse and Lion	1
Greece	Birth of Athena	3
Greece	Persephone	3
Greece	The Wooden Horse	3
Greece	Icarus	4
Greece	Midas and Apollo	4
Greece	Midas's Wish	4
Greece	Odysseus and the Cyclops	4
Greece	Prometheus	4
Greece	Theseus and the Minotaur	4
India	Monkeys and Hats	1
India	The Lion's Roar	1
India	The Bird and the Forest Fire	2
India	The Elephant's Fury	2
India	The Marriage of Ganesh	3
India	The Scorpion and the Frog	3
India	Three Brothers and the Polar Bear	3
India	Three Dolls	3
India	Rama and Sita	4
India	Bird in Hand	6
India	Five Wise Trainings	6
India	The Diamond Dream	6
India	The Power of Stories	6
India	What Happens When you Really Listen!	6
India	Who is the Husband?	6
Indonesia	The Tiger's Whisker	5
Inuit	Skeleton Woman	6
Iran/Arab	Cause and Effect	5
Iran/Arab	Hitting the Target	5
Iran/Arab	Looking on the Bright Side	5
Iran/Arab	Nasseradeen and the King's Hunting Party	5
Iran/Arab	Nasseradeen and the Light	5
Iran/Arab	Nasseradeen and the Turnips	5
Iran/Arab	Nasseradeen and the Perfect Wife	5
Iran/Arab	Nasseradeen Teaches Empathy	5
Iran/Arab	Nasseradeen Teaches Justice	5
Iran/Arab	Nasseradeen's Nail	5
Iran/Arab	Nasseradeen Speaks Truth	5
Iran/Arab	The Neighbour's Cockerel	5
Iran/Arab	Stop Eating Sweets	5
Iran/Arab	Who do you Trust?	5
Iraq	The King and the Cockerel	2
Iraq	The Boots of Abu Kassim	5
Iraq	A Drop of Honey	6
Iraq	Everything You Need	6
Iraq	Gilgamesh	6
Ireland	One Wish	3
Ireland	The Shepherd's Dream	4
Ireland	Jack and Jackie	5
Islam	The Nest and the Web	1

Country	Story Title	Year
Japan	The Land of the Deep Ocean	4
Japan	Heaven and Hell (1)	4
Japan	Who is the Thief?	5
Jewish	Snip-Snip	1
Jewish	Feathers in the Wind	4
Korea	The Story Bag	3
Mexico	Godmother Death	5
Native American	Fruit of Love	3
Native American	Little Burnt Face	3
Native American	The Fox and the Healer	3
Native American	How Butterflies Came to Be	4
Native American	The Eagle Who Thought He Was a Chicken	4
Native American	Jumping Mouse	5
Native American	Why the Seagull Cries	5
Norse/Viking	Baldur	6
Norway	Three Billy Goats Gruff	1
Palestine	How Jerusalem Began	4
Roman/Italy	Ericython	6
Russia	The Giant Turnip	1
Russia	Baba Yaga's Black Geese	3
Russia	Three Questions	6
Saudi	The House That Has Never Known Death	5
Scotland	The Island of Fairies	2
Scotland	Death in a Nutshell	3
Scotland	Half a Blanket	3
Scotland	The Lighthouse Keeper and the Selkie	3
Scotland	The Piper's Boots	4
Scotland	The Woman of the Sea	4
Serbia	The Woodcutter and the Snake	6
Spain	The Prince and the Birds	5
Sweden	Three Wishes	3
Switzerland	Stone Soup	1
Thailand	The Freedom Bird	1
Uganda	How a Boy Learned to be Wise	3
USA	More!	1
USA	The Dancing Harmonica	1
USA	The Talkative Turtle	1
USA	How Coyote Brought Fire to Earth	2
USA	The Snake and the Frog	2
USA	Traveller at the Gates of a City	6
Wales	The Two Dragons	2
West Africa (Ghana)	The Sweet-Talking Potato	1
West Africa	Strength	2
West Africa	The Blind Man and the Hunter	4
West Africa	The Hunter and the Leopard	5
World (Christian)	The Birth of Jesus	1
Zimbabwe	Children of Wax	6
Origin unknown	Bat Learns to Dance	1

Story Titles in Alphabetical Order

Title	Page
A Drop of Honey	352
A Husband for Miss Mouse	48
Awongalema	52
Baba Yaga's Black Geese	150
Baldur	309
Bandits and Berries	68
Bat Learns to Dance	12
Beowolf	251
Bird in Hand	361
Birth of Athena	187
Cap of Rushes	145
Cause and Effect	297
Children of Wax	300
Cinderella	124
Death in a Nutshell	159
Ericython	312
Everything You Need	344
Feathers in the Wind	239
Five Wise Trainings	336
Fruit of Love	184
Gawain and the Green Knight	331
Gawain Gets Married	340
Gilgamesh	348
Godmother Death	258
Goldilocks and the Three Bears	22
Goose Girl's Wings	57
Half a Blanket	182
Heaven and Hell (1)	240
Heaven and Hell (2)	241
Hitting the Target	285
Honey and Trouble	94
How a Boy Learned to be Wise	174
How Coyote Brought Fire to Earth	97
How Butterflies Came to Be	206
How Jerusalem Began	226
Icarus	208
Jack and Jackie	272
Jack and the Beanstalk	76
Jack and the Dancing Trees	164
Jumping Mouse	269
Language Lesson	281
Lazy Jack	147
Little Burnt Face	167
Little Red Riding Hood	74
Looking on the Bright Side	283
Luckily Unluckily	279
Midas and Apollo	218
Midas's Wish	216
Monkeys and Hats	2
More!	73
Mother Sun and Her Daughters	334
Mouse and Lion	60
Nasseradeen and the King's Hunting Party	291
Nasseradeen and the Light	293
Nasseradeen and The Perfect Wife	286
Nasseradeen and the Turnips	296
Nasseradeen Speaks Truth	292
Nasseradeen Teaches Empathy	297
Nasseradeen Teaches Justice	294
Nasseradeen's Nail	289
Odysseus and the Cyclops	228
One Wish	186
Persephone	178
Prometheus	202
Quetzalcoatl Brings Chocolate to Earth	314
Rama and Sita	236
Rumplestiltskin	120
Skeleton Woman	318
Skinny Old Lad	30
Sleeping Beauty	118
Snip-Snip	36
Snow White	132
Stone Soup	46
Stop Eating Sweets	284
Strength	115
The Apple Tree Man	255
The Bee's Treasure	108
The Bird and the Forest Fire	92
The Birth of Jesus	8
The Birth of Osiris	200
The Blind Man and the Hunter	196
The Boots of Abu Kassim	246
The Boy who Learned to Shudder	320
The Building of St Paul's Cathedral	238
The Dancing Harmonica	63
The Diamond Dream	359
The Eagle Who Thought He Was a Chicken	204
The Elephant's Fury	103
The Fox and the Healer	162
The Fox's Sack	25
The Four Dragons	230
The Freedom Bird	33
The Giant Turnip	18
The Gingerbread Man	10
The House That Has Never Known Death	274
The Hunter and the Leopard	244
The Island of Fairies	106
The King and the Cockerel	88
The King and the Moon	39
The Land of the Deep Ocean	233
The Lighthouse Keeper and the Selkie	157
The Lion's Roar	54
The Little Red Hen	4
The Lode Stone	189

The Magic Paintbrush	130
The Magic Porridge Pot	41
The Marriage of Ganesh	142
The Monk and the Thieves	169
The Neighbour's Cockerel	288
The Nest and the Web	62
The Noisy House	16
The Pedlar of Swaffham	113
The Pied Piper of Hamlyn	111
The Piper's Boots	213
The Power of Stories	358
The Prince and the Birds	264
The Princess and the Pea	28
The Scorpion and the Frog	191
The Shepherd's Dream	211
The Snake and the Frog	100
The Stonecutter	82
The Story Bag	171
The Sweet-Talking Potato	44
The Talkative Turtle	66
The Talking Skull	101
The Thirsty Frog	71
The Tiger's Whisker	253
The Two Dragons	136
The Unlucky Man	85
The Weaver's Dream	261
The Woman of the Sea	224
The Woodcutter and the Snake	325
The Wooden Baby	20
The Wooden Horse	180
Theseus and the Minotaur	220
Three Billy Goats Gruff	14
Three Brothers and the Polar Bear	152
Three Dolls	154
Three Little Pigs	6
Three Questions	328
Three Wishes	192
Traveller at the Gates of a City	362
Warrior	302
What Happens When You Really Listen!	357
Who do you Trust?	295
Who is the Husband?	356
Who is the Thief?	248
Why the Seagull Cries	276

Appendices

Sources and Resources

This section provides more detail on the various sources I drew upon when first learning to tell any given story. Other variants are also included which may be of interest to teachers for watching and listening to in the classroom. There are picture books and storybooks, which may be used to link the story to reading and research activities in various ways, and also web clips and other web resources for the class to experience as they go deeper into the story.

Chapter 1   Year 1 Stories   383

Chapter 2   Year 2 Stories   391

Chapter 3   Year 3 Stories   398

Chapter 4   Year 4 Stories   403

Chapter 5   Year 5 Stories   408

Chapter 6   Year 6 Stories   412

Chapter 1   Year 1 Stories

Monkeys and Hats

This is a great storyteller's favourite and is on many, many storytellers' repertoires. It is reported as both an Indian and African folktale. In my retelling, I try to emphasise the way that storytelling is validated by the tale. There are loads of written storybook versions around, sometimes called *Monkey See, Monkey Do*. I can't remember where I first heard it: it never ceases to be wonderful!

Children's Books
Adeney, Anne; Bretschnedeir, Christina (2006) *Monkey See, Monkey Do: Blue level 2 (Reading Corner)* Franklin Watts, imprint of Hachette Children's Books, London.

Guillain, Adam; Bernadini, Cristian (2011) *Collins Big Cat Phonics - The Hat Maker and the Chimps: Blue/Band 4* Collins Educational, imprint of HarperCollins, London.

Diakite, Baba Wague (1999) *The Hatseller And The Monkeys* Scholastic Press, New York.

Lupton, Hugh; Fatus, Sophie (2001) *The Story Tree: Tales to Read Aloud* Barefoot Books Inc., Oxford (Book and CD)

Web Sources
Smith, Chris (2009-2014) *The Monkeys and the Hats* Story Museum:
http://www.storymuseum.org.uk/1001stories/detail/79/the-monkeys-and-the-hats.html

Unknown Year Four Student, Pegasus School (Unknown) *The Monkeys and the Hats Storytelling Schools* http://www.storytellingschools.com

Little Red Hen

This is an ever-popular English fable. The web has many versions of Pie Corbett and school children retelling this popular folktale, which I first learned from Pie himself.

Children's Books
Muldrow, Diane; Miller, J. P. (1954, 1982, 2001) *The Little Red Hen (Little Golden Book)* Random House Inc., New York. Random House Canada Limited, Toronto.

Galdone, Paul (1985, 2001) *The Little Red Hen (Paul Galdone Classics)* Clarion Books, imprint of Houghton Mifflin Company, New York.

Ottolenghi, Carol; Holladay, Reggie (2002) *The Little Red Hen* Brighter Child, imprint of Carson-Dellosa Publishing LLC, Greensboro.

Pinkney, Jerry (2006) *The Little Red Hen* Penguin Group Inc., New York.

Ada, Alma Flor; Tryon, Leslie (2004) *With Love, Little Red Hen* Simon and Schuster Children's Publishing Division, New York.

Downard, Barry (2004) *The Little Red Hen* Simon and Schuster Children's Publishing Division, New York.

Paul, Miranda; Majumder, Antara (2010) *The Little Red Hen* iStory Books, a division of InfoMarvel Business Solutions Inc.

Three Little Pigs

There are so many versions of this old classic. In early versions of this story the first two pigs often get eaten, although this has been removed from many recent literary tellings. I like the original because it underlines more clearly the purpose of the tale, which is to emphasise consequences of not being safe. You can see my version on the Story Museum website. Children seem to really like this version despite the reservations of some adults and publishers. Personally I think that stories are great to explore and rehearse difficult feelings and situations, so that we can learn to deal with such feelings in real life.

Children's Books
Baxter, Nicola; Lewis, Jan (1999, 2011, 2012) *The Three Little Pigs: Ladybird First Favourite Tales* Ladybird Books, a division of Penguin Books Ltd., London.

Seibert, Patricia; Elena, Horacio (2002) *The Three Little Pigs (Brighter Child: Keepsake Stories)* Brighter Child, imprint of Carson-Dellosa Publishing LLC, Greensboro.

Amery, Heather; Cartwright, Stephen (2003) *3 Little Pigs (First Stories)* Usborne Publishing Ltd., London.

Johnson, Richard (2007) *Three Little Pigs (Flip-Up Fairy Tales)* Child's Play International Ltd., Swindon.

Scieszka, Jon; Smith, Lane; Hoffman, Kurt (1989, 1991, 1996) *The True Story of the Three Little Pigs (Picture Puffin)* Penguin Books USA Inc., New York.

Trivizas, Eugene; Oxenbury, Helen (2003) *The Three Little Wolves and the Big Bad Pig* Egmont UK Ltd., London.

Brooke, Leonard Leslie (1905) *The Story of the Three Little Pigs* Frederick Warne and Company, now Public Domain.

Banta, Milt; Walt Disney Studios; Golden Books (2005) *Three Little Pigs (Little Golden Books (Random House))* Random House Inc., New York.

Tucker, Stephen; Sharrat, Nick (2009) *Lift-the-Flap Fairy Tales: The Three Little Pigs* (with CD) Macmillan Children's Books, imprint of Pan Macmillan, London.

Birth of Jesus

Obviously the main source here is the New Testament gospels. Thanks to the teachers at John Fisher Roman Catholic Primary School in Oxford for helping develop this version, which is great for whole school assemblies. I hope it conjures some of the magic of the tale without detracting from its sacredness.

Gingerbread Man

Here's another hugely popular English fable, on the theme of runaway food! I added a little song to evoke the character of the fox a bit more.

Children's Books
Macdonald, Alan (2011) *The Gingerbread Man: Ladybird First Favourite Tales* Ladybird Books, a division of Penguin Books Ltd., London.

Corke, Estelle (2007) *The Gingerbread Man (Flip-Up Fairy Tales)* Child's Play International Ltd., Swindon.

Mccafferty, Catherine; Bowles, Doug (2002) *The Gingerbread Man (Brighter Child: Keepsake Stories)* Brighter Child, imprint of Carson-Dellosa Publishing LLC, Greensboro.

Sims, Lesley; Temporin, Elena (2011) *The Gingerbread Man (Usborne Picture Story Books)* Usborne Publishing Ltd., London.

Southgate, Vera; Howarth, Daniel (2012) *Ladybird Tales: The Gingerbread Man* Ladybird Books, a division of Penguin Books Ltd., London.

Corbett, Pie (2008) *Storyteller: The Gingerbread Man and other stories for 4–7 year-olds* Scholastic Ltd., London.

Bat Learns to Dance

I first heard this story from storyteller Tom Phillips, who kindly gave permission for me to publish a written version based on his telling. He told me he got it from Kevin Walker. There is also video version by Peter Chand in the StorySpinner series called *Stories from around the World* with videos of top storytellers for classroom use. I haven't managed to track down a written source or country of origin yet!

Three Billy Goats Gruff

Here's another classic favourite, with some picture book alternatives.

Children's Books
Yates, Irene (2011) *The Three Billy Goats Gruff: Ladybird First Favourite Tales* Ladybird Books, a division of Penguin Books Ltd., London.

Edgson, Alison (2007) *Three Billy Goats Gruff with CD (Flip-up Fairy Tales)* Child's Play International Ltd., Swindon.

Southgate, Vera (2012) *Ladybird Tales: The Three Billy Goats Gruff* Ladybird Books, a division of Penguin Books Ltd., London.

Carpenter, Stephen (1995) *The Three Billy Goats Gruff* HarperCollins Publishers Inc., London.

Hornsby, David (2002) *The Three Billy Goats Gruff Big Book and E-Book (Inside Stories Traditional Tales)* Kingscourt.

Tucker, Stephen; Sharrat, Nick (2010) *Lift-the-Flap Fairy Tales: The Three Billy Goats Gruff (with CD)* Macmillan Children's Books, imprint of Pan Macmillan, London.

Finch, Mary; Arenson, Roberta (2007) *The Three Billy Goats Gruff (Book & CD)* Barefoot Books Ltd., Bath.

Edgson, Alison (2007) *Three Billy Goats Gruff with CD (Flip-up Fairy Tales)* Child's Play International Ltd., Swindon.

Audio
Greig, Tamsin; Mangan, Stephen (2012) *The Three Billy Goats Gruff and Other Stories* (BBC Audio) AudioGo Ltd., Bath.

The Noisy House

I first heard this story from Dr. Fattin Massaad who used it to explain foreign policy in the Occupied Palestine. Later I heard a version from early years advisor Megan Carberry which I adapted for my own telling. It's best known in this form as a Jewish rabbi story.

Children's Books
Murphy, Jill (1980, 2007) *Peace at Last* MacMillan Children's Books, division of Pan Macmillan, London.

Other Print Versions
Macdonald, Margaret Read (2000) *Shake-It-Up Tales!* August House Publishers Inc., Atlanta.

Web Sources
Zerah, Aaron (Accessed online 09/01/2014) *The Way You Like It* Belief Net: http://www.beliefnet.com/Love-Family/Parenting/2000/10/Teaching-Tales-The-Way-You-Like-It.aspx

Traditional Polish/Jewish (Accessed online 09/01/2014) *It Could Be Worse* UUA: http://www.uua.org/re/tapestry/children/home/session4/sessionplan/stories/60031.shtml

Oats, Simon (2013) *The Noisy Little House – A Yiddish Folktale* Youtube: http://www.youtube.com/watch?v=jj7xgCMKir0

The Giant Turnip

This popular fable about working together is a Russian folktale rewritten by Tolstoy himself. It's a great repeating and accumulating tale. The chant/song is there to make it even more fun.

Children's Books
Walker, Lois; Guthridge, Bettina (2007) *Collins Big Cat – The Gigantic Turnip Tug: Band 12/Copper* Collins Educational, imprint of HarperCollins, London.

Yates, Irene (2012) *The Enormous Turnip: Ladybird First Favourite Tales* Ladybird Books, a division of Penguin Books Ltd., London.

Cerretti, Cristiana (2011) *The Enormous Turnip (Flip-Up Fairy Tales)* Child's Play International Ltd., Swindon.

Daynes, Katie; Overwater, Georgien (2006) *The Enormous Turnip (Usborne First Reading: Level 3)* Usborne Publishing Ltd., London.

Southgate, Vera (1982) *The Enormous Turnip (Well-loved Tales)* Ladybird Books, a division of Penguin Books Ltd., London.

Chambers, Mark; James, Robert (2010) *The Enormous Turnip (Leapfrog Fairy Tales)* Franklin Watts, London.

Tolstoy, Aleksei; Sharkey, Niamh (1998, 2006) *The Gigantic Turnip (Book and CD)* Barefoot Books Ltd., Bath. Barefoot Books Ltd., Cambridge, USA.

The Wooden Baby

I have heard this from many storytellers over the years, and noticed a Neolithic variant popping up in Ben Haggarty's amazing graphic novel *Mezolith* (David Fickling Books). It seems to originate with a Czech folktale which has been made into a film *Little Otik* (Otesánek) by Jan Svankmajer (DVD, 2003). The filmmakers cite *Otesánek* by K.J. Erben Otesánek as their main source for the film, and also describe various other print versions suggesting that this is a well-known tale in Slovakia and the Czech Republic.

Children's Books
Weatherill, Cat (2005) *Barkbelly* Penguin Books Ltd., London.

Other Print Versions
Bateson, Catherine; Carmody, Isobel; Mcnab, Nan (2011) *Tales From the Tower: The Wicked Wood* Allen and Unwin, Crows Nest, Australia.

Erben, K. J.; Gissing, Vera (1969) *Tales from Bohemia* Littlehampton Book Services Ltd., West Sussex.

Goldilocks and the Three Bears

This story has evolved into one of the most popular English Language fairy tales, with many many print versions available.

Children's Books
Amery, Heather; Cartwright, Stephen (2003) *Goldilocks and the Three Bears (First Stories)* Usborne Publishing Ltd., London.

Davidson, Susanna; Gordon, Mike; Gordon, Carl (2012) *Goldilocks and the Three Bears (Usborne Picture Books)* Usborne Publishing Ltd., London.

Ladybird (2010) *Goldilocks and the Three Bears: Ladybird Touch and Feel Fairy Tales (Ladybird Tales)* Ladybird Books, a division of Penguin Books Ltd., London.

Child, Lauren; Jenkins, Emily; Borland, Polly (2009) *Goldilocks and the Three Bears* Puffin Books, Penguin Books Ltd., London.

Muller, Gerda (2011) *Goldilocks and the Three Bears* Floris Books, Edinburgh.

Loewen, Nancy; Avakyan, Tatevik (2012) *Believe Me, Goldilocks Rocks! The Story of the Three Bears as Told by Baby Bear (The Other Side of the Story)* Raintree Publishing, Basingstoke Hants.

Askew, Amanda (2011) *Goldilocks and the Three Bears (Storytime Classics)* QED Publishing, a division of Quarto Publishing PLC., London/New York.

The Fox's Sack

This is a great old English repeating story that you can find in the classic collection *Folk and English Fairy Tales* by Joseph Jacobs (1890).

Children's Books
Galdone, Paul (1982, 1987) *What's in Fox's Sack? An Old English Tale* Clarion Books, imprint of Houghton Mifflin Company, New York.
Other Print Versions
Harley, Bill; Holt, David; Mooney, Bill (2000) *More Ready to Tell Tales From Around the World* August House Inc., Atlanta.

Web Sources
Johnson, Charles (2011) *The Fox's Sack* Youtube: http://www.youtube.com/watch?v=lewmHxI4G5w

Johnstone, Sarah (2006) *What's in Fox's Sack* Blogspot: http://caloundrastorytime.blogspot.co.uk/search?q=fox%27s+sack

The Princess and the Pea

This tale was popularised by Hans Christian Anderson who reported he heard it as a child, and is possibly a Swedish folktale. It has now become a very commonly retold fable.

Children's Books
Sanderson, Ana; Shulman, Dee; Umansky, Kaye (2004) *Three Rapping Rats: Making Music with Traditional Stories (A&C Black Musicals)* A & C Black Publishers Ltd., London.

Child, Lauren; Borland, Polly (2006) *The Princess and the Pea* Puffin Books, Penguin Books Ltd., London.

Davidson, Susanna (2004) *The Princess and the Pea: Gift Edition (Usborne Young Reading Series 1)* Usborne Publishing Ltd., London.

Grey, Mini (2003) *The Pea and the Princess* Jonathan Cape, imprint of Random House Children's Books, London.

Hart, Caryl; Warburton, Sarah (2013) *The Princess and the Peas* Nosy Crow Ltd., London.

Stockham, Jess (2009) *The Princess and the Pea (Flip-Up Fairy Tales)* Child's Play International Ltd., Swindon.

Southgate, Vera (2013) *Ladybird Tales: The Princess and the Pea* Ladybird Books, a division of Penguin Books Ltd., London.

Andersen, Hans Christian; Dusikova, Maja (2012) *The Princess and the Pea* Floris Books, Edinbugh.

Christy, Jana; Andersen, Hans Christian (2013) *The Princess and the Pea (Little Golden Book)* Golden Books, imprint of Random House Children's Books, division of Random House Inc., New York.

Gresham, Xanthe; Miss Clara (2013) *The Princess and the Pea (Book and CD)* Barefoot Books Inc., Oxford.

Skinny Old Lady

This is a great African tale that I learned from my friend Adam Guillain. He calls it *Mze Kidogo*. I haven't found any other sources for this lovely story yet.

Web Source
Gullain, Adam (2009-2014) *Mze Kidogo* Story Museum: http://www.storymuseum.org.uk/1001stories/detail/143/mze-kidogo.html

The Freedom Bird

This story was brought to the West by David Holt who reports being told it in Thailand by his guide during a trip there. It is a fantastic story full of play and wit. Thanks for finding it David!

Other Print Versions
Holt, David; Mooney, Bill (1994) *Ready-to-Tell-Tales* August House Inc., Atlanta.

Harley, Bill; Miller, Teresa; Pellowski, Anne; Livo, Norma (1988) *Joining In: An Anthology of Audience Participation Stories and How To Tell Them* Yellow Moon Press, Cambridge MA.

Web Sources
Stewart, Joanie (2012) *Freedom Bird* Youtube: http://www.youtube.com/watch?v=IjgOGLjtKGM

Smith, Chris (Accessed online 13/01/2014) *Freedom Bird* Storytelling Schools: http://www.storytellingschools.com/

Snip-Snip

This is retelling of a very popular Jewish Traditional folktale. I first heard it from Adele Moss and then from the wonderful David Bash. It is a favourite of many storytellers around the world.

Children's Books
Lupton, Hugh; Fatus, Sophie (2001) *The Story Tree: Tales to Read Aloud* Barefoot Books Inc., Oxford (Book and CD)

Web Sources
Cargill-Strong, Jenni (2013) *The Blue Coat* Youtube: http://www.youtube.com/watch?v=PvlURrAB2Os

Cargill-Strong, Jenni (2010) *The Blue Coat* StoryTree: http://www.storytree.com.au/the-blue-coat-a-jewish-folktale-inspired-by-a-retelling-by-hugh-lupton/

Wagner, Maureen (2010) *The Blue Coat* Blogspot: http://strongstart.blogspot.co.uk/2010/12/story-blue-coat.html

Smith, Chris (2009-2014) *Snip-Snip (two minute version)* Story Museum: http://www.storymuseum.org.uk/1001stories/detail/130/snip-snip-two-minute-version.html

The King and the Moon

I first heard this Dominican Republic story from a teacher at Rose Hill Primary School in Oxford, who asked me to develop it for oral retelling.

Children's Books
Hawkes, Alison; Gamble, Nikki; Heapy, Teresa; Slater, Kate (2011) *Oxford Reading Tree Traditional Tales: Level 2: The King and His Wish* Oxford University Press, Oxford.

Web Sources
Teachprimary (2011) *The King and His Wish* Youtube: http://www.youtube.com/watch?v=bGeD51IyRsc

Bennet, William; Michel, John E. (2009) *Building our own Towers to the Moon* af.mil: http://www.grandforks.af.mil/news/story.asp?id=123143089

Magic Porridge Pot

This is another much loved and much told tale was originally collected by the Brother's Grimm.

Children's Books
Macdonald, Alan (2012) *The Magic Porridge Pot: Ladybird First Favourite Tales* Ladybird Books, a division of Penguin Books Ltd., London.

Hurt-Newton, Tania (1999) *First Favourite Tales: The Magic Porridge Pot* Ladybird Books, a division of Penguin Books Ltd., London.

Ladybird (2008) *The Magic Porridge Pot: Ladybird Tales* Ladybird Books, a division of Penguin Books Ltd., London.

Grimm, Jacob; Grimm, Wilhelm; Dickins, Rosie; Gordon, Carl; Gordon, Mike (2012) *The Magic Porridge Pot (Usborne Picture Books)* Usborne Publishing Ltd., London.

James, Robert; Leplar, Anna C. (2009) *The Magic Porridge Pot (Leapfrog Fairy Tales)* Franklin Watts, a division of Hachette Children's Books, London.

Other Print Versions
Grimm, Wilhelm; Grimm, Jacob (1812) *Children's and Household Tales/Grimm's Fairy Tales* Not Applicable.

The Speaking Sweet Potato

I first heard this from Pie Corbett, who has spread this story all over the country with the main vegetable as a Papaya. There are many West African versions using different characters and objects within the same plot idea. I use the sweet potato as an easier reference for young children.

Children's Books
Medearis, Angela; Vitale, Stephano (1996) *Talk Too Much* Walker Books Ltd., London.

Web Sources
Corbett, Pie (Accessed online 13/01/2014) *The Papaya That Spoke* Scholastic: http://images.scholastic.co.uk/assets/a/13/a4/papaya-sip-106416.pdf

Guillain, Adam (2009-2014) *The Yammering Yam* Story Museum: http://www.storymuseum.org.uk/1001stories/detail/145/the-yammering-yam.html

Ashanti Folk Tale (Accessed online 13/01/2014) *The Day the Yam Spoke* Itisdschools: http://ltisdschools.org/cms/lib/TX21000349/Centricity/Domain/1314/The Day the Yam.pdf

Riedman, Kathie (2009) *Yammering Yam! A Folktale from Ghana* The Free Library: http://www.thefreelibrary.com/Yammering+yam!+A+folktale+from+Ghana.-a0198472004

Stone Soup

This is a much-told European trick tale, sometimes using a stone, sometimes a nail or other inedible objects. There is a town in Portugal that claims to be the capital of stone soup, where you can eat it in the cafes!

Children's Books
Forest, Heather; Gaber, Susan (1998, 2000) *Stone Soup* August House Publishers Inc., Atlanta.

Sims, Lesley; Overwater, Georgien (2009) *Stone Soup (First Reading) (Usborne First Reading)* Usborne Publishing Ltd., London.

Ross, Tony (1987) *Stone Soup* Andersen Press Ltd., London.

Muth, Jon J. (2003) *Stone Soup* Scholastic Ltd., London.

Sommer, Carl; Denman, Michael (2013) *Stone Soup (Sommer-Time Story Classic Series)* Advance Publishing Inc., Houston.

Paul, Miranda; Majumder, Antara; Ray, Maya (2012) *Stone Soup* iStory Books, a division of InfoMarvel Business Solutions Inc.

Other Print Versions
Liao, Bill (2009) *Stone Soup: The Secret Recipe for Making Something from Nothing* Bookshaker, Great Yarmouth.

A Husband for Miss Mouse

This is a long and lovely variant of the *Who is the strongest?* tale. I first read it in a battered collection of tales I found in a second hand bookshop on Yangoon. It can also be found in the ancient *Panchatantra* collection from India (3rd Century BC).

Other Print Versions
Sarma, Visnu; Rajan, Chandra (1993, 2006) *Pancʹatantra* Penguin Classics, Penguin Books Ltd., London.

Hashimoto, Yasuko (1981) *A husband for Miss Mouse, and other tales (Tales of a Japanese grandmother)* Casalinda Bookshop, Batanes.

Griffis, William Elliot (1911) *The Unmannerly Tiger and Other Korean Tales* Thomas Y. Crowell and Company, New York.

Carey, Martha Ward (1887) *Fairy Legends of the French Provinces* Thomas Y. Crowell and Company, New York.

Awongalema

I learned this one from Adam Guillain; it's a popular African story, sometimes called the *Awongalema Tree* and sometimes called the *Tree of Life*.

Children's Books
Williamson, Melanie; Don, Lari (2012) *The Tortoise's Gift: A Story from Zambia* Barefoot Books Ltd., Bath.

Web Sources
Loebe, Laurie; Sharpe, Stephen (Accessed online 13/01/2014) *The Awongalema Tree* Spellbinders: http://www.spellbinders.org/store/p16details57.php

Groper, Micki (2013) *The Awongalema Tree* Youtube: http://www.youtube.com/watch?v=q_3HyRGwpF8

Webb, David (Accessed online 13/01/2014) *The Tortoise and the Tree of Life* SoundCloud: https://soundcloud.com/augustine-leudar/allwangullema

The Lion's Roar

This story is a retelling of a tale from the Jataka collection, which tells legends of the lives of the Buddha. The complete set of tales is published in English by the Pali Text society. It has an obvious parallel with the *Chicken Licken* story, though a very different ending!

Other Print Versions
Cowell, E. B. (1990) *Jataka Stories* Pali Text Society, Wiltshire.

Martin, Rafe (1999) *The Hungry Tigress* Yellow Moon Press, Cambridge MA.

Meller, Eric (2013) *The Rabbit Who Overcame Fear (Jataka Tales)* Dharma Publishing, Cazadero CA.

Goose Girl's Wings

I first came across this lovely story in Yellow Moon's excellent book *Joining In* (Yellow Moon Press) where Diane Wolkstein explained how to tell the story in a participative way.

Children's Books
Wolkstein, Diane; Miller, Teresa; Pellowski, Anne; Livo, Norma (1988) *Joining In: An Anthology of Audience Participation Stories and How To Tell Them* Yellow Moon Press, Cambridge MA.

Wolkstein, Diane; Parker, Robert Andrew (1992) *The Magic Wings: A Tale from China (Picture Puffin)* Puffin Books, Penguin Books Ltd., London.

Burton, Marilee Robin; Sokolova, Valerie (2000) *The Goose Girl: A Traditional Chinese Tale* Scholastic Press, New York.

Mouse and Lion

I first learned this story from my friend Amaranatho as a fable about friendship. It can be found in the fables of Aesop.

Children's Books
Pinkney, Jerry (2011) *The Lion and the Mouse* Little Brown Books for Young Readers, Hachette Children's Books, London.

Broom, Jenny; Noj, Nahta (2013) *The Lion and the Mouse (Turn and Tell Tales)* Templar Publishing Company Ltd., Surrey.

Mackinnon, Mairi; Endersby, Frank (2008) *The Lion and the Mouse (Usborne First Reading: Level 1)* Usborne Publishing Ltd., London.

Echeverri, Catalina (2013) *Lion and Mouse* Jonathan Cape Publishing, imprint of Random House Group, London.

Tomato, Tomzi (2013) *The Lion and The Mouse – Aesop's Fables Retold – Kids Story and Activities* Tomzi Press.

Burkert, Nancy Ekholm; Burkert, Rand (2011) *Mouse & Lion* Scholastic Press, New York.

Marwood, Diane; Axworthy, Anni (2009) *The Lion and the Mouse (Tadpoles Tales)* Franklin Watts, imprint of Hachette Children's Books, London.

The Nest and the Web

This is a legend of the life of the prophet Mohammed and how he escaped assassins to reach Medina in safety.

Children's Books
Mccaughrean, Geraldine; Willey, Bee (2001) *100 World Myths and Legends* Orion Publishing Group Ltd., London.

Other Print Versions
Smith, Chris; Al-Gailani, Noorah (2004) *The Islamic Year* Hawthorn Press, Stroud.

The Dancing Harmonica

There are so many stories about instruments, which force people to dance when being played for one reason or another. This version is based on a story created by George Shannon called *Lazy Peter*. George kindly agreed for me to retell his version of the story.

Children's Books
Power, Rhoda (1969) *The Big Book of Stories from Many Lands* Franklin Watts, imprint of Hachette Children's Books, London.

Talkative Turtle

This story is both popular and global. I once heard the great Native American teller Dovey Thompson tell a wonderful version of the story.

Children's Books
Peters, Andrew Fusek; Cooke, Charlotte (2011) *The Talkative Tortoise (Traditional Tales with a Twist)* Child's Play International Ltd., Swindon.

Other Print Versions
Sarma, Visnu; Rajan, Chandra (1993, 2006) *Panc´atantra* Penguin Classics, Penguin Books Ltd., London.

Cowell, E. B. (1990) *Jataka Stories* Pali Text Society, Wiltshire.

Audio
Pease, Robert (2005) *Talkative Turtle & Other Tales* Kulture Kids, CD Baby (CD)

Bandits and Berries

This has been retold from a telling by Linda Fang (Holt, David; Mooney, Bill [2000] *More Ready-to-Tell Tales From Around the World* August House Inc., Atlanta.) called *Sweet and Sour Berries*. She cites Hsiao-chin: filial anecdotes as her own source. Linda kindly gave permission for me to retell her lovely version of the story.

The Thirsty Frog

This is one of the most popular aboriginal tales from Australia. You will find many version and clips on the web. It is sometimes called *The Greedy Frog, The Thirsty Frog* or simply *Tiddalick*.

Children's Books
Roennfeldt, Robert (1981) Tiddalick: *The Frog Who Caused a Flood (Picture Puffin)* Penguin Books USA Inc., New York.

Carthew, Mark; Rogers, Greg (2007) *Tiddalick the Thirsty Frog: Collins Big Cat: Ruby/Band 14* Collins Educational, imprint of HarperCollins, London.

Nunes, Susan; Chen, Ju-Hong (1990) *Tiddalick the Frog* Hodder Headline Australia Children's Books.

Troughton, Joanna (1994) *What Made Tiddalik Laugh (Puffin Folk Tales of the World)* Penguin Ltd., London.

More!

My source for this retelling is Carol Birch's story called *Bracelets*, found in the anthology *Joining In* (Birch, Carol; Miller, Teresa; Pellowski, Anne; Livo, Norma [1988] *Joining In: An Anthology of Audience Participation Stories and How To Tell Them* Yellow Moon Press, Cambridge MA.). Her telling is retold from a story by Laurel Hodgden, a psychologist with the Headstart Program in Ithaca, New York. She wrote this story in 1974 as part of a grant. In keeping with the oral tradition, Diane Wolkstein heard it from a student in her storytelling class, adapted it, and began to tell it. Carol Birch heard it from Diane, further adapted it, and wrote it down in *Joining In: An Anthology of Audience Participation Stories and How to Tell Them*. My version is adapted from Carol's. Carol kindly gave permission for me to retell from her version of the story.

Little Red Riding Hood

There are so many versions of this ever-popular story, and you can read many of them in Jack Zipes' seminal *The Trials and Tribulations of Little Red Riding Hood: Versions of the Tale in Sociocultural Context* (Zipes, Jack [1993] Routledge Inc., New York)

Children's Books
Ransom, Candice F.; Lyon, Tammie (2002) *Little Red Riding Hood (Brighter Child: Keepsake Stories)* Brighter Child, imprint of Carson-Dellosa Publishing LLC, Greensboro.

Shaskan, Trisha Speed; Guerlais, Gerald (2012) *Honestly, Red Riding Hood was Rotten! The Story of Little Red Riding Hood as Told by the Wolf (The Other Side...)* Raintree Publishing, Basingstoke Hants.

Grimm, Wilhelm; Grimm, Jacob; Gordon, Mike (2013) *Little Red Riding Hood (Usborne Picture Books)* Usborne Publishing Ltd., London.

Ross, Mandy (2011) *Little Red Riding Hood: Ladybird First Favourite Tales* Ladybird Books, a division of Penguin Books Ltd., London.

Tocher, Timothy; Lansky, Bruce (2012) *Newfangled Fairy Tales: Classic Stories with a Funny Twist Book #1* Meadowbrook Press, Minnetonka.

Cartwright, Stephen; Amery, Heather (2003) *Little Red Riding Hood (First Stories)* Usborne Publishing Ltd., London.

Don, Lari; Chauffrey, Célia; Staunton, Imelda (2012) *Little Red Riding Hood* Barefoot Books Ltd., Bath (Book and CD)

Stockham, Jess (2007) *Little Red Riding Hood (Flip-Up Fairy Tales)* Child's Play International Ltd., Swindon (Book and CD).

Jack and the Beanstalk

My main source for this retelling was in *Folk Tales of the British Isles* (Crossley-Holland, Kevin [1986] *Folk Tales of the British Isles* Faber and Faber Ltd., London). I find this old version so much more satisfying than later versions because the back-story of Jack's father makes sense of the rest of the plot.

Children's Books
Treahy, Iona (2012) *Jack and the Beanstalk: Ladybird First Favourite Tales* Ladybird Books, a division of Penguin Books Ltd., London.

Ottolenghi, Carol; Porfirio, Guy (2002) *Jack and the Beanstalk (Brighter Child: Keepsake Stories)* Brighter Child, imprint of Carson-Dellosa Publishing LLC, Greensboro.

Watt, Fiona; Wells, Rachel; Daynes, Katie; Mounter, Paddy (2006) *Jack and the Beanstalk (Usborne Young Reading)* Usborne Publishing Ltd., London.

Lines, Kathleen; Jones, Harold (2013) *Jack and the Beanstalk: A Book of Nursery Stories* Oxford University Press, Oxford.

Rivers, Ruth (1999) *First Favourite Tales: Jack & the Beanstalk* Ladybird Books, a division of Penguin Books Ltd., London.

Kellog, Steven (1998) *Jack and the Beanstalk* William Morrow and Company Inc., New York.

Tucker, Stephen; Sharrat, Nick (2010) *Lift-the-Flap Fairy Tales: Jack and the Beanstalk (with CD)* Macmillan Children's Books, imprint of Pan Macmillan, London.

Vagnozzi, Barbara (2007) *Jack and the Beanstalk (Flip-Up Fairy Tales)(With CD)* Child's Play International Ltd., Swindon.

Walker, Richard; Hope, Richard; Sharkey, Niamh (2006) *Jack and the Beanstalk (Book & CD)* Barefoot Books Ltd., Bath.

Chapter 2   Year 2 Stories

The Stonecutter

I can't remember where I first heard this lovely Chinese fable, which is also sometimes quoted as a Japanese tale. The web is full of clips of retelling, songs and text versions. It is also found in collections of Zen Buddhist tales as teaching us acceptance and the comedy of always wanting more. It has obvious uses for teaching about nature and interdependence.

Children's Books
Taylor, Sean; Curmi, Serena; Moon, Cliff (2005) *The Stone Cutter-Collins Big Cat* Collins Educational, imprint of HarperCollins, London.

Sims, Lesley (2010) *Illustrated Stories from Around the World* Usborne Publishing, London.

Barella, Laura (2012) *The Stonecutter (Flip-Up Fairy Tales)* Child's Play International Ltd., Swindon.

Benton, Lynne; Cosgrove, Lee (2009) *The Stonecutter (Usborne First Reading)* Usborne Publishing, London.

Heddle, Becca; Gamble, Nikki; Dowson, Pam; Hunt, Meg (2011) *Yoshi The Stonecutter (Oxford Reading Tree Traditional Tales: Level 6)* Oxford University Press, Oxford.

Williams, Rose; Barret, Robin T. (1997) *Fairies: Nature Spirits from Around the World* Barefoot Books Ltd., Bath.

Other Print Versions
Lang, Andrew (1903) *The Crimson Fairy Book* Folio Society.

Web Sources
Newton, Pam (2011) *Stonecutter Short Story* Youtube: http://www.youtube.com/watch?v=7ChOYWJV2U4

Unkown (Accessed online 14/01/2014) *The Stonecutter* Meaningful Stories: http://www.meaningful-stories.com/taleweb/p000325/online_stories/the_stonecutter

Unknown (Accessed online 14/01/2014) *The Story of the Stonecutter* comcast: http://home.comcast.net/~jptillman/stonecutter.html

Lang, Andrew (Accessed online 14/01/2014) *The Stone-Cutter* Read Book Online: http://www.readbookonline.net/readOnLine/4739/

The Unlucky Man

This English story is very popular with UK storytellers and with UK schools. My favourite telling was by the great French storyteller Abbi Patrix.

Other Print Versions
Horsely, Katrice; Keding, Dan; Douglas, Amy (2005) *English Folktales* Libraries Unlimited Inc., Westport.

Hook, Derek; Neelakantan, Radhika (2013) *He walked and he walked and he walked: Cracking Good Tales* Karina Library Press, California.

Web Sources
Smith, Chris; Gulbenkian, Vergine (2009-2014) *The Unlucky Man* Story Museum: http://www.storymuseum.org.uk/1001stories/detail/215/the-unlucky-man.html

Unkown (2013) *A good story with a moral: The Unlucky Man* Reddit: http://as.reddit.com/r/CampFireStories/comments/xejfj/a_good_story_with_a_moral_the_unlucky_man/

Hook, Derek; Neelakantan, Radhika (2013) *The Unlucky Man* Cracking Good Tales: http://www.crackinggoodtales.com/flip-book

Evans, Matt (Accessed online 14/01/2014) *The Unlucky Man* Ultimate Camp Resource: http://www.ultimatecampresource.com/site/camp-activity/the-unlucky-man.html

Moorcroft, John Henry; Zarraga, Paul Henry (2012) *The Unluckiest Man in the World* Wordpress: http://thehenrybrothers.wordpress.com/2012/09/21/the-unluckiest-man-in-the-world-co-constructed-storytelling/

Unknown (Accessed online 14/01/2014) *Folklore Every Culture*: http://www.everyculture.com/wc/Afghanistan-to-Bosnia-Herzegovina/Pashtun

The King and the Cockerel

I first heard this tale on a story tape called Aerabian Nights from the 1001 Nights collection. I can't find the original storyteller's name, but thankyou! A similar story is found in Hungarian Folktale, often known as *The Little Rooster* and *The Diamond Button*. This story is almost identical, though it features a diamond rather than a coin.

Children's Books
Macdonald, Margaret Read; Terry, Will (2007) *Little Rooster's Diamond Button* Albert Whitman and Company, Illinois.

Lottridge, Celia Barker; Fitzgerald, Joanne (2001) *The Little Rooster and the Diamond Button: a Hungarian Folktale* Groundwood Books, Toronto.

Web Sources
Uusmets, Reena (2011) *The Little Rooster and the Diamond Ring* Slide Share: http://www.slideshare.net/reenauusmets/the-little-rooster-and-the-diamond-ring

Smith, Chris (2009-2013) *The King and the Cockerel* Story Museum: http://www.storymuseum.org.uk/1001stories/detail/85/the-king-and-the-cockerel.html

The Bird and the Forest Fire

This is another Jataka story, telling legends of the life of the Buddha. You can hear me tell it on the Story Museum website, and find it in any number of collections of Jataka and Buddhist stories. It's sometimes called *The Brave Little Parrot* or *The Brave Little Quail* if you go story hunting! There is a very similar South American folktale that features a Hummingbird.

Children's Books
Martin, Rafe; Gaber, Susan (1998) *The Brave Little Parrot* G. P. Putnam's Sons, imprint of Penguin Ltd., New York.

Yahgulanaas, Michael Nicolli; Maathai, Wangari (2010) *The Little Hummingbird* Greystone Books, Vancouver.

Nagaria, Dharmachari; Tancredi, Sharon (2010) *Buddha at Bedtime* Duncan Baird Publishers Ltd., London.

Web Sources
Unknown (2012) *The Little Bird that Stops a Fire* Wordpress: https://buddhiststories.wordpress.com/2012/11/04/the-little-bodhisattva-bird/

Honey and Trouble

This much-told story comes from Haiti and has also been attributed as an African folktale. I first heard it from storyteller Ben Haggarty. It has a number of titles including *Honey and Suffering*, and *Honey and Misery and Papa God*. I like using the word trouble rather than misery, which I believe was initially coined by Ben. I find trouble is more easily understood by UK children, and makes the joke better. Many retellings cite Diana Wolkstein as their source in *The Magic Orange Tree and other Haitian Folktales* (Wolkstein, Diane; Henriquez, Elsa [1978] Schocken Books, imprint of Random House Group Ltd., London.)

Children's Books
Lupton, Hugh; Sharkey, Niamh (1998) *Tales of Wisdom and Wonder* Barefoot Books Ltd., Oxford (Book and CD)

Other Print Versions
Bausch, William J. (2012) *An Anthology of Saints: Official, Unofficial and Should-Be Saints* Twenty-Third Publications, New London.

Web Sources
Smith, Chris (2009-2014) *Honey and Trouble* Story Museum: http://www.storymuseum.org.uk/1001stories/detail/95/honey-and-trouble.html

Gardner-Hammond, Irma (Accessed online 16/01/2014) *How The Monkey Found Misery* Arts Are Essential: http://www.arts-are-essential.org/saproject06/lesson_plans/Authenticstory2.pdf

Wall, Nikki (2011) *The Little Monkey and Papa God* Blogspot: http://ninny-noodle-noo.blogspot.co.uk/2011/10/little-monkey-and-papa-god.html

Audio
Dreamcatchers (2004) *Ride a White Stallion* DreamCatchers (CD)

How Coyote Brought Fire to Earth

This cracking Native American tale originates with the Karok people. I have heard it told with various helper animals over the years. It is popular with UK storytellers as it has great drama and a lovely twist at the end.

Children's Books
London, Jonathan; Pinola, Lanny; Long, Sylvia; Lang, Julian (2013) *Fire Race: A Karuk Coyote Tale* Chronicle Books LLC, San Francisco.

Web Sources
Unknown (Accessed online 16/01/2014) *How the Coyote Stole Fire* fs.fed: http://www.na.fs.fed.us/fire_poster/nativeamer.htm

Unknown (Accessed online 16/01/2014) *Coyote's Gift* Weingart Design: http://www.weingartdesign.com/TMaS/Stories/tmas2-Coyote.html

Unknown (Accessed online 16/01/2014) *Native Lore: How Coyote Stole Fire* ilHawaii: http://www.ilhawaii.net/~stony/lore06.html

Unknown (Accessed online 16/01/2014) *How Coyote Brought Fire to the People* First People: http://www.firstpeople.us/FP-Html-Legends/How_Coyote_Brought_Fire_To_The_People-Karok.html

The Snake and the Frog

My source for this charming story is Jon Spelman in *More Ready-to-Tell-Tales* (Spelman, Jon; Holt, David; Mooney, Bill [2000]-August House Inc., Atlanta.), who cites it simply as an old tall tale. Jon kindly gave me permission to publish my retelling in this book. Learn more about Jon at http://www.jonspelman.com

Web Sources
Ahearn, William Francis (2010) *The Frog and the Snake* Remarkable Journeys: http://remarkablejourneys.net/2010/11/04/the-frog-and-the-snake/

The Talking Skull

This story, sometimes called *The Skull that Refused to Talk*, is discussed at length in *African Folktales* by Roger D. Abrahams [1983] Pantheon Books, imprint of Random House Inc., New York). The author cites it as one of the most commonly told folktales in all Africa.

Other Print Versions
Bascom, William Russel; Udechukwu, Obiora (1976) *African Folktales in the New World* Indiana University Press, Indiana (valuable for numerous versions/sources).

Forest, Heather; Boston, David (1995) *Wonder Tales from Around the World* August House Inc., Atlanta.

Lowbury, Edward; Patten, Brian (2006) *The Puffin Book of Modern Children's Verse* Puffin Books, imprint of Penguin Books Ltd., London.

Web Sources
Lowbury, Edward (Accessed online 16/01/2014) *The Huntsman* Blogspot: http://childhoodsongs.blogspot.co.uk/2008/10/huntsman-by-edward-lowbury.html

Smith, Chris (2009-2014) *The Talking Skull* Story Museum: http://www.storymuseum.org.uk/1001stories/detail/196/the-talking-skull.html

Frobenius, Leo; Fox, Douglas G. (Accessed online 16/01/2014) *The Talking Skull* Nexus Learning: http://www.nexuslearning.net/books/holt_elementsoflit-3/Collection%203/talking%20skull%20a%20nigerian%20folk.htm

The Elephant's Fury

This is another tale from the Buddhist Jataka collection of stories of the Buddha's past lives. It can be found in various Jataka translations.

Web Sources
Unkown (Accessed online 16/01/2014) *The King's Elephant* Clear-Vision: http://www.clear-vision.org/Schools/Students/Ages-4-7/story-of-Kings-elephant.aspx

The Island of Fairies

I first read this story in *Around the World in 80 Tales* by Saviour Pirotta (Pirotta, Saviour; Johnson, Richard [2007] Kingfisher Publications Plc., London.)

Other Print Versions
Thomas, W. Jenkyn (1907, 2001) *The Welsh Fairy Book* Dover Publications Inc., New York.

Ashliman, D. L. (2006) *Fairy Lore: A Handbook* Greenwood Press, imprint of Greenwood Publishing Group Inc., New York.

The Bee's Treasure

I first read this story in a variant called *The Man Who Bought a Dream* by Timmy Abell (Abell, Timmy; Holt, David; Mooney, Bill [2000] *More Ready-to-Tell-Tales* August House Inc., Atlanta.). Timmy Abell cites *Folktales Told Around the World* (Dorson, Richard M. [1975] The University of Chicago Press, Chicago/The University of Chicago Press Ltd., London.)

Children's Books
Long, Jan Freeman; Ono, Kaoru (1996) *The Bee and the Dream: A Japanese Tale* E. P. Dutton and Co., imprint of Penguin Group USA LLC.

Web Sources
Abell, Timmy (1998) *The Man Who Bought a Dream* timmyabell: http://www.timmyabell.com/mandream.htm

Act!Vated Story Theatre (Accessed online 16/01/2014) *Follow the Buzz* Activated Story Theatre: http://activatedstorytheatre.com/folktales/buzz.html

The Pied Piper of Hamlyn

Collected by the Grimm Brothers, there are many wonderful retellings of this tale in various formats.

Children's Books
Morpurgo, Michael (2013) *Of Lions and Unicorns: A Lifetime of Tales from the Nation's Favourite Storyteller* HarperCollins Publishers Ltd., London.

Corrin, Sara; Corrin, Stephen; Cain, Erol Le (1991) *The Pied Piper of Hamelin* Houghton Mifflin Harcourt, Boston.

Other Print Versions
Grimm, Wilhelm; Grimm, Jacob (1812) *Children's and Household Tales/Grimm's Fairy Tales* Not Applicable.

Browning, Robert; Greenaway, Kate (1888, 2009) *The Pied Piper of Hamelin* Pook Press, Unkown.

Lasko, Danny (2012) *The Children of Hamelin* StickyPitch Press, Unkown (A novel that picks up where Robert Browning ends).

Web Sources
Browning, Robert (Accessed online 16/01/2014) *The Pied Piper of Hamelin* Indiana.edu: http://www.indiana.edu/~librcsd/etext/piper/text.html

Ashliman, D. L.; Grimm, Wilhelm; Grimm, Jacob (199-2013) *The Pied Piper of Hameln and related Legends of Other Towns* pitt.edu: http://www.pitt.edu/~dash/hameln.html#grimm245

Bellingham, Daryl (1996) *The Pied Piper of Hamelin* storytell: http://www.storytell.com.au/stories/PiedPiper.html

The Pedlar of Swaffham

This is a much-told Norfolk tale. A popular variant *In Baghdad Dreaming of Cairo* appears in many *1001 Nights collections*, and was also retold by the popular Persian mystic Jalaladin Rumi.

Children's Books
Lupton, Hugh; Sharkey, Niamh (1998) *Tales of Wisdom and Wonder* Barefoot Books Ltd., Oxford (Book and CD)

Unkown (1997) *The Jackanory Story Book* Book Club Associates in arrangement with the British Broadcasting Association.

Jacobs, Joseph; Stobbs, William (1969) *The Crock of Gold* Bodley Head Children's Books, imprint of Random House Group Ltd., London.

Other Print Versions
Hartland, Edwin Sidney (1890, 2008) *English Fairy and other Folktales and The Science of Fairytales* Book Revivals Press, trademark of Amadio Inc., California.

Crossley-Holland, Kevin; Gordon, Margaret (1971) *The Pedlar Of Swaffham* Macmillan, imprint of Pan Macmillan, London.

Pearce, Phillipa; Fowler, Rosamund (2001) *The Pedlar of Swaffham* Scholastic Inc., New York.

Web Sources
Unkown (Accessed online 16/01/2014) *The Pedlar of Swaffham* e2bn: http://myths.e2bn.org/mythsandlegends/textonly11-the-pedlar-of-swaffham.html

Unkown (2012) *The Pedlar of Swaffham* Around Swaffham: http://www.aroundswaffham.co.uk/general/history

Smith, Chris (2009-2014) *The Pedlar of Swaffham* Story Museum: http://www.storymuseum.org.uk/1001stories/detail/214/the-pedlar-of-swaffham.html

Dgeorgiou (Accessed online 16/01/2014) *The Pedlar of Swaffham* Aniboom: http://www.aniboom.com/animation-video/298688/The Pedlar of Swaffham/

Strength

My source for this tale was *Peace Tales* by Margaret Read Macdonald (Macdonald, Margaret Read [1992] August House Inc., Atlanta). She cites *Limba Stories* and *Storytelling* by Ruth Finegan (Finegan, Ruth [1981] Greenwood Press, imprint of Greenwood Publishing Group Inc., New York.) as a fine variant. Margaret kindly gave me permission to publish my retelling in this book.

Sleeping Beauty

I based my retelling of this story on the Grimm Brothers' version of the story found in *Complete Fairy Tales: Grimm* (Grimm, Wilhelm; Grimm, Jacob; Colum, Padraic; Campbell, Joseph; Scharl, Josef [1948, 2002] *Grimm: Complete Fairy Tales* Routledge & Kegan Paul, Routledge Classics, imprint of the Taylor and Francis Group, Oxford.)

Children's Books
Hyman, Trina Schart (1997) *The Sleeping Beauty* Little, Brown Book Group, London.

Perrault, Charles; Crane, Walter (Unknown) *The Sleeping Beauty Picture Book* Dodd, Mead and Company, New York (kindle edition)

Grimm, Wilhelm; Grimm, Jacob; Drescher, Daniela (2013) *An Illustrated Treasury of Grimm's Fairy Tales* Floris Books, Edinburgh.

Evans, C. S.; Rackham, Arthur (1920, 2008) *The Sleeping Beauty* Dodo Press, Unknown.

Web Sources
Grimm, Wilhelm; Grimm Jacob (Accessed online 16/01/2014) *Sleeping Beauty* usf.edu: http://etc.usf.edu/lit2go/68/fairy-tales-and-other-Traditional-stories/5102/sleeping-beauty/

Perrault, Charles (Accessed online 16/01/2014) *The Sleeping Beauty in the Wood* pitt.edu: http://

www.pitt.edu/~dash/perrault01.html (Contains the rarely told second half of the story)

Rumpelstiltskin

This story was collected by the Grimm Brothers and can be found in various translations of their collection. Personally, I like *Grimm: Complete Fairy Tales* published by Routledge (Grimm, Wilhelm; Grimm, Jacob; Colum, Padraic; Campbell, Joseph; Scharl, Josef [1948, 2002] Routledge & Kegan Paul, Routledge Classics, imprint of the Taylor and Francis Group, Oxford.) Teachers may also wish to look at the old English story *Tom Tit Tot* for comparison. There is a good version of this in Alan Garner's *Book of British Fairy Tales* (Garner, Alan; Collard, Derek [1984] William Collins Sons and Co. Ltd., London).

Children's Books
Morpurgo, Michael; Fine, Anne; Geras, Adele; Pullman, Philip; Wilson, Jacqueline; Various (2011) *Magic Beans: a Handful of Fairytales from the Storybag* David Fickling Books, a division of Random House Children's Books, a Random House Group Company, London.

Southgate, Vera (2012) *Rumpelstiltskin: Ladybird Tales* Ladybird Books, a division of Penguin Books Ltd., London.

Mayo, Margaret; Norman, Philip (2003) *Rumpelstiltskin (First Fairy Tales)* Orchard Books, London.

Stockham, Jess (2009) *Rumpelstiltskin (Flip-Up Fairytales)* Child's Play International Ltd., Swindon.

Ladybird (2011) *Rumpelstiltskin - Read It Yourself with Ladybird: Level 2* Ladybird Books, a division of Penguin Books Ltd., London.

Ladybird (2008) *Rumpelstiltskin: Ladybird Tales* Ladybird Books, a division of Penguin Books Ltd., London.

Davidson, Susanna; Guicciardini, Desideria (2006) *Rumpelstiltskin* Usborne Publishing Ltd., London

Other Print Versions
Duffy, Carol Ann; Prachaticka, Marketa (1999) *Rumpelstiltskin and Other Grimm Tales* Faber and Faber Ltd, London.

Web Sources
Grimm, Jacob; Grimm, Wilhelm (Accessed online 17/01/2014) *Rumpelstiltskin* East of the Web: http://www.eastoftheweb.com/short-stories/UBooks/Rum.shtml

Cinderella

This ever popular story, now global, can also be found in the Grimm collection, which I used as a basis for this retelling (Grimm, Wilhelm; Grimm, Jacob; Colum, Padraic; Campbell, Joseph; Scharl, Josef [1948, 2002] *Grimm: Complete Fairy Tales* Routledge & Kegan Paul, Routledge Classics, imprint of the Taylor and Francis Group, Oxford.). In Grimm collections it is often titled *Ashputtel*. Teachers may also wish to read the old English story *Mossycoat* for comparison (Garner, Alan; Collard, Derek [1984] *Book of British Fairy Tales* William Collins Sons and Co. Ltd., London), as well as *Little Burnt Face,* which can be found in Chapter Three of this book.

Children's Books
Perrault, Charles; Cain, Erol Le (1976) *Cinderella or The Little Glass Slipper* by Picture Puffin, Puffin Books, imprint of Penguin Books Ltd., London.

Ladybird (2014) *Cinderella: Ladybird First Favourite Tales* Ladybird Books, a division of Penguin Books Ltd., London.

Ray, Jane (2012) *Cinderella: A Three-Dimensional Fairy Tale Theatre* Walker Books Ltd., London.

Grimm, Wilhelm; Grimm, Jacob; Dennis, Sarah (2013) *Cinderella: A Paper-Cut Book* Tango Books Ltd., London.

Roberts, Lynn; Roberts, David (2011) *Cinderella: An Art Deco Love Story* Pavilion Children's, imprint of Anova Books Group, London.

Eilenberg, Max; Sharkey, Niamh (2012) *Cinderella* Walker Books Ltd., London.

Other Print Versions
Duffy, Carol Ann; Prachaticka, Marketa (1999) *Rumpelstiltskin and Other Grimm Tales* Faber and Faber Ltd, London.

Grimm, Jacob; Grimm, Wilhelm, Funke, Cornelia; Cruikshank, George (2012) *Fairy Tales from the Brothers Grimm* Puffin Books, imprint of Penguin Books Ltd., London.

Web Sources
Grimm, Jacob; Grimm, Wilhelm (Accessed online 17/01/2014) *Ashputtel* Authorama: http://www.authorama.com/grimms-fairy-tales-35.html

Perrault, Charles (Accessed online 17/02/2014) *Cinderella; or, the Little Glass Slipper* pitt.edu: http://www.pitt.edu/~dash/perrault06.html

Grimm, Jacob, Grimm, Wilhelm; Reed, Quentin (2012) *Ashputte Audiobookl* Youtube: http://www.youtube.com/watch?v=vNGhaY5rSgQ

The Magic Paintbrush

I can't remember where I first heard this story, which has become well known through Julia Donaldson's lovely picture-book retelling of the tale. Julia Donaldson kindly gave her blessing for this retelling to be published.

Children's Books
Donaldson, Julia; Stewart, Joel (2003) *The Magic Paintbrush* Macmillan Children's Books, imprint of Pan Macmillan, London.

Powell, Jillian; Amazova, Elena; Shvarov, Vitaly (2011) *The Magic Paintbrush: A Chinese Tale* Hachette Children's Books, London.

Demi (1988) *Liang and the Magic Paintbrush* Square Fish, imprint of Macmillan Children's Books, Pan Macmillan, New York.

Other Print Versions
Yep, Laurence; Wang, Suling (2000) *The Magic Paintbrush* Harper Collins Publishers Inc., London.

Web Sources
Unknown (Accessed online 17/01/2014) *A Magic Paintbrush: The Story of Ma Liang* Cultural China: http://traditions.cultural-china.com/en/211Traditions9846.html

Bushyhead, Leta (2011) *The Magic Paintbrush* Youtube: http://www.youtube.com/watch?v=YVSzTvvDOcc

Snow White

Here's another Grimm standard with no end of variants and picture book options.

Children's Books
Ray, Jane (2009) *Snow White: A Three Dimensional Fairy Tale Theatre* Walker Books Ltd., London.

Grimm, Jacob; Grimm, Wilhelm; Garcia, Camille Rose (2012) *Snow White* Harper Design, an imprint of Harper Collins Publishers Inc., London.

Cotton, Katie; Johnson, Richard (2013) *Snow White: A Classic Fairtale Pop-Up Books with Sounds* Templar Publishing, The Templar Company Ltd., Dorking, Surrey.

Danson, Leslie (2006) *Snow White (Flip-Up Fairy Tales)* Child's Play International Ltd., Swindon.

Other Print Versions
Duffy, Carol Ann; Prachaticka, Marketa (1999) *Rumpelstiltskin and Other Grimm Tales* Faber and Faber Ltd, London.

Grimm, Wilhelm; Grimm, Jacob; Colum, Padraic; Campbell, Joseph; Scharl, Josef (1948, 2002) *Grimm: Complete Fairy Tales* Routledge & Kegan Paul, Routledge Classics, imprint of the Taylor and Francis Group, Oxford.

Pullman, Philip (2012) *Grimm Tales for Young and Old* Penguin Classics, Penguin Books Ltd., London.

Web Sources
Grimm, Jacob; Grimm, Wilhelm (Accessed online 17/01/2014) *Little Snow-White* pitt.edu: http://www.pitt.edu/~dash/grimm053.html

The Two Dragons

For older children you can add in the two other curses of the land: gossiping goblins and hoarding hoarders. See these references for details!

Children's Books
Thomas, Gwyn; Jones, Margaret; Crossley-Holland, Kevin (2006) *Tales From the Mabinogion* Y Lolfa, Aberystwyth.

Other Print Versions
Davies, Sioned (2007) *The Mabinogion* Oxford University Press, Oxford.

Guest, Lady Charlotte (2000) *The Mabinogion* Dover Publications Inc.

Gantz, Jeffrey (1976) *The Mabinogion* Penguin Classics, Penguin Books Ltd., London

Chapter 3   Year 3 Stories

The Marriage of Ganesh

I found this lovely and little known Ganesh story in *The Bronze Cauldron: Myths and Legends of the World* (Mccaughrean, Geraldine [1999] Margaret K. McElderry Books, imprint of Simon and Schuster, London.) Geraldine McCaughrean kindly gave her blessing to the retelling in this book. The back-story of how Ganesh got his elephant head may also be of interest; I recommend Novesky, Amy; Wedman, Belgin K. (2004) *Elephant Prince: The Story of Ganesh* Mandala Publishing, Unknown.

Web Sources
Unknown Author (2013) itimes : http://ww.itimes.com/blog/story-of-kartikeya-and-ganesh-51613cccc51d8

Smith, Chris (2009-2013) Story Museum: http://www.storymuseum.org.uk/1001stories/detail/97/the-marriage-of-ganesh.html

Smith, Chris (2009-2013) Story Museum: http://www.storymuseum.org.uk/1001stories/detail/125/how-ganesh-got-married.html

Cap of Rushes

This tale is an English Folktale standard, first collected by joseph Jacobs in the 19th century.

Children's Books
British Broadcasting Corporation (1979) *The Jackanory Story Book* The Book Club Associates, Norfolk.

Other Print Versions
Jacobs, Joseph (1890, 2005) *English Fairy Tales* Public Domain Books.

Web Sources
Ashliman, D.L. (1998-2013) *Love Like Salt: folktales of types 923 and 510*: http://www.pitt.edu/~dash/salt.html

Authorama Public Domain Books/Jacobs, Joseph *English Fairy Tales*: http://www.authorama.com/english-fairy-tales-13.html

Lazy Jack

Lazy Jack is another English Folktale collected by Joseph Jacobs (Jacobs, Joseph [1890, 2005] *English Fairy Tales* Public Domain Books). It is a favourite of English Storytellers and there are many picture book versions.

Children's Books
Ross, Tony (1997) *Lazy Jack* (Puffin Picture Story Book) Puffin Books, imprint of Penguin Books Ltd., London.

French, Vivian; Ayto, Russel (1996) *Lazy Jack* Walker Books Ltd., London.

Gallagher, Belinda (2011) *Lazy Jack and Other Five-Minute Stories* Miles Kelly Publishing Ltd., Thaxted, Essex.

Biro, Val (1996) Lazy Jack Oxford University Press, Oxford.

Web Sources
Jacobs, Joseph *English Fairy Tales* Authorama: http://www.authorama.com/english-fairy-tales-30.html

Guillain, Adam (2009-2013) Story Museum: http://www.storymuseum.org.uk/1001stories/detail/142/lazy-jack.html

Natasha; Deakin, Claire (Accessed online 17/01/2014) *Lazy Jack* Storynory: http://www.storynory.com/2008/04/21/lazy-jack/

Baba Yaga's Black Geese

I learned this Russian tale from Adam Guillain, who tells the story on the Story Museum website (Guillain, Adam [2009-2013] *Baba Yaga's Black Geese* Story Museum: http://www.storymuseum.org.uk/1001stories/detail/136/baba-yaga-s-black-geese.html).

Children's Books
Lurie, Alison; Souhami, Jessica (2007) *Baba Yaga and the Stolen Baby* Frances Lincoln Publishers, London

Sims, Lesley (2010) *Illustrated Stories from Around the World* Usborne Publishing Ltd., London.

Mayer, Marianna; Craft, K.Y. (1994) *Baba Yaga and Vasilisa the Brave* William Morrow and Company Inc., New York.

Other Print Versions
Carter, Angela (2005) *Angela Carter's Book of Fairy Tales* Virago Press, London.

De Blumenthal, Vera Xenophontovna Kalamatiano (1903) *Folk Tales from the Russian* Rand McNally and Co., New York.

Web Sources
Barberton, Zan (2012) *Baba Yaga and the Black Geese* Vimeo: http://vimeo.com/51125282

Three Brothers and the Polar Bear

While developing a story for a project about global warming, I reset this tale in the arctic. Since then the setting has stuck with me. Originally I know this story as an Indian tale with a lion instead of a polar bear. I first found the tale in a collection of Goblin stories (Ryder, Arthur W. [2008] *22 Goblins* MacMay22, Unkown).

Other Print Versions
Zimmer, Heinrich (1971) *The King and the Corpse: Tales of the Soul's Conquest of Evil* Motilal Banarsidass Publishing.

Web Sources
Smith, Chris (2009-2013) *The Three Brothers* Story Museum: http://www.storymuseum.org.uk/1001stories/detail/106/the-three-brothers.html

Lupton, Hugh (2013) *The Cow-Tail Switch* Youtube: http://www.youtube.com/watch?v=Dvse_vHQ9v0

Three Dolls

Most versions of this tale use a King as the main protagonist. I have chosen to reset the tale in a school to illustrate the relevance of its message to the Storytelling School's model for education. It sums up the value of storytelling so well! I first read this tale in *Ready-to-Tell-Tales* (Novak, David; Holt, David; Mooney, Bill [1994] August House Inc., Atlanta.). David Novak reports hearing it from an Indian storyteller, Mr. Dasgupta.

Web Sources
Smith, Chris (2009-2013) *The Three Dolls* Story Museum: http://www.storymuseum.org.uk/1001stories/detail/98/the-three-dolls.html

Heathfield, David (Accessed online 17/01/2014) *The Three Dolls* WorldStories: http://www.worldstories.org.uk/stories/story/36-the-three-dolls

Morganschatzblackrose (2013) *The Three Dolls* Wordpress: http://morganschatzblackrose.wordpress.com/2013/05/01/the-three-dolls/

Bhagavân S'rî Sathya Sai Baba (Accessed online 17/01/2014) *The Three Dolls* helloyou: http://askbaba.helloyou.ch/stories/s1004.html

Al-Mukhtar Standard Schools (2013) *Secret of the Three Dolls* Youtube: http://www.youtube.com/watch?v=Y6gapQG8_fg

Taletimestories (2013) *The Three Dolls: A Story about Storytelling* tes: http://www.tes.co.uk/teaching-resource/The-Three-Dolls-A-Story-about-Storytelling-6316374/

The Lighthouse Keeper and the Selkie

Scottish Lore is full of tales where a seal becomes a wife and then later returns to the sea. I can't remember where I first heard this one, though it is often referred to as *The Selkie Bride*. For further sources and resources see also *The Woman of the Sea* in Chapter Four of this book.

Web Sources
Unknown (Accessed online 17/01/2014) *The Selkie Bride: A Scottish Folktale* WeinGartDesign: http://www.weingartdesign.com/TMaS/Stories/tmas1-SelkieBride.html

Mccrorie, Walter (2011) *The Selkie Bride* Youtube: http://www.youtube.com/watch?v=vQM2nGpMrtU

Black, Frank (2010) *The Selkie Bride* Youtube: http://www.youtube.com/watch?v=vmWNBtJU2u8

Muir, Tom *Story of a Selkie* Education Scotland: http://www.educationscotland.gov.uk/scotlandsstories/aselkiestory/index.asp

Towrie, Sigurd (1996-2013) *The Goodman O' Wastness* Orkney Jar: http://www.orkneyjar.com/folklore/selkiefolk/wastness.htm

Death in a Nutshell

I first heard this story from Jane George of Coral Arts, Oxford. My retelling is similar to this and to the Norwegian version, which can be found in *Norwegian Folktales* (Asbjørnsen, Peter Christen; Moe, Jørgen; Werenskiold, Erik; Kittelsen, Theodor; Shaw, Pat; Norman, Carl [1982] *Norwegian Folktales* Pantheon Books, a division of Random House Inc., New York).

Children's Books
Maddern, Eric; Hess, Paul (2005) *Death in a Nut* Frances Lincoln Publishers, London.

Williamson, Duncan (2013) *The Flight of the Golden Bird: Scottish Folktales for Children* Floris Books, Edinburgh.

Web Sources
Smith, Chris (2009-2013) *Death in a Nutshell* Story Museum: http://www.storymuseum.org.uk/1001stories/detail/123/death-in-a-nutshell.html

The Fox and the Healer

I first heard this from storyteller Ashley Ramsden at Emerson College. Later I read it in *Tales of Wisdom and Wonder* (Lupton, Hugh; Sharkey, Niamh [1998] Barefoot Books Ltd., Oxford). Hugh Lupton cites Howard Norman (Norman, Howard [1982] *Where the Chill Came From: Cree Windigo Tales and Journeys* North Point Press, San Francicso.). Hugh Lupton kindly gave me permission to publish this retelling.

Web Sources
Allison, Daniel *The Fox in the Snow* Among the Wild Deer: http://www.amongthewilddeer.com/thefoxinthesnow/

Jack and the Dancing Trees

This story is also known by the name *Auld Cruivie*.

Web Sources
Robinson, Stanley *Auld Cruivie* Education Scotland: http://www.educationscotland.gov.uk/scotlandsstories/auldcruivie/

McNicol, Claire (2013) blogspot: http://nicerailittleblog.blogspot.co.uk/2013/05/auld-cruivie-or-jack-and-dancing.html

Little Burnt Face

This story is sometimes known as *The Algonquin Cinderella*, as well as variations on *Sootface* or *The Rough-Face Girl*. It is a Micmac Native American Tale.

Children's Books
Martin, Rafe; Shannon, David (1992) *The Rough-Face Girl* Putnam Berkley Group Inc., New York.

San Souci, Robert D.: San Souci, Daniel (1994) *Sootface* Bantam Doubleday Dell Publishing Group Inc., New York.

Johnson, Edna; Scott, Carrie (1935) *Anthology of Children's Literature* Houghton Mifflin Co., Boston.

Lock, Kath; Kennet, David (1997) *Little Burnt Face* Era Publications Pty, Brooklyn Park, Australia.
Olcott, Frances Jenkins (1917, 2006) *The Red Indian Fairy Book* Houghton Mifflin Co., Boston. Republished Yesterday's Classics LLC, Unkown.

Other Print Versions
Shah, Idries (1979) *World Tales* Penguin Books Ltd., London.

Web Sources
Shepard, Aaron (1996) *The Hidden One* Aaron Shep: http://www.aaronshep.com/stories/046.html

Unknown (Accessed online 17/01/2014) *Little Burnt Face: A Micmac Tale from North America* Sur LaLune: http://www.surlalunefairytales.com/cinderella/stories/littleburntface.html

The Monk and the Thieves

My source for this was Saviour Pirotta's retelling (Pirotta, Saviour; Johnson, Richard [2007] *Around the World in 80 Tales* Kingfisher Publications Plc., London.)

The Story Bag

I first heard this told by storyteller Daniel Morden in one of his amazing shows full of music and stories. It is a storytelling favourite, with dozens of versions all over the internet.

Other Print Versions
So-Un, Kim; Eui-Hwan, Kim; Higashi, Setsu

(1989) *The Story Bag: A collection of Korean Folk Tales* Tuttle Publishing, North Clarendon.

In-Sob, Zong (1952) *Folk Tales from Korea* Routledge and Kegan Paul, London.

King, Nancy R.; Gersie, Alida (1989) *Storymaking in Education and Therapy* Jessica Kingsley Publishers Ltd., London.

Web Sources
Zun, Mun Czang; Mimi The Storyteller (2011) *The Story Spirits* youtube: http://www.youtube.com/watch?v=SVnGGh7DccI

Ehrmen, Kelly (2013) *The Bag Full of Stories* Lavender's Blue Home School: http://lavendersbluehomeschool.com/story-the-bag-full-of-stories/

How a Boy Learned to be Wise

I found this story in an amazing collection of stories from Uganda: Baskerville, Mrs. George; Morris, Mrs. E. G. (1922, 2008) *The King of the Snakes and Other Folk-Lore Stories from Uganda* The Sheldon Press, London. Reprinted Dodo Press, Gloucester.

Persephone

I first read this as a child in my favourite book of Greek Myths: *The God Beneath the Sea* (Garfield, Leon; Blishen, Edward; Keeping, Charles [1977, 201]) Doubleday Children's, imprint of Random House Children's Publishers UK, London.). There are countless versions in print and online.

Children's Books
Mccaughrean, Geraldine: Clark, Emma Chichester (1992) *The Orchard Book of Greek Myths* Orchard Books, London.

Clayton, Sally Pomme; Lee, Virginia (2009) *Persephone: a Journey from Winter to Spring* Frances Lincoln Ltd., London

Williams, Marcia (1991) *Greek Myths* Walker Books, London.

Milbourne, Anna; Stowell, Louie; Temporin, Elena; Bursi, Simona (2010) *Usborne Book of Greek Myths (Usborne Myths and Legends)* Usborne Books, Oxon.

Other Print Versions
Graves, Robert (1995) *Greek Myths* Penguin Books Ltd., London.

D'Aulaire, Ingri; D'Aulaire, Edgar Parin(1962) *D'Aulaire's Book of Greek Myths* Delacorte Press, imprint of Random House Inc., New York.

The Wooden Horse

This is another Greek standard. Homer is the main original source (*The Iliad*) of which there are many translations. Hugh Lupton and Daniel Morden have a great show based on the Iliad, in which this story is included.

Children's Books
McCaughrean, Geraldine: Clark, Emma Chichester (1992) *The Orchard Book of Greek Myths* Orchard Books, London.

Milbourne, Anna; Stowell, Louie; Temporin, Elena; Bursi, Simona (2010) *Usborne Book of Greek Myths (Usborne Myths and Legends)* Usborne Books, Oxon.

Punter, Russel; Pincelli, Matteo (2011) *The Wooden Horse (Young Reading)* Usborne Publishing Ltd, London.

Meister, Cari; Harris, Nick (2012) *Wooden Horse of Troy* Raintree Publishing, Basingstoke Hants.

Pirotta, Saviour; Lewis, Jan (2006) *Odysseus and the Wooden Horse (First Greek Myths)* Orchard Books, London.

Other Print Versions
Graves, Robert (1995) *Greek Myths* Penguin Books Ltd., London.

Half a Blanket

I first read this story in a Scottish version by Maggi Pierce in *Ready-to-Tell-Tales* (Peirce, Maggi Kerr; Holt, David; Mooney, Bill [1994] August House Inc., Atlanta.) It turns up in all sorts of places: below there is a Jewish version, a Native American version and a Medieval European version.

Other Print Versions
Schram, Peninnah (2008) *The Hungry Clothes and Other Jewish Folktales* Sterling Publishing, New York.

Web Sources
Jordan, Elaine Marie (2002-2013) The Divided Horsecloth Tradition In Action: http://www.traditioninaction.org/religious/h032rp.Horsecloth_Jordan.html

Takatoka (2010) This Blanket is for You Manataka: http://www.manataka.org/page2356.html

Fruit of Love

I first heard this told by the Native American storyteller extraordinaire Michael Moran.

Children's Books
Bruchac, Joseph; Vojtech, Anna (1998) *The First Strawberries: A Cherokee Story (Picture Puffins)* Puffin Books, Penguin Putnam Books for Young Readers, New York.

Other Print Versions
Mooney, James (1900, 2003) *Myths of the Cherokee* Dover Publications Inc., Unknown.

Web Sources
Traditional (Accessed online 17/01/2014) *Strawberry Legend* First People: http://www.firstpeople.us/FP-Html-Legends/StrawberryLegend-Cherokee.html

Brill, Steve (Accessed online 17/01/2014) *The Origin of Strawberries* Wild Man Steve Brill: http://www.wildmanstevebrill.com/Plants.Folder/Strawberry.html

Warren, Barbara Shining Woman (Accessed online 17/01/2014) *The First Strawberries* Powersource: http://www.powersource.com/cocinc/articles/strwbry.htm

Unkown (Accessed online 17/01/2014) *The Origin of Strawberries: A Native American Folktale* Blogspot: http://storytellingcookingandkids.blogspot.co.uk/2010/06/origin-of-strawberriesa-native-american.html

Smith, Chris (2009-2013) *Fruit of Love* Story Museum: http://www.storymuseum.org.uk/1001stories/detail/207/the-fruit-of-love.html

One Wish

This is a great little Irish tale, rather like a riddle tale and very popular with teachers and storytellers. Short and satisfying! The commonly told story involves three problems: wanting a baby, restoring the sight of a mother and having more money. My own version is an example of story innovation, recycling the original plot with a footballing twist. Very different from, say, the version where Ganesh is the wish granter.

Web Sources
Bukowiec, Annette (2012) *One Wish, Irish Folktale* Blogspot: http://geowonderland.blogspot.co.uk/2012/03/one-wish-irish-folktale.html

Chowdhury, Rohini (Accessed online 17/01/2014) *How the Old Woman Got Her Wish* Long Long Time Ago: http://www.longlongtimeago.com/llta_folktales_oldwomanwish.html

Smith, Chris (2009-2013) *One Wish* Story Museum: http://www.storymuseum.org.uk/1001stories/detail/129/one-wish.html

Moss, Adele (2009-2013) *The Wise Wish* Story Museum: http://www.storymuseum.org.uk/1001stories/detail/118/the-wise-wish.html

Birth of Athena

I first read this story as a child in my favourite book of Greek Myths: *The God Beneath the Sea* (Garfield, Leon; Blishen, Edward; Keeping, Charles [1977, 201]) Doubleday Children's, imprint of Random House Children's Publishers UK, London.). There are countless versions in print and online. More collections of Greek Myths can be found in the sources for *Persephone*, earlier in this chapter.

Children's Books
Milbourne, Anna; Stowell, Louie; Temporin, Elena; Bursi, Simona (2010) *Usborne Book of Greek Myths (Usborne Myths and Legends)* Usborne Books, Oxon.

Other Print Versions
Graves, Robert (1995) *Greek Myths* Penguin Books Ltd., London.

D'Aulaire, Ingri; D'Aulaire, Edgar Parin(1962) *D'Aulaire's Book of Greek Myths* Delacorte Press, imprint of Random House Inc., New York.

Deacy, Susan (2008) *Athena* Routledge, Oxon.

The Lode Stone

I cannot remember where I first heard this one, except that it was in Eric Maddern's wood in Wales and I haven't found any other sources yet!

Web Sources
Smith, Chris (2009-2013) *The Lode Stone* Story Museum: http://www.storymuseum.org.uk/1001stories/detail/205/the-lode-stone.html

The Scorpion and the Frog

I first heard this story from Ashley Ramsden at Emerson College; he used it as a powerful metaphor for the dangers of anger. This fable is known by other names, including *The Scorpion and the Turtle* and *Kalil and Dumina*, and can be found in *Aesop's Fables* as well as collections of the *Panchatatra*, which is a collections of ancient Hindu Fables. This story also turns up in the 1992 film *The Crying Game*, when a prisoner uses it to explain how he ended up in prison.

Children's Books
Publisher, Phantom; Odu, Tn (2010) *The Lady Frog and The Scorpion* Phantom House Books Ltd., Nigeria.

Other Print Versions
Sarma, Visnu; Rajan, Chandra (1993, 2006) *Panc´atantra* Penguin Classics, Penguin Books Ltd., London.

Web Sources
Unknown *The Scorpion and the Frog* Short Stories: http://shortstoriesshort.com/story/the-scorpion-and-the-frog/

Three Wishes

There are so many versions of this story featuring various misguided wishes, and many can easily be found online.

Children's Books
Melling, David (2007) *The Three Wishes* Hodder Children's Books, London.

Sims, Lesley; Squillace, Eilsa (2009) *The Three Wishes* Usborne Publishing Ltd., London.

Harrison, Joanna (2000) *The Three Wishes* HarperCollins, London.

Other Print Versions
Sylvester, Doug (1987) *Folkfest: Folktales from Around the World* Rainbow Horizons Publishing, San Diego.

Djurklou, Nils Gabriel; Braekstad, H, L. (1901) *Fairy Tales from the Swedish* J. B. Lippincott Company, Philadelphia and New York.

Chapter 4 Year 4 Stories

The Blind Man and the Hunter

This is a story with many sources; Alexander McCall Smith's version, titled *Blind Man Catches a Bird*, can be found in *The Girl Who Married a Lion and Other Tales From Africa* (Smith, Alexander Mccall [1989, 1999, 2004] Random House Inc., New York.). Alexander McCall Smith attributes this story as an Ndebele tale from Zimbabwe. There is also a version by Hugh Lupton, who says that he heard the story from Duncan Williamson.

Children's Books
Lupton, Hugh; Sharkey, Niamh (1998) *Tales of Wisdom and Wonder* Barefoot Books, Oxford.

Other Print Versions
Macdonald, Margaret Read (1992) *Peace Tales* August House Inc., Atlanta.

Web Sources
Lupton, Hugh (2009-2013) *The Blind Man and the Hunter* Story Museum: http://www.storymuseum.org.uk/1001stories/detail/155/the-blind-man-and-the-hunter.html

Unknown (2007) *A Blind Man Catches a Bird* Wordpress: http://littleganeshas.wordpress.com/2007/05/31/a-blind-man-catches-a-bird/

Timpanelli, Gioia *A Blind Man Catches a Bird* PRX: http://www.prx.org/pieces/91629-a-blind-man-catches-a-bird - description

Rhino Girl; Frankel, Nina; Wood, Noah (2013) *The Blind Man and The Hunter Fight For Rhinos*: http://fightforrhinos.com/2013/04/11/the-blind-man-and-the-hunter/

The Birth of Osiris

I first read this story in the lovely picture book *Egyptian Myths* (Morley, Jacqueline; Casselli, Giovanni [1999] Peter Bedrick Books, New York.).

Children's Books
Coley, Mike; Alston, Nick (2013) *Osiris* Bellykids, Unkown (UK)

Other Print Versions
Tyldesley, Joyce (2010) *Myths and Legends of Ancient Egypt* Penguin Books Ltd., London.

Web Sources
Unknown (2005-2010) *The Children of Nut the Lady of Heaven*: http://www.legends.egyptholiday.com/children_of_nut.htm

Furst, Dan (2001) *The Stories of Thoth and Ma'at*: http://www.hermes3.net/thoth6.htm

Prometheus

Again, as with many of the Greek Myths in this book, I first came across this as a child in *The God Beneath the Sea* (Garfield, Leon; Blishen, Edward; Keeping, Charles [1977, 201]) Doubleday Children's, imprint of Random House Children's Publishers UK, London.). *Prometheus* retellings can be found in countless collections.

Children's Books
McCaughrean, Geraldine: Clark, Emma Chichester (1992) *The Orchard Book of Greek Myths* Orchard Books, London.

Williams, Marcia (1991) *Greek Myths* Walker Books, London.

Milbourne, Anna; Stowell, Louie; Temporin, Elena; Bursi, Simona (2010) *Usborne Book of Greek Myths (Usborne Myths and Legends)* Usborne Books, Oxon.

Other Print Versions
Graves, Robert (1995) Greek Myths Penguin Books Ltd., London.

D'Aulaire, Ingri; D'Aulaire, Edgar Parin(1962) *D'Aulaire's Book of Greek Myths* Delacorte Press, imprint of Random House Inc., New York.

Web Sources
Baldwin, James (1895, reissued 2006) *Old Greek Stories* Dodo Press, Slough. Available online at: http://www.authorama.com/book/old-greek-stories.html

The Eagle Who Thought He Was A Chicken

I can't remember where I first heard this great little story, which can be found in many different versions. It is often attributed as a Native American story, although African versions have also been published. There are many retellings on the web, as this story is often used as a parable for fulfilling your potential.

Children's Books
Gregowski, Christopher; Daly, Niki; Tutu, Desmond (2000) *Fly, Eagle, Fly!* Frances Lincoln Ltd., London.

Web Sources
Larson, Jonathan P. (2011) *The Eagle Who Thought He Was A Chicken* Youtube: http://www.youtube.com/watch?v=4JtOlRmLbMk

Smith, Chris (2009-2013) *The Eagle Who Thought He Was A Chicken* Story Museum: http://www.storymuseum.org.uk/1001stories/detail/208/the-eagle-who-thought-he-was-a-chicken.html

Somaiah, Rosemarie (2001) *The Eagle Who Thought He Was A Chicken* Spoken Stories: http://www.spokenstories.org/the-eagle-who-thought-he-was-a-chicken/

How Butterflies Came To Be

Storyteller Michael Moran told me this Native American Papago tale, which went by the name *Why Butterflies are Silent*. I have emphasized the joy rather than the silence in my retelling.

Children's Books
Bruchac, Joseph; Caduto, Michael J. (1991) *Keepers of the Animals: Native American Wildlife Stories and Activities for Children* Fulcrum Publishing Inc., Colorado.

Other Print Versions
Erdoes, Richard; Ortiz, Alfonso (1984) *American Indian Myths and Legends* Pantheon Books, Random House Inc., New York.

Mccarthy, Tara (1992) *Multicultural Fables and Fairytales* Scholastic Inc., New York.

Web Sources
Unknown *How the Butterflies Came to Be* First People: http://www.firstpeople.us/FP-Html-Legends/HowTheButterfliesCameToBe-Papago.html

Sanjit *How Butterflies Came to Be* Planet Oz Kids: http://www.planetozkids.com/oban/legends/how-butterflies-came-to-be.htm

Conner, Buck (2006-2013) *Butterflies* Butterfly Pages: http://www.butterflypages.com/stories.php

Icarus

Icarus is a popular fable for primary schools with its clear lessons and potential for dramatization. Personally I love Ted Hughes' retelling in *Tales from Ovid* (Hughes, Ted [1997] Faber and Faber Ltd., London).

Children's Books
Pirotta, Saviour; Lewis, Jan (2006) *The Boy Who Could Fly (First Greek Myths)* Orchard Books, London.

Williams, Marcia (1991) *Greek Myths* Walker Books, London.

Milbourne, Anna; Stowell, Louie; Temporin, Elena; Bursi, Simona (2010) *Usborne Book of Greek Myths (Usborne Myths and Legends)* Usborne Books, Oxon.

McCaughrean, Geraldine: Clark, Emma Chichester (1992) *The Orchard Book of Greek Myths* Orchard Books, London.

Other Print Versions
Ovid; Raeburn, David; Feeney, Denis (2004) *Metamorphoses: A New Verse Translation* Penguin Books Ltd., London.

Graves, Robert (1995) *Greek Myths* Penguin Books Ltd., London.

D'Aulaire, Ingri; D'Aulaire, Edgar Parin(1962) *D'Aulaire's Book of Greek Myths* Delacorte Press, imprint of Random House Inc., New York.

Web Sources
Henson, Jim; Minghella, Anthony (1987) *The Storyteller; Daedalus and Icarus* The Jim Henson Company. Available to buy on iTunes: https://itunes.apple.com/us/tv-season/jim-hensons-storyteller-complete/id319062204

Watch an extract on youtube: http://www.youtube.com/watch?v=7yp_igX-sDs

The Shepherd's Dream

I love this Irish story, with its curious puzzle solving and potential to prompt fascinating discussions about life, dreams and souls.

Children's Books
Lupton, Hugh; Sharkey, Niamh (1998) *Tales of Wisdom and Wonder* Barefoot Books, Oxford.

Other Print Versions
O'Sulliva, Sean; Dorson, Richard M. (1974) *Folktales of Ireland* The University of Chicago Press, London and Chicago.

Crossley-Holland, Kevin (1985) *Folktales of the British Isles* Pantheon Books, a division of Random House Inc., New York.

Web Sources
Smith, Chris (2009-2013) *The Shepherd's Dream* Story Museum: http://www.storymuseum.org.uk/1001stories/detail/200/the-shepherd-s-dream.html

The Piper's Boots

This cracking yarn, sometimes called *The Piper's Revenge*, has spread throughout the UK storytelling community. I can't remember where I first heard it. You can find a print version by Bill Teare in *More Ready-to-Tell Tales From Around the World* (Teare, Billy; Holt, David; Mooney, Bill [2000] August House Inc., Atlanta.). Billy Teare kindly gave me permission to publish my retelling.

Other Print Versions
O'Lochlainn, Colm (1965) *More Irish Street Ballads* Pan Books, London.

Pearson, Maggie (2002) *Short and Shocking!* Oxford University Press, Oxford.

Trevor, William (1989, reissued 2010) *The Oxford Book of Irish Short Stories* Oxford University Press, Oxford.

Web Sources
Jacob-McDowell, Barra (2013) *Why The Piper *Had* To Take His Revenge* Blogspot: http://adventuresinbarding.blogspot.co.uk/2013/03/why-piper-had-to-take-his-revenge.html

Midas' Wish and Midas and Apollo

These two tales of Midas are much told. I really love the Ted Hughes retelling in *Tales from Ovid* (Hughes, Ted [1997] Faber and Faber Ltd., London). It's great to listen to him on CD if you get the chance.

Children's Books
Demi (2002) *King Midas: The Golden Touch* Margaret K. McElderry Books, imprint of Simon and Schuster Children's Publishing Division, New York.

Coats, Lucy; Lewis, Anthony (2002) *Atticus the Storyteller's 100 Greek Myths* Orion Publishing Group Ltd., London.

Milbourne, Anna; Stowell, Louie; Temporin, Elena; Bursi, Simona (2010) *Usborne Book of Greek Myths (Usborne Myths and Legends)* Usborne Books, Oxon.

McCaughrean, Geraldine: Clark, Emma Chichester (1992) *The Orchard Book of Greek Myths* Orchard Books, London.

Craft, Charlotte; Craft, Kinuko Y. (1999) *King Midas and the Golden Touch* William Morrow and Company Inc., New York.

Sims, Lesley; Gordon, Carl; Gordon, Mike (2009) *King Donkey Ears* Usborne Publishing Ltd., London.

Other Print Versions
Ovid; Raeburn, David; Feeney, Denis (2004) *Metamorphoses: A New Verse Translation* Penguin Books Ltd., London.

Graves, Robert (1995) *Greek Myths* Penguin Books Ltd., London.

D'Aulaire, Ingri; D'Aulaire, Edgar Parin (1962) *D'Aulaire's Book of Greek Myths* Delacorte Press, imprint of Random House Inc., New York.

Theseus and The Minotaur

My main source for developing this story was Robert Graves' Greek Myths (Graves, Robert [1995] Greek Myths Penguin Books Ltd., London.)

Children's Books
McCaughrean, Geraldine: Clark, Emma Chichester (1992) *The Orchard Book of Greek Myths* Orchard Books, London.

Milbourne, Anna; Stowell, Louie; Temporin, Elena; Bursi, Simona (2010) *Usborne Book of Greek Myths (Usborne Myths and Legends)* Usborne Books, Oxon.

Williams, Marcia (1991) *Greek Myths* Walker Books, London.

Milbourne, Anna; Stowell, Louie; Temporin, Elena; Bursi, Simona (2010) *Usborne Book of Greek Myths (Usborne Myths and Legends)* Usborne Books, Oxon.

Coats, Lucy; Lewis, Anthony (2002) *Atticus the Storyteller's 100 Greek Myths* Orion Publishing Group Ltd., London.

Lupton, Hugh; Morden, Daniel; Henaff, Carole (2013) *Theseus and the Minotaur* Barefoot Books Ltd., Oxford.

Other Print Versions
D'Aulaire, Ingri; D'Aulaire, Edgar Parin (1962) *D'Aulaire's Book of Greek Myths* Delacorte Press, imprint of Random House Inc., New York.

Web Sources
Baldwin, James (1895, reissued 2006) *Old Greek Stories* Dodo Press, Slough. Available online at: http://www.authorama.com/book/old-greek-stories.html

The Woman of the Sea

I am not sure where this one came from; there are many many versions of Selkie stories. Several versions appear under the name *The Goodman of Wastness*.

Children's Books
Riordan, James; Hall, Amanda (1996) *Stories from the Sea* Barefoot Books Ltd., Bristol.

Doherty, Berlie; Bailey, Sian (1996) *Daughter of the Sea* Penguin Books Ltd., London.

Other Print Versions
Dennison, W. Traill (1893) *Scottish Antiquary VII (The Goodman of Wastness)* Edinburgh University Press.

Black, G. F. (1903) *Country Folklore III* Unknown publisher.

Crossley-Holland, Kevin (1985) *Folktales of the British Isles* Pantheon Books, imprint of Random House Inc., New York.

Web Sources
Muir, Tom *Story of a Selkie* Education Scotland: http://www.educationscotland.gov.uk/scotlandsstories/aselkiestory/index.asp

Towrie, Sigurd (1996-2013) *Orkney Jar*: http://www.orkneyjar.com/folklore/selkiefolk/wastness.htm

Morris, Jackie; Crossley-Holland, Kevin (2011) *The Sea Woman* Youtube: http://www.youtube.com/watch?v=VeIP3ut9R_U

How Jerusalem Began

This story was reportedly collected in Palestine by a visiting Christian from a Muslim storyteller. It then became popular in Jewish Europe and is now firmly established as a Jewish tale while it is still told by Palestinians. There are now hundreds of versions online. You can read my retelling as a picture book in *One City, Two Brothers* (Smith, Chris; Fronty, Aurelia [2007] Barefoot Books Ltd., Oxford.).

Odysseus and the Cyclops

This story originates with Homer's *Odyssey*. My primary source for this was Robert Graves' *Greek Myths* (Graves, Robert [1995] Penguin Books Ltd., London.)

Children's Books
Milbourne, Anna; Stowell, Louie; Temporin, Elena; Bursi, Simona (2010) *Usborne Book of Greek Myths (Usborne Myths and Legends)* Usborne Books, Oxon.

McCaughrean, Geraldine: Clark, Emma Chichester (1992) *The Orchard Book of Greek Myths* Orchard Books, London.

Coats, Lucy; Lewis, Anthony (2002) *Atticus the Storyteller's 100 Greek Myths* Orion Publishing Group Ltd., London.

Other Print Versions
Ovid; Raeburn, David; Feeney, Denis (2004) *Metamorphoses: A New Verse Translation* Penguin Books Ltd., London.

The Four Dragons

I first came across this lovely tale in *Dragon Tales: A collection of Chinese Stories* (Wang, Fuyang; Cheng, Shu-Fang [1988] Chinese Literature Press, Beijiing.).

Other Print Versions
Life, Man V. (2012) *MianJian Gushi Chinese Folktales* Amazon eBook.

Web Sources
Unknown (2008-2013) *The Four Dragons* World of Tales: http://www.worldoftales.com/Asian_folktales/Asian_Folktale_6.html

Scott, David *The Legend of the Four Dragons: A Chinese Tale retold* Abandoned Towers: http://abandonedtowers.com/stories/the-legend-of-the-four-dragons-a-chinese-fairy-tale-retold/

The Land of the Deep Ocean

There are many variants of this tale involving travel to an ocean land and returning to a later age. Often this story is called *Urashimo Taro*, and it is sometimes cited as the oldest example of time-travel occurring in a story.

Children's Books
Sakade, Florence; Hayashi, Yoshio (2008) *Urashima Taro and Other Japanese Children's Favorite Stories* Tuttle Publishing, Tokyo.

Other Print Versions
Lear, David (2013) *Urashima Taro and Other Tales* Firestone Books.

Martin, Rafe (1989) *Ghostly Tales of Japan* (available as CD or book) Yellow Moon Press, America.

Ozaki, Yei Theodora (1903 first publishing, reissued 2007) *Japanese Fairytales* BiblioBazaar, imprint of Barnes and Noble Inc., New York.

Tyler, Royall (1987) *Japanese Tales* Pantheon Books, imprint of Random House Inc., New York.

Rama and Sita

The original source for this story is the *Ramayana*, two versions of which are included below.

Children's Books
Clayton, Sally Pomme; Herxheimer, Sophie (2010) *Rama and Sita: Path of Flames* Frances Lincoln Ltd., London.

Milbourne, Anna; Edwards, Linda (2004) *Stories From India* Usborne Books, Oxon.

Souhami, Jessica (1997) *Rama and the Demon King* Frances Lincoln Ltd., London.

Other Print Versions
Nagra, Daljit (2013) *Ramayana: A Retelling* Faber and Faber Ltd., London.

Valmiki; Sattar, Arshia (2010) *Ramayana* Penguin Books Ltd., London.

The Building of St Paul's Cathedral

This little tale, often going by the name *The Three Bricklayers* is popular with management trainers and business consultants for obvious reasons.

Web Sources
Asimus, Lindy (2012) *The Three Bricklayers* Design Business Engineering: http://www.designbusinessengineering.com/lib_3_bricklayers.htm

Drdebbrown (2009) *Job Satisfaction: The Story of the Three Bricklayers* intentblog: http://intentblog.com/job-satisfaction-story-three-bricklayers/

Wren, Christopher, Coker, Greg (2012) The Recovering Bricklayer the cathedral institute: http://www.thecathedralinstitute.com/2012/05/13/the-recovering-bricklayer/

Feathers in the Wind

I first heard this story from Doug Lipman on his lovely CD *Milk from the Bull's Horn: Tales of Nurturing Men* (Lipman, Doug [1986] Yellow Moon Press, Cambridge MA.) The story is originally attributed to Rabbi Levi Yitzhak of Berdichev.

Children's Books
Forest, Heather; Cutchin, Marcia (2005) *Feathers* August House Inc., Atlanta.

Web Sources
Brombacher, Shoshanna (2009) *A Pillow Full of Feathers* Chabad: http://www.chabad.org/library/article_cdo/aid/812861/jewish/A-Pillow-Full-of-Feathers.htm

Smith, Chris (2009-2013) *Feathers in the Wind* Story Museum: http://www.storymuseum.org.uk/1001stories/detail/124/feathers-in-the-wind.html

Netsmartz *Feathers in the Wind* TeacherTube: http://www.teachertube.com/viewVideo.php?video_id=3790

Heaven and Hell (1) and (2)

You can find both these stories in many collections, including:

Kornfield, Jack; Feldman, Christina (1991) *Soul Food: Stories to Nourish the Spirit and the Heart* HarperOne, imprint of Harper Collins Publishers, San Francisco.

Nick Owen (2001) *The Magic of Metaphor* Crown House Publishing, Carmarthen.

Chapter 5 Year 5 Stories

The Hunter and the Leopard

This story is known under several names, including *Brave Hunter* and *The Buffalo Woman*. I first heard this told by the wonderful storyteller Jan Blake.

Other Print Versions
Smith, Alexander McCall (1989, 1999, 2004) *The Girl Who Married A Lion and Other Tales From Africa* Random House Inc., New York.

Web Sources
Blake, Jan; Sereba, Raymond (2012) *The Buffalo Woman* hayfestival:
http://www.hayfestival.com/c-209-archive.aspx?ManufacturerFilterID=0&VectorFilterID=4810&GenreFilterID=23

The Boots of Abu Kassim

This comical tale can be found in most of the larger *1001 Nights* translations, although it is often omitted from shorter ones. Also known as *Abu Kassim's Slippers*.

Children's Books
Mccaughrean, Geraldine; Fowler, Rosamund (1982) *One Thousand and one Arabian Nights* Oxford University Press, Oxford.

Other Print Versions
Zimmer, Heinrich; Campbell, Joseph (1948, 1957, 1975) *The King and the Corpse: Tales of the Soul's Conquest of Evil* Princeton University Press, West Sussex.

Web Sources
Lowe, Chris; Speake, Malcolm (Accessed on the internet 06/01/20134) *Abu Kasim's Slippers* speakeandlowestories: http://www.speakeandlowestories.talktalk.net/abu_kasim%27s_slippers.htm

Who is the Thief?

This story also goes by the name *The Wise Judge* or *A Just Judge*, I first read this in *Ready-to-Tell Tales* (Holt, David; Mooney, Bill; Klein, Susan [1994] August House Inc., Atlanta.)

Other Print Versions
Tolstoy, Leo; Blaisdell, Bob; Weiner, Leo; Dole, Nathan (1904, 2001) *Classic Tales and Fables for Children* Prometheus Books, New York.

Web Sources
Unknown (Accessed online 07/01/2014) *The Young Judge* Wattpad: http://www.wattpad.com/5143165-wise-short-stories-from-arab-old-times-in-english

Unknown (Accessed online 13/01/2014) *The Turkish Judge* Stories to Grow By: http://www.storiestogrowby.com/stories/one_man.html

Beowulf

There are many retellings of this Anglo-Saxon Classic.

Children's Books
Morpurgo, Michael; Foreman, Michael (2006) *Beowulf* Walker Books Ltd., London.

Crossley-Holland, Kevin; Keeping, Charles (1999) *Beowulf* Oxford University Press, Oxford.

Sutcliff, Rosemary; Keeping, Charles (1961, 2001) *Beowulf: Dragonslayer* Bodley Head, republished by the Random house Group Ltd., London.

Jones, Rob Lloyd; Tavares, Victor (2009) *Beowulf* Usborne Publishing Ltd., London.

Harris, John; Morgan-Jones, Tom (2007) *The Geat: The Story of Beowulf and Grendel* notreallybooks, UK.

Nye, Robert (1968, 2004) *Beowulf* Dolphin, an imprint of Orion Children's Books, a division of the Orion Publishing Group Ltd., London.

Other Print Versions
Heaney, Seamus (2000) *Beowulf: A New Verse Translation* Farrar, Straus and Giroux, New York.

Alexander, Michael (1973, 2001) *Beowulf: A Verse Translation* Penguin Group, Penguin Books Ltd, London.

The Tiger's Whisker

This is a much-told tale with many versions in print and on the web. It can be found in both Asia and Africa

Children's Books
Day, Nancy Raines; Grifalconi, Ann (1995) *The Lion's Whiskers: An Ethiopian Folktale* Scholastic Trade.

Woods, Rosemary; Mike, Jan M. (2000) *The Lion's Whiskers: An Ethiopian Story* Pearson Scott Foresman, Pearson Educations Inc., Unkown (US).

Henderson, Kathy Carman (2013) *The Tigers Whisker: A Story to Learn and Draw* By CreateSpace, Unkown.

Other Print Versions
Courlander, Harold; Arco, Enrico (1995) *The Tiger's Whisker and Other Tales from Asia and the Pacific* Henry Holt & Company, New York.

Forest, Heather (1996) *Wisdom Tales from Around the World* August House Inc., Atlanta.

Ashabranner, Brent K.; Davis, Russel G., Siegl, Helen (1997) *The Lion's Whiskers and Other Ethiopian Tales* Linnet Books, The Shoestring Press Ltd., New Haven.

Web Sources
Smith, Chris (2013) *The Tiger's Whisker* Story Museum: http://www.storymuseum.org.uk/1001stories/detail/193/the-tiger-s-whisker.html

Ali, Fatima (Accessed online 07/01/2014) *The Woman and the Lion* Ethiopian Folktales: http://www.ethiopianfolktales.com/en/benishangul-gumuz/88-the-woman-and-the-lion

The Apple Tree Man

This is a great English standard, occasionally found in collections of Christmas stories for children.

Other Print Versions
Jacksties, Sharon (2012) *Somerset Folktales* The History Press, Stroud.

Web Sources
Thomas, Taffy (Accessed online 06/01/2014) *The Apple-Tree Man* Wordpress: http://thecompanyofthegreenman.wordpress.com/2009/01/23/the-apple-tree-man/

Traditional (Accessed online 13/01/2014) *The Apple Tree Man* lynnoel.com: http://www.lynnoel.com/crosscurrents/programs/seasonal_round/ritual_songs_poems_for_the_/the_apple_tree_man.html

Godmother Death

My original source for this tale was Doug Lipman's retelling of a Mexican version in *Ready-to-Tell Tales* (Lipman, Doug; Holt, David; Mooney, Bill [1994] August House Inc., Atlanta.). Doug Lipman kindly gave his blessing for the retelling in this book.

Other Print Versions
Wratislaw, A. H. (1890) *Sixty Folk-Tales from Exclusively Slavonic Sources* Houghton, Mifflin and Co., Boston.

Yolen, Jane; Datlow, Ellen; Windling, Terri (1997) *Black Swan, White Raven* Avon Books, UK.

Web Sources
Yolen, Jane (1997) *Godmother Death*: http://www.endicott-studio.com/rdrm/rrGodmother.html

Traditional (Accessed online 06/01/2014) *The Candles of Life: The Story of a Child for Whom Death Stood Godmother* World Of Tales: http://www.worldoftales.com/European_folktales/Czechoslovak_folktale_30.html

The Weaver's Dream

Children's Books
Heyer, Marilee (1989) *The Weaving of a Dream* Puffin Books, imprint of Penguin Books Ltd., London.

San Souci, Robert D.; Gál, Lászlo (1993) *The Enchanted Tapestry* Puffin Books, London.

Pirotta, Saviour; Johnson, Richard (2007) *Around the World in 80 Tales* Kingfisher Publications Plc., London.

The Prince and the Birds

I first found this in *Spanish Fairy Tales* (Marks, J; Cook, Hazel [1957] Cladpole Books, West Sussex.). There is also a beautiful picture book version by Amanda Hall (Hall, Amanda [2005] *Prince of the Birds* Frances Lincoln Ltd., London.).

Jumping Mouse

This is a very popular and inspiring Native American story. According to the First People website, its tribal origin is Unknown. I first heard this story years ago from storyteller Katy Cawkwell.

Children's Books
Pattern, Brian; Moore, Mary (2010) *Jumping Mouse* Hawthorn Press, Stroud.

Steptoe, John (1984) *The Story of Jumping Mouse* William Morrow and Company, Inc., New York.

Web Sources
Forman, Carole (2008) *Jumping Mouse* Youtube: http://www.youtube.com/watch?v=HTZU9hh0T6c

Storm, Hyemeyohsts (1996) *The Story of Jumping Mouse* StoneE Producktions: http://www.ilhawaii.net/~stony/lore116.html

Jack and Jackie

I first heard this from Ben Haggarty, who has told this tale far and wide. I believe it was also told by the great Scottish storyteller Duncan Williamson.

Other Print Versions
Ryder, Arthur W. (2008) *22 Goblins* MacMay22, Unknown.

Web Sources
Martin, Richard (2013) *Jimmy No-Story* Vimeo: http://vimeo.com/74531121 Note: video not complete.

Audio
Martin, Richard (2003) *Jack Goes Hunting and Other Tales* Audio Recording, Unknown licenser: http://www.cdbaby.com/cd/richardmartin

The House That Has Never Known Death

I first found this in Bushnaq's definitive collection *Arab Folktales* (Bushnaq, Inea [1987] Pantheon Books, New York.). There is a similar and well-known legend of the life of Buddha called *The Mustard Seed* or *The Parable of the Mustard Seed*.

Children's Books
Conover, Sarah; Wahl, Valerie (2001, 2011) *Kindness: A Treasury of Buddhist Wisdom for Children and Parents* Skinner House Books, imprint of the Unitarian Universalist Association, Boston.

Urry, Paul (2004) *Brilliant Stories for Assemblies* Brilliant Publications, Bedfordshire.

Web Sources
Martin, Richard (2013) *The House That Has Never Known Death* Vimeo: http://vimeo.com/78922641

Ashlimann, D. L. (1999-2002) *The Parable of the Mustard Seed*: http://www.pitt.edu/~dash/mourn.html - mustardseed

Smith, Chris (2013) *The House Which had Never Known Death* Story Museum: http://www.storymuseum.org.uk/1001stories/detail/206/the-house-which-had-never-known-death.html

Why the Seagull Cries

This is a Native American Tale attributed to various tribes of the North West Coast. There are a number of more complex versions.

Children's Books
McDermott, Gerald (1993, 2001) *Raven: A Trickster Tale from the Pacific Northwest* Harcourt, Inc., New York.

Dixon, Ann; Watts, James (1992) *How Raven Brought Light to People* Margaret K. McElderry Books, imprint of Simon and Schuster Children's Publishing Division, New York.

Web Sources
Traditional (Accessed online 06/01/2014) *How Raven Brought Fire to the Indians* World of Tales: http://www.worldoftales.com/Native_American_folktales/Native_American_Folktale_59.html

Traditional (Accessed online 06/01/2014) *Seagull's Daylight Story* Boy Scout Trail: http://www.boyscouttrail.com/content/story/seagulls_daylight-1692.asp

Traditional (Accessed online 06/01/2014) *Raven, Seagull and the Coming of Light* Raven Lore: http://www.shadowraven.org/lore4.htm

Luckily Unluckily

This is a Chinese Taoist tale with many variations. It is sometimes called *A Blessing in Disguise*.

Web Sources
Hancock, Elise; Chu, Ching-Ning; Langer, Ellen J.; Graham, Angus C. Yen, Duen Hsi (2006) *The Story of the Taoist Farmer* noogenesis: http://www.noogenesis.com/pineapple/Taoist_Farmer.html

Yang, Jwing-Ming (2007) *A Blessing in Disguise (Chinese Folktale)* ymaa: http://ymaa.com/articles/stories-proverbs/blessing-in-disguise

Language Lesson

I can't remember where I first heard this charming story!

Web Sources
Lucy (2010) *Dog as a Second Language* eslpod: http://www.eslpod.com/eslpod_blog/2010/01/12/dog-as-a-second-language/

Nasseradeen Tales

These tales and many more can be found in the various collections of stories which go by the names *Nasreddin*, *Juha* or *Hodja Tales*.

Other Print Versions
Husain, Shahrukh; Archer, Micha (2011) *The Wise Fool: Fables from the Islamic World* Barefoot Books Ltd., Oxford.

Solovyov, Leonard (1957, 2009) *The Tale of Hodja Nasreddin; Disturber of the Peace* Translit Publishing, Toronto.

Shah, Idries; Williams, Richard; Cain, Errol Le (1968, 1971, 1993) *The Pleasantries of the Incredible Mulla Nasrudin* Penguin Books Ltd., Middlesex.

Web Sources
Bashir, Hajji Abdu Settar Mohammed (Accessed

online 07/01/2014) *Sheikh Nasreddin in the Rain, Sheikh Nasreddin at the Fork, Sheikh Nasreddin counts the Donkeys, Sheikh Nasreddin and the Miser* Ethiopian Folktales: http://www.ethiopianfolktales.com/en/harar

Chapter 6 Year 6 Stories

Children of Wax

I first heard this from storyteller Michael Moran, who found it in *Children of Wax: African Folk Tales* by Alexander McCall Smith (Smith, Alexander Mccall [1989, 1999] Interlink Publishing Group, Northampton.)

Web Sources
Welch, Tessa; Lorato, Trok; Jager, Wiehan De (Accessed online 13/01/2014) *Children of Wax* fundza.mobi: http://live.fundza.mobi/home/books/fiction-childrens-stories/children-of-wax/

Otrovskii, A. (Accessed online 07/01/2014) *The Snow Maiden* pitt.edu.: http://clover.slavic.pitt.edu/tales/snow_maiden.html

Warrior

This popular story often goes by the name *The Black Prince*.

Other Print Versions
Simm, Laura; Holt, David; Mooney, Bill (1994) *Ready- to-Tell Tales* August House Inc., Atlanta.

Zagloul, Ahmed; Zagloul, Zane; Armstrong, Beverly (1971) *The Black Prince and Other Egyptian Folk Tales* Doubleday, imprint of Transworld Publishers, Ealing.

Web Sources
Palache, Abbie (2013) *Abbie Palache* Youtube: http://www.youtube.com/watch?v=ZxvKw5AHJ2E

Baldur

Baldur will be found in most collections of Norse Myths. It's a wonderful story about the beginning of the end.

Children's Books
Ardagh, Philip; May, Steven (1997) *Norse Myths and Legends* Belitha Press Ltd., imprint of Chrysalis Children's Books, London.

Frith, Alex; Stowell, Louie; Pincelli, Matteo (2013) *Norse Myths* Usborne Books, Oxon.

Other Print Versions
Crossley-Holland, Kevin (1980, 1982, 1983, 1993, 2011) *Norse Myths: Gods of the Vikings* Penguin Books Ltd., London.
Picard, Barbara Leonie (1953, 1994, 1996, 2001) *Tales of the Norse Gods* Oxford University Press, Oxford.

Web Sources
McCoy, Dan (2012, 2014) *The Death of Baldur* Norse Mythology: http://norse-mythology.org/tales/the-death-of-baldur/

Ericython

Also spelt *Erysichthon* and *Erisichthon*, roughly pronounced Err-Ees-Ick-Thon. I particularly enjoy Ted Hughe's version in *Tales from Ovid* (Hughes, Ted [1997] Faber and Faber Ltd., London.

Children's Books
McCaughrean, Geraldine; Clark, Emma Chichester (1999, 20013) *The Orchard Book of Roman Myths* Orchard Books, London.

Other Print Versions
Fantham, Elaine (2004) *Ovid's Metamorphoses* Oxford University Press Inc., New York.

Quetzalcoatl Brings Chocolate to Earth

Children's Books
Parke, Marilyn (1995) *A Quetzalcoatl Tale of Chocolate* Fearon Teacher Aids, Unkown.

Lowery, Linda; Keep, Richard; Porter, Janice Lee (2009) *The Chocolate Tree: A Mayan Folktale* Millbrook Press, imprint of Lerner Publishins Group, Minneapolis.

Skeleton Woman

This story has become hugely popular with storytellers as a result of its inclusion in the seminal book *Women Who Run With the Wolves : Contacting the Power of the Wild Woman Rider* (Estés, Clarissa Pinkola [1992, 1998, 2008] imprint of Ebury Publishing, a Random House Group Company, London.)

Children's Books
Villoldo, Alberto; Yoshi (2008) *Skeleton Woman* Simon and Schuster Children's Books, Simon and Schuster.

Web Sources
Pieperhoff, Edith; Morrison, Mary (2004, 2005) *Skeleton Woman* RedKite Animation: http://redkite-animation.com/_redkite/projects/skeleton-woman/

Smith, Chris (2009-2013) *Skeleton Woman* Story Museum: http://www.storymuseum.org.uk/1001stories/detail/102/skeleton-woman.html

The Boy Who Learned to Shudder

Grimm, Wilhelm; Grimm, Jacob (1812) *Children's and Household Tales/Grimm's Fairy Tales* Not Applicable.

Pullman, Philip (2012) *Grimm Tales for Young and Old* Penguin Books Ltd., London.

Grimm, Wilhelm; Grimm, Jacob; Hunt, Margaret (2006) *The Story of the Youth Who Went Forth to Learn What Fear Was* SurLaLune: http://www.surlalunefairytales.com/authors/grimms/4youthfear.html

The Woodcutter and the Snake

I first heard this told by Ben Haggarty many years ago.

Other Print Versions
Lee, F.H. (1931) *Folktales From All Nations* George Harrap and Co. Ltd, London.

Web Sources
Lupton, Hugh (2002) *The Snake of Dreams* Healing Story: http://healingstory.org/the-snake-of-dreams/

Friedman, Amy; Gilliland, Jillian (1999) *The Snake's Prophecy* Spartanburg Herald Journal: http://news.google.com/newspapers?nid=1876&dat=19990617&id=N0IfAAAAIBAJ&sjid=yc8EAAAAIBAJ&pg=6718,5571747

Eynon, Terri (Accessed online 08/01/2014) *The Snake and the King's Dream* alderoak: http://www.alderoak.co.uk/26101/26401.html

Three Questions

Tolstoy has made this Russian tale very popular.

Children's Books
Muth, Jon J. (2002) *The Three Questions* Scholastic Press, Scholastics Inc., New York.

Other Print Versions
Tolstoy, Leo (1885, 2004, 2007 2008,) *What Men Live By and Other Tales* Kessinger Publishing, Dodo Press, Tark Classic Fiction.

Gawain and the Green Knight

There are many versions of this classic of Medieaval literature.

Children's Books
Courtauld, Sarah; Davidson, Susanna; Daynes, Katie; Dickins, Rosie; Punter, Russel; Sebag-Montefore; Sims, Lesley (Unknown) *One Hundred Illustrated Stories* Usborne Children's Books, Usborne, Books Ltd., London.

Ashley, Mike (2005) *The Mammoth Book of King Arthur* Constable and Robinson Ltd., London.

Morpurgo, Michael; Foreman, Michael (2004) *Sir Gawain and the Green Knight* Walker Books Ltd., London.

Other Print Versions
Armitage, Simon (2007) *Sir Gawain and the Green Knight* Faber and Faber Ltd., London.

O'Donoghue, Bernard (2006) *Sir Gawain and the Green Knight* Penguin Classics, Penguin Books Ltd., London.

Tolkien, J. R. R.; Tolkien, Christopher (1975) *Sir Gawain and the Green Knight, Pearl and Sir Orfeo* Random House Publishing Group, New York, by arrangement with Allen and Unwin Ltd.

Mother Sun and Her Daughters

I found this story in a wonderful collection called *Primal Myths: Creation Myths Around the World* (Sproul, Barbara C. (1992) HarperOne, imprint of Harper Collins Publishers, San Francisco).

Five Wise Trainings

I came across this tale in one of Andrew Lang's collections. He calls it *The Five Wise Words of the Guru*.

Other Print Versions
Lang, Andrew (1907) *The Olive Fairy Book* Longmans, Green and Co, London. Now in the Public Domain.

Web Sources
Lang, Andrew (Accessed online 08/01/2014) *The Five Wise Words of the Guru* Sacred-Texts: http://www.sacred-texts.com/neu/lfb/ol/olfb16.htm

Gawain Gets Married

This is another classic of Arthurian legend with many literary retellings.

Children's Books
Courtauld, Sarah; Davidson, Susanna; Daynes, Katie; Dickins, Rosie; Punter, Russel; Sebag-Montefore; Sims, Lesley (Unknown) *One Hundred Illustrated Stories* Usborne Children's Books, Usborne, Books Ltd., London.

Hastings, Selina; Wijngaard, Juan (1985,1987) *Sir Gawain and the Loathly Lady* Walker Books Ltd., London.

Ashley, Mike (2005) *The Mammoth Book of King Arthur* Constable and Robinson Ltd., London.

Other Print Versions
Hahn, Thomas (1995) *Sir Gawain: Eleven Romances and Tales* Medieval Institute Publications, Kalamazoo, Michigan.

Hahn, Thomas (1995) *The Wedding of Sir Gawain and Dame Ragnelle* University of Rochester: http://d.lib.rochester.edu/teams/text/hahn-sir-gawain-wedding-of-sir-gawain-and-dame-ragnelle

Everything You Need

This rather harsh salutary tale was collected by C.G. Campbell in Iraq in the 1930's.

Campbell, C. G.; Buckland-Wright, John(1949, 1980, 2008) *Tales from the Arab Tribes* Lindsay Drummond Ltd., Unknown, Arno Press, New York.

Gilgamesh

I first heard this told by Ben Haggarty, whose storytelling of this tale was truly inspirational. There are many translations and versions of what is possibly the oldest surviving written story.

Children's Books
McCaughrean, Geraldine; Parkins, David (2002) *Gilgamesh the Hero: The Oldest Story Ever Told* Oxford University Press, Oxford.

Other Print Versions
Mitchell, Stephen (2004) *Gilgamesh: A New English Version* Profile Books Ltd., London.

Bryson, Bernarda (1966, 2012) *Gilgamesh: Man's First Story* Pied Piper Press, Sacramento.

George, Andrew (1999) *The Epic of Gilgamesh* Penguin Books Ltd., London.

A Drop of Honey

This story is in many 1001 Arabian Nights collections, and variations of it can be found in Burma, Thailand and Iran

Other Print Versions
Macdonald, Margaret Read (1992) *Peace Tales* August House Inc., Atlanta.

Aung, Maung Htin; Trager, Helen G.; Tiset, Paw Oo (1968) *A Kingdom Lost for a Drop of Honey And Other Burmese Folktales* Parent's Magazine Press, Unknown.

Web Sources
Heathfield, David (Accessed online 23/01/2014) *The Drop of Honey* World Stories: http://www.worldstories.org.uk/stories/story/35-the-drop-of-honey

Unknown (Accessed online 23/01/2014) *A Drop of Honey* UUA: http://www.uua.org/re/tapestry/adults/harvest/workshop10/workshopplan/stories/142312.shtml

Chand, Peter (209-2014) *A Drop of Honey* Story Museum: http://www.storymuseum.org.uk/1001stories/detail/174/a-drop-of-honey.html

Who is the Husband?

This story comes from an ancient Indian collection of riddle tales. I found it in *22 Goblins* (Ryder, Arthur W. [2008] MacMay22, Unknown).

What Happens When You Really Listen!

I found this delightful tale in *Folktales from India: A Selection of Oral Tales from Twenty-Two Languages* (Ramanujan, A. K. [1991] Pantheon Books, a division of Random House Inc., New York. Simultaneously published by Random House of Canada Ltd., Toronto.)

Other Print Versions
Richman, Paula (1991) *Many Ramayanas: The Diversity of a Narrative Tradition in South Asia* University of California Press, Berkeley and Los Angeles.

Web Sources
Richman, Paula (1991) *Many Ramayanas: The Diversity of a Narrative Tradition in South Asia* cdlib: http://publishing.cdlib.org/ucpressebooks/view?docId=ft3j49n8h7&chunk.id=d0e3172&toc.depth=100&brand=eschol

Smith, Chris (2009-2014) *What Happens When You Really Listen* Story Museum: http://www.storymuseum.org.uk/1001stories/detail/192/what-happens-when-you-really-listen.html

The Power of Stories

I also found this one in *Folktales from India: A Selection of Oral Tales from Twenty-Two Languages* (Ramanujan, A. K. [1991] Pantheon Books, a division of Random House Inc., New York. Simultaneously published by Random House of Canada Ltd., Toronto.)

Web Sources
Baltuck, Naomi (1994) *Telling It To The Walls: Storytelling as a Healing Art* Naomi Baltuck: http://www.naomibaltuck.com/Npages/HealingArt-ARTICLE.html

The Diamond Dream

I first came across this in a version by Jim May called *The Ruby* (May, Jim; Holt, David; Mooney, Bill [2000] *More Ready-to-Tell Tales From Around the World* August House Inc., Atlanta.). Jim kindly approved my retelling in this book.

Bird in Hand

I first heard this story from storyteller Eric Maddern. It was also used by Toni Morrison in her acceptance speech when receiving the Nobel Prize for literature. Trauma specialist Mooli Lahad uses a version with a butterfly and therapist in his book below.

Other Print Versions
Lahad, Mooli (2000) Creative Supervision: *The Use of Expressive Arts Methods in Supervision and Self-Supervision* Jessica Kingsley Publishing, London and Philadelphia.

Jaffe, Nina; Zeitlin, Steve; Segal, John (1993) *While Standing on One Foot: Puzzle Stories and Wisdom Tales from the Jewish Tradition* Henry Holt and Company LLC, New York.

Kornfield, Jack; Feldman, Christina (1991) *Soul Food: Stories to Nourish the Spirit and the Heart* HarperOne, imprint of Harper Collins Publishers, San Francisco.

Bartholome, Paula; Wacker, Mary B.; Silverman, Lori L. (2003) *Stories Trainers Tell: 55 Ready-to-Use Stories to Make Training Stick* Pfeiffer, imprint of John Wiley and Sons Inc., San Francisco.

Web Sources
Bartholome, Paula (2003) *The Wise Man and the Baby Bird* Say It With A Story: http://www.sayitwithastory.com/articles/WiseManBabyBird.pdf

Unkown (Accessed online 08/01/2014) *The Power of Choice: Bird in the Hand* Mockingbird Education: http://www.mockingbirdeducation.net/choicebird-in-hand-story.html

Traveller at the Gates of a City

I came across this great little tale in *Soul Food: Stories to Nourish the Spirit and Heart* (Kornfield, Jack; Feldman, Christina [1996] HarperCollins, San Francisco.)

Web Sources
Ashliman, D.L. (Accessed online 23/01/2014) *The Traveler and the Farmer* Pitt.Edu: http://www.pitt.edu/~dash/traveltales.html

Unknown (Accessed online 23/01/2014) *The Traveller* cityyear: http://www.cityyear.org.uk/new-founding-stories.pdf

Storytelling Schools Series

Available Spring 2014
The Storytelling School: Handbook for Teachers
Storytelling Schools Series Volume I
Chris Smith and Adam Guillain, Foreword by Pie Corbett

This handbook describes a revolutionary way of delivering primary education. In a storytelling school all children learn to be storytellers, retelling and improvising stories from memory as a way of learning both language and subject content across the curriculum. Children graduate with a repertoire of their own stories to tell. This approach has been shown to raise standards and fire imaginations in schools throughout the UK.

Chris Smith and Adam Guillain show you how to make this happen in practice. The handbook draws on more than ten years' experience researching and developing this way of teaching. Piloted, researched and up-dated, this second edition includes new chapters on non-fiction teaching and cross-curricular integration across the school. It is packed with practical activities, examples, theory, charts, diagrams and photocopiable pages.

ISBN: 978-1-907359-38-5; 210 x 297; Ringbound: Paperback

Available Autumn 2014
History Stories for Primary School Children to Retell
Storytelling Schools Series, Volume III
Chris Smith and Adam Guillain

This unique collection of history-related stories includes commonly taught topics for primary schools together with suggestions on ways to link the story to the teaching of history. The approach has been adjusted to fit with the 2014 primary national curriculum for England and Wales, and focuses mainly on British history from the end of the last ice age to the present day.

ISBN: 978-1-907359-44-6: 210 x 297mm Ringbound; Paperback

Science Stories for Primary School Children to Retell
Storytelling Schools Series, Volume IV
Jules Pottle and Chris Smith

The authors have created a collection of stories for children to retell as a springboard for primary science teaching. Some of the stories have been created to contain the content of the science curriculum. Others are traditional stories that fit well with science topics and are great for oral retelling. The authors explain how to tell the stories, suggest ways of using them as a starting point for science teaching and also show how to link them to the teaching of literacy. This book will be of interest to all primary teachers who are looking for new ways to engage and inspire their classes about science.

ISBN 9789-1-907359-45-3: 210 x 297mm
Ringbound: Paperback

Future publications
A Storytelling Approach to Primary–Secondary Transition
Storytelling Schools Series, Volume V
Chris Smith and Nanette Stormont

A smooth transition between primary and secondary school is an important and often neglected part of the educational system. Here the authors have produced a step-by-step guide to help children navigate this unsettling change by using a single story to form a bridge between the old and new schools. Issues of change, uncertainty and fear are addressed in the story, which is begun at the end of year 6, and completed at the beginning of year 7.

Designed with Storytelling Schools in mind, this is a model which can be adapted for all primary-secondary transitions.

Model Primary Storytelling School Scheme
Storytelling Schools Series, Volume VI
Nanette Stormont and Chris Smith

The Storytelling School approach to education uses oral storytelling as a springboard for learning language, raising standards in writing and teaching in almost any topic of the primary curriculum. This scheme provides a detailed example of a whole Storytelling School system, featuring:

- traditional and fiction stories for retelling
- sample plans for teaching narrative writing
- links to reading
- non-fiction topics and texts
- sample plans for teaching non-fiction
- sample plans for cross curricular links
- tools for monitoring, evaluation and supervision

It is intended as a reference for schools wishing to become Storytelling Schools; as a blueprint to be imitated and innovated as needed.

The Storytelling School, Early Years Handbook
Storytelling Schools Series, Volume VII
Chris Smith and Adam Guillain

Storytelling and storymaking are an integral feature of early years education, providing a crucial spur for child development in those first few years. Exposure to a rich storytelling environment builds language and social development in a natural and enjoyable way.

In this handbook the authors provide a step-by-step guide to developing storytelling in these settings, with guidelines for working with children from birth to 5 years. Areas include:

- ways of telling stories to children
- teaching the children to retell stories
- group storymaking and retelling
- the storytelling corner
- storymaking in free play
- storytelling and communication with babies and toddlers
- using chants and ritual to support the rhythm of the day

Stories, Chants and Rhymes for Early Years Children to Retell
Storytelling Schools Series, Volume VIII
Chris Smith and Adam Guillain

Every early years practitioner needs a repertoire of stories, songs, chants and rhymes so that they can create a rich story environment in their setting. In this volume the authors have collected a set of wonderful stories and rhymes that can be used to build the repertoire of every early years worker.

Barefoot Books

For more stories from Barefoot Books, visit **www.barefootbook.com**

The Adventures of Achilles
Retold and narrated by Hugh Lupton and Daniel Morden, illustrated by Carole Hénaff (hardback with 2 CDs, 2010). Ages 8 and up.

The Adventures of Odysseus
Retold and narrated by Hugh Lupton and Daniel Morden, illustrated by Christina Balit (hardback with 2 CDs, 2006). Ages 8 and up.

The Arabian Nights
Retold by Wafa' Tarnowksa, illustrated by Carole Hénaff (hardback, 2010). Ages 8 and up.

The Barefoot Book of Animal Tales
Retold and narrated by Naomi Adler, illustrated by Amanda Hall (paperback with 2 CDs, 2006). Ages 6 - 11.

The Barefoot Book of Buddhist Tales
Retold by Sherab Chödzin and Alexandra Kohn, illustrated by Marie Cameron (paperback, 1997). All ages.

The Barefoot Book of Earth Tales
Retold by Dawn Casey, illustrated by Anne Wilson (paperback, 2009). Ages 6 – 11.

The Barefoot Book of Jewish Tales
Retold by Shoshana Boyd Gelfand, illustrated by Amanda Hall (hardback, 2013). All ages.

The Snow Queen
Retold by Sarah Lowes, illustrated by Miss Clara, narrated by Xanthe Greshham (hardback with CD, 2013) Ages 6 – 11.

The Story Tree: Tales to Read Aloud
Retold and narrated by Hugh Lupton, illustrated by Sophie Fatus (paperback with CD, 2004) Ages 3 to 7.

Storytime: First Tales for Sharing
Retold by Stella Blackstone, illustrated by Anne Wilson, narrated by Jim Broadbent (paperback with CD,) Ages 3 to 7.

Hawthorn Press

Ordering books

If you have difficulties ordering Hawthorn Press books from a bookshop, you can order direct from: Booksource, 50 Cambuslang Road, Glasgow G32 8NB
Tel: (0845) 370 0063, E-mail: orders@booksource.net
or you can order online at www.hawthornpress.com

For further information or a book catalogue, please contact:
Hawthorn Press, 1 Lansdown Lane, Stroud, Gloucestershire GL5 1BJ
Tel: (01453) 757040, E-mail: info@hawthornpress.com
Website: **www.hawthornpress.com**